African Traditional Religion
in the Modern World

Second Edition

African Traditional Religion in the Modern World

Second Edition

Douglas E. Thomas

McFarland & Company, Inc., Publishers
Jefferson, North Carolina

LIBRARY OF CONGRESS CATALOGUING-IN-PUBLICATION DATA

Thomas, Douglas E.
    African traditional religion in the modern world /
Douglas E. Thomas. — Second edition.
        p.   cm.
    Includes bibliographical references and index.

    ISBN 978-0-7864-9607-5 (softcover : acid free paper) ∞
    ISBN 978-1-4766-2019-0 (ebook)

    1. Africa—Religion.   2. Christianity—Influence.
3. Islam—Influence.   I. Title.

BL2400.T47 2015
299.6—dc23   2015011426

BRITISH LIBRARY CATALOGUING DATA ARE AVAILABLE

Cover images © 2015 Zoonar/iStock/Thinkstock

Printed in the United States of America

McFarland & Company, Inc., Publishers
  Box 611, Jefferson, North Carolina 28640
    www.mcfarlandpub.com

To my sons James Edwin and Myles Douglas.
May this work serve as a continual reminder
to you of your African roots and culture.
For it is through remembering that the best
of Africa will live on inside of you.
This is the sacred mandate that I charge you
to transmit from generation to generation.

Table of Contents

Preface

African traditional religion (ATR) is a highly non-dogmatic spiritual lifestyle that is practiced by millions of people around the world. Some argue that it is related to the religion practiced by the African Nubians of Ta-seti who created what would become known as Egyptian religion. The Ta-seti also developed the world's first writing system which we call hieroglyphics. This book, a second edition of my 2005 publication by the same name, continues to examine the nature of African traditional religion, or Traditional African Cultural Forms (TACF), to determine the common attributes of the religion practiced on the continent and by millions throughout the Americas. It focuses on West Africa and the religious experiences of black people throughout the Americas and is based on an intertextual, synchronic analysis of traditional African cultural forms by isolating key elements in the Yoruba, Dagara, and Ibo cultures. It was discovered that enough intertextual relations exist in oral and written literatures of the West Africans and practitioners of TACF in the New World to define a common response to the environment.

Principal elements studied included sacrifice, salvation and culture, modes of revelation, divination, and African resilience in the face of invasions and colonization. Our analysis of traditional norms and values undergirding Yoruba cultural forms, particularly as they relate to cosmology, symbolism and ritual, were found to be the fundamental basis for traditional African religion.

This study was also written to fill an academic void on the topic of African religion. John Mbiti's classic text *African Religions and Philosophy* was published more than 45 years ago and has become the standard text on African religion. Mbiti explored the diverse nature of religion primarily practiced in West Africa, but ignored the rich tradition practiced by millions of black people throughout the Americas. Also, because of his own Christian biases, Mbiti

1

neglected to view traditional African religion as a system capable of "saving" African people, without the aid of Christianity or Islam.

We have determined that African traditional religion is the most viable sacred source available to black people, which can assist them in restoring the solidarity that is found among the Arabs and the Europeans who are the overseers of Islam and Christianity. For African people to become whole, they cannot continuously neglect those time-honored traditions such as rites of passage and other rituals that predate the incursion of Islam and Christianity.

Although there are many books on the market that explore the role of traditional religion in Africa and in the Americas, few, if any, attempt to analyze traditional African cultural forms as a spiritual system on par with the Abrahamic religions—Judaism, Christianity and Islam. This work uses meta-studies and interviews from practitioners of African religion and explicates hundreds of texts written primarily by African scholars. The copious use of information is designed to substantiate our working hypothesis: African traditional religion is a world religion and fully saving "faith." It is indeed worthy of the respect given to other belief systems. One of the main differences between African religion and the Western faiths is that African religion is rooted in mores that have their foundation in the myths and traditions of African people. Such myths have become venerated and are observed not only by those on the continent, but by millions of black people throughout the New World, such as those in Cuba, Trinidad, Haiti, Brazil, the Caribbean, and the United States. Each place created anew from their new environment and reinterpreted African myths to preserve the religion of their ancestors.

This book will be of great value to undergraduate students and lay persons as an introduction to African religion. Also, to maintain academic continuity we utilize texts and articles from present writers to those scholars who pioneered the scholarship of African traditional religion. This study will prove invaluable for seminarians who are interested in creating dialogue between students of African and Western religions. Since many academic institutions of late require their students to learn about African religion, this work will provide them with a perspective from the view of an insider.

Also, in recent years many African Americans have become obsessed with the recovery of their historical roots. This book will answer many of their questions regarding the cultural, historical, spiritual, and psychological role religion served in the lives of their ancestors prior to them becoming Christians. Many African Americans and other non–Europeans are beginning to look outside of the "Western" faiths to find meaning for their lives. They are searching for their cultural and spiritual identities in ways that are not openly celebrated in Christianity and Islam. This book's philosophical departure does not celebrate imperialism in the name of religion. We have seen what happens when an ideology cloaks itself in religious garb, but is in reality an extension of Western militarism.

Introduction

African religion is a spirituality that has been operating in the lives of traditional Africans for thousands of years. It was in existence for several millennia before the Hebrews gave birth to the Abrahamic faiths—Judaism, Christianity, and Islam. We witness African traditional religion (ATR) or Traditional African Cultural Forms (TACF) at their apex in Egypt, and observe them taking various forms after Egypt's decline. African traditional religion has not been given the academic attention it deserves since most scholars conducting research of TACF have little interest in African traditional religion, apart from the curiosities and Hollywood caricatures surrounding Egypt. Others show a great deal of interest in Egypt because European scholarship has managed to isolate Egypt from Africa. Until more scholars not beholden to mimicking the Western narrative begin to unearth the riches that lie buried beneath the African soil, many will continue to look outside their culture for spiritual sustenance and worse, seek salvation from the cultural myths of foreigners. Many Africans continue to embrace another people's culture and venerate the deeds of strangers instead of honoring their own noble men and women.

In part, the focus of this study was taken from an idea expressed in the foreword of the classic text *Critical Race Feminism* by Derrick Bell, which discussed the role black women have served throughout American history. What he said sparked my interest in African culture as a means of salvation and wholeness for African people. Since Africans on the continent and throughout the diaspora were forced to abandon traditional forms of African religion and, in some instances, forced to adopt Christianity or Islam, I was interested in ascertaining what, if anything, is redemptive within African culture? Does African culture possess any sacred cultural elements that can heal and serve as a guide in the lives of African people?

We utilized and reviewed hundreds of academic journals and books on

African religion to complete this study. It involved interviewing several practitioners of African religion, in an effort to substantiate one of our working theories: African traditional religion and culture are a viable source of cultural redemption for Africans on the continent and black people of African descent throughout the diaspora. Most of the previous studies failed to view African religion as a "faith" capable of providing "salvation" on the same level as Christianity or Islam. Most of these studies were conducted by Europeans and Americans who were extremely biased and primarily focused their scholarship on comparing African religion with Christianity or Islam. These scholars were very narrow minded and focused their attention on how African religion lacks those life-affirming qualities that are in Islam and Christianity. African traditional religion has been viewed primarily by most European and American scholars as a culture that is *prolegomena* to Christianity and Islam.

This study analyzes African religion and culture (religio-culture) as the primary means of spiritual development and healing for black people everywhere. It uncovers how traditional religion and various forms of African spirituality have historically served the Africans as a unifying force.[1] Traditional African religion continues to survive at the cultural subconscious center of most Africans, regardless of their allegiance to Islam or Christianity. It is therefore important to analyze the nature of its role in African communities, especially as it functions within the lives of black people throughout the world. TACF survived the cruel middle passage and are more than capable of providing them with the spiritual knowledge and sustenance to experience an abundant life.

Bell suggests in *Critical Race Feminism* that black women have historically served a vital role in the community. "Just as we acknowledge women's power to give life, we must come to recognize their power to sustain us in life during the critical times to come. Black women have always been the salvation secret of our people. It is time for them to assume formally the positions they have always held in fact."[2] These words sparked my interests into researching the role of culture, and how it has historically served those Africans who practice traditional religion, especially prior to Islam and Christianity. By explicating African creation myths we can begin the long journey of unearthing the tradition that sustained African communities and provided them with the norms and values that undergird the traditional African "belief" system.

Many ethnic groups have created myths that explain their understanding of existence and especially the nature of the cosmos. For instance, the Hebrew-Jewish scripture and the Arabic Qur'an begin their sacred narratives with traditional myths. Since the incursion of Islam into West Africa from the 7th to 14th centuries, later followed by the Anglo-Christian colonization in the 15th to 20th centuries, Africans were systematically programmed for over one thousand years to reject their cultural myths and adopt traditions that emerged from another people's myths. John Mbiti argues that although many Africans have outwardly embraced Christianity or Islam, they have not totally abandoned those traditional forms of life rooted in African religio-cultural norms. Mbiti argues that the acceptance of Christianity or Islam signifies that many Africans may outwardly "come out of African religion but they don't take off their traditional religiosity. They come as they are. They come as people whose world view is shaped according to African religion."[3]

Laurenti Magesa notes that,

> because of the cultural form in which it is clothed, the Christianity of the missionaries cannot be assimilated, nor can it help [our] people face up to difficult situations.... These people struggle to respond to the Christian calling, but they are compelled from within to do so without denying their culture, the conception and understanding of life that defines them as Africans.[4]

Those sacred elements in Christianity and Islam that entire nations of Africans have adopted as their religion are also available in the traditions of Africans. Since all religion is in part culturally constructed, Africans should consider re-embracing their tradition before abandoning it for one not suited to address their existential needs. As Magesa makes clear in the above statement, Africans may attempt with all their heart to embrace Christianity or Islam. Yet, there are some things within these cultures that "cannot be assimilated." Those Africans who have adopted Christianity or Islam cannot fully rid themselves of traditional ways of life. The African Christian and Muslim cannot completely reject their traditional belief system, because it is ingrained within their cultural DNA. It is in the air they breathe.

For example, Mercy Oduyoye wrote, "Culture and religion are so significant within African life that neither Muslim nor Christian in Africa can be totally free of the values that emanate from the traditional African religions."[5] Religion and culture are so intertwined throughout Africa that it is impossible to speak of one without the other. (I have termed this phenomenon "religio-culture.") Even after Christianity and Islam forcefully fed Africans their ideology premised on their historical cultural myths, it is a testament to African people that despite their open rejection of their traditional ways of being, still TACF have not been completely obliterated. In fact, to eliminate all forms of African religio-cultural forms from African communities would have in essence destroyed all of Africa. Those who operated the plantation systems in the New World were aware of the power that culture wields in the lives of Africans. Thus, they passed laws forbidding Africans from participating in several African cultural forms.

For instance, it was considered a crime for enslaved Africans to practice their religion and culture, which is the very thing that Clifford Geertz argues completes humanity. "We are, in sum, incomplete or unfinished animals who complete or finish ourselves through culture—and not through culture in general but through highly particular forms of it."[6] The restoration of certain aspects of TACF has the potential to heal and equip Africans with the tools for surviving in a hostile environment.

Christianity and Islam have not provided Africans with the communal stability needed in moments of crisis and existential despair. Only the religio-culture that has existed in Africa for thousands of years can speak to those deep yearnings that the foreign faiths are unequipped to address. The impact that Christianity, Islam, and modernity have upon traditional forms of existence have not fulfilled the existential yearnings of African people.

> In these [existential crisis] circumstances, Christianity and Islam do not seem to remove the sense of frustration and uprootedness. It is not enough to learn and embrace a faith which is active once a week, either on Sunday or Friday, while the rest of the week is virtually empty. It is not enough to embrace a faith which is confined to a church building or mosque, which is locked up six days and opened only once or twice a week. Unless Christianity and Islam fully occupy the whole person as much as, if not more than, traditional religions do, most converts to these faiths, will continue to revert to their old beliefs and practices for perhaps six days a week, and certainly in times of emergency and crisis.[7]

African creation myths are the raw materials from which the culture-affirming values of Africans are constructed and housed. Creation myths are the building blocks for maintaining strong cultural and group affiliations. Traditional African political and social mores were developed from the myths that are the foundational stones of their society. It is important to explicate a people's myths because they shape perspective and form their ideological understanding of life. Undergirding such narratives lie the people's notion of existence. Africans have numerous myths that should be explicated and adopted by Africans on the continent and those throughout the diaspora. The adoption of these stories can forge the common link that is essential for the establishment of a collective African consciousness. In *African Religions*, Benjamin Ray employs creation myths, rituals, folktales, and trickster stories, to explicate African religion.

> Most African myths tell the origins of human life and the creation of social order. As such, they describe the social and cultural building blocks of African societies and give meanings to life-cycle events and the moral rules for everyday life.... These sacred stories established the models and standards by which the Batammiliba organize their society.[8]

It is important for African people everywhere to accept their cultural narratives as sacred mediums to govern their lives. The veneration of deities from another people's mythical tradition is perhaps responsible for some of the instability experienced in black communities throughout the world. For it is quite possible that some of the social problems confronting black people throughout the diaspora may be due to their adoption of a foreign belief system. The absorption of ideas that are antithetical to one's primal culture and foreign to their social cognitive thought processes has the potential to create mental chaos. The human mind can function under severe pressure, but chaos is a formidable psychological weapon that causes the mind to shut down. The acceptance of one's cultural-self brings mental clarity, especially when one embraces those aspects of their tradition that Europeans have programed black people to hate. Those life-affirming values that support the whole human being are ingrained within one's cultural traditions. These sacred elements should never be discarded so one can fit into another people's social framework. We become fully human through "particular" forms of culture, because there are no universal cultural referents that can be imbibed by those alien to that particular tradition. After one embraces the cultural values that are in alignment with their socio-historical tradition, then they can eliminate much of the chaos that occurs from adopting other people's traditions. African cultural myths function as building blocks for the construction of societal norms by supplying the community with positive referents from within their traditions, which provide guidance for the individual. Myths also serve to shape one's perspective of other important events that occur throughout life.

> In African societies, traditionally, one finds many myths that attempt to explain the reality of how anything ever came into existence. Through various myths, the people try to understand the natural realities and facts of life. In the religious sense, myths are testimonies in narrative form designed to instruct or give explanations ... about the relationships between the natural and the supernatural.[9]

Since myths serve as cultural building blocks in African traditional societies, practices that pay homage to such myths are essential for maintaining communal order. Practicing various rituals and attending to shrines or pouring libations, are ways by which traditional Africans maintain their connection with the past and future. Africans may never be perceived as fully human if they continue to appropriate another people's myths that are not tied to African culture.[10] Rituals and initiations function to support the myths that are indispensable for cultural stability. Many sacred rites are practiced to maintain cosmic and communal harmony and to ignore these rituals may result in an imbalance, which is the precursor to instability. Imbalance is harmful in all its forms and cannot produce anything of value. Therefore, certain cultural rituals must be maintained to prevent upsetting the balance that keeps society intact. Our lives must be lived in a way that we are conscious to avoid offending the ancestors who are the guardians of communal order.

African religion and culture is premised upon maintaining harmony with all the forces in nature. Any breech in the social order, whether involving the ancestors, divinities, or nature, must be avoided at all cost. Somé notes in his book, *Of Water and the Spirit*, that chaos will pursue those who defy cosmic and communal order. He argues that many of the problems confronting humanity may be due to our refusal to maintain ontological harmony between the forces of nature. "It is my belief that the present state of restlessness that traps the modern individual has its roots in a dysfunctional relationship with the ancestors.... Unless the relationship between the living and the dead is in balance, chaos results."[11] Thus, to avoid creating disharmony, practitioners of traditional African religion perform rituals to maintain harmony that is crucial for communal and cosmic happiness.

For example, in *Of Water and the Spirit*, Somé explains that myths give rise to ceremonial rituals and are essential for establishing a positive identity. He offers insight into the minds of those who kidnapped him and colonized his people in Burkina Faso. The lingering effects experienced by the victims of colonialism created a tension that conflicted with their traditional understanding of community and self. This internal chaos can be remedied by adhering to traditional practices that aim at restoring one's fragmented psyche. Initiations in particular are important because they provide the initiate with the tools needed to reprogram their thinking and to see themselves anew. Somé wrote that his initiation functioned to restore in him a respect for his people, something which was lost during his Western training.[12] This new sense of self came into being because of the conversion one undergoes through initiation. In traditional African communities, the rite of passage is equivalent to what Christianity refers to as the "born-again" experience. For without undergoing this process, which aims at awakening one to one's real purpose in life, one will forever remain a child and be unable to function in a world that hides from the uninitiated.

Those African communities that were forced to live under the terror of enslavement and colonialism suffered a great communal loss. The way of life that had guided them for thousands of years was taken away and labeled criminal in some places and called witchcraft in others. When Africans refused to abandon their culture and insisted on maintaining those "heathen" customs practiced by their ancestors, they were isolated from the community or killed. When one's life is placed in danger for practicing their culture, one is forced to choose between honoring the tradition of the elders, or adopting the traditions of those who invaded their land.[13]

Only by practicing the time-honored traditional African religio-cultural forms created by his ancestors was Somé able to escape the natural hatred one develops for those who treat them less than human. Some's new mind-set engendered love instead of hate, which is the logical attitude that victims have for their attackers. His escape from the imprisonment of hatred resulted from his participation in various African rituals, which attempted to restore in him a sense of communal consciousness and responsibility. Even his view of those who kidnapped him was looked upon differently after under-going his initiation. Hence, the name "Malidoma" means friend of enemy or stranger—the befriender of one's enemy.

By adhering to the ideas that emerged from traditional African creation myths, one participates in the maintenance of African religion and culture. A positive communal identity must be rooted in traditional African forms of existence. Maintaining a strong sense of community and personal identity results from embracing one's own religio-cultural story. Those who embrace the cultural narratives that are in alignment with the philosophy undergirding their way of being will experience cultural unity and national pride. Thus, practitioners of traditional African cultural forms adhere to myths that have their origin in their culture and not another's.[14]

African religion and culture are so intertwined that we can speak of African culture as a religion or at least as serving a religious function. This phenomenon is so pervasive throughout African society that those who con-verted to Islam and Christianity are never free of its influences. Culture and religion are so significant within African life that neither Muslims nor Chris-tians can be totally free of the values that emanate from traditional African religion. In other words, religion is not independent from or free of cultural influences. Where one observes the practicing of particular cultural forms such as dress, dance, or what Robert Thompson refers to as "mystic coolness," this too is a function of religion. Hence, African culture is maintained and perpetuated when black people partake in traditions that emanate from their environs.

Also, honoring ancestors and praying for the not-yet-born are forms of cultural expressions in which one participates within traditional African communities. Naming ceremonies and storytelling are also cultural forms to which one honors in order to maintain cosmic and individual harmony. Pour-ing libations and the use of saliva are also important rituals that serve a vital function within traditional society. Participating in such acts are the locus by which one maintains right relations with the divinities, the ancestors, and the community. Those who refuse to participate in such time-honored customs may be responsible for creating an ontological disharmony between the forces that govern human activity. For example, disharmony is thought to account for sickness, natural catastrophes, and according to Somé, mental illness. "[T]he inability to understand, to indigenous people is symptomatic of an illness."[15] This illness may occur when one rejects their cultural traditions and elevates another people's myths to the status of sacred.

Geertz maintains that culture completes humanity. However, he also asserts correctly that culture is not universal but people specific. Culture functions in a specific way within various environs. Not all cultural environs complete the human process by using the same cultural referents and parameters. Geertz argues that all cultures are unique and that there is no such thing as a *consensus gentium*. Those unique webs that embody culture are essentially the building blocks of a society. "We are, in sum, incomplete or unfinished animals who complete or finish ourselves through culture—and not through culture in general but through highly particular forms of it."[16] It is these "highly particular forms" that I argue can be found only in one's primal culture. The cultural template that is used to complete the human process will inevitably favor one people over another. There is no cultural consensus gentium, and it is a myth contrary to rational thought to assume that cultural elements function the same in completing the human process. The rhetoric of preserving culture when espoused by the group in power, inevitably means the destruction of the other's way of life.[17]

Adherents of traditional African cultural practices validate the idea that culture does indeed serve a redemptive role. Certain cultural practices include participating in art guilds, secret societies, and becoming an expert in identifying and using traditional medicine. This kind of knowledge is required to master skills involving techniques, where one "celebrates the powers of the underworld, where the true nature of the natural order is administered by the gods, [and] becomes the greatest healing tool that a community can have."[18] In addition, in traditional Dagara societies the *boburo* are practitioners of medicine who possess an extensive knowledge of physical and spiritual illnesses. This kind of knowledge is very limited and has its origin in the underworld and continues to be a sacred cultural form practiced throughout West Africa.

Participating actively in traditional cultural practices is therapeutic. Somé argues that practicing religions alien to one's cultural template imprisons an individual's ability to think critically. "Religious colonialism tortures the soul. It creates an atmosphere of fear, uncertainty, and general suspicion."[19] Hence, participating in religious activities that originate from within one's culture enables the participant to experience freedom without negating their unique religio-cultural story. On the other hand, when people reject their cultural story or adopt another people's religious cosmology as the guiding force for their lives, they are essentially rejecting themselves. As James Cone argued in *Black Theology and Black Power,* black people must reject all religio-cultural narratives that are not tied to the empowerment of black people.[20]

If Africans want to maintain the religio-cultural forms of existence that emerged from the environment that birthed the world's first religion, they must reject all forms of religious tyranny that have forced them to abandon their sacred traditions in exchange for myths tied to alien narratives. For example, Somé points out that after he was kidnapped he was forbidden to speak the Dagara language. "After Father Maillot heard us greet him in French, he declared that speaking Dagara at school was now a sin, so Mantié declared Dagara illegal within the precinct of the mission."[21] The prohibition against speaking his primal language was an effort by the priest to destroy all remnants to his culture. Therefore, all forms of pressure to abandon one's religious culture must be rejected in order to preserve the traditional ways of existence.

Traditional African cultural forms are maintained by speaking the language of one's nationality and ancestors. Language is not simply a form of communication, but as Martin Heidegger so aptly states, "Language is the house of being." It is essential in transmitting and preserving those cultural nutrients that are essential for building a strong community. Even those forced to think in another people's language may be unable to understand the full complexities of life or what Heidegger deemed the question of the age: What is the meaning of existence?

Therefore, it is crucial that African people maintain those traditional religio-cultural forms that keep them connected to the past, present, and future. A breach in this connection is thought to result in chaos and to set in motion certain problems that Western religio-cultural systems are unequipped to address.[22] African cultural systems sustain and nurture the practitioners of traditional thought systems. As more people become practitioners of TACF and reflect more deeply upon African religion, many who have become lost in the Western desert will see the light that emanates from this rich tradition. Mbiti has attempted to systematize some of those sacred ideals undergirding African thought in *African Religions and Philosophy.* He argued that there are five guiding principles that encompass African religious ontology. They include the Creator, spirits, human beings, animals, and phenomena that include nonhuman entities.

> In addition to the five categories, there seems to be a force, power or energy permeating the whole universe. God is the Source and ultimate controller of this force; but the spirits have access to some of it. A few human beings have the knowledge and ability to tap, manipulate and use it, such as the medicinemen, witches, priests and rainmakers, some for the good and others for the ill of their communities.[23]

If Africans continue to view this religious ontology as devoid of values and look outside of their sacred system for spiritual sustenance, they will never reach their full potential as human beings. Those who reject their religio-cultural traditions will always view themselves and the world through alien lenses that depict them as less than. By rejecting their cultural worldview, they are forced to interpret the world through an alien lens that has proven to be detrimental to the survival of African people. By rejecting the ideological foundations from which their cultural system is based, Africans have committed the worst of all sin by worshipping foreign idols. Kwame Gyekye observes that "philosophy is essentially a cultural phenomenon; it is part of the cultural experience and tradition of a people."[24] Since philosophy is culturally constructed, one must venerate the myths from within African culture if they are to have relevance for their lives.

> I have already observed that there are universal human experiences, ideas, values, sentiments, ideal.... But the fact still remains that the forms of such (alien) philosophies were hammered out on the anvil of the cultural and historical experience of other peoples. I suggest therefore that *the starting points, the organizing concepts and categories of modern African philosophy be extracted from the cultural, linguistic, and historical background of African peoples,* if that philosophy is to have relevance and meaning for the people, if it is to enrich their lives.[25]

Africans must turn to African myths, folklore, art, and social phenomena in order to construct an African philosophy of religion. The concepts that embody African philosophy of religion are not solely found within written texts, at least not to the same degree that Western philosophy of religion is housed within the written text. "Philosophical concepts, ideas, and propositions can be found embedded in African proverbs, linguistic expressions, myths and folktales, religious beliefs and rituals, customs and traditions of the people, in their art symbols, and in their sociopolitical institutions."[26] Philosophers can systematize these myths that give rise to thought. This could involve addressing "various fundamental questions about human life, conduct, and experience and to provide the necessary conceptual or theoretical trimming for those elements."[27]

It is important that African people respect those traditional narratives passed down by their ancestors regarding cosmology, existence, ethics and religion. It is a European myth that Africans are incapable of reflecting upon self and the universe. Marcel Griaule attempted in his book, *Conversations with Ogotemmêli*, to show that Africans are capable of thinking deeply about the nature of existence. Griaule seeks to show, contrary to the popular opinion of his time (second quarter of the twentieth century), that the Dogon have myths that reveal the order of existence and explore the nature of existence.[28] Unless Africans fully explore their own philosophical system, which provides the ideological impetus for governing all modes of existence, one erroneously places themselves under another people's philosophy that is not culturally attuned to the specific cultural etiquettes of outsiders. When a people embrace cultural norms that were created for a particular people to address their unique needs, they will be unable to experience the fulfillment that comes from honoring those cultural norms that provide nourishment for a particular people. Unfortunately, this is the problem millions of black people experience daily. They are trying to live within a European framework and find it difficult or impossible of deriving the same kind of satisfaction and contentment that their European or American counterparts experience. They will continue to experience this existential void because one cannot serve the cultural gods of another people and find fulfillment. The Greeks created a unique culture for their people, not to provide cultural nutrients for Africans and Chinese. One would be foolish to believe that Chinese culture alone can humanize a European. It can aid in the humanization process, but the European will not experience total fulfillment from the nutrients of a foreign culture. Instead, they will experience the same sense of estrangement that people of African descent encounter as they try to live in a world that was not designed for them to thrive in. They can only survive from one moment to the next. Very few people are expected to thrive in a cultural environment that is hostile to one's cultural inclinations. The thoughts governing African philosophical-religious culture are housed within African culture alone:

> African philosophical thought is expressed both in the oral literature and in the thoughts and actions of the people. Thus, a great deal of philosophical material is embedded in the proverbs, myths and folktales, folk songs, rituals, beliefs, customs, and traditions of the people.[29]

Myths house the cultural lore of a people's origins and religion. For instance, Yoruba myths are an extrapolation of mythical events that function to substantiate the ideas they have of themselves and the cosmos. Yoruba myths provide answers to questions that experience alone cannot reveal. "The myths thus serve the manifold purposes of statements of doctrinal beliefs, confirmation of faith in the mind, liturgical credo, simple metaphysics."[30] More importantly, embedded within myths are ideas about God, life, death, and much of what confronts the existent throughout life. "To get at the full philosophical import of myths, however, requires detailed examination."[31]

African philosophy is based on practicality. "The crucial concern of philosophy is to reflect upon the fundamental ideas that shape and influence the life of humanity."[32] If African people are unable to develop ideas reflective of their own cultural ideology, this bespeaks to the nature of their value as human beings. The major Enlightenment philosophers argued that the hallmark of humanity is rationality. A people who cannot reflect upon the world and the nature of existence fuels the erroneous ideas that certain European philosophers advocated in the past and some still advocate about the intellectual ability of Africans.[33]

Philosophy is embedded within folklore, proverbs, and wisdom literature. It is explicated through storytelling. "This is, I think the reason for the teaching of moral values embedded in proverbs and folktales to children in the process of their socialization; the moral instructions are meant to habituate them to moral virtues."[34] Unearthing African myths serve a crucial role for millions of practitioners of traditional African cultural forms. African myths are critical for the survival of black people everywhere because it provides them with an alternative vision from the Abrahamic perspective. African myths provides Africans with a system of thought that is more in tune with their cultural axiological grid. "[U]nless a philosophy interacts with the mentalities and core values of a people, it will not endure but will sooner or later atrophy."[35]

1

The Sacred Role of Culture in African Religion

A variety of Traditional African Cultural Forms (TACF) emerged throughout Western Africa that birthed African religion. All religions are connected to a particular people who venerate their culture as sacred. For example, Islam has its origins within Arabic cultural forms that emerged from ideals within their tradition. These values were articulated in the Koran and elevated to the status of sacred. Christianity has its roots in Alexandria, Egypt, but in the fourth century was taken over by Constantine. From that point until today, Christianity has been articulated through a European cultural lens. We can speak of Christianity as a religion dominated by men, who have elevated European cultural forms to the status of sacred. They developed their concept of deity from their cultural myths and those proselytes who have adopted these religions are, in fact, participating in the veneration of Arab and European cultural forms. Likewise, African spirituality is rooted in traditional African ways of being. Those practitioners of traditional African cultural forms have also elevated their value system to the sacred realm.

In some traditional communities prior to colonialism, human beings were sacrificed to deliver a message to the spirit world. Sacrifices were deemed essential because they demanded the attention of the divinities, which could intervene on the behalf of a suffering community. In times of national crisis such as war and drought, a human being was sacrificed to provide the community direct access to the Other World. Most traditional Africans believed that especially in times of communal crisis, such sacrifices would immediately bring about a positive response, thereby stopping the carnage. Some African traditional cultures would offer their oldest son as a sacrifice.[1] This tradition was later changed and a stranger would be selected as a sacred offering. In Dogon traditional culture the younger son was sacrificed, but later an albino or captured stranger would be offered up as an offering.[2]

Sacrifices aim at restoring communal balance and remain an important feature of African religion. "Among the [most] important religious actions which they [practitioners of TACF] lay down, that of sacrifice is one of the most serious for the faithful of the African religions."[3] Sacrifices can consist of an animal or a monetary offering.[4] "The mechanism of the sacrifice is explained by the possibility of liberating, transmitting and directing the 'vital dynamism,' which would be particularly concentrated in the blood, that of animals and of men.... One of the present principles is that of sub-stitution as one can recognize in the sacrifices accompanying sacrificial animal[s,] [which] are placed one against the other, sometimes with both enveloped in the same sheets, demonstrating in this way that the animal is being immolated in the place of the man and offered in his name to a Spirit."[5]

Sacrifices are the primary means by which traditional Africans maintain and restore relations with deity, ancestors, and the community. John Mbiti maintains that sacrifices "are acts of restoring the ontological balance between God and man, the spirits and man, and the departed and the living."[6] Imbal-ance creates disharmony, which is equivalent to the Christians notion of sin. Without honoring deity and the ancestors through sacrifices, chaos will upset the delicate balance between the physical and non-physical worlds. Sacrifices are also performed to restore health and prevent sickness. Sacrifices "are intended to avert sickness, or to promote recovery from an illness, or to avert failure in business, or some other form of ill-fortune attributed to the influ-ence of some evil spirit, but more often to witchcraft."[7]

Theologically, sacrifices must be understood as a medium used to restore and maintain communal relations. Sacrifices in traditional African culture are in essence "acts and occasions of making and renewing contact between God and man, the spirits and man. When they are directed to the departed, they are a symbol of fellowship, a recognition that the departed are still mem-bers of their human families, and tokens of respect and remembrance of the departed."[8] E. Bóláji Ìdòwú wrote: "The basic purpose of sacrifice is right relationship between man and the Deity; the more urgent the need for the maintenance or restoration of that relationship, the higher the condition man is prepared to fulfil."[9]

Sacrifice is a form of petition to higher forces, much the same as prayer, which is intricately related to sacrifice in communities were TACF are observed. Prayers are requests to helper-spirits and are designed to establish a relation-ship between the devotee and the divinity. In traditional societies when one enters into a relationship with the divinities, they expect to be protected and rewarded. The relationship is based on a promise made between the two parties. The devotee must feed the spirit and in return, the orisha must provide one with good fortune. For example, when one is wedded to an orisha in Yoruba-Santeria tradition, they agree to serve the spirit in return for protection, good health, and overall success in life. In essence, one allows the spirit to use their body and mind and the devotee expects to be rewarded in this life. Prayer and sacrifices are premised upon the contract between the human being and the spirit world. Therefore, when the community or individual is facing difficulty, they can expect their *orisha* to intervene on their behalf and to assist them in overcoming life's obstacles.

Practitioners of traditional African cultural forms are communal-oriented. As a communal people, traditional Africans not only prayed for their own welfare, but for the community. Within traditional African thought there is barrier between the "I" and the "We." Traditional Africans prayed for the well-being of their community because it was the most visible representation of themselves. It is commonly accepted that prayer is the primary medium, whereby Africans communicate their deepest desires to the divinities.[10] Traditional Africans believe that sacrifices and prayer are an integral part of their spirituality. Most importantly, for activating God's functionaries, "sacrifices are offered to a spirit ... who is supposed to be more powerful than human beings in the natural state. Sometimes sacrifices are offered to the ancestors who, now spirits, are more powerful than the living, and in a few rare instances to the Supreme God."[11]

Certain divinities function as communal harmonizing spirits. Within Yoruba traditional culture, "Ela" (one who keeps in safety) is viewed as a preserver or savior, who restores individual and communal order.[12] Some African Christian theologians have incorrectly made comparisons between *Ela* and Jesus Christ.[13] However, Okot p'Bitek warned us that such comparisons create epistemic problems for which there is no remedy. The use of sacrifices throughout traditional communities implies that the practitioners of TACF believe that African religion is a viable source of communal cohesion and for upholding ones cultural traditions. The unity of African culture cannot occur while Africans reject their traditional values and venerate another people's cultural forms. African traditional cultural forms are praxis-centered. Africans must reject utopian theology and focus their attention on the here and now. There is no salvation for Africans outside of the cultural forms created by their ancestors. As long as Africans rely upon foreign paradigms for spiritual sustenance, they will remain imprisoned to a constructs that will never set them free.

Types of Sacrifices and Offerings

Bishop Charles Remi Rakotonirina of Madagascar wrote that the bull in Madagascar is a sacred symbol. It symbolizes the Creator and is representative of the ultimate sacrifice for divine appeasement. Offenses are transferred to the bull and relieves one from carrying guilt. "For us the sacred animal *par excellence* is the bull. This is offered to the Creator both in sacrifices of respect and in rites of reconciliation. Whenever, for instance, it concerns reestablishing in the vital flow a son who has seriously offended his father, then one resorts to the bull. The bull which replaces the guilty son is called 'a substitute of guilt' (*Sòlo hèloka*) or 'a substitute of the offence' (*sòlo vòina*)."[14] Generally, within African traditional communities, sacrifices are a mode of communication between the visible and invisible worlds. "Traditionally, sacrifices and offerings are believed to be a means of contact or communion between man and the deity. They are said to be man's best way of maintaining an established relationship between himself and his object of worship."[15] To expand upon Mbiti's comments, we can view sacrifices and offerings as acts of restoration, which aim to heal any brokenness between the departed and the living. If this relationship is not maintained one will experience many misfortunes throughout life. Sacrifices and offerings help, at least psychologically, to maintain a positive relationship between all life forces.[16]

We can distinguish between at least four major types of sacrifices and offerings in traditional African communities:

(1) Meal and Drink Offerings, which are performed daily at shrines and on sacred days[17];

(2) Thanks Offerings, which are daily rituals that express one's appreciation to deity for bringing success to one's family (successful businesswomen in the markets are known for making these offerings,[18] which includes the use of money or animals[19]);

(3) Propitiatory Offerings and Sacrifices, which were once known throughout the Yoruba cultural traditions as *ebo etutu*. The propitiatory sacrifices were conducted to avert a catastrophe or major crisis.[20] The entire community was involved in this type of sacrifice, which was very expensive. Whenever the community was facing a major crisis that threatened the life of the community, making a propitiatory sacrifice was needed to appease the offended beings. In ancient times a human being was offered up to appease the offended deity during moments of extreme communal crisis. The sacrifice was either burned or covered in oil.[21] This offering

was premised on the ideal that such an act would appease the offended party and once accepted, communal harmony would be restored. The human being cannot experience wholeness if there is a breach in the relationship between the ancestors and deity; and

(4) Vicarious Sacrificial Offerings, which were conducted to undo offenses committed against a divinity.[22] The sacrificial elements usually involved a sheep that was rubbed against the body of an offender to transfer their guilt onto the sheep. The sheep was then burned in the place where the offense was committed, and the offender was spared from the wrath of god.[23]

Sacrifices and worship in traditional African cultures speaks to the people's desire to maintain communal and cosmic relations with all of creation. The maintenance of this delicate balance is one of the primary occupations of every practitioner of TACF. Worship in African traditional societies is most commonly expressed in the form of rituals, rites of passages, ceremonies, and in honoring sacred traditional norms.[24] The veneration of these cultural norms may occur in one's home-shrine or at a public-shrine. Such worship may begin in a rather orderly way, but soon become spontaneous-driven, which may appear disjointed but these acts are governed by the success of prior experience.[25] The veneration of one's ancestors and serving the *orisha, neteru* or *lwa*, is the primary aim of African worship. "It [Worship-Veneration] is a means by which man makes a devout supplication to, and enters into communion with, the object of worship."[26] These cultural objects can be physical or non-physical.[27] Sacrificial offerings and prayers to deities and ancestors occur when the community offers thanksgiving or makes petition to their divinities or ancestors.[28] Awolalu interestingly points out that within the Yoruba tradition, prayer is rarely a time where one confesses faults.[29] "This does not mean that the people do not have a sense of sin; the idea behind their action is that when they bring thank-offerings before their divinities they do so with joy and gratitude as they ask for a continuance of the benefits."[30] However, during times of communal crisis, Africans immediately consult an oracle to determine if they have offended a divinity or ancestor. If so, they confess their sin, knowing that the calamity will continue until remedied by the spirits.[31] This act, "a rite of purification ... implying confession of sin as well as cleansing from sin and impurity, comes in when the worshippers feel the need to assuage the divine wrath."[32]

Communal-harmony and brotherhood was not an abstract ideal in traditional African communities. Harmony is not an abstract notion one hopes to experience in the next world. Communal-harmony must be experienced in this life. Otherwise, chaos will reign and disrupt the delicate balance between the devotee and their divinity. Communal-harmony and unity is expected in this life. The ideals, principles, and rituals needed to bring about this goal, undergirded the ideology that governed traditional African cultural norms. Traditional Africans seemed to know something important about communal and individual wholeness that many in modernity have yet to understand. That explains why one must focus their spiritual attention on embracing who they are and to assist the community in doing the same. Such communal principles and traditional values were designed to bring about communal transformation. This explains why the traditional view of religion does not separate the sacred from the profane. Even the gods were not separate from one's daily activities. "In Africa, religion, culture and custom are closely related to such an extent that many African peoples have no separate words for them."[33] African traditional culture is community based and has no tolerance for the type of individualism that has become the hallmark of Western thought. There is no such idea as one having a "personal savior" because either the entire community is in harmony with the forces that control the cosmos or all will suffer together. African traditional cultural forms is a collective-based system that aims at reaching every member in the community. Traditional Africa religion is not a private affair because we are all tied to each other. "It is of much concern to me whether Mr. X whom I may never have met in my life is religiously behaving himself well or not. If he is not, I have the right and duty to have him dealt with as he deserves.... [E]verybody is everybody else's keeper. Individualism has no place."[34]

There was little space given to "feed" the "self," or ego, in traditional society because isolation from the community signaled death. Africans seemed to know what modern physics has only recently discovered. That we are all biologically connected and the individual "cell" has no existence, at least not in any meaningful way, outside of a loving community. Those who choose to isolate themselves from the community experience chaos that affects the entire community. The traditional African's notion of communal and cosmic harmony is so interconnected with culture that we have used the term "religio-culture" throughout this text to show how difficult it is two separate the two. There are no dividing lines between religion and society in traditional African communities. "The profane is impregnated with the sacred."[35] African religion and culture are inseparable, which is also why within most traditional African communities, "no word exists for 'religion' and one can understand why. When religion invades all areas of life, to the extent that the sacred is contained in the profane, how does one distinguish and *name* such a phenomenon?"[36]

Many students of religion maintain that Christianity is a faith-based belief-system, which is principally guided by faith-propositions. On the other hand, Islam is also a belief-system purportedly guided by principles based upon action. African religion or the elevation of traditional African cultural forms to the status of sacred are praxis-centered. It emerged from traditional African values that honor communal unity, cosmic harmony, and the nurturing of each member in the community. This is accomplished by passing down cultural traditions through rituals, ceremonies, and writings. Since human beings are in a constant battle to maintain a positive sense of belonging, African values stress the importance of upholding one's dignity. "The man who is apparently the poorest is rich in this nobility; it may not perhaps give him the means to live but it gives him reason for living."[37] The value of dignity is a noble trait and those who lack this attribute, will usually succumb to the forces that threaten human autonomy.

In addition to maintaining one's sense of dignity, African tradition views the family as a sacred unit. "The family remains the soil in which the person is rooted, and his refuge in difficult hours. In the family home the African mother, of whom the poets sing, is the object of almost religious respect for fruitfulness and her material love for her sons."[38] However, colonialism with its raping and pillaging, and the incursions of Arabism into Africa, caused many to waver in their traditional faith. In the nineteenth and early twentieth century, most notably after receiving a Western education, many Africans became ashamed of their traditional culture. They abandoned it for Islamic and Christian cultural forms, and worse, rejected their traditional belief system, and adopted Arab and European myths. Anything was better than their traditional culture, which was a cursed paganism, their Western schools taught them to despise. After being mis-educated by the Europeans, they ran far away from their traditions and into the arms of another god. They rejected the traditions of their forefathers not because the religions were better, because Islam and Christianity were connected to external powers. Those who outwardly abandoned the religion of their ancestors, lacked the concept of real power, which is internal and derived from one's primal cultural values. African traditional culture was perceived by many Western educated Africans as unable to feed them spiritually, as the foreign gods "supposedly" could. African deity were abandoned by African people because they were mythologically defeated by Arab and European gods. The African gods were abandoned because they could no longer deliver African people from life's woes. They certainly were no match for the Arab and European gods who entered the modern world as conquerors. Yet, with the Western educated Africans efforts to isolate themselves from the religio-culture of their ancestors and to adopt gods foreign to their religio-mental construct, rather than experiencing the abundance they so desperately sought in their adopted religion, they have instead participated with the foreigner in destroying traditional culture.[39] Isolation from one's primal culture is a clear sign of intellectual death. Not even the gods of Abraham can save those who have abandoned their tradition from the cultural genocide that has engulfed the continent. When a people abandons the religion of their ancestors they are unconsciously engaging in a war against themselves. Even the Western educated African cannot contend with the psychological warfare that has encircled him. He cannot win this type of battle adhering to the same ideals espoused by his enemies. A return to the sources that sustained his ancestors is the only way to victory.

Salvation for African people is available to them from within their own sacred traditions. Even some African Christian scholars are struggling to accept this reality. They were trained by men and women who were Eurocentric in their outlook, which is a perspective that views all things through the lens of Europe. A few courageous white scholars wrote positively about African religion, at a time when black people throughout the world were considered incapable of conceiving Deity. Hagel's remarks regarding Africans as being outside of history remains the position of most white scholars. This view is still maintained by most non-black scholars throughout the world. Cheikh Anta Diop deconstructed the pathology undergirding Eurocentric thought. He argued that the world's first great thinkers came from the very heart of Africa along the Nile River and that all inquiry into the origins of philosophy must begin in Africa.

P'Bitek also argued that many Western trained African scholars have committed a grave injustice by attempting to interpret African phenomena through a European context and hermeneutic. He questioned Christianity's interests in dialoguing with African traditional religions (ATR). P'Bitek was suspicious of Christians who say they wanted to form a bridge between traditional value systems and Christianity, especially when they continued to view Africans as subhuman. P'Bitek questioned the sincerity of Christian missionaries, who only recently became interested in dialogue: "[D]uring the colonial period ... the missionaries found nothing good at all in the African religions, ascribing its practices to the Devil. After Independence, however, they declared that they found little difference between African religion and Christianity. They might ... have had the courage of their convictions, however misguided."[40]

P'Bitek seems to imply what some African bishops have also recognized: that Christianity and Roman Catholicism, in particular, cannot survive without inculcating and acculturating African people. P'Bitek was correct to question the sincerity of the missionaries in Africa. (Today, p'Bitek would certainly question the presence of AFRICOM throughout Africa, which is a malevolent humanitarian strategy used by the United States government and European powers to re-colonize Africa. This renewed mission may prove more volatile than slavery and colonialism.) The postcolonial missionaries were just as concerned with saving Christianity as an institution, as they were in converting Africans to Christianity. The missionary came to Africa to further propagate and expand European hegemony. They certainly were not there to save the "unsaved." In their so-called efforts to save Africans, Christian missionaries deliberately created distrust among the people. Bishop Anthony Maanicus of Bangassou, at the Fourth Synod of Bishops, noted that converted Africans are not at home in their new Christian identity.[41] This new identity has created a tension in which the traditional person is always colliding with his foreign faith. Maanicus argued that this tension leads to a schism, in which African Christians must battle to maintain their mental and emotional health. "In the opinion of many laymen committed to the apostolate and also of many bishops and priests, the African lives ill at ease in the Church as far as the majority of the circumstances of his life are concerned."[42] This is due to the dual nature that develops within those Africans who abandon the traditions of their forefathers. These converts to Christianity or Islam lack knowledge of the relationship between religion and culture. They do not know that one's religio-cultural worldview has been genetically implanted within their DNA. (Or so it seems.) "Traditional religion in Africa is still alive and still informs the customs and ways of thinking of many," uttered a priest who taught religion to male African students preparing for college.[43] Even though all his students were "confessing" Christians, African traditional cultural forms were not unfamiliar to any. "Each boy felt within him, with greater or lesser intensity, a loyalty to the Christianity in which he was being educated and a loyalty to the religion and customs of his people."[44] This pressure to serve Christianity with one hand and to uphold the tradition of the ancestors with the other hand created in Africans a schism that can be overcome by choosing between the god of their culture and the foreign gods who destroyed their cultural memory. Or, can they serve both (serving with both hands) much like the New World Africans in the Caribbean and the Americas?

Unity of African Religion

Are their cultural values within African traditional religion worthy of elevation to the realm of sacred? Or should Africans continue to venerate

Arab and European cultural forms, from which they derive their values and sense of being? Do black people need rescue from estrangement or human despair? If so, whose cultural norms and values would best assist them in becoming whole? Is the entire question of cultural values as nodes of salvation unnecessary in the modern world, which is attempting to construct a global value system? African traditional religion is culturally rich and should be the primary vehicle from which Africans tap to shape their perceptions. It's highly abstract and use of numerous rituals attests to its unceasing devotion to keep humanity and the world in harmony with the forces that govern the cosmos. Traditional African cultural forms are perhaps the most ritualized in the world. They employ several mediums in which to communicate with the deity. Based on its constant pursuit of attaining the perfect way of life, Africa's ritualized traditional religion is capable of providing black people with the knowledge needed to experience a full life. "[W]e have good reasons to see and acknowledge it [traditional religion] within its own context and world-view as full and fully-salvatory revelation as could be expected in any genuine religion including Christianity."[45]

Any inquiry into the socio-cultural aspects of a particular phenomenon is best conducted from a general approach. Many scholars of TACF agree that African religion can be spoken of in the singular. They acknowledge that a broad approach to studying African religion is a good starting point, but there is also a need to specialize in the study of particular African cultural forms, such as Yoruba cultural forms, Dagara cultural expressions, and New World African religion expressions. Father Chidi Denis Isizoh suggests the following approach to studying African religion:

> [A] study designed to embrace all the African religions [cultures] cannot fail to be general, and it will, in its turn, show that the main culture fields will need definite special guides which will adapt descriptions and suggestions to the local realities. There can be no question of giving an account of every religious [cultural] form to be found in a world which contains perhaps more than a thousand of them, or even of pronouncing on the religious originality of any particular region.[46]

The study of traditional African cultural forms covers an array of cultures that requires a multi-disciplinary approach because, unlike the Abrahamic faiths, most TACF are not canonized. Several hundred languages and dialects have been identified that house these complex knowledge systems. Still, scholars agree that a certain level of unity exists among African cultural groups.[47] Therefore, any inquiry into the nature of African religion should be conducted with the understanding that there is a unity of diversity that exists throughout these cultural forms. For example, Father J. H. Greenburg classified and numbered more than 700 languages or dialects throughout Africa.[48] He concluded that there are "major areas of unity.... At the present time, African studies all lean towards the unity of all the African peoples; *it is something that can now no longer be denied*."[49] The following observation by Father Greenberg was made in a study involving the Mandé of West Africa. Once part of the great Mali Empire that included Senegal, Sudan, Ivory Coast, Ghana, Togo, and parts of Guinea: "The principles of their unity are expressed in the course of a ceremony held at Katanga every seventh year, in the loop of the river Niger, for the renovation of a sanctuary called 'the Vestibule of Mandé.'"[50] During the five-day ceremony, participants cite cosmological myths, especially myths of human origin.[51]

More importantly, mythical genealogies are carefully cited, which helps the people maintain a sense of unity and keeps them connected to their sacred past. These gatherings are built upon a common belief that started in the thirteenth century with an organization known as Sun Diata, which was the name of a Mandé Chief who presided over the gathering. Beyond the Mali Empire there exists among many Africans, a sense of unity that was however challenged by the brutal incursions carried out by Arabs and Europeans. Even after withstanding such vicious attacks, traditional African cultural forms are still practiced in various degrees throughout West Africa and the Americas. Rituals that at first glance seem bizarre to outsiders, upon closer examination, exhibit the "same religious beliefs and proceed from a common mental structure. At the inner core of this system, opposing social forms are considered as complementary[,] this being supposed necessary to the functioning of the whole."[52]

It is important to recognize the similarities that exist among traditional African cultural forms, so that African people can more easily organize around a common cultural identity. Religion has been shown to have the power to separate, but if used properly, it has a much greater potential to bring people together. Explicating the common cultural elements shared by black people throughout the world is the key to Kwame Nkrumah's vision to "unite all of Africa." A common religio-cultural norm should be the starting point from which to begin discourse regarding cultural unity and the salvation of African people. Westerners have perpetuated the myth of African disunity, which may in part be responsible for the high murder rate of black men in the United States and for the raging wars taking place throughout the continent. Although differences do exist between the different African cultural forms, there are enough common religio-cultural traits that should not be ignored. "Between the African societies, in addition to an apparent diversity, there are bonds of symmetry, of contrast and of complement, the root cause of which is very probably the unity of character among Negro-Africans and even among Negro-Berbers."[53] Africans share a common religious and cultural bond. This must be the starting point from which to begin any serious inquiry into the unit of Africans.

> We can begin by admitting that there is in the black world a certain unity of conception of a spiritual character. But it is a unity in a great diversity of forms. In fact we find an extreme variation in the rituals of the traditional religions. The cause of this must be sought in the ethnocentric character of these religions, in which God is often the creator of the tribal ancestor, ... whence arises the attachment of each ethnic unit to its own rites, and the complete absence of proselytism.[54]

African religion is culturally situated and holistic in its approach to ministering to human beings. It is not one in search of converts because it is not a "religion" in the Western sense of the world, but more so a unique way of existing in the world. African traditional religion is culture-based and therefore has no interests in seeking out converts. On the other hand, Islam and Christianity have violent histories as missionary religions because their dogma compelled them to make converts and force others to prostrate themselves before the gods created from their cultural myths. Africans were educated to reject the cultural narratives of their ancestors and to venerate the god created by Arabs and Europeans. The need to force others to accept a foreign god is a clear sign that such a religion and the people it produces can never be peaceful. In traditional African cultures one is born into a particular culture, which provides them with the cultural lens by which they perceive the world. In traditional African communities one's family cult (culture) was also their "religion." Culture is religion and it has proven difficult or nearly impossible for those born and bred in the bush to embrace alien cultural forms developed in the mountains of Europe. Those who adopt another people's culture as their religion will inevitably experience tension that is not easily overcome. Students of traditional religion discovered that African cultural unity is based on diversity. Rituals that seemingly have no connection with a neighboring culture may, in fact, be an attempt at addressing a similar need. "In fact African religions, like the other non–Christian religions, constitute a whole which must be grasped in its entirety. One cannot, even in a good cause, select this belief or that rite, and declare them acceptable, while eliminating others as worthless observances. The whole religious life of a given civilisation is presented at one bound."[55]

A basic premise of African traditional religion is that all life forms are guided by spiritual principles. "This attitude to spiritual things puts man into the presence of God and makes him view the visible world from a spiritual standpoint. It allows him to go beyond the present moment and to accept a more spiritual idea of time. Even the values of African humanism take on a richer meaning and are marked by this spiritual attitude."[56] The spiritual ideals that govern traditional African cultural forms permeates every aspect of one's existence. How Africans view the Supreme Being and others is based upon certain spiritual laws that effect how they perceive the world. Many traditional African communities govern their society according to common spiritual principles. Those who reside "in the bush" developed a different perspective of deity than those who live by the sea. "The image of the Supreme Being which each constructed for himself could not have been the same in the gloom of the forest and in the brightness of the savannah."[57] Nonetheless, "at the heart of all the traditional religions we find similar structures and aspirations, so that in spite of the varieties in beliefs and rites we can realise that we are dealing with homogeneous forms and we can affirm a certain African religious unity."[58]

Since there is now consensus that TACF emerged from a common African source, African religion should be viewed as a world religion. Cardinal Hyacinth Thiandoum of Dakar, Senegal, maintained that African religion is "a valid partner in dialogue as much as any other organised world religion."[59] However, is African religion really "organized" in the sense that Cardinal Thiandoum uses the word? Does it have to be so "organized" to acquire legitimacy? And what does the word "organize" reference itself? Yet, African religion is a spiritual phenomenon that may go unrecognized by European scholars, but it is alive in the hearts of millions of people throughout the world. For one to speak of TACF as a single religio-cultural phenomenon, or as, "homogenous forms," should no longer be a point of contention. The consensus among scholars is to use the term "African traditional religion" (singular): "There seems [*sic*] to be sufficient common features in traditional religion in Africa to justify the usage."[60] This monumental consensus is based on meta-data which identified a common thread that runs through the various African cultural forms. "The accounts of the traditional religion in different parts of Sub-Saharan Africa are very similar, and this fact underlines the fundamental unity of this religion despite the difference in actual practices; the world-view at bottom seems identical."[61]

Africans are not new at grappling with the God concept. Thousands of years before the Hebrews, the Europeans, and Arabs birthed their belief systems, Africans along the Nile River had already developed the world's first theological system. This is common knowledge, but for centuries Westerners have questioned whether African people were even capable of understanding God. How could this be when the historical record clearly shows that "Black"

Africans have always known God and have proverbalized that knowledge in many sayings? There are common proverbs such as "You don't have to teach a small child about God." This proverb reveals their understanding of the divine as being part of one's heritage. Africans believed that each human being was created with a sense of the Creator wired into their DNA. Still, the question remains for some, did African people really know God before the Arabs and Europeans arrived?

Africans have a long history of pursuing the force that some have called God or Ultimate Reality. "[T]here was good and adequate knowledge of God in African Religion long before the advent of the new religions of Islam and Christianity—and such knowledge of God could only be possible through God's own self-disclosure.... [T]he reality of revelation is very much there in African Religion. Otherwise there would be no knowledge of God at all.... Whenever there is knowledge of God, it can only come from revelation, i.e., God in his own initiative disclosing his presence, his nature and his will to men thus making it possible for them to have a relationship with him in response."[62] Yet it is extremely difficult for many Westerners, particular religion scholars, to accept God's activity among non–white peoples. "The earliest western views on African Religion were characterised by excessive racial prejudice, ignorance and also by the dominant influence of the theory of evolution."[63] Therefore, the Western perspective of Africans has been propagated by "the views which saw the African as a primitive savage who was at the bottommost rung of the imaginary ladder of human evolution while western man was at the pinnacle of that ladder. African religion and other so-called primitive religions were viewed similarly, and all kinds of disparaging terms were employed to describe it, e.g., animism, idolatry, magic, superstitions, ancestor worship, fetishism, and the like. It too, like the people who practised it, was placed at the bottommost rung of the imaginary ladder of religious evolution while Christianity was at the pinnacle of that ladder."[64]

The early Western-trained scholars of traditional African cultural forms used a biblical and Euro-cultural template to conduct their analysis.[65] Kibicho points out that both approaches were based on a racist model that preferences European hermeneutics. The missionaries' disdain for African religion is partly rooted in the Christian view of revelation. The Christian attitude against foreign religions in general is "determined by our Christian idea of Revelation."[66] In Western scholarship, Judaism, Christianity, and Islam have been viewed as superior to other religions because of their theological view of deity.[67] This ignores the fact that African religion is comprised of several cultural systems governed by a philosophy rooted in the unity of diversity. Case in point, African Egyptians were the first people to exhibit a belief in one God. Such common knowledge is usually relegated to the margins or ignored when discussing the history of monotheism. Traditional African conceptions of a Supreme Being are expressed in their "proverbs, short statements, songs, prayers, names, myths, stories and religious ceremonies."[68] God has never been absent from the lives of African people. An Ashanti proverb encapsulates the Africans' comprehension of God's self-disclosure: "No one shows a child the Supreme Being."[69] African people are genetically wired to know God. So much, that "in traditional life there are no atheists."[70]

The future scholarship of African religion must view the diverse cultural forms that house traditional ways of being as expressing a singular meaning. Africa is a vast continent and culturally diverse, but there remains a common theological view of the Supreme Deity to which the majority of black Africans subscribe. For example, "it is remarkable that in spite of great distances separating the peoples of one region from those of another, there are sufficient elements of belief which make it possible for us to discuss African concepts of God as a unity on a continental scale."[71] The God perspective emerges from a people's cultural foundation. "The basis of Religion is the conviction that some higher [usually spiritual and invisible] being or power exists, and that he or it can or does exercise some influence on the believer's life."[72] This idea includes African peoples' passion for rituals and objects that assist them in acquiring the knowledge required to communicate with deity. Such knowledge is acquired through God's self-disclosure, which is the unveiling of the mysterious that are hidden behind the mundane. "Revelation therefore is not inspiration, the special grace with which one is believed to be endowed by a deity.... Revelation deals purely and simply with the contents of Religion, what is to be believed as true or rejected as untrue. It deals with the Deposit of Faith."[73]

In traditional thought, revelation is not static but happens daily, as opposed to the Abrahamic religions, where it has become fixed and canonized. Within the Abrahamic religions revelation is recorded within their scriptures and traditions.[74] It is a past event that ceased to exist with the death of their prophets. Islam has certain dictates within the Qur'an that safeguard revelation, such as the belief that Muhammad is the last prophet and no other revelation to humanity will follow him. Christianity has similar views concerning Jesus, who was not only a prophet but also the very "Son of God." These faiths operate in the lives of millions, yet in some respects, their theology is static and out of touch with our ever changing world. Both subscribe to a stringent dogma that does not accept revelation outside of the scriptures. "But when we enter the realm of Traditional Religions we appear to be at a loss. The religious ideas here can hardly be said to be organized. There are no written documents or body of doctrines, one explaining another or validating it."[75] This is not a sign of weakness or inability to organize a written record to house their sacred history. Many "Black" African societies have left well-documented written histories, which are discussed elsewhere in this book. The fact that African religion is not completely canonized speaks to its organic nature and its openness to new revelation. The misconception that African religion is without scriptures has led many to harbor negative attitudes toward African people. Thereby placing Africa and black people at the bottommost rung of the evolutionary ladder. Some have even suggested that Africans be placed at a lower stage of development, somewhere "between animism and polytheism, which came to be known as polydaemonism [a stage involving some classification of spirits, some higher than others]."[76] Evolutionary interpretations of African culture dominated early studies of Africans and their religion. Many of these negative attitudes have since slightly changed, but the idea that African people in general are less human than whites in particular, remains the underlying philosophy that continues to pervade Western thought. Such thinking has changed only recently, with the advancement of African scholars conducting research, which has provided the world with a more accurate assessment of TACF. Nonetheless, even African scholars are guilty of attacking their own culture, and in particular, many African Christian and Muslim scholars harbor negative attitudes toward traditional African cultural forms.[77]

Christian Theology and Revelation

African Christians' negative view of their traditional culture was not of their making alone. These views were first propagated and advanced by the most respected white scholars. Karl Rahner advanced the hegemonic view that anyone who followed certain principles were "anonymous Christians."[78] All that was good in the world was attributed to the great values upheld within Christendom. Rahner even proposed that those outside of Christendom could be saved without accepting Jesus, providing that they exhibit "fruits of the spirit."[79] He further rationalized that one who possesses these traits must certainly have received them from Christ, and even if they are ignorant of Christianity.[80] Kibicho rejected Rahner's arrogant perspective and accused him of advancing Western hegemony. "This to me smacks of Christian imperialism, as it seeks to claim for itself all that it regards as the best in human qualities wherever it is to be found."[81] This model is the same as the acculturation strategy that European missionaries used to destroy TACF and convert Africans to Christianity.

Another theory advanced by Western theologians to explain the nature of revelation is the general theory of revelation, which explains that all good knowledge comes from the Christian God. However, this form of self-disclosure is only preparatory and not complete. Those who possess this type of revelation cannot have a full-saving, conceptual knowledge of God. "I consider traditional religions," writes Mbiti, "Islam and the other religious systems to be preparatory and even essential ground in the search for the Ultimate. But only Christianity has the terrible responsibility of pointing the way to that ultimate Identity, Foundation and Source of being."[82] Mbiti goes a step further, so that no one mistakenly places him in the camp of African traditionalists: "Christianity should be presented as the fulfillment of that after which, in all its richness, African traditional religiosity has groped."[83]

The Christian interpretation of God's self-disclosure is not uniform.[84] For instance, Kibicho describes one of many perspectives advanced in Christendom as the evolutionary theory of revelation: "This is the view which sees religion in general as going through an evolutionary process: from the most primitive stages [variously described as animism, dynamism, shamanism] through polydaemonism and polytheism, to henotheism, and finally to monotheism. The different religions are then classified in one or other of these evolutionary stages."[85] The evolutionary theory of revelation is, in part, advocated by some Christian fundamentalist throughout black Christendom in the United States. Especially their passionate belief that all views of God apart from those advocated outside of Christendom are false. This narrow-minded perspective is dangerous and ignores the common trait that all cultures share; namely, that "all religions represent sinful man's confused and misdirected efforts to reach God on his own and on his own terms."[86] The general Christian theory of revelation or G-d's self-disclosure is divisive and does not make allowances for different perspectives. As long as the black churches remain faithful to the visions staunchly advocated by white fundamentalists, they will be unable to embrace those who practice the religion of their ancestors.

The general perspective of revelation is the most common and closely tied to natural revelation. Natural revelation is premised on the notion that nature is a witness of God's presence. All of nature, including plant and animal life, testifies to a power greater than itself. Natural revelation is available to those who do not know Christ, whereas, special revelation is for those in the Christian church, who have been endowed with special grace through faith. This special revelation "is contained in the Christian biblical history comprising the old and the new testaments and culminating in the Incarnation of God, the one and only full and fully saving Revelation, Jesus Christ."[87]

The various Christian views of revelation may differ slightly, but share a common unity that holds them together. Each position advocates that Christianity is the superior medium by which God self-discloses. "All these theories have this one thing in common: they all end up in their various ways and degrees denying complete and fully saving revelation to other religions.... They are incomplete in themselves and they find their fulfillment in Christianity."[88]

The Christian concept of revelation is tainted and therefore incapable of analyzing African views of God. Kibicho condemns the Christian theories of revelation and charges that they are inadequate for explaining African conceptions of the divine. "The way I see it, none of the views considered is adequate to interpret the revelation we have in African Religion."[89] Even general revelation that is supposedly given by God to all God's creation, cannot sufficiently explain African concepts of God. For, according to Western scholars, natural revelation is incapable of bringing one to a full awareness of deity. Still, practitioners of TACF hold that they indeed possess a "fully-saving" knowledge of deity. Africans must not accept those who say they have access only to natural revelation because they have as much right as any other people to experience the fullness of God. "This incomplete revelation would also imply at worst no salvation at all [as many Africans were taught to believe and still believe about African Religion and other non–Christian religions]. At best it means an incomplete and inferior type of salvation, which in actuality means no salvation."[90]

Kibicho argues rather strongly that African religion is "fully-saving," and that its practitioners have a clear perception of deity. "[R]evelation in this religion is as complete and fully salvatory as any religion could be expected to be, including Christianity."[91] Racism permeates Western scholarship and prevents European and Arab scholars from respecting African religion and its people. The Kikuyu people have a proverb that expresses the racial dilemma within Western scholarship: "*Gutiri muthungu na mubia'* [There is no difference between the Mzunga (settler) and the Mzungu (missionary)]."[92] Both seem intent upon denying African people respect as human beings. Neither respected Africans as capable of governing their socioeconomic and religious destiny. "To this day in South Africa and parts of the United States of America, some of the most 'saved' Christians are among the most notorious racists, and they use Christianity to support their racism."[93] African traditional cultures have always existed with knowledge of God as Supreme Being and creator of all things in existence. There has never been a time when Africa and its people were in need of receiving knowledge about God from Arabs or Europeans: "There is ample and strong empirical evidence in pre–Christian African communities of faith which shows that there was full and fully saving knowledge of God, as full and fully saving, that is, as can be attained [or appropriated] by any human communities of faith."[94]

This "saving" knowledge of God, which existed before the arrival of the Arab and European, attests to the historical relationship with the divine, which existed thousands of years before the Hebrew faith, which in part, gave birth to Judaism, Christianity, and Islam. Modern Judaism did not flourish until the destruction of the temple around 70 CE. Even most ancient European historians recorded that African Egyptians had an elaborate religious system in place for at least two thousand years before giving birth to Western religion. It was not until the fifteenth century CE that European historians began to deviate from their predecessors and revise history. The post-enlightenment Europeans were indeed the first revisionists of the modern era. It was because of their hegemonic and imperialist perspectives and African enslavement, which they created a new African that had always existed in a state of servitude. Kibicho studied the attitudes of those who harbor such thinking, including Africans. He determined that many self-hating Africans' thinking was largely shaped by Christian missionaries: "Some of the older converts from Kikuyu Religion to Christianity I have talked to were made to believe that they had really been in total darkness or ignorance of God, that their religion was of Satan with hardly anything good in it."[95]

Black people throughout the world were programmed by Christian missionaries to think of themselves as a people without cultural values. The missionaries were embedded with the occupying colonial forces in Africa and taught African converts that their religion and culture was barbaric and would lead them to hell. Even so-called friendly European scholars, such as Marcel Griaule and Fr. Placide Tempels, did not seek to advance African religion as an appropriate source worthy of elevation to the status of sacred. They simply sought to show that Africans were not completely uncivilized as their scholars had reported. Many of these like-minded missionary-scholars did however record that Africans did indeed possess a rational knowledge of God: "Thus, as the missionaries themselves ultimately realised, the idea of God was not something new which they had to introduce to the Africans. And even the missionaries' claims that the African conception of God had serious deficiencies have been shown to be false, and due mainly to the missionaries' own prejudices and preconceived ideas about African Religion and African peoples generally."[96]

Africans had not only a valid concept of God, but also a highly developed spirituality and theology that undergirded their cultural traditions. African people are highly spiritual and one cannot understand anything about them without first realizing that their perception of reality is governed by spiritual laws. Mbiti comments on this matter: "To understand their religious ethos and philosophical perception it is essential to consider their concepts of the spiritual world in addition to concepts of God."[97] Their concepts of the inner working of the spirit world reveals that their highly ritualized culture was capable of developing those essential elements that provide healing for the community. Their ability to recognize that the individual and the cosmos are involved in a delicate relationship places African religion at the pinnacle of religious systems with a cosmic consciousness.

> [E]mpirical evidence for full and fully saving knowledge of God among pre–Christian communities of faith is the strong presence there of what would be described in Christian terms as "the fruits of the Spirit." ... [J]udged by the "fruits of the Spirits" (even as Jesus said that human beings must ultimately be judged on this question rather than by their professed faith) these societies were certainly more God fearing, and therefore had better existential saving-knowledge of God, than the colonialist Christian societies to which the missionaries who came to evangelize them belonged.[98]

That many African communities initially resisted the invasions by Arabs and Europeans is indicative of their willingness to preserve an essential part of their existence. They knew what many are now coming to understand— that if one becomes estranged from their cultural center, they lose their connection to the values that house their way of being. When a people are violently uprooted from their cultural center they become vulnerable to imbibing alien values that push them further away from their inner core. Those who fought against the Arabs and Europeans to prevent the destruction of traditional African cultural norms were the true patriots of the faith. Many African freedom fighters turned to the paradigms that had sustained their forebearers. In effect, they rejected the God of imperialism, especially when they realized that Christianity had taught them to accept their enslavement and to wait until death, when they will then enter the afterlife and live in eternal bliss. African freedom fighters rejected this utopianism and trusted the spirits who had helped their ancestors. This type of thinking would eventually free them from the unrelenting enemies who had destroyed their culture.

In retrospect we have to conclude that those cultural groups that resisted Christianity and Islam possessed a vision of God that the invaders were incapable of possessing. Those who resisted colonialism and Christianity understood an important concept that remains the hallmark of liberation theology: God is always on the side of the oppressed.[99] The true believers were not the missionaries who came along with the colonizers to steal, kill, and destroy.

The true believers could not have been the Christian missionaries who destabilized the African continent, with so-called information that would "civilize"
and "save" the savages. It was the duty of African people to reject Christianity
and Islam. Rejecting Islam and Christianity was the moral responsibility of
African elders, and may have saved what remains of those TACF scattered
throughout the continent. "God was on their side and ... all true believers
must also be on the same side of justice, the African freedom fighters were
standing solidly within the Africa revelation or conception of God which
they brought with them into Christianity and which still formed the core of
their conception of God."[100] Kibicho concluded his study by remarking
that the Christian missionary's conception of revelation in traditional Africa
is deeply flawed: "[T]he traditional Christian attitude towards African Religion ... in the various interpretations of the Christian idea of Revelation ...
is in error, and does not do justice to the conceptual and experiential revelation which we see in African communities of faith.... [I]t is erroneous
and out of keeping with empirical evidence to describe the revelation or
the knowledge of God we have in African Religion [from the pre–Christian
period to the present], as general and incomplete revelation, to regard it
as merely preparatory or latent, or condescendingly to call it 'anonymous
Christianity.' Rather, we should recognize there is indeed in all genuine religions, and be bold enough to acknowledge, a full and fully saving revelation,
as full and fully saving, that is, as would be possible in any human situation,
and in accordance with the world-view of the community of faith in question."[101]

If students of religion are serious in dialoguing across the religious
divides, they must be willing to accept the reality of African religion. After
all, it is the oldest religion in the world today. It possesses a full revelation of
deity and its practitioners possess an elaborate, esoteric understanding of
spiritual beings. Their knowledge of the divine is independent of Islam and
Christianity.[102] If Christian academics are to accept traditional African cultural forms as constituting a world religion, worthy of the respect given to
other faiths, then and only then can a genuine dialogue across the religio-
cultural divide occur. The Creator has certainly spoken to African people
and has disclosed Her will to them. God has indeed appeared to all people
and the first human beings certainly would not have missed the opportunity
to seek God's mind. Africa remains a society that survives on a religious
ontology rooted in cosmic harmony and are in possession of a spirituality
our modern world desperately needs. Geluwe's position on African religion
and its conception of God is very positive, with the exception that he holds
Africans do not have written religious records. (This is not his fault because

those educated in Western schools were taught to separate Egypt from the rest of Africa. Not knowing that the Arab is a newcomer to Egypt, an interloper who has no claim to its history.) African people have perhaps the first and oldest religious records extant. Aside from Geluwe's inability to embrace Egypt as a part of Africa's heritage, his observations shed light on TACF nondogmatic posture and their unique perspective on revelation. "Media of Revelation in African Traditional Religion" describes the flexibility and tolerant nature of African religion. As the Africans' sense of unity is within diversity, so also are his concepts of God hidden in a paradox:

> He does not see any inconsistency in a good and kind God creating and acting through a spirit which is essentially evil. He is not bothered by his belief that a malevolent spirit can be a manifestation of an all-merciful God. For him, the moral order is ultimately constituted according to principles which often elude men; experience and tradition reveal them, and no human action can change them.... The African bases himself on experience. And experience teaches him that fortune and misfortune happen.[103]

Geluwe perceives African revelation as that grounded in ideals that were also expressed by David Hume, who argued that knowledge is acquired through the senses and contingent on experience: "The contents of revelation in Traditional Religions appear to affect only what man has experienced or does experience. And based on this experience, Africans have come to define four distinct categories of spiritual entities or potencies."[104] The first element within Geluwe's experiential schema involves the African conception of deity. "He is kind and benevolent to man—the source of all the good things that man experiences, such as water, food, good health, wealth, old age and fame. He is ... the final explanation of all phenomena."[105] Second is the role of helper spirits that assist the Creator in carrying out various duties. These helpers can be either spiritual beings or deified ancestors, which function as mediums and provides a channel by which communication is made possible between the visible and invisible realms. These spiritual forces can be good or otherwise. Prophetic voices can speak truth or advocate falsehoods. "Like the Supreme Being himself the good ones are a source of blessings for man, while the evil spirits cause havoc, diseases, even death. The good spirits act as counteracting agents on the evil spirits."[106] The third force operating in the traditional African perception of God's self-disclosure is the roll of ancestors who must always be given honor. "In Africa people's welfare and rights are safeguarded by the ancestors. It is the ancestors who ultimately punish wrongdoing, by sending trouble or illness, even death, to the transgressor. When trouble comes, the diviner's makes inquiry into the reasons behind an illness or misfortune, from there determines which of the ancestral laws have been broken. In this way abuses are corrected and people are given an opportunity to make amends and turn their lives around."[107]

African elders were expected to live extraordinary lives and die a good death. Even African Christian bishops have charged those who accuse Africans of worshiping ancestors as misinformed. "It would be better to speak of 'presence of ancestors,' 'service of ancestors.'"[108] African culture is family centered and the love for family is so great that it is inconceivable for traditional Africans to accept that death can eternally separate them from those they love. Africans live out this belief by honoring their loved ones who have passed on. In agricultural regions of Africa the first harvest is presented to the ancestors.[109] The offering is received by the ancestors as a sweet odor in their nostrils. In Madagascar, the honoring of ancestors is at the center of their religious ideology. They view the ancestors as givers of all good gifts.[110] Ancestors "have become their counselors, judges and leaders.... These ancestors are so highly esteemed that they receive a divine name when they are eminent, which is *Zanahary*" (one who possesses a noble scent).[111] Throughout traditional Africa, it is not the Supreme Being who functions to bestow blessings and gifts upon humanity but his emissaries. "The ancestors are said to bring blessings, both spiritual and material to the living; they may decide to come back to life to accomplish a duty which they may have left undone or unfinished."[112] In traditional African communities, the ancestors are honored and venerated because unlike the Creator who is perceived as being far away, the ancestors have lived among the people. "They [Ancestors] look at us as an extension of themselves, and so as a result, their own extension must be made either to grow up to the level of vision that they have, or must be adjusted in one way or another so as to keep continuity on their side."[113] An interdependent relationship exists between humanity and the spirit world. "There is a reciprocity here that really cancels out the whole sense of hierarchy.... This is an important idea, because the same sense of hierarchy is found in the thinking of some Westerners that romanticizes the indigenous world and indigenous life."[114]

The fourth revelatory medium used for disclosing God's will is nonhuman entities. Traditional Africans have been accused of worshipping nature, but this is a misreading because they believe that they are intricately connected to nature. Plants and minerals function as divine mediums and modes of communication between the visible and invisible worlds. Therefore, nature must be honored and venerated in much the same way as respect is rendered to God.

Revelation in traditional communities is not confined to a religious hierarchy limited to professional clergy. Anyone, including a child, can be used as a divine medium to communicate the creators will. Revelation is not confined to Christian dogma, but is available to every human being regardless of their religious preference. Revelation has its validity authenticated in the lives of everyday people. "The African's awareness of the possibility and his wholehearted acceptance of private revelation as a regular feature, very much enlarge the contents of Revelation…. It is commonplace in Africa for any person to announce that it has been revealed to him to give alms or not to go on a journey or to divorce his wife!"[115] Thus, private revelation is the primary means by which the spirit world communicates to humanity. There is really no need for someone to teach another human being about God because human beings are programmed to know God. "There are no formal religious classes, except in the case of an exclusive few for whom some secret knowledge is deemed essential for their work, as for example, priests or custodians of shrines."[116] Those who enter the ministry do not place themselves above those with whom they minister. African ministers do not live one way on Sunday and another on Monday. There is no dichotomy between ethical behavior in business and behavior at the shrine. "He does not dichotomize between his religious activity and any other aspect of his life. Whether he is hunting or farming, or deciding a case, or enjoying himself through dancing, or whatever else he is doing, he is deeply involved in a religious experience."[117] Revelation in traditional society is one of praxis. Discussing theories of life for the sake of hearing oneself speak is not in the interest of traditional Africans. African people are spiritually driven and are constantly listening for what the spirit is saying. In turn, they conduct the affairs of their life based on their communication with the ancestors and helper-spirits.

Kibicho identified several modes of revelation in traditional African religion. He described one as the created order, which highlighted the role of nature as a medium used to communicate the will of the divine for one's life. "The whole of nature or creation, by its very existence, beauty, its mystery; by its orderliness & dependability, and by the life it continually brings forth and sustains even in the face of great dangers and tragedies—by all these and other related features of it the whole of creation has always and constantly pointed the African peoples to the Creator and to his wonderful nature."[118] Kibicho described the relationship traditional Africans have with nature as sacramental.[119] "This sacramental nature of the universe is especially noted in relation to the most prominent and awe-inspiring natural phenomena such as celestial bodies[,] especially the sun, and also mountains…. This explains in part why we find among various African [peoples] apparent identification of God with natural phenomena. Such identification, however, is not real identification but only apparent and symbolic."[120] Mbiti stated that the African perception of God is "one of the most fundamental religious heritages of African peoples."[121]

God discloses God's-Self through people, but more often uses nature as a medium. For instance, whether God speaks in a still small voice or through lightning and rain, Africans wait patiently and listen, to ascertain the meaning and purpose of the act. "Quite apart from human beings, Africans believe that God and the gods and ancestors speak to them through happenings, and dreams. An unusual or unexpected event may easily be considered a kind of revelation from the spirits."[122]

In the Ashanti and Yoruba traditions, to simply stumble over one's feet and hit their big toe is a divine sign that should not be ignored.[123] Those who dream about certain animals also are receiving a revelatory sign.[124] In fact, divination may be the ultimate source of revelation within African traditional cultures. It is by far the most abstract feature of all revelatory systems. "[M]eans of divination like pots, cola nuts, poisoned chickens, cowry shells as a key element in the attempt to know the hidden or the future are a universal feature in African Religions."[125]

Revelation is not an abstract event but a medium used for communicating between the physical and nonphysical realms. The Christian concept of revelation should never be used as the criteria to critique African religion. "[T]he traditional Christian idea of revelation ... the concept of General & Special Revelation, is distorting and inappropriate to describe the knowledge of God evident in African Religion; that both the ideas of God found in Africa, and the accompanying religious and humanistic values [fruits of the spirit]—show that the revelation there is as full and as salvatory as could be expected in any religion including Christianity; ... full revelation and salvation are available and possible in non–Christian religions, and it has actually occurred, e.g., in African Religion; and that you can know where such full revelation is, by the high religious-humanistic values and qualities which it fosters [fruits of the spirit]."[126]

People are also an important medium used for disclosing God's will. "It may be described as a uniquely human quality, a sort of higher wisdom or deep intuition of otherwise hidden but most important features of reality; it is like a sixth sense."[127] Human beings are a unique medium of revelation described by the Kikuyu people as "*meciria* [reason and more]."[128] There is also a mode of revelation situated in those gifted men and women who are the few in every society. Many of these individuals function as priest, priestess, prophet, and prophetess. Some may have no title at all but possess extraordinary insight to see beyond the veil. The men and women who possess the gift to see beyond circumstances, and understand what is happening in the spirit world, are highly sought out in traditional African communities.

Extraordinary acts of God are perceived as a medium of revelation. (God is trying to tell us something.) Whether those acts are mediated through natural disaster or sickness, these events are viewed as mediums or modes of revelation that should not be ignored. For example, "the Meru of Kenya have a wonderful tradition in which they relate how God delivered them from slavery on a certain island [Mbwa], and guided them through difficult periods, to their present land on the slopes of Mt. Kenya."[129]

Revelation is experiential and pragmatic. The norms undergirding traditional Africans perception of religion are sewn into the cultural fabric of the society. "Through their various acts of worship, sacrifices and prayers, rites and ceremonies and festivals[,] etc., God's presence among the people is kept alive, heightened[,] passed on from generation to generation."[130] Modes of revelation are kept alive in "myths and legends…, proverbs and wise sayings through which important beliefs and values are kept alive, strengthened and passed on."[131] African religion and revelation emerged from traditional African cultural norms that were first established by the ancestors. Despite the cultural wars waged against Africans by Arabs and Europeans, the elevation of African cultural values to the status of sacred has kept alive Africa's most sacred gift to the world. Religion remains a vital force in the lives of those practitioners of African cultural forms observed by millions of people throughout the world. TACF permeate every aspect of one's life and shape how they perceive themselves and the world. "[T]he African has [a] pragmatic and utilitarian outlook on religion: Religion must prevent man from being harmed; Religion must make man happy; Religion must neutralize the evil forces, both physical and psychical that surround man—or else Religion loses its meaning."[132]

This may explain why Christianity and Islam are incapable of sustaining the Africans' appetite for religion. Africans who worship at the feet of European and Arab gods will remain unable to embrace their full humanity. Divided Africans cannot be happy in their adopted religio-cultures, whether Euro-Christian or Arab-Islamic. These cultural systems may appeal to Africans, but they do not address those existential yearnings for which only those cultural values from within their sacred culture has the answer. "If God is at work in the traditional African religions, and if man responds to this divine activity, the African religions contain the element of revelation and the help of divine grace, because God, from the beginning of time, seeks to make himself known to men, and this response of man to God is religion."[133] Although many Africans willingly follow the religio-culture of the Arabs and others embrace various forms of Euro-Christianity, Africans must not abandon their traditional value systems. They should remember how it sustained their forebearers prior to the creation of Christianity and Islam. "African religion is a divinely inspired vehicle, which includes the human response as a vital ingredient, through which man and God and other ultrahuman powers keep in communication. And through this divine-human relationship and interaction, plus the resultant human and extrahuman wisdom, creativity and innovations [as found especially in great diviners—doctors, prophets and seers, charismatic judges and elder-leaders]. Man ... receives the vision of reality and the appropriate orientation to it which enable him to survive and to live a fulfilled, satisfying and happy life."[134] Kibicho's meticulous analysis TACF has shown that African religion is sacred and culturally attuned to the deepest needs and aspirations of African people.[135]

2

African Culture and Western Attitudes Toward African Religion

Western society has committed a grave injustice by its continuing role in the destabilization and destruction of traditional African cultural forms. Yesterday it was slavery and colonialism that was needed to assuage the Euro-Anglo appetite for world dominance. Today it's Africom and the re-colonization of former colonies, especially by the United States and France. In addition to the Anglo-Europeans' insatiable drive to control the world, traditional African communities have also suffered from the global and technical nature of world events. Advancements in technology have allowed people to travel over vast territories to import their religio-cultural ideologies. For example, every non-black person on the continent of Africa, especially the Arabs, have to some degree used religion to justify their attack on African culture. Christianity and Islam have been the single greatest factors leading to the erosion of African tradition and culture. These Abrahamic religions are partly responsible for the disunity and chaos that has destabilized black communities across the world. For when one is violently separated from their religion and culture and classified as pre-human, instability becomes their constant companion. E. O. Babalola was a leading scholar of African culture who affirmed that proponents of Islam and Christianity have negatively labeled African culture and by extension, its people, as a "non-reality."[1] Not only have Arabs and Europeans perpetrated such negativity and worse, but ironically, many African Christians also view traditional ways of being with disdain. This should not be surprising since most were educated in Western schools where they were taught to hate themselves. This deep-seated hatred has become one of the main sources of the crisis that plagues Africa and people of African descent throughout the world. After Africans were forced to abandon their traditional cultural referents, they entered a world where they were no longer viewed as human beings. In a world created by and for the white man, Western-educated Africans became their tokens and apologists and are used to advance European and Arab values.

Babalola further argued that European and Arab scholars characterized traditional cultural values as unworthy of elevation to the status of sacred. While they have elevated their own traditional values to the status of religion, they cannot conceive of Africans elevating their tradition to the status of a "religion." Many continue to mis-judge African traditional culture because it is viewed through a European or Arab lens. Compared to what they deem as valuable within their traditions, they determine that African traditional culture lacks similar values. African cultural values must be critiqued by tools forged from within its cultural milieu. How could the Abrahamic religions be "accurately" evaluated from a traditional African perspective? Of course their obsession with monotheism seems strange to traditional Africans. Yet, traditional Africans do not condemn them for their one god theory. We should not remain ignorant of the nature of religion and how all religions emanate from someone's culture. Organized religion is simply the elevation of one's cultural values and traditions and the uplifting of one's cultural heroes and heroines to the realm of divinity. Thus, if we are to adequately understand any religion we must view it as the elevation of a people's cultural values and traditions to the realm of sacred. The same is true of African traditions, which can be explored in their fullness through the medium of culture. Babalola maintains, "To understand African Traditional Religion properly[,] the religion must be seen against the back drop of the traditional people."[2] Traditional African cultural forms can only be adequately critiqued in light of black cultural norms and values. There are no European or Arab standards or cultural templates, which can rightfully evaluate TACF. Even many African Christian are incapable of evaluating the religion of their forbearers, because most African Christians who attended Western schools were systematically taught to reject their culture. Especially those traditional customs that contradict Christian dogma, such as venerating the ancestors and allowing helper-spirits to guide one's life. The same is true of African Muslims who will defend Arab nationalism with their lives. The propagators of Islamic and Christian expansion into Africa effectively destabilized many African traditional cultural forms. Islamic and Christian crusaders successfully propagandized negative myths about African people, particularly their inherent inability to conceptualize Deity.[3] This thinking is very much alive and can be witnessed in the hiring practices of major universities in the United States.

African Religion and Western Domination
of Sacred Discourse

Few scholars of African descent serve as full faculty members in religion departments in the United States. Some suggest this is due to the historical racist ideology that undergirds the thinking of many whites in positions of authority. Such ideas may stem from what former Secretary of State Dr. Condoleezza Rice calls "America's original birth mark." (I prefer to think of racism as America's original birth-defect.) Comments in *The Journal of Blacks in Higher Education* on the prevailing attitude regarding black scholars in academia shed light on this subtle but higher form of racism, noting "the once prevailing view that black people were inherently lazy, stupid, and wholly lacking in aptitude in historical analysis and abstract mathematics—but it is something of a mystery why the scholarly penetration of blacks is almost nil in their stronghold of religion and theology."[4] Religion has been and, some would argue remains the vehicle *par excellence* that has stabilized the physical and mental hemorrhaging that began when millions of Africans were ripped from their homeland and forced to breed and produce in order to advance capitalism, which in many ways is the religion of the Anglo-European "race." African people have been barred from entering the religion departments where their story could be told, and quite possibly, the next generation of white leaders may have a change of heart. If the black narrative is taught to the next ruling white elite—the 1 percent—maybe history will not repeat itself. Maybe fewer white police officers would kill unarmed black men if they were required to take religion and law enforcement classes taught by black men.

The major academic institutions in the United States continue to view African people as incapable of serving as professors in religion departments. One would think that African Americans would at least be represented in the field from which most of the civil-rights leaders hailed, but this is not the case. In fact, African American students have been terrorized in religion departments and black scholars of religion have been deliberately kept out of religion departments throughout country. Due to the major influence religion has on the black community and society at large, it is only reasonable to expect their presence in the place where it is supposedly most objectively propagated. However, in the year 1995, only two black candidates earned doctorates in religion, which was less than two percent of the degrees awarded in the field. Even Howard University, the place where black minds are supposedly allowed to think and develop, did not produce one Ph.D. during its golden years of the civil-rights era. African Americans are twice as likely as whites to attend divinity schools, yet, they are still grossly underrepresented as faculty in the nation's best departments of religion.

For instance, in the 25 highest-ranked universities in the United States as of 1995, only two black scholars held endowed chairs and only 12 African Americans were on the faculty of their religion departments, barely 3 percent of the total religion faculty in those universities. Only Princeton and Cornell had more than one black professor in their department of religion. Ten of the schools—Yale, Stanford, Brown, Rice, the University of Pennsylvania, Northwestern, Washington, the University of Michigan, the University of Virginia, and the University of California at Berkeley—as of 1995, did not have a single African American faculty member in their religion departments. This is the state of objective religion and so-called liberal education in North America. There are no black-operated or black-owned universities in North America that grant a Ph.D. in religion. Considering that African Americans are kept out of a field that has questioned their intelligence and advanced theories that dehumanized them may explain why African traditional religion has also been demonized in Western scholarship. White Christian missionaries or converted African Christians (whose self-identity is a major issue) have conducted many of the studies we have on African religion. Some of the studies have been so negative toward African people that it is impossible to deem their work as scholarly—and certainly not objective.

The most critical analysis of Western scholarship by an African scholar was carried out by the late Okot p'Bitek. In a small book entitled *African Religions in Western Scholarship*, he begins by attacking Western scholarship for its derogative choice of language used to describe African people. For example, to refer to African cultural groups or families as "tribes" was at one time widespread throughout academia. P'Bitek argued that the word "tribe" must be discontinued within academia because of its history. The term "tribe" had become synonymous with "people living in primitive or barbaric conditions." And each time it is used, as in the sentence "I am a Kikuyu by tribe," implies that the speaker is a Kikuyu who lives in a primitive condition. When we read of "tribal law," "tribal economics," or "tribal religion," Western scholars mean that the law, economics, or religion under review are those of primitive and barbaric peoples.[5]

Since meaning is encoded within discourse, Westerners' propensity to use such negative descriptors points to their perception of themselves. Westerns are generally taught to view their society as superior to all others. "Western scholarship sees the world as divided into two types of human society: one, their own, civilized, great, developed; the other, the non–Western peoples, uncivilized, simple, undeveloped."[6] This binary remains the controlling ideology that undergirds Western thinking. It was with this negative view of African people that so-called objective scholars traveled to Africa in the late nineteenth and early twentieth century to study the "undeveloped" and "pre-modern" Africans. Many of these studies were openly biased and riddled with methodological problems. In the Obama era the United States government continues to fund studies on Africa for strategic and economic purposes. The U.S. government has little concern for African people and are entirely focused on controlling their resources.

From the earliest of times when white aristocrats began to travel outside of Europe they were both enthralled and dismayed with African people and their religion. P'Bitek asserts that the European interest in Africa and its people dates back to the very "dawn of Western scholarship."[7] One can witness the Europeans' fascination with Africa early as the Homeric poems. Homer's poetry, especially the *Iliad*, reveals the Greeks' obsession and admiration for Africans in Ethiopia.[8] The Greek gods and scholars were always eager to visit Africa. "Zeus, followed by all the gods, went to feast with the blameless Ethiopians where he remained for 12 days. Poseidon also visited Ethiopia to receive a hecatomb of bulls and rams."[9] Pythagoras spent twenty-two years studying in the Egyptian temples and later taught the Egyptian system as his own.

Herodotus of Harlicarnassus was one of the earliest white historians to visit Africa and carefully record the people's way of life. He was intrigued by their religious devotion to justice, which prompted him to advance the theory that the Greeks borrowed much of their mythology and many of their deities from African lore.[10] Around 751 BCE, when the African Kushite King Piankhi, who was founder of the twenty-fifth dynasty, invaded Egypt, African deities were subsumed into Greek mythology.[11] It was upon these myths that the Greeks built their society. Seneca wrote that "myths reveal either philosophical views on the basic nature of things or ethical doctrines."[12] Since myths have the potential to reveal the essential thought processes of a society, early scholars who investigated African religion should have first explicated the peoples' myths prior to writing their theories and misrepresentations of a people who created the ancient world.

Evans Pritchard and Placide Tempels were among the first white scholars who consulted Africans mythical history. Both men concluded that it was misleading to view Africans as godless or incapable of conceptualizing deity. How could their findings prove otherwise when they knew that Africans possessed a very complex perception of deity and were conscious of their cultural creation of the deity. Pritchards and Tempels discovered that Africans did indeed possess very complex notions of deity, that in many cases, were closed to outsiders.[13] However, the classical Western academic view of African religion outside of Egypt has been generally negative. "[T]he picture of African societies and people painted by the classical scholars is that of anarchy, promiscuity and cruel living. Some African peoples are even denied ... truly human form. They are described as strange and miserable folk who barely exist in continual hunger and fear."[14] This attitude is rooted in the Westerners' cultural identity crisis. Western scholarship is premised upon limiting binaries and misconceptions, such as things are either good or bad and there can be no middle ground. For instance, ideas are usually compared and or contrasted; ideas can be similar or dissimilar. "You are either with us or with the terrorists." You must either support the United States government's inhumane domestic and foreign policy or risk being arrested as a terrorist. These binaries reveal a people who are engaged in a war with nature. This constrictive binary may, in fact, be the hallmark of Western scholarship. "One of the most perplexing and amazing phenomena of Western scholarship is its almost morbid fascination and preoccupation with the "primitive," and the hostile and arrogant language of the philosophers, historians, theologians and anthropologists."[15]

The Western binary puts "barbarians" against the "humane" and Muslim against Christian. Western discourse preferences white males and of lately, white females, who are placed in positions of power throughout the white world. Former President George W. Bush placed the entire world into two camps as though there were no other options. This binary logic is without question the hallmark of Western discourse.[16] The narrow lens through which academics view African religion has changed very little since the early days of European conquests. It is important to note that even today Western scholarship has not abandoned its racist view of Africa. The world is still divided into the "civilized" west and the "primitive" non–Western world, now politely referred to as "the Developing Countries."[17] The language may have changed, but the West still perceives itself as superior to all other groups. "For over two thousand years, from Herodotus and Diodotus to Trevor-Roper and Levi-Strauss, Western scholars have provided the most powerful ideology for Western dominance over the rest of mankind. By systematic and intensive use of dirty gossip they have justified and explained away the plunder, murder and suppression carried out by Western man."[18]

P'Bitek's keen observation of Western scholarship and its negative attitude of African people has not changed since the early 1900s, when Europeans finally penetrated the interior of West Africa. The study of African religion has utilized three strategies to explicate African traditional cultural forms: (1) Christian apologists; (2) African priest-scholars; and (3) Ecumenical dialogue.[19] All three methods are used in varying degrees throughout academia and by professional Christian missionaries. The Christian apologists are the most prevalent throughout departments of religion. They privately discourage those who stray too far from the political correct religious mainstream, and as professors, they encourage their students to conduct studies that show how the Christian view can assist whatever religion is under investigation. The current fad is to find ways to dialogue across the religious divides between Asian and Abrahamic religions. There are only a few scholars in academia, particularly the Afrocentrists, who are committed to preparing black students to understand and respect their culture. This kind of educator is committed to the transmittal and propagation of African cultural forms. The third category is also represented throughout academia. Their strategy is to appear to have a genuine interest in all religious faiths. Yet, one will search far and wide to find any meaningful efforts to create dialogue between Christian and practitioners of African religion. Religion scholars in the United States who are Christian or Muslim have found it difficult to accept African religion on the same level as their own. Without at least bracketing or controlling their biases, meaningful dialogue between African and Abrahamic religions will remain sidelined. Even when meager attempts are made to speak about African religion the discourse usually occurs with the Abrahamic religions lurking overhead as the final evaluators of African traditional cultural forms.

P'Bitek was also critical of those scholars who were viewed as friendly in furthering the study of African religion. Men such as Pritchard, Parrinder, Mbiti, and many other Christian missionary scholars were critiqued by p'Bitek and considered as enemies of African religion. They were not concerned with furthering African traditional cultural forms, but were Christian apologists who sought to show that the "noble savage" or "pagan" was capable of religious thought and that Jesus Christ was the fulfillment of their blind allegiance to their gods. P'Bitek points out that Pritchard, Parrinder, Mbiti, and others, however friendly they appeared, may have spoken positively about African tradition, but would never have considered abandoning their culture to worship at the feet of African gods. He concludes that these early pioneers of African religion were, in fact, imposters, masquerading as friends. They utilized African culture and deities to show the world that these "primitives" did indeed possess a knowledge of God. However underdeveloped or misguided, they did indeed possess a remote knowledge of the Christian God.[20]

Since p'Bitek's critical analysis several decades ago, many students of African religion are reviewing the works of Tempels, Mbiti, Pritchard, and other scholars who pioneered the study of African religion. Couched within their friendly veneer was their hidden belief that African religion is incomplete and in the process of becoming an Abrahamic religion. These men never intended to propagate African religion as an ideal religio-cultural system to be embraced by African people. Instead, after carefully scrutinizing their work, one finds their preference for Christianity. Even many Christian African scholars who undoubtedly have good intentions of reporting on their religio-culture, have erred greatly when they dress up African deity in European garb. For example, when scholars attempt to explicate African religio-cultural forms by utilizing European tools, structure, and schema, a methodological problem arises that has no easy remedy. A point clearly articulated by p'Bitek: "African scholars, smarting under the insults from the West, claimed that African peoples knew the Christian God long before the missionaries told them about it. African deities were selected and robed with awkward hellenic garments by Jomo Kenyatta, J. B. Danquah, K. A. Busia, W. Abraham, E. B. Ìdòwú and others."[21]

P'Bitek directly levels this indictment against those African Christians who were considered by many as the giants of African religio-culture. He directs much of his criticism at their efforts to make African religion conform to European norms. P'Bitek is especially concerned about the methodological dilemma created when one analyzes African religion through a Western lens. He even accuses the sons of Africa as misguided by failing to view African religion as a sacred cultural system within its own rights. Instead of respecting their own sacred religio-cultural forms, these men denied the traditional cultural values worthy of worship and veneration. Instead of making every effort to uphold their traditional values these African Christians were supporting a strategy designed to destabilize and destroy traditional African cultural forms.

P'Bitek further criticizes Mbiti for what he calls "hellenizing" and "Christianizing" African deity. "Mbiti's books are intended to show to the world not only that "African peoples are not religiously illiterate," but also that the African deities are but local names of the One God who is omniscient, omnipresent, omnipotent, transcendent and eternal."[22] The one God according to Mbiti and Ìdòwú is the God of Christianity and Jesus is his only begotten Son. This theology of dominance brought great harm to African people. Many abandoned their sacred culture because men like Mbiti and others convinced them that Jesus was the only way. They were correct to claim Jesus's authority as a divine being on par with the orisha and lwa. Yet, to attack the sacred cultural system of their forbearers unveils a pathology rooted in their psyche that is at war with the cultural forms that formed their identity. In such a condition one can never be at peace within themselves because mental chaos is the fruit that accompanies confusion.

We must be careful of the language used to communicate thought. Terms used to discuss African religion are in many ways foreign to African traditional cultural forms. In most traditional African societies the word religion as understood by the Western world does not exist. The language of Western theology is a bearer to meaningful dialogue between proponents of African and Abrahamic religions. "The interpretation of African deities in terms of the Christian God does not help us understand the nature of the African deities as African peoples conceive them. Furthermore, 'The attributes of our God and their [Dinka] Nhialic are not identical.... [T]o use the word God would raise metaphysical and semantic problems of our own for which there is no parallel among the Dinka.'"[23]

Missionary interests in African religion were premised on the condescending ideal that the "primitives" are in need of conversion to Christianity. For example, "the mission of the Church ... consists in extending Christ's life throughout the world and in helping mankind to participate in his mysteries; and in order to achieve this the church adapts itself to the thoughts, culture, customs, and languages of different ages and peoples."[24] Theoretically, this is the mission of the church and in some ways it is an accurate statement because in Latin America and throughout the Caribbean enslaved Africans adopted certain elements of Roman Catholicism, primarily to safeguard their sacred tradition. This engrafting became so pervasive throughout Roman Catholicism outside of Europe that the Church was forced to reluctantly accept certain aspects of African culture that did not conflict with church dogma. Since most scholars of Western religion in the early twentieth century were followers of the Abrahamic faiths, one is justified in linking the interests of evangelism with Western scholarship. Hence, it is Western Christian terminology that was used to view African people and their traditional cultural forms as lacking value. The military and economic dominance of Western values have influenced hermeneutics. Thus, African cultural forms cannot have any value apart from their connection with Anglo-European values. Such thinking is the microcosm of the dilemma distorting African scholarship. Due to Western dominance of discourse, African religion has primarily been observed and explicated via Christian dictates. "When students of African religions describe deities as eternal, omnipresent, omnipotent, omniscient, etc., they intimate that African deities have identical attributes with ... the Christian God.... African peoples may describe their deities as 'strong' but not 'omnipotent,' 'wise,' not 'omniscient,' 'old,' not 'eternal,' 'great,' not 'omnipresent.' The Greek metaphysical terms are meaningless in African thinking."[25]

Again, such comparison are the primary reason why African cultural forms have not been accepted even by African Christian scholars. Furthermore, p'Bitek charges most African scholars with hellenizing African religion, thereby placing it out of the reach of those who admire their traditions. "Like Danquah, Mbiti, Ìdòwú, Busia, Abraham, Kenyatta, Senghor and the missionaries, modern Western Christian anthropologists are intellectual smugglers. They are busy introducing Greek metaphysical conceptions into African religious thought. The African deities of the books, clothed with the attributes of the Christian God, are, in the main, creations of the students of African religions. They are all beyond recognition to the ordinary Africans in the countryside."[26]

This keen analysis of the ongoing dilemma facing African and non–African scholars of religion is equally true of all theological analysis regarding African people and culture. The quasi-scientific approach known as theology, by virtue of its privileged location within white-dominated educational institutions, separates itself from the practitioners of the faith. Rarely are the researchers true advocates of the religion or the people they study. Academia does a disservice to their people and scholarship when they attempt to explain local phenomena in foreign structures that were culturally situated to evaluate a specific religio-cultural group: Namely, Abrahamic cultural forms and the people that represent those religio-cultural traditions. African religion cannot adequately be assessed with language and tools designed to critique Christian theology. "The aim of the study of African religions should be to understand the religious beliefs and practices of African peoples, rather than to discover the Christian God in Africa."[27]

Since Western scholarship has analyzed traditional African cultural forms from a Christian perspective, the real study of African religion has barely been explored. Even those Africans who have embraced Christianity have not been able to abandon their "pagan" past. In some ways Christianity has been unable to bring complete fulfillment to Africans, especially those who were raised to celebrate their own sacred narratives. In this regard, "Christianity has barely touched the core of the life of most African peoples."[28] Some scholars have estimated that, in places such as northern Uganda, only a few decades ago, 90 percent of the population relied on indigenous cultural forms to assist them in moments of crisis.[29] Although many black people throughout Africa and in the Americas were forced to abandon their gods and embrace the god of Abraham, in moments of existential crisis, they revert to the faith of their forebears. P'Bitek remarks that the Africans' adoption of Arabic and Anglo cultural forms was understood by most Africans as nothing more than accepting another god into their large pantheon of divinities. They viewed Jesus and Muhammad as just another divinity who could assist them in much the same way as their divine intermediaries. This perspective is also supported by several scholars who argued that African theology is naturally tolerant of multiple deities and that the addition of new deities naturally functions to enhance the rhythmic nature of life: "The African tradition encourages a kind of 'catholicity' in religious thought and practice," argues Booth. "It [TACF] looks with favor on any power, new or old, that may be available for the healing and enhancing of man's life, especially in the communal context. An attempt to relate rather than to separate is characteristic of the African religious perspective."[30]

Islam and Christianity should be viewed as good ideas that African people perceived as palpable to their pantheon of divine entities. "It seems to me that the new God of Christianity was taken by many African peoples as just another deity, and added to the long list of the ones they believed in. So that many African Christians are also practitioners of their own religions."[31] Booth's scholarship further substantiates p'Bitek's thesis that Africans who accepted another people's culture as their religion initially did so to enhance their connection to the divine. They had no intention to completely abandon their cultural forms, which they turn to when facing a life crisis. The early African converts to Western cultural forms did not begin attacking traditional religion until they started attending schools operated by missionaries. The educated African assisted the Arabs and Europeans in destroying traditional African culture and values. The early scholars who studied African cultural norms and values did so to formulate strategies in which to attack TACF. They had no intentions of celebrating traditional African culture but were simply attempting to further the Christian agenda, which aimed to bring all men to Christ. Africans attended Western schools not to attain the highest form of knowledge, which is self-knowledge. Instead, they were given a Western education so they could learn to hate themselves and accept the white man's interpretation of Christianity as the only voice of God. "Throughout the long history of Western scholarship African religions have never been the object of study in their own right. African deities were used as mercenaries in foreign battles, not one of which was in the interest of African peoples…. The Christian Fathers had no intention of presenting African deities as they really were. Their main aim was to condemn and then destroy what they called 'demons,' and replace them with the Christian faith."[32]

These sentiments are not confined to a historical moment but can be witnessed throughout the history of Christendom. "We hear echoes of the same battle cry from the fifteenth century onwards, when hordes upon hordes of barbarians from Europe disguised as Christians leapt from ships, bible and gun in hand, to attack, plunder, murder and enslave the inhabitants of the whole world."[33] Few scholars of that time, much like today, were concerned with the atrocities committed against "nonentities." Such acts of barbarism then and now, were viewed as collateral damage. Most people of African descent and, in particular, Muslims, are still viewed by elite whites (the 1 percent) as non-entities. Christianity and Islam has done little in their battle to correct this negative view. It is as though Christianity, which verbally promotes values, is itself without an ethical guide. "The writers of that long period of Western domination set out to justify the colonial system by preaching that the world was sick and needed Western suppression ... in order to survive."[34] The fact that few men in positions of authority spoke out against European expansion and atrocities committed by white men throughout Africa and the Americas speaks to the general attitude many have for nonwhite people. P'Bitek argued that such silence is itself a strategy and weapon of mass destruction used to justify white barbarism. These acts of violence continue to be committed by Western military powers, whose sole intentions are to control the cosmos. They have been quite successful in enslaving most of the world through their inhumane form of capitalism. Many of the so-called wise men in the Western world play a vital role in the suppression and destruction of African people and their culture. Western scholars in general—particularly anthropologists and philosophers—remain primary agents whose writings and views are used to justify the dehumanization and destruction of black people throughout the world.

> The speculations of the eighteenth century philosophers and those of the nineteenth century anthropologists were not meant to give a true picture of African religions. These people were not interested in the proper study of African societies, because if they were, they would have come to Africa to carry out researches. Their works were "apologies" for the colonial system, their task was to demonstrate the superiority of Western culture over those of colonized peoples.... Terms ... used by Western writers in their imaginary speculations are not only meaningless, they are a nuisance in the proper understanding of African religions.[35]

Initially the systematic and comparative studies of African religion were positively viewed as a more objective approach to the study of African people and their culture. Nonetheless, these approaches that at first appeared "objective" were, in fact, tools used by academia and imperialist governments to confuse, destabilize, and eventually destroy African culture. P'Bitek notes the following regarding so-called objective scholarship: "For the first time in Western scholarship, the systematic study of African religions through field work began about forty [now ninety] or so years ago. A golden opportunity presented itself for the recording and understanding of African religious conceptions as they really are. But, alas, the materials collected from these researches have been interpreted in such a way that African deities became distorted beyond recognition. And, once more, African religious conceptions were drafted by Christian scholars to fight on their side against European non-believers. The hellenic armours with which African deities were clothed were not primarily for their protection, but to make them appear like the Christian God."[36]

Academia should be embarrassed over how they used their scholars not to advance knowledge, but as agents of a nefarious imperial agenda. Worst, educated Africans were bribed to participate in the destruction and demise of their own culture. P'Bitek begged African intellectuals not to collaborate with white scholars in distorting the reality of their culture and people. The notion that African religion can be interpreted or understood within a European context is absurd. The African mind-set cannot be conceptualized, categorized, or clothed within Greek or Roman garb. "The first duty of an African scholar is to remove these rusty Greek metaphysical dressings as quickly as possible, before African deities suffocate and die inside them in the same manner as the Christian God has perished."[37] Furthermore, since African religion has barely been studied from an African point of view, p'Bitek argues that the "proper study of African religions [remain] untouched."[38]

The study of African religion remains untouched because those who control finance and access to institutions where original fieldwork can be performed do not deem it necessary to study African religio-culture from an African perspective. Thus, we remain in the dark regarding the racial origins of African-Egyptians, Jesus, and any idea of cultural and historical value is deliberately hidden from African people. There seems to be a conscious effort within academia, which is clearly controlled by the government, to use every means possible to prevent black people from discovering who they are. Black people on the continent and throughout the Americas know very little of their history. They attend schools were they are required to study European history and pay tribute to European heroes and heroines. Under these conditions, one cannot expect black people to ever experience mental freedom. Those few black students who study black culture and religion usually do so through a hellenized Abrahamic lens; a perspective that distorts and misrepresents African people and culture. Black people cannot embrace African cultural forms when they are prevented from seeing them in their fullness. This is a strategy used by the elite to keep black people in a state of dependence and servitude. Blacks will never be able to embrace the values and principles that built their noble cultures if they simply rely on white munificence. In this confused state of mind one naturally moves towards what they have been programmed to know. In the black communities, one moves toward the bible and other utopia doctrines that leads them away from the answer and solution to their dilemma. The Abrahamic faiths look quite stable in a world were authenticity is associated with external power. In a world created by Abrahamic principles and values, black people have much to overcome. "Certain assumptions deriving from Christian theology—that amalgam of Platonic and Aristotelian ways of thinking and Judaic concepts and Christian claims—ought not to be brought in when Christian students approach the study of African religion."[39] Western discourse bases its presuppositions on cultural values and ideals that are alien to black culture. Thus, many black scholars continue to argue against the use of Western language and schema when studying African religion. Western presuppositions are rooted within Greco-Roman Platonic thought, which is culturally attuned to white Euro-American's axiological grid. European epistemological tools are unable to analyze phenomena outside of that cultural milieu. The presuppositions that govern African society have their origin within pre–Christian/Islamic African religio-cultural norms. It is the colliding of cultural presuppositions and norms which makes it impossible to analyze another people's cultural system with tools that are foreign to that culture. P'Bitek writes:

> The assumptions of western man have their roots in Judaism, the Greek and Roman experiences, the Christian faith and industrialization. True Uhuru [revolution] means the abolition of Western political and economic dominance from Africa, and the reconstruction of our societies on the basis of African thought systems. The study of African religions is one important way of understanding African ways of thought.[40]

Echoing the same arguments advocated by the African American revolutionary David Walker in the early 1800s, p'Bitek places an extra amount of cultural responsibility upon black scholars. Like Walker who decried that African scholars would one day scrutinize the historical record, which was fabricated by whites. P'Bitek likewise charges African scholars with correcting the misconceptions that have been recorded about Africa and its people, especially by academia. This momentous task falls at the feet of black scholars and they are obligated by the ancestors to spread peace and correct misinformation. Also, they owe those who were murdered and tortured to not have given their lives in vain. Thus, black scholars must actively attack the racist ideology that has been sewn into the fabric of Western society. Subtle racist ideologies that may no longer be on the surface undergird an on-going campaign to malign and destroy African people. This stratagem has been in place from the time of Alexander in 332 BCE to the height of colonialism in the fifteenth century. It must be attacked and dismantled by African scholars. They must also be committed to imparting knowledge and at the same time waging a battle to correct the slander against African people that is inherent within Western discourse. P'Bitek suggests that

> only a process of counter-selection can correct this, and African historians have to concentrate on those aspects which were ignored by the disparaging mythologies. So commitment to the correction of human error in this case might involve purposive discrimination in terms of what is emphasised and what is augmented in the pool of human information. And yet to correct error is as respectable an aim as to increase knowledge. And African scholars could legitimately serve scholarship in the very enterprise of counter-selection.[41]

Counter-selection may prove to be the factor missing in the African's attempt to liberate himself from the shackles of white domination. It will prove to be a difficult task since most black scholars depend on white benefi-cence and funding. Most African scholars work at white institutions and can hardly imagine attacking the hand that feeds them. This is a job that only the courageous can undertake. It is not a task for cowards. Thus, African scholars must also be warriors because they are presented with a two-pronged approach that simultaneously involves imparting knowledge and at the same time correcting misconceptions. Henry L. Gates, Jr., speaks about this double responsibility imposed upon the black race in his book *Thirteen Ways of Looking at a Black Man*. This dual role in which African scholars must operate should not be viewed as an unnecessary burden, as Gates speaks of it,[42] but rather, as a sacred responsibility that either history or fate has forced upon the race. Dr. Martin L. King Jr. spoke about this responsibility not with the burdensome terms used by Gates. King recognized what he needed to con-front not only to keep his humanity, but to restore the confidence in those who were left devastated by white racism. King viewed his task as a "beautiful struggle." This dual responsibility is a necessary duty which African scholars must undertake. It is a sacred role that functions to restore ontological—and, more importantly, epistemological—balance throughout the community.

In many respects, information that transforms thinking is less available now than it was prior to the informational explosion. Today most of the information available to the public is either propaganda or deeply embedded in phrases that the average citizen is not equipped to decode. In the United States, the public is bombarded with sensational stories involving celebrities and rarely are they exposed to substantive information. This is an effective strategy designed to control what people think. Thus, when the United States government uses misinformation to justify imperialism it creates an atmosphere where the overwhelming majority do not know what to think.

The media is used to control how one is supposed to think and there is little room for free thinkers. The think-language that dominates discourse has also been used as a weapon in academia, especially regarding the real history of African people. Western discourse is racist and preferences white males. Language used to describe a "tribe" in one part of the world is a "cultural group" in another.[43] With the same language used to celebrate a freedom fighter in one part of the world, one is called a terrorist elsewhere. The Syria rebels are a terrorist organization fighting to over through a democratic elected government. The United States provides them with weapons and money. When the Syrian rebels cross the border to fight in Iraq against Western powers they are called terrorists by the United States government. This pathological way of being in the world was developed by those who create war to expand their financial empires. Language is a lethal weapon used by external powers to keep the masses in a perpetual state of ignorance. The elite's control of language is an extreme form of psychological warfare. Just in case one is unaware of its existence, Guantanamo Bay continues to house innocent men and boys who are forced to stay alive so they can be tortured by Christian doctors.

Christianizing African Religion

The proper study of African religion has yet to receive its due, especially by those within higher education. Although many Western scholars have stressed the need to study African religion, those trained in the discipline continue to interpret traditional African cultural forms through a Christian lens. This practice continues across the disciplines, because every discipline is studied and interpreted through a European lens. Proponents of neutral scholarship continue to distort reality and the true nature of traditional forms of culture. "In the study of religion, African deities were duly dressed in resplendent garments and robes reminiscent of religious services in the Vatican and Canterbury."[44] P'Bitek's potent analysis of TACF and how they have been misinterpreted speaks to the continual need to expose those who deny Africans the opportunity to tell their story. P'Bitek "Enters the temple thus erected by the first wave of African religious scholars and indignantly pulls off those resplendent robes, in an attempt to reveal the real essence of African deities."[45] P'Bitek uncovers the most common errors that plague most students of African religion. Their attempt to place African religion within a European framework, and worse, comparing or contrasting African religion with Christianity. The African traditional worldview is as far removed from the Anglo perspective, as the sun is from the earth. Once again, p'Bitek challenges students of African religion.

> Why should there be a constant search to fit African conceptions of God into notions like omnipotence, omnipresence and omniscience? Why should there be a constant exploration for one supergod in African societies, almost as if one was trying to discover an inner monotheism in traditional Africa belief systems? Why should African students of religion be so keen to demonstrate that the Christian God had already been understood and apprehended by Africans before the missionaries came?[46]

Again, p'Bitek argued that the Christianization of African deities was a strategy carried out by scholars such as Mbiti, Ìdòwú, Parrinder, and others who studied African religion to advance the Christian agenda. They explored traditional values not as proponents of African culture, but as Christian apologists. Most of the early scholars of African religion were devout Christian men whose main duty was to remain faithful to Christian scripture and dogma. Most importantly, African religion was not viewed by any of these men as a religion with sacred cultural values and norms, which were independent of Christian dictates. If so, why would not these men, especially the African scholars, worship and venerate their own cultural history and sacred religious myth? Why would Africans be urged to convert to Christianity if they already had a culture capable of providing them with salvation?

For instance, Mbiti is viewed by many as a great scholar of African religion. At the same time, he is a faithful African Christian and ordained minister whose scholarship could never be free of Christian biases. "[B]eing a devout Christian, he [Mbiti] has not always succeeded in resisting the temptation to see the divine will of Jesus operating in Africa even before the missionaries came."[47] This propensity to view all things African through a Euro-Christian lens is not an isolated incident, but a trend that marks the scholarship of Western religion in general. "The first wave of African socialistic theoreticians were [sic] also inclined to look at traditional African institutions and ideas, and describe them in language borrowed from Western ideologies."[48] The analysis of African religion through Western spectacles creates major theological issues. "It is a question of looking at the African phenomena with the spectacles borrowed from a different experience. It is a question of analysing [sic] African experience with a rhetoric borrowed from a different cultural universe."[49] This Eurocentric approach to the study of traditional African cultural forms is incapable of yielding reliable data. It is even more alarming when an entire country utilizes the European paradigm to determine if non-white countries have broken international mores or cultural norms that Euro-Americans have declared as laws. Of course, if these laws are violated in any way, the white powers that enforce them violently and will use their militaries to make the offending country pay by indiscriminately bombing their women and children without impunity.

These same ideas of dominance control academia and most scholarly interests must conform to Eurocentric norms. If not there will be no funding for their projects. P'Bitek confronted Western scholars of African religion much the same as Martin Luther attacked Roman Catholicism. For example, he criticized academia much the same as James Cone condemned Christian arrogance in his classic text *Black Theology and Black Power*. Like Cone and others who continue to criticize Christianity's propensity for empty propositions, p'Bitek was "not interested in proving that traditional Africans were capable of metaphysical thought.... He persuasively asserts that those African scholars who seek to do this are simply trying to pay homage to Western criticism in the terms dictated by the West. Africa's religious respectability ought not to depend on how nearly Hellenistic African conceptions of the 'transcendental' really were."[50]

P'Bitek's analysis of Western scholarship is encapsulated in the following: "What emerges from this brief survey is a distorted and pale picture of African religious beliefs, their deities buried under thick layers of the prejudices of the students of African societies."[51]

Strategies to Destabilize Traditional African Cultural Forms

The principal medium used to propagate Christianity and Islam was executed in the name of enculturation. The Model of Enculturation (MOE) was effectively used by Christian missionaries to supposedly acculturate and civilize pagan Africans. Normally, enculturation is a natural process and takes place from within ones family and cultural group. Yet, Arabs and Europeans labeled Africans as a people without respectable cultural values. If they possessed anything of value it needed to be infused from a superior culture. The Christians required Africans to adopt Christianity and the cultural values of the European to become civilized. Without inculcating these life-sustaining European-Christian cultural values, Africans would remain on the lower must rung on the evolutionary ladder. Therefore, to acquire the skills needed to become fully human, black people would need to accept the cultural nutrients from Europeans and Arabs since they lacked these life-affirming values in their own culture.

For instance, the Arabs initially resorted to physical and economic force to force their tradition and cultural values upon Africans.[52] They resorted to acts of barbarism to enforce their culture on Africans, but such acts of violence were later modified and instead of utilizing force to make converts, other forms of persuasions were successfully employed. Soft force was used as a strategic weapon to seduce Africans to adopt Arab culture as their religion. Islam is among many other things the veneration of Arab culture. Yes, Africans have done a spectacular job in making it fit into their cultural template. Still, Islam is the deification of Arab culture and, at its best, remains the highest form of Arab nationalism. The Arabs' veneration of traditional Arab cultural forms and the celebration of their mythology is the source Islam's power.

A similar strategy was later used by European Christians to enforce their religio-cultural worldview upon Africans. Like the Arabs who came before them, Christian colonizers also utilized various strategies to force their perceptions on Africans. This too was a demeaning process designed to impoverish both African people's sense of reality and to destabilize or destroy the memory of their culture. (Today we can glimpse certain aspects of the Model of Destabilization (MOD) in Syria, Libya, Iraq, Venezuela, and Ferguson, Missouri). Wherever these strategies are employed they aim to destabilize or destroy the social fabric of a society. If effective all that remains is a shell. The Roman Catholic Church and other white powers have effectively used several MODs to create what some call the New World. The Church does not view these incursions or MODs as hostile to human beings. It is part of their divine mission as a religious institution. After all, the historical mission of the Church is to propagate its values as a divine mandate. "And the Word became flesh.... The content of what would come in time to be called 'inculturation' is contained in these words of the Gospel according to Saint John. God became man so that human beings might become his children."[53]

Christianity in general and the Roman Catholic Church in particular has a historical record of one incursion after another, destabilizing and destroying nonwhite cultures throughout the world. These episodes of violence are actually acts of terror, involving the pillaging, raping, and killing of innocent people. The Christian Church has utilized theology to justify their barbarism. "The process of the Church's insertion into people's cultures is a lengthy one. It is not a matter of purely external adaptation, for inculturation 'means the intimate transformation of authentic cultural values through their integration in Christianity and the insertion of Christianity in the various human cultures.'"[54]

These acts of violence make sense only if one subscribes to the ideals advocated by some proponents of chaos theory. Violence is primary to the

life of the church and without these acts of blood-letting, these casual cleans-
ings, or what an Israeli government official called "mowing the lawn" (referring to the need to keep Gaza in check by occasionally bombing Hamas).
The Catholic Church has historically viewed its incursions into Africa, the
Caribbean, South America, and elsewhere, as part of their divine mission
authorized by God. Supposedly these incursions are religious in nature and
focus on adopting another people's cultural values that are deemed church-
worthy. The adoption of other people's cultural values is a divine mandate
of the Roman Catholic Church. This process allows both the "worthy" values
within those non–European cultural groups, and those who imbibe these
"worthy" values, into the fellowship of the Church. These incursions take
their cue from divine mandate, especially from the words attributed to Jesus
in Matthew 28:20. This biblical mandate is used to justify acts of terror. Saint
Paul supported strategies of incursion by invading gentile territories with a
new interpretation of the Gospels.[55] The church views the process of cultural
displacement as an act of grace. African cultural values are replaced or refur-
bished by Euro-Christian cultural values. This is the mission of Christendom
throughout the black world. It sees its work in Africa in particular, as civilizing those in darkness and living in pre-civilization conditions. The mission
of the Church is to serve as inculcators of cultural values and to civilize the
pagan.

> [I]nculturation does not consist only in transforming the mentality of human
> beings or groups of people, but also implies approaching cultures in such ways
> that they are enabled, from within themselves, to be fertile. Christianity
> becomes itself enriched when through inculturation it enters into dialogue
> with peoples and with their cultures. An inculturated evangelisation will help
> peoples give flesh to evangelical values in their language and symbols, their
> history, politics, business life and own ways of developing.[56]

The question for African scholars and practitioners of TACF must ask
themselves is why African people need to be inculcated with European values
to experience the divine? Could it be possible that these treasures already
exist within African culture? If so, why are not white Americans and Europeans converting to African religion and venerating African heroes and heroines? Until these questions are fully explored, Africans should not reject their
traditions to worship another people's myths.

The inculturation model functions to purify those traditional African
cultural forms deemed incomplete or outside of Christianity. "Inculturation
facilitates not only the integration of cultural values but also the purification
of those elements not in keeping with the exigencies of the gospel."[57] The
Church is morally obligated to civilize the cultural systems of traditional

Africans. How else could African culture be made palpable to Euro-Christianity? Again, the Church justifies its actions as divine mandates that are in alignment with their dogma. "In the answers to the *Lineamenta* the necessity and the urgency of inculturation are justified in Africa."[58]

As one analyzes the theological dogma used to justify the church's justification for its destruction of TACF, it becomes clear that achieving their objectives would destroy millions of black people. Enculturation by its very nature annihilates and destroys another people's sacred story. One cannot not live a fruitful and fulfilling life if they lack a cultural referent. African scholars should scrutinize all missionary activities. The failure to do so is equivalent to participating in the cultural genocide of their people. Sadly, numerous African bishops and, of late, many Christian mega church leaders are actively participating in the destruction of traditional black culture. They too justify their acts of barbarism in the name of Jesus. "Inculturation is looked upon by the great majority of the Particular Churches in Africa as a task that is urgent, necessary and even a priority. It consists, in face [*sic*], of a process by which Christian belief takes flesh in the cultures, a process inherent in the announcing of God's Good News. Because the incarnation of the Son of God was concrete and integral, it was a cultural incarnation."[59]

The Church justifies its strategy by claiming Jesus' appearance in Palestine was a "cultural incarnation." How could that be when he was born at a time when his culture was under Roman occupation? A cultural incarnation would be limited to his people alone, which is why scripture states he came to "save" his people from their sins. In truth, Jesus was in fact attempting to encourage the Jewish leadership to abide by the words of their prophets. He never taught them to abandon their religious traditions and deify the gods of their Roman occupiers. This is exactly what the Church has taught Africans to do. They have misused biblical language to justify their acts of violence. Anytime a people abandons their cultural myths and adopts the gods of their enemies, they have unknowingly aborted their future. Even the missionary would never think of abandoning Jehovah for an African or Taino god. Missionaries are warned to distance themselves from the objects associated with African gods. Lay Christian and clergy are encouraged to study African religion for the exclusive purpose of equipping themselves with knowledge of how best to convert Africans to Christianity. The Church's main interests in African people is to inculcate them with Euro-Christian cultural values. Secondly, to educate Africans to reject traditional cultural ideals that challenge Western hermeneutics. The study of African culture is limited by their questionable agenda. "It is not enough to be able to describe customs and to recite poetry. A thorough knowledge [of African religion]

... enables Christ's ambassador who is equally well equipped with the knowledge of his message, to compare tradition and gospel and pass judgment on the former in the light of the latter."[60]

The passing judgment on African religion from a supposedly more advanced culture rules out any meaningful dialogue between Christians and proponents of African traditional culture. How can the Christian scripture judge a people who do not subscribe to its tenets? "It is not adequate to base such judgments on the scriptural texts of a single culture." We need a "cross cultural criteria" to make the kinds of judgments that would yield meaningful results. The Church's interests in African religion lies not in unearthing its rich cultural traits for salvific purposes, but in finding ways to dismantle traditional African cultural forms. Those Christian-worthy elements in African religio-culture are saved and adopted by the Church, all else is rejected and abandoned.

> Inculturation requires a deep understanding of the religious and cultural context from which we [African Roman Catholic clergy] continue to live. The dynamic interaction between faith and culture is a two-way process. Rites of passages which are very important in the lives of our people ... can cause considerable tension for devout Catholics. These rites should be thoroughly examined in order that they can be integrated fully into the life and liturgy of the Church.[61]

Here we have African clergy admit that there are elements of value within traditional African cultural forms, which should be adopted by the Roman Catholic Church. After careful scrutiny of African rituals and sacred rites of passage, the African bishops suggest that the Church borrow certain Euro-Christian-worthy elements, and perhaps, adopt them to save their dying faith. The syncretization of African and Euro-Christian cultural forms would then become the religious and cultural property of the Church. The borrowing of traditional African cultural forms and then repackaging them as something New Age is not new at all. African religio-cultural elements deemed worthy of re-adaptation for usage in Roman Catholic liturgy has already created problems for many African Christians.

> Christianity remains for many Africans "a stranger religion," there being some part of their very selves and lives that stays outside the gospel. This is the source of a certain double quality in living their beliefs, holding them divided between their faith in Jesus Christ and custom's traditional practices.[62]

Many of the early Africans converts to Christianity were aware that they would have to reject a vital part of themselves to worship the white man's god. They sacrificed an essential aspect of their being to become Christian. But what really is Christianity? It is only one minor aspect of Christendom, which is a global system and adjunct of Western hegemony, which encompasses much more than saving ones soul. Christianity as a faith tradition is the least part of this vast ideology, which involves economics, politics, entertainment, race, sociology, culture and more. Euro-Christians devised an effective strategy to convert Africans and other non–Europeans, including the use of "hidden psychological and emotional forces," that assisted them in manipulating Africans into rejecting their culture. Still, many African Christians continue to experience a crisis of identity until they thoroughly investigate the process Europeans used to Christianize them. The process used for the cultural displacement of Africans was an effective strategy. "Without inculturation the faith of the African will remain fragile and superficial, lacking depth and personal commitment."[63] However destructive the inculturation model may have been, the Church has since dedicated itself to preserving certain African cultural forms for the sake of preserving Christianity. The "use of certain African cultural traditions helps the African better understand and live the sacraments."[64] Certainly based on the latter statement, African traditional cultural forms are being used to save the Catholic Church, which is a dying institution that can no longer hide from the light. Even though there are millions of dedicated believers who live out the sacraments, the Church as an institution is morally bankrupt. Therefore, the borrowing of TACF may be the Church's best chance to save itself.

What appeared to be genuine respect for traditional African cultural forms turns out to be a search for African traditional norms to be injecting into the veins of a dying religion. The borrowing of traditional cultural forms by the Church is more than simply seeking for those cultural nutrients that can be of use by the Church. In spite of the multiple strategies used to separate African people from their culture, some African Christians do retain some traditional views, which at times collide with Christian doctrines. (This is true of Catholics in Cuba, Haiti, Brazil, and many places throughout the black Atlantic world.) "Most Ghanaians and Christians … still hold on to some of the strong beliefs in African Traditional Religion, because they have been part of the cultural heritage from which they come and within which they live."[65] It is important to point out that the views of most Christians are not as strict against traditional African cultural forms as are most African bishops. No matter how much Christianity enforces itself upon traditional ways of being, they cannot replace the cultural heritage that guided Africans before the Abrahamic religions were created. Remember, as Mbiti and several other African scholars make clear, "the African is still not at home with Christianity, it is European in almost everything—theologies, spirituality, style of worship, prayers, rites, structures and even architecture."[66]

The enculturation model is an effective imperial strategy used throughout Africa by clergy and Western militaries. From the beginning, Christianity has been used by Western powers as a military strategy. Chaplains have been embedded with the United States military in nearly every major war. They were in Iraq when mothers were running through the streets clutching to their dead babies as bombs lit up the skies over Bagdad. The converting of Africans to Christianity utilized a military strategy which just happened to use evangelism as a medium to achieve a sinister agenda. "It is in the domain of liturgy that the great majority of attempts at acculturation have been undertaken. The development moved rapidly from simple adaptations to creative efforts."[67] The church has been used by imperial powers since the fourth century to spread Euro-Christian values and to destabilize non–European traditional cultural forms throughout the world. For instance, by using certain African cultural elements within worship services, one is more likely to draw the suspicious African into Christian service. By utilizing African dress, music, and art, the nominal adoption of these cultural elements were used to lure Africans into Christianity. The Church converted millions of unsuspecting Africans through the "use of African art in liturgical clothing, in decorating places of worship and in sacred vessels; and use of traditional forms to express certain elements of the faith: drum strokes, hand-claps, dancing and body language."[68] By employing such deceptive strategies, African bishops and white evangelicals have drawn Africans away from the traditional cultural forms that offers them real salvation. "The better African Traditional Religion is understood, the better the Gospel can be preached."[69] Africans are engaged in a cultural war to save what remains of their sacred tradition. Unfortunately, many are unaware of the war being waged against them. Those who know of its existence can prepare themselves to win and protect their offspring. Those who reject reality have surrendered themselves over to secularism and Abrahamism. There are forces beneath the surface fighting to take away what remains of traditional cultural forms.

Religion is the primary medium used by Western imperialists to execute their nefarious agenda, which includes much more than introducing someone to a man named Jesus for which there are no historical records documenting his existence. Those who remain naïve about the war being waged against them will become the elite's cannon fodder. The enculturation strategy is a weapon used by Christendom to spread more than the good news. The Church justifies the strategies it uses to reach "the lost." It is one of Christendom's divine mandates to acculturate those who lack cultural nutrients of value. "With inculturation properly conducted," as Vatican II affirms, "the Christian life will be adapted to the *mentality* and *character* of each culture, and local traditions together with the special qualities of each national family, illumined by the light of the gospel, will be *taken up* into a Catholic unity."[70]

> [W]hatever good is found sown in the minds and hearts of men or in the rites and customs of peoples ... not only are preserved from destruction, but are *purified, raised up, and perfected* for the glory of God" (LG 17; cf. GS 58)....
> Everything in a culture that is compatible with the gospel and communion with the universal Church can be assumed by the Church. The rest must be "purified, raised up, and perfected," anything incompatible must be abandoned.[71]

The process of "purifying" and "raising up the incompatible cultural nutrients" is an attack against non–Christian cultures. How much clearer can such words of war become before black people realize that Christianity, as articulated by white missionaries and governments, is hostile to black existence? It has destroyed much of their traditional culture and has left many educated Africans in a state of lostness. Those so-called Western educated Africans in particular, spend most of their lives trying to undue their Western education, especially after discovering that it taught them to hate themselves. Those African cultural forms adopted by the Church must undergo a process that involves removing any "sinful" African elements that are not Church-worthy. The borrowing of traditional cultural elements "involves excising anything that is sinful, redeeming and raising up what is humanly good; or, to put it briefly, it is the process of incarnation reaching unto redemption."[72]

John Paul II's encyclical *Redemptoris missio* describes the process of acculturation thusly: "Through inculturation the Church makes the gospel incarnate in different cultures and at the same time introduces peoples, together with their cultures, into her own community."[73] While Pope John Paul II was traveling throughout Africa in 1982, he made the following remark with regards to the Church's commitment to converting Africans: "The passage to the state of the African church requires, as one of its basic duties, the evangelisation of its culture. African culture is a magnificent 'substratum' which is awaiting incarnation into Christianity.... There are multiple links, between the message of salvation and culture. God, in revealing Himself to his people unto the full manifestations of Himself in His incarnate Son, spoke according to the cultures peculiar to each epoch."[74]

The Catholic Church recognizes that religion and culture are inseparable and we cannot disrupt one's culture without affecting the entire society. Still, the aim of enculturation is to disrupt indigenous belief systems and to replace them with foreign cultural systems that they must pay homage. Such acts of cultural displacement should be viewed as crimes against humanity. For how can one feel at home in a world that forces some to abandon their cultures, and adopt a lens foreign to one's cultural aesthetic? In such a condition they will be unable to see the world as it truly exists. Still the church views its acts of enculturation as a means to provide Africans and other cultural misfits, with cultural nutrients not available to them in their cultures. Every act of violence or cultural destabilization taken by the church is theologically justified. "Inculturation is the *irruption and epiphany of the Lord which provides destabilisation….* It means the insertion of Christian faith into a culture, generally outside the Western Judaeo-Christian context and that culture's response to the Christian message."[75]

Would the enculturation model work in Europe, which is supposedly a Christian region? [Or, at least it was Christian before the recent Muslim migration.] Models of cultural destabilization were not designed for Europeans, but by them as strategies and weapons to destroy non–European nations without firing a gun. Christianity is the missionary-militaristic arm of Christendom. Many African bishops welcomed the inculturation model as a means to provide civilization for those who practice traditional African cultural forms. Yet, these bishops have no idea who they have aligned themselves with. Supposedly, inculturation allows certain non-offensive elements of African religio-cultural forms to be adopted by the Church; thus making Roman Catholicism and Christianity more appealing to practitioners of African religion. Inculturation functions within Africa "to correct the impression that Christianity is a white man's religion."[76]

The Church's acculturization model is an open assault upon African traditional cultural forms and the people who value these traditions. Regardless of how Christian dogma is used to justify its naked aggression, it remains a military strategy that must be viewed as an attack on black culture and African people everywhere. The Church's justification for disrupting and destroying black culture must not be taken lightly. It is their use of soft power to achieve an object that would otherwise require the shedding of much blood. The Church's soft approach to the destruction and destabilization of African culture is always couched in theological terminology. Such "holy" language serves to soften its blow and cause blacks to feel it can't be bad, since no one is bleeding, at least not in public. "The Incarnation of Christ is the theological reason for inculturation; in fact, it is not a strategy to win over converts, but a tenet of our faith."[77]

Enculturation and Destabilization Strategies

Theological dialogue is the current fad used to improve dialogue across the religio-cultural divide. The discourse is mostly confined to academia and a few progressive churches because rarely do practitioners of Western faiths desire to accept the outsider. Within academia cross-cultural dialogue is situated around establishing contact between Asian, Islamic, and Jewish-Christian traditions. Rarely are African traditional cultural forms recognized as a worthy partner for such discussions. Furthermore, within most religion departments in the United States, very few courses are taught on African religion. When courses are offered in the religion department, they are usually taught by men or sometimes women who imbibed the missionary model. Cross-cultural dialogue is really designed to enculturate non–Westerners and prepare them to accept Christianity from an Anglo perspective. Such discourse is not premised upon mutual respect, but exists for the express purpose of finding within other people's traditions, symbols or customs that point to their fulfillment in Christianity. "It would be easy to find ... 'stepping-stones' to Christianity such as, their notion of the Supreme Being and other spiritual principles that animate man; of the next world; of putting to death and ritual resurrection apart from the rites of passage; of prayer and sacrifice."[78]

Such dialogue is not sincere because it is primarily focused on what can be discovered within traditional African cultural forms, which can used to further Christian dominance. Their cross cultural rhetoric is actually a search for ways on how best to deceive Africans, while at the same time, appearing to celebrate African culture? This strategy has been successfully executed throughout Africa and elsewhere, especially among nonwhite populations. It has worked very well for missionaries and other evangelicals who are foot soldiers for white imperialism. Once they discovered that Africans were childlike and appeared gullible, they were convinced they could easily make them salves. This childlike trait was also by Columbus observed among the Indigenous people in the Caribbean. It was because they were naïve in the white man's eyes that Columbus suggested that it would be easy to enslave them. P'Bitek and other conscious men and women condemned African scholars who participated in the destruction of their own culture. Many educated black men and women throughout the world continue to make themselves available to assist the white in the destabilization and destruction of black traditional cultural forms. Such men and women have no respect for themselves or their culture. Those black men and women who use their talents to assist the white man with his endeavors to destroy the world are, in fact, more dangerous than the oil magnates who come to Africa and hire "educated" African men to silence outspoken critics, who contest the white man's belief that he has a divine right to pollute the environment. Throughout the world the white power structure continues to enrich itself, and provide crumbs to a few greedy Africans, while the overwhelming majority of their people remain in a state of abject poverty.

In addition to the model of enculturation used to exploit African people, the continuity model is to explicate African cultural forms for the expressed purposes of discovering elements that point to their fulfillment in Anglo controlled discourse. The continuity model is premised on the refusal of Western religionists to accept TACF and to acknowledge that they are alive and capable of acculturating Africans. Black people have never needed alien cultural forms to civilize them, especially those that are hostile to black humanity. The continuity model uses condescension and other forms of dehumanization as strategies, premised on the idea that Africans may be spiritually inclined, but their culture lacks the essential ingredients necessary for human growth and development. "[T]he *aspirations* of the African religions are valuable, the wish for life, for spiritual and human fecundity, for cleansing from faults, for communion with those who are in the next world. All of these aspirations can be evoked and can serve as a point of departure in a dialogue with African spirituality, detached from religious techniques properly so called."[79]

Dialogue between Christians and practitioners of TACF starts by discussing non-debatable ideas and then the Church can proceed to bring the unconverted Africans into the true knowledge of god. This is needed to complete the Africans evolution to full humanity because their cultural norms are ill-equipped to accomplish this monumental task. This is the preferred model *par excellence* used by Christians to convert Africans. The continuity model is an effective strategy, centered upon the belief that all religio-cultures prior to Jesus Christ were simply *prolegomena* or stepping stones, which served to lead humanity to a more perfect path. Or, as Mbiti has written elsewhere, Africans "groped in darkness" until rescued by Christians. Therefore, how could African religion be anything other than something temporary? How could anyone expect to find anything of eternal value within a culture that is incomplete without prostrating themselves before the white man's god? Of course Africans' path to humanity and redemption are elsewhere because Africa is outside of history and incapable of producing anything of value.

> In the same way that the religion of Babylon was "pedagogic" for Abraham, while it taught him to be the servant of God, though it was finally bypassed in order to allow him to accomplish his providential destiny, the African religions have been and still are "pedagogic" to prepare the way for Christ.[80]

How can a "pedagogic" religion provide anything of lasting value to modernity? The products of such cultures are good for nothing other than to be controlled by cultures of dominance. Those cultural groups who possess the nutrients black people need to become whole. Yet, if all religions are "ped-agogic" prior to Christianity, does this not include Judaism, Islam, Hinduism, and every religion in the world that is not Christian? If all religion are "ped-agogic" outside of Christendom, then the majority of the world's inhabitants are in trouble. The notion that the superior race and dominant culture must save the world is without question the foundation of white supremacy. It is a common feature shared by all religions that are missionary directed. Missionary religions are militaristic because they resort to force to carry out their agenda. Non-missionary communities are forced to prostrate themselves before the gods of those in power. Any rational analysis of missionary religions will immediately identify the arrogance embedded within their theology. Such thinking appears to be inherent within missionary religions, which explains why Christianity and its Islamic counterpart are very dangerous belief systems. The Abrahamic religions are based on dominating others by any means necessary. One must reject reality or be quite naïve to expect peace from systems whose theologies are undergirded by violence. Missionary religions believe that "salvation" is not fully possible outside of their dogma, at least not for Africans who are perceived by Western theologians as people without cultural values.

We can find many sources that gave birth to such thinking. For example, the Christian doctrine of revelation which is discussed elsewhere. However, the theology of continuity and those who advance this perspective reluctantly admit that there may be cultures outside of Christendom that possess elements of social and theological value. All good things belong to those who possess the greatest amount of external power. Even salvation of the soul is controlled by those who dominate the world.

> There were and still could be *an exceptional way to salvation* for a section of humanity of which we only catch a glimpse…. As St. Justin said, speaking of Plato and of certain philosophers of antiquity whose search for wisdom was in fact a search for God: "Everything good that they have said has benefited us Christians, because the ancient authors had insight into reality thanks to the innate action of the Logos" [*Apol.* II, Col. 13].[81]

As an outreach of these ideas, the Catholic Church has encouraged its educational institutions to include the teaching of African religion within their curricula. This will serve to inform the whole body on how best to con-vert non–Christians and those who practice African cultural forms. The teaching of African religion within catholic institutions of higher learning will also assist in systematizing African sacred thought to make it easier for the non–African mind to digest. By organizing African religion into a system comparable to the systemization of Christian theology, white theologians can gain a better understanding of African cultural forms and, most importantly, align certain ideals expressed in traditional religion with Western logic. These studies may also encourage Catholic and Christian scholars to discontinue using offensive terminology when referring to aspects of TACF, which seem antithetical to Euro-Christian cultural etiquette.[82]

The Catholic Church remains committed to changing "the mentality and the religious manifestations of the great majority of the continent's peoples."[83] This is one of the main goals of missionary activities in Africa. Africans can no longer remain ignorant regarding the goals of Christian and Catholic missionaries. Historically, the white man did not come to Africa to save African people. Richard Wright wrote in his book *Black Power* that the white man came to Africa to save himself. Catholics and Christians, who are soft powers or handmaidens of global white power, are in Africa to save themselves. Christianity may appear to be growing, but its theology has been greatly challenged by New Thought. The world created from the white Christian construct is quickly dying. Catholicism and Christianity have run their course and as Western imperialism disintegrates, they will do likewise. Christianity is beyond redemption and if it can be saved, it must gather in more Africans and Latinos. Otherwise, it will die of starvation, especially since it feeds off the minds of the misinformed.

Practitioners of TACF have kept alive those traditions passed down by their forbearers. These sacred African cultural forms have not been tainted by the white man's thoughts. Even the educated Africans who were taught by the white man to hate themselves have been unable to completely forsaken their tradition. Like the biblical character Nicodemus who sought out Jesus under the cover of darkness, millions of brain-dirtied African Christians visit shrines and consults oracles when the sun goes down. Even the Christian preacher slips into the backdoors of African wise men and women, to seek what his white god cannot offer him. Maybe there is something within the dark world that can save Christianity. In this regard, dialogue is of utmost importance.

> Some of the intellectual elite in some African countries are declaring themselves adherents of African Traditional Religion…. More of the intellectual elite than in former years are declaring themselves its adherents…. Study and understanding of African Traditional Religion will therefore promote evangelisation…. Many Christians, at critical moments in their lives, fall back to practices of the traditional religion or have recourse to prayer houses, or healing homes or "prophets," or witchcraft or fortune-tellers, or they join some sect.[84]

Millions of Africans abandoned their traditions because they mistakenly associated materialism with spirituality. Christianity is controlled by the white power elite who are afraid because this system which was created to advance European imperialism has reached a saturation point. They are finding it ever more difficult to deceive Africans into rejecting their culture in exchange for another people's superstitions. The controllers of Christendom are concerned that several educated Africans are openly voicing their preference for the culture they once rejected. This will greatly undermine the strategies used by the Church to miseducate black people, as they have also done throughout the Americas. Education is a strategy that has been the primary weapon used by white regimes to destroy and separate one from their cultural norms. Now millions are awakening throughout the black world and realizing their errors, especially the rejection of their culture for the elevation of European values hidden under the garb of Christianity. Black people are beginning to look beyond Christian rhetoric and are recognizing the ever-widening gap between words and action. Dialogue within academia with regard to the interpretation of African religion from a Christian perspective has resulted in the destruction of several traditional African cultural forms. The missionary-intellectuals who prefer rhetoric over reality claim to be guided by neutral scholarship. "It is less easy to see how scholars can be neutral? Where such neutrality is claimed, must it not be some kind of preference?" Western theologians must be seen as agents of Western imperialism. They have never been concerned with furthering African cultural forms. Instead, they seek for ways how they can be engrafted into Christianity. These so-called objective scholars who study African religion for purpose of comparing it with Christianity must be seen as enemies of African culture. What followed the dismantling of African cultural forms was the near destruction of African people. The aim of all missionary religions is to displace or destroy those who serve a different god. There can only be one dominant cultural form and it must have a military presence to execute its dogma. There is but one god who is the representative of the superior cultural groups. All others must be prepared for war or be displaced. Missionary-cultures have sworn an allegiance to protect the one true god. There can be no other gods before Him. Africans are miseducated to ensure that he accepts the Europeans' god, because He has already proven that He alone has the power to kill, steal, and destroy.

Africans were systematically taught to distrust the gods of their culture. They did not know then what we now all know, that all gods emanate from a particular culture. Africans were taught to hate certain aspects of their culture, and worse, to believe it inferior to Arab and European cultural forms. An incomplete culture cannot assist one in becoming fully human. Africans were taught to believe that they needed to adopt the white man's culture to complete their humanity. Black people throughout the world were educated by the white man to receive their gift of life, which only they could offer. The role of missionary-centered schools is to teach nonwhite people to reject their culture and adopt a one that can civilize them.

The Roman Catholic Church instructed its theologians to conduct a thorough systematic study of African religion to "organise [*sic*] a Catholic university [or several] that will help to elaborate an African Christian thought, in dialogue with living experience of the great Catholic tradition and a living experience of the Africa of yesterday."[85] The Catholic and Christian educational centers study African religion and use the knowledge to convert Africans. The study of African religion is designed to provide missionaries with the arsenal necessary to persuade Africans to abandon their cultural system, and adopt the more superior cultural form. Church affiliated schools throughout the Western world instruct their missionary to following certain methods for conducting a systematic study of African religion:

> The traditional religion could be studied as to its name, its major objects of belief, especially God the Creator, the place of the spirits and the ancestors, the fundamental rites in this religion, sacrifice, priesthood, prayer, marriage, the human soul, life after death, religion and moral life. Values such as sense of the sacred, respect for life, sense of community, family spirit, a spiritual vision of life authority as sacred, and symbolism in religions worship, could profitably be studied.[86] These areas of study in African religion certainly have the potential to reveal many strengths of the religion that are culturally situated, and obscured to an outsider. It is clear that the European's focal on African culture does not aim at advancing African traditional cultural forms but, they aim to find ways on how to counter its effects upon the believers. Additionally, Isizoh the African Catholic apologists, argues, "The study should be an objective and factual work so that the heralds of the Gospel will see more clearly the positive and the negative in the religious and cultural situation of the people to whom the Gospel is being brought."[87]

(Isizoh is an African who has made himself available to the Roman Catholic Church to assist them in how best to convert his people, mainly through the use of highly deceptive strategies. The researchers are to appear objective as though they are genuinely concerned with traditional African cultural norms. But the real object of their studies are unclear to the participants. Hence, they deceive the people who unknowingly are assisting them in the destabilization and destruction of traditional African cultural forms. For the missionary educators use the information they gather from traditional Africans to argue against them and eventually, this knowledge was used to convert them to Anglo-European Christianity and Catholicism.)

Deception nullifies any objectivity as the departure point for conducting an impartial study of traditional African cultural forms. Academia's so-called objective perspective is the preferred approach for scholarly studies cultural phenomena. Western academia commits an injustice to the real study of African cultural forms by claiming to be impartial, while at the same time analysing African phenomena through a Euro-Christian lens. Of course the findings are tainted and cannot be trusted. P'Bitek and many conscious African scholars condemned such hypocrisy and argued that the study of African religion has yet to be undertaken. Until African cultural forms are critiqued by tools forged within the culture, not to find their affinities with Christianity or Islam, but as a viable cultural forms that are equipped with the cultural nutrients capable of humanizing Africans, then p'Bitek's attack of Christendom and its aggressive missionary activities remains true. Christianity remains an aggressive missionary religion that serves as the handmaiden for Western militarism. Many who study African cultural forms are representatives of the Western imperialist agenda. Therefore, the real study of African religion has yet to be fully conducted because one cannot trust Western scholarship when it is controlled by a militaristic agenda. The Christian model of continuity is a military strategy used to entrap Africans. It taught them to reject their cultural myths and adopt the European narrative. This disqualifies many Western scholars, who gather information to supposedly objectively analyze African phenomena. The theological rhetoric used to speak about "man's" relationship with Christ must be scrutinized because there is nothing that comes out as Christendom which is separate from the Europeans agenda to control the world. The language of religion has proven to be the most effective medium in which ones hides from truth.

> The good news of Christ continually renew[s] the life and culture of fallen man; it combats and removes the error and evil which flows from the ever-present attraction of sin. It never ceases to purify and elevate the morality of peoples. It takes the spiritual qualities and endowments of every age and nation, and with supernatural riches it causes them to blossom, as it were, from within; it fortifies, completes and restores them in Christ [GS 58].[88]

Is it possible to conduct sincere dialogue across the cultural divide, when Christian dogma places itself at the top of the hermeneutical pinnacle? The Vatican Council on missionary activity, *Ad gentes*, outlines the Church's commitment to infusing African cultural forms with Anglo norms and values; thereby making it a viable culture. Yet, it is the Holy Church that is dying and cannot survive in Africa or anywhere without dismantling traditional cultural forms and replacing them with what they call "gifts of grace."

> The seed which is the Word of God sprouts from the good ground watered by divine dew. From this ground the seed draws nourishing elements which it transforms and assimilates into itself. Finally it bears much fruit.... From

the customs and traditions of their people, from their wisdom and their learning, from their arts and sciences, these Churches borrow all those things which can contribute to the glory of their Creator, the revelation of the Saviour's grace, or the proper arrangement of Christian Life.... Particular traditions, together with the individual patrimony of each family of nations can ... be taken up into Catholic unity. Finally, the individual younger churches, adorned with their own traditions, will have their own place in the ecclesiastical communion, without prejudice to the primacy of Peter's See, which presides over the entire assembly of charity."[89]

While some see this as the destruction of traditional cultural forms, the Roman Catholic Church claims they are engaged in a process to enrich non Western cultures? Supposedly, this has always been an important mission of the faith beginning with the early church.

As it moved from the Jewish to the Hellenic world the early Church felt it necessary to inculturate the message and to share our responsibilities (cf. Acts 6, 1–6). At the Council of Jerusalem the Hellenists had to accept—for the sake of unity (cf. Acts 15, 28)—to maintain what was strictly necessary.[90]

The Church remains committed to inculcating its version of Christianity throughout the world. It carries out its mission most effectively by utilizing Africans and other sleepwalkers who believe it is their divine duty to bring the Christian light to those who grope in darkness. No matter how enshrined in Christian grace such rhetoric may appear, the displacement of another peoples way of living is no laughing matter. All cultures are guided by principles and norms that undergirds their thought processes. Why would the so-called culture of the Gospel be gifted with the grace to transcend every other culture, without being subjected to any? Again, one must be leery of theological rhetoric, especially when it comes out of the mouth of those wield power. For such rhetoric is the language of war neatly couched in the words of Christian grace.

Several years ago Pope Paul VI strongly emphasised the importance of inculturation as part of the Church's evangelising mission. "The Gospel, and therefore evangelisation, are certainly not identical with culture, and they are independent in regard to all cultures. Nevertheless, the kingdom which the Gospel proclaims is lived by men who are profoundly linked to a culture, and the building up of the kingdom cannot avoid borrowing the elements of human culture or cultures. Though independent of cultures, the Gospel and evangelisation are not necessarily incompatible with them; rather they are capable of permeating them all without becoming subject to any of them."[91]

Some have interpreted the incursions of Christianity and Islam in Africa as effective destabilization strategies that displaced many traditional African cultural forms. The effects of Arabic and European invasions on African people precipitated the speedy destruction of traditional institutions that housed

African cultural forms. Cultural destabilization introduced ever deepening levels of confusion and forced many African nations to accept their status as a broken people under foreign cultural occupation. Many scholars have written about these changes, especially with regard to their impact upon African religion. Githige points out that several of these writers such as Ìdòwú, Mbiti, Kenyatta, and Parrinder interpreted African religion from a perspective that created deeper levels of confusion. Githige points out that these men were devoted Christians whose primary views "were greatly influenced and even biased by their [loyalties] to their faiths and professions."[92] Githige maintains that Mbiti's contribution to the study of African religion was driven by his efforts to prove that modernity was the primary cause of West Africa's decline. Mbiti makes no mention of Christian hegemony, which only served to accelerate Africa's inevitable decline. Yet there was nothing natural about the mercenary tactics used by Western powers to destabilize traditional African cultural forms. The displaced African cultural forms were replaced by an Anglo paradigm, which served the plans of Western hegemony. Such strategies were not natural or acts of god, but the result of conquest and Western dominance. The militarization of missionary activity undermined African cultural forms.

Githige charges that traditional African communities were not prepared to deal with the sudden changes first triggered by Arab aggression followed by Euro-Christian missionary activities. Education was the preferred medium used by Christian missionaries to entice Africans into adopting a worldview at odds with their cultural DNA. Both the Islamic and Christian worldviews were connected to a new kind of power; an external force not available to black African nations. Education was used as a weapon to force upon Africans, a worldview that placed them at the bottom-most rung on the evolutionary ladder. Arab and Euro-missionary education was not liberal or designed to cause Africans to yearn for freedom. Missionary education by nature must be narrow and dogmatic. It is designed to "Europeanize" or "Arabicize" those who lack cultural values. Today we witness the lingering effects this process continues to have on African people. The Boko Harem (haters of Western education) are killing women and children because they resent what Western education has done to their people. Thus, in their distorted logic, those who embrace Western education are not worthy of living.

The incursion of Islam and Christianity upon African cultural forms, created what seems to be an irreparable rupture in the communal fabric that held them together. This rupture has left many Africa nations unable to diagnose the real source of their problems. Christianity was intricately connected to the new changes sweeping across the continent, even more so than Islam, which had made its entry into West Africa a thousand years before Christianity. Once

Christianity arrived in West Africa, it was tied to Anglo-European military power and this power was the real god and representative of white power. Jesus was an afterthought compared to the external power that appealed to Africans. Still, they accepted white power and his god, of whom they thought could be called upon to assist them in time of need. White power appealed to those Africans who confused external power with real power. Africans mistakenly thought that converting to Christianity would provide them access to white power. Some sacrificed everything for the bright lights of Europe, only to later realize that they had sold their birthright for a morsel of stale bread.

> The coming of Christianity was actually accompanied by these changes.... It was the missionaries who started schools, hospitals, and it was in collaboration with them that administration, cash economy and social changes found their way into African societies.[93]

The educated Africans benefited from their covenant made with the white god. They quickly began to disassociate from their uneducated brothers and sisters. The Western-trained African thought that he had finally arrived on the world stage. He had become Christian and, by extension, an honorary European. "This resulted in their alienation from the way of life of their predecessors in general and from African traditional religion in particular."[94] The strategies used by Western powers to lure Africans away from their cultural traditions and reach for what appeared of greater value was a brilliant strategy that would have made Emperor Constantine proud. This was a well thought-out plan which clearly reveals that from the very beginning the Europeans used a systematic approach to dismantle traditional African cultural forms. European missionaries seduced Africans into selling their cultural birth rights for what the most civilized European viewed as trash.

With the rise of Western education came the anti–African notion of individualism. African communalism was under assault as more Africans converted to Christianity and isolated themselves from their community. Some moved to Europe never to return and the few who returned began to fight against those traditional cultural forms they were trained to despise. A communal people were attacked from an ideology born in the cold mountains of Europe, where nature forced each person to kill or be killed. In such a hostile environment, the focus upon self was key to survival. There was no need for communalism when food was scarce and life was harsh. Even Mbiti recognized the impact individualism had on traditional African ways of being: "Live as individuals, but are dead to the corporate humanity of their forefathers."[95] The European obsession with "I" was a foreign concept in traditional African societies. One could not become human outside of the community. For traditional Africans to live outside of one's community only occurred under conditions when one was placed in isolation for violating societal norms. Black people have somehow forgotten that isolation from the community is a sign of death. The Western educated Africans' rejection of "corporate humanity" continues to have negative repercussions throughout Africa and wherever people of African descent reside.

The European sense of individualism functioned as a military strategy that challenged African communalism and traditional principles.[96] Still, Africans have shown themselves to be adaptive and resilient. For example, after Arabism forced itself upon Africa, Africans eventually adapted to Islam by accepting and modifying it, while at the same time, many continued to observe those essential elements within traditional African cultural forms.[97] Not surprisingly, Mbiti has viewed the incursion of Christianity into Africa as a positive force. He argues that Africans were without hope before the arrival of Christianity.[98] Mbiti views Christian imperialism as a positive force because it provided Africans with hope. Certain crises have accompanied these changes, which may be responsible for Africa's socioeconomic and political instability.[99] Much like the earlier Arab missionary models that spread like a virus throughout the continent of Africa, Christian missionaries employed a strategy of "radical discontinuity" to destabilize traditional cultural forms and replace them with alien cultural forms that have corrupted black thought. These white cultural forms imbibed by Africans were like time bombs that infiltrated their psyche and rewired cognitive circuitry to view the world through a white lens. Several scholars agree that when Christianity invaded certain parts of West Africa, it created social tension and cultural instability. One scholar discovered in his studies of African religion that tension mounted "among Africans when they realised the assault that had been waged on their customs."[100] After Western educated Africans awoke from their dark slumber, they discovered that the type of Christianity they adopted undermined their traditions. Thus many have since departed in droves from the white churches they once faithfully served. They established independent African churches, where they could continue to honor traditional values and norms.[101] In part, independent African churches signal their reluctance to fully reject the traditions of their ancestors.[102]

African Traditional Cultural Forms Within Hostile Environments

African traditional cultural forms continue to play a vital role in the decision-making process of many Africans. Whether one honors Arab or European cultural forms as religions, many aspects of traditional culture remains deeply engrained within the psyche. Githige maintains that African traditions have become deeply ingrained within Islam, but in some ways these TACF continue to resist Christianity.[103]

> It is becoming increasingly accepted that the type of missionary Christianity that came to Africa, beginning from the last century, was in collaboration with colonialism. This type of Christianity was brought by missionaries, most of whom did not know the nature of African traditional religion, and had preconceived ideas about what they termed as "primitive and pagan" religions.[104]

Unlike Islam, which initially resorted to violence to advance Arabism as a religion, Christianity entered Africa in the same fashion of its stringent faith-claims that are defended by the black church. For instance, "If you do not accept Jesus, you will go to hell," was an effective scare tactic used by missionaries to frighten some into becoming Christians. Christian missionaries rode into West Africa in the early nineteenth century with the crusading military objective to erase, realign, or destroy African culture and, if necessary, the people who honor that tradition. Traditional African cultural forms are viewed by most whites as subhuman. The missionaries' primary objective was to destabilize and destroy traditional African cultural form and, by doing so, the disintegration of African cultural unity would be certain. "Their basic aim on arrival was to erase these religions and to start a new religious chapter in Africa."[105] Many Africans who converted to Christianity during the missionaries' first incursion into Western Africa converted out of economic necessity. "Conversion into the new faith was motivated by material, academic, economic and other reasons, more than by faith."[106] Other factors that prompted Africans to accept Christianity was their way to escape the bondage of colonialism and to obtain new allies.

> Freedom from slavery as well as the need for political allies were some of the reasons that attracted Africans into the new religions. It can be argued that the nature of this conversion was more apparent than real. It was not a "turning away" from traditional religion into the new, but rather an acceptance of some good aspects of the new so as to mix them with the good elements of the old.[107]

This is perhaps an accurate explanation of why many Africans converted to Islam and Christianity. Throughout the New World where Africans were enslaved and forced to work on plantations in Haiti, Cuba, Trinidad, and elsewhere, they never completely abandoned traditional ways of being. They simply adopted certain aspects of white Christianity and cultural values to add to their tradition. Africans "turning away" from traditional ways of living is a common theory advanced by several scholars, including Ìdòwú, Kibi-cho,[108] and Booth. Again, the idea that Africans embraced foreign cultural forms is not new and can be witnessed in the New World where enslaved Africans adopted nominal forms of Catholicism and Christianity to protect their cultural traditions. Arabism did not destroy the natural African rhythm as did Christianity, which was more of a destabilizing force. At least in some instances, Islam was as willing to receive from traditional African cultural forms as it was to give of its cultural tradition. Some have even argued that African divination practiced by the Yoruba is an esoteric tradition adopted from Arab traditions? "Divination, belief in spirits [jinns], magical practices, witchcraft, rainmaking ceremonies, charms as well as rites of passage are some of the elements of ATR which Africans carried over into Islam."[109] However, the "tolerance" once shown by Islam in West Africa, has since changed. Today, Christianity by far is more embracing of "non-offensive" TACF. In spite of the violent attacks from Arab and European evangelizers, African traditional cultural forms remain a vital part of black survival strat-egy throughout the world.

There are indeed certain African traditions that are offensive to many. Those Christians seeking to dialogue with practitioners of TACF insist on what traditions should remain and what should be abandoned. This is the exact type of Christian arrogance that caused Africans to create African inde-pendent churches. Mbiti argued that African independent churches address Africans' need to maintain ties to their tradition whereas Christianity allows them to enter the realm of modernity.[110] The Africans' move to establish inde-pendent churches attests to their desire to maintain a relationship with the tradition of their ancestors.[111] Within some independent African churches traditional practices such as polygamy and female circumcision are main-tained.[112] Independent churches are reflective of the identity struggle that has plagued Africa since Alexander invaded the continent in 332 BCE. From that time, Africans have accepted a perspective of life that conflicts with their perception of reality. They remain torn between two dimensions and are forced to exist in both worlds. Within the independent churches, they exist within this bifurcated sphere where they feed the gods of Christianity with one hand and serve the ancestors with the other.

From the beginning of Western dominance, there were some Africans who rejected the alien cultural forms forced upon them by Arabs and Euro-peans. For example, Parrinder noted in his early study of African culture in the mid-twentieth century, certain West African societies rejected Christi-anity. Those cultural groups that rejected Christianity and Islam have been referred to by some practitioners of traditional African cultural forms as the faithful remnant that kept the African gods alive. The African remnant scattered throughout the diaspora and survived numerous attacks from those who promote violence, which is a concomitant of white power. African culture has survived despite the forces it battles on a daily basis. These forces aim to drive black culture, and the people who honor their heritage, out of existence. The African remnant that survived modernity struggled to keep alive the knowledge passed down to them. Proponents of African culture struggle against those who insist that all people must serve the god of Western imperialism. After all, He alone has shown himself strong and immutable. He defeated African culture and even communalism. He destroyed all the indigenous gods in the New World. Today he stands alone as god of the cosmos. Since the Western god has shown himself to be the only true god, it is only reasonable that all prostrate themselves before Him. Those who resist are targeted for death by drone or other higher forms of killing.

The re–Africanization of the black mind began to gather momentum in the mid-twentieth century after African nations were emancipated from European tyranny. This new sense of freedom created mass movements by Africans on the continent and throughout the New World. In Africa the return to African cultural forms was called "Utamaduni." In the United States it was known as the Black Power Movement. Later, a more conscious and refined movement emerged—Afrocentricity. "The revival was strengthened by the realisation that there really was nothing to be ashamed of in the African culture and heritage; contrary to the European attitude that most of what was in the African culture was bestial in nature."[113]

Throughout the Caribbean and particularly in Cuba, Trinidad, and Haiti, there is a movement underway to re–Africanize traditional African "creole" cultural forms. If this movement proves successful it will mark a new beginning for black people everywhere. Until black people begin to scrutinize the white gods that have sworn allegiance to destroy black existence, they will remain imprisoned to a construct that has crippled their growth and developed. Black awakening movements, including the Pan-Africanists, Negritude, and personality movements,[114] were incapable of freeing the black mind from white bondage because these movements lacked the cultural unity that proceeds real freedom.

Githige recognized another force that added in the cultural transmission of traditional African values, which aims at promoting African consciousness. He criticized African scholars for providing more theory than concrete analysis. African scholarship is of little relevance for the average person because "the goals and aims behind the revival are far away from the context in which these traditional elements were practiced in reality in our societies."[115] The re–Africanization movements such as Afrocentricity are also attempting to reconnect with an authentic African aesthetic. Such cultural movements are indications of a people's unwillingness to embrace a hermeneutic that does not demand them to prostrate themselves before the altars of whiteness. Any people forced or deceived to prostrate themselves before alien gods, or any other forces outside of their cultural milieu, places the entire black world in danger. Which is why China refuses to allow certain Western religious organizations from entering their country. The Chinese know that there is no religion which is not connected to an external power. Only traditional religions are without such external power, which is the real sign of their authenticity.

The future of African traditional cultural forms looks bright, providing that those who define them are also practitioners. As was noted elsewhere, most fieldwork into TACF has been conducted by Christian scholars, whose analysis is centered within a Euro-Christian framework. These scholars are imprisoned by a hermeneutic that is incapable of clearly seeing the world except through a Christian lens. Christian missionaries and their academic counterparts promote a diluted version of African religion to advance a common agenda because both were trained to view TACF as possessing little value. Their findings are flawed because they were designed to create in Africans a sense of religious inadequacy. Western scholarship is nothing more than an appendage of Western imperialism. It is designed to show that African culture is inferior to whiteness in all its guises. Again, Western education is the handmaiden of Western imperialism and has historically been used as a weapon to attack African traditional cultural forms. Ìdòwú noted that such biases were centered in post enlightenment Eurocentrist ideologies. These teachings and similar strategies instilled in them a hatred for all things African: "They learn this from books most of which are written by foreigners who have been biased against African culture and religion. What our students get is therefore a biased view, and the end result is that they learn to hate themselves and to be ashamed of their heritage."[116]

This observation is quite telling, especially since it was uttered by a devout African Christian clergy. Yet, he recognized that the missionaries were using education to inculcate or brainwash African students with ideas, which would lead them to hate their culture. Such self-hatred is meticulously instilled into nonwhite Western educated students. Post-colonial Africans seemed to have little choice but to accept Christianity. It offered them access to the type of lifestyle they witnessed among Europeans. Supposedly, African traditional cultural forms could not provide Western educated Africans with those creature comforts offered to even nominal Christians. Thus, TACF were viewed as inferior to the Euro-Christian construct, even though many converts continued to visit traditional healers for ailments that modernity, and their white god had no remedy. African Christians were systematically taught to hate themselves, as pointed out by Ìdòwú. This was a powerful strategy that continues to have negative repercussions throughout the black world. Still, it is difficult to divorce oneself from their primal culture and as a result, many Africans continue to adhere, consciously or otherwise, to certain aspects of traditional cultural forms. This is due to the relationship between religion and culture because in traditional Africa, religion is synonymous with culture.

For example, any assault on the United States is an attack upon the entire white world and the Euro-Christian principles they adhere too. If these sacred principles that govern whiteness are attacked anywhere in the world, it is understood as an attack upon those nations and cultural groups that adhere to the norms that govern Euro-Christian values. The same is true of Africa and its sacred cultural forms. Those corporate-controlled Christian missionaries who invade Africa with alien cultural forms are in essence waging a war against African people everywhere. Traditional African cultural forms have been under attack since Alexander invaded Africa in 332 BCE, which has led some scholars to believe its future is bleak. The Reverend Ìdòwú and Mbiti argued that African traditional culture would not survive modernity because it is ill-equipped to survive in the modern world.

Both seem to have forgotten about the survival of African traditional cultural forms in the Americas. Robert Farris Thompson described the replantation of African cultural forms in the New World as one of the greatest religio-cultural migrations in world history. Ìdòwú and Mbiti seem to have either overlooked or disregarded such evidence, which overwhelmingly speaks to the resiliency of African cultural forms, especially in Cuba, Haiti and Brazil. Ìdòwú believed that Christianity would eventually take over all of Africa and at the same time and maintained that it may be Africa's greatest hope.[117] This bleak view of TACF was also echoed by Mbiti, who suggested that African religion would ultimately pass away. Its death was inevitable, cried Mbiti, but not all scholars hold such bleak views.

For example, Githige argued that Mbiti's logic was premised upon his interpretation of traditional Africans concept of time. Mbiti argued that African religion was doomed because its foundation is rooted in the Zamani period, which is a concept of time very different from the west.[118] Mbiti argued that African religion is situated in period which lacks a clear perspective of the future.[119] "Zamani is the graveyard of time, the period of termination, the dimension in which everything finds its halting point.... Zamani is the period of the myth, giving a sense of foundation or 'security' to the Sasa period;

and binding together all created things, so that all things are embraced within the Macro-Time."[120]

Traditional Africans lack a sense of future and by extension are unable to survive in an ever-changing world. In the modern world where drastic changes are the norm, African religion is static and will become less significant, eventually passing away.[121] "Time is meaningful [only] at the point of the event and not at the mathematical moment."[122] Throughout traditional communities time is confined to the here and now and lacks a concept of future events. With this restrictive view of time, Mbiti surmised that African religion was incapable of providing the people with a positive outlook on life. Time is not a "commodity which must be utilized, sold and bought; but in traditional African life, time has to be created or produced."[123]

There are at least two modes of time expressed in traditional societies: "no-time" and "potential time."[124] The no-time covers the period that has not yet occurred, which is similar to what some recognize as future time. Potential time is linked to natural events, such as agriculture and cycles of nature.[125] The traditional view of time is linked to a "composition of events which have occurred, those which are taking place now and those which are inevitably or immediately to occur."[126] Traditional time is two-dimensional and involves a long past and a present. "The future is virtually absent because events which lie in it have not taken place, they have not been realized and cannot, therefore, constitute time."[127]

Since traditional African societies have a different concept of time, Mbiti argues that African religion is incapable of long-term survival. Cross-conversion is occurring across faith lines, argued Mbiti, with the exception of traditional African religion.[128] When those few convert from Christianity or Islam to traditional religion, Mbiti terms this conversion as apostasy or backsliding.[129] This kind of thinking substantiates the words of p'Bitek, who condemned Africans who attack the religion of their ancestors. It also speaks to the depth of self-hatred inculcated into the hearts of Western educated Africans. Mbiti's analysis of African cultural forms as a dying religion is completely inaccurate. Not only have TACF survived Western hegemony and in particular, Christian imperialism, but these sacred forms have recreated themselves throughout the black Atlantic world. TACF will become significant in the lives of more black people when non–Abrahamic scholars record their findings, without the Christian propaganda carried by Mbiti and others. Githige decried that "the views of Africans as presented by Mbiti and Ìdòwú with regards to the nature of ATR today, and its prospects for the future, are greatly determined and even biased by their loyalties to their religion and by their task of Christian evangelisation."[130]

The African Christians have had a deadly impact on traditional ways of being. However, it was Arabs who were the first outsiders to use religion as a weapon. They used Arabism to attack Africans perception of the sacred. They were the first invaders to successfully transplant Arab traditional cultural forms also known as Islam first in North Africa and throughout most of Africa by the end of the first millennium CE.[131] The Euro-Anglo cultural forms in the garb of Christianity did not penetrate the interior regions of African until the nineteenth century CE Arabism and Europeanisms introduced cultural prejudices because their scriptures obligated them to convert the heathen (Qur'an 4:48; Psalm 135:15).[132] Although a few independent Christian organizations have become "outwardly" accepting of certain aspects of traditional African cultural forms, African Muslims on the other hand, are becoming less tolerant[133] (for example, Boko Haram and Islamic State).

The core of such problems are theological and based on hermeneutics and concepts of the Divine. Muslim and Christian scholars do have certain things in common such as both share a disdain for TACF. There remains much contention between advocates of traditional religion and proponents of the Abrahamic faiths. Such contention is partly based on cultural myths from which all theology is derived. Christian and Islamic theologians are responsible for creating a distorted view of African reality.

For instance, p'Bitek highlighted the problems that occur when scrutinizing traditional African cultural forms with theological tools designed to evaluate the Abrahamic faiths. Patrick Ryan at the University of Ghana in Legon charged that such templates are not universal and for the most part, are ill-equipped to critique TACF. "Not only outside observers but also certain African Christian insiders have perpetuated a tendency, perhaps unconscious, to describe African conceptions of the transcendent in Semitic or Indo-European theological categories that are still basically foreign."[134] Ryan further argued that these foreign structures impose "alien patterns of thought" on African piety.[135] In essence, it is highly unlikely to accurately evaluate traditional African cultural forms with theological tools designed to evaluate the Abrahamic faiths.

These "alien patterns of thought" are culturally restrictive because they were developed by Europeans to evaluate Abrahamic thought. Western theological schematics are inadequate for mapping TACF. Ryan even suggested that the very language used to speak about the divine creates theological issues, especially when comparisons are made between traditional and Abrahamic religions. Ryan maintains that language is one of the primary barriers preventing Euro-Christian paradigms from accessing. African languages are more suitable for analyzing TACF because "the Yoruba and Akan populations of West Africa are better equipped linguistically than are Semites, Greeks, Romans and their inheritors to express the absolute uniqueness of God."[136]

The colonizers used education as a weapon to separate Africans from their culture. Education was used to distance Africans from their traditions and replace it with a Western construct contrary to traditional ways of being. The closer one becomes to emulating white aesthetics and mannerisms, the more human they were perceived by the colonizer—then and now. For instance, during the colonial era the Catholic Church controlled many training centers throughout West Africa.[137] At the turn of the nineteenth and the beginning of the twentieth centuries, their interests in African religion was driven by evolutionary theories developed by anthropologists.[138] The anthropologists were guided by ethnocentrism and cultural empiricism, especially the idea that Africans were inherently inferior to whites. These theories functioned as the departure point by which nearly every inquiry into African culture were based until the middle of the twentieth century, when a few white scholars hinted that African culture may have within it principles and values capable of humanizing Africans. It was not until the phenomenological approach to the study of religion became the new fad and that comparative studies of TACF began.[139]

The phenomenological approach was initially considered free of the prejudices that contaminated most of Western scholarship. Today, the phenomenological approach has been abandoned because it too carries its own "cognitive baggage." M.F.C. Bourdillion argued in his article entitled "Anthropological Approaches to the Study of African Religions" that no discourse is neutral or free of biases. "The problem of avoiding ethnocentrism in the study of religions cannot be avoided simply by abstaining from judgment." The phenomenologist or the positivist approach to the study of religion can't avoid contaminating what it observes. Since one cannot avoid being biased in their research, the researcher must acknowledge his or her position from the beginning. Honesty must be the departure point for all inquiry. When the scholar is openly honest about their biases and admit their limitations, "We can enter into academic debate," writes Bourdillion. "In an undogmatic way, ready to listen and learn." Biases cannot be avoided when making observations, especially when those under observation are from a different cultural and "racial" group. Still, evaluation is a critical intellectual skill that cannot be ignored because not every perspective is equally valid. There must be some way of making distinctions, especially in a time of Boko Harem and drones. Bourdillion challenges scholars not to shy away from making judgments. We all have a right to our opinions, but when those opinions or doctrines result in the killing of innocent lives, we must boldly make judgments against the perpetrators of such violence. "When religion results in conflict, we can [must] make a judgment about this kind of religion." (For example, both the Palestinians and Israelis cannot be right. Someone is deadly wrong. We cannot avoid making judgments in such matters of life and death.)

Colonial missionary-scholars used various strategies to study traditional African cultural forms, trying to avoid facing their own biases. "In British anthropological studies, based on field work, religion has often been portrayed mainly as a reflex of the social order."[140] James Cone is the premier scholar of black theology who argued three decades ago that there has always been a direct relationship between theology and the social order. Cone argued in his groundbreaking studies of pre–Civil War black churches that social location plays a pivotal role in how religion is interpreted. Yet many white scholars ignore what is known by most. They continue to claim that religion is something more than a reflection of the social order. They argue that religion is more than an image of the socioeconomic order.[141] How can that be when people create the social order? The development of societal norms are "man-made." God has nothing to do with the institutions that are developed to govern society. Human beings create from their imagination. The God-concept is itself a creation from "man's" morbid imagination. Whatever this divine force may be, it appears to be as far removed from "man's" imagination as the heavens are from the earth.

Many early scholars of African religion were not theologians but anthropologists.[142] We have now discovered that the methods they used for gathering information were distorted and yielded data that is quite unreliable. For example, Westerlund maintains that "the writings of Western anthropologists have usually been ignored or viewed critically in works by African scholars of religion."[143] P'Bitek criticized the anthropological analysis of African religion because of its distorted views on race. "There has been a conspicuous interest in research with a comparative rather than a locally limited perspective."[144] The comparative approach was used to assist scholars in their efforts to systematize African religion, but it has been criticized for being too general. Therefore, some have suggested that a local approach be employed when studying TACF, which provides a richer analysis of TACF. The comparative study of African religion has proven itself to be inadequate, especially when the Western worldview remains the single criteria by which TACF are judged. Bourdillion maintains that, "when we use a European or western category to cover institutions in African societies, we must be ready to fit the institutions, rather than distort our accounts of the institutions to fit the categories."

Some scholars adopted the phenomenological approach to study African phenomena to avoid contaminating their research, which often results from prejudices and biases of the researcher. Although the phenomenological approach made sincere efforts to avoid several of the biases that contaminated most of Western scholarship, its preoccupation on description rather than theoretical explanations is equally inadequate.[145] Whatever approach one employs to study TACF, honesty and academic integrity are important principles that must be honored. "The study of African religion ... is the 'master-key' to understanding Africans."[146] TACF function as the nerve center of all things African. Without recognizing those foundational elements that comprise African ways of being, it is impossible to understand how religion "has shaped their [African] cultures, their social life, their political organizations and economic activities."[147] Spirituality plays a vital role in the lives of African people.[148]

Academia and African Traditional Religion

An accurate assessment of TACF can be realized when more practitioners of TACF study African phenomena, although the "insider" perspective does not guarantee one's findings will be bias-free because they too have their own biases. Insiders often take for granted the dominant ideology of their community and do not notice how much behavior diverges from this ideology.... Insiders often obscure what is supposed to happen, rather than what does happen. Judgments cannot be avoided but we can reduce the amount of contamination that taints most studies by stating our intentions from the start. If the relationship between the researcher and the people under study is to be one of equality, researchers must be open about their study and clearly state what they are doing and why. Honesty, before all else must be the departure point for those who aim at reducing the level of biases that so easily creep into ones research. There is no way one can completely avoid being bias, but to admit our biases in the beginning, and not be deceptive by claiming ones work is purely objective.

For example, the study of TACF as an academic discipline began in institutions controlled by Protestant and Roman Catholic academic-missionaries. It was not until the 1940s that the Universities of Ghana and Ibadan created departments of religion, where TACF could be analyzed, in part, outside of Christian dogma that preferences whiteness. The University of Ghana and Ibadan were still under the control of Western missionaries who provided the lion share of their funding. It was not until the 1960s that a secular religion department appeared in an East African university, which was combined with the philosophy department.[149] In the early 1980s, Makerere established a separate department for the study of religion.[150] It was at Makerere in Kampala, Uganda, that the first department of religion was founded at an East African university.[151] Many African countries where the study of traditional religion was established encountered challenges from Muslim students opposed to studying any religion except Islam.[152] Both students and not a few professors were hesitant about studying TACF as an academic discipline. They had so little regard for the traditions of their forbearers. One would think they were Arab or born in Saudi Arabia. Some did lighten up and a professor at Kampala stated that "Muslim scholars are conservative, although a few of them are beginning to change their attitudes toward African religion."[153] At the University of Ghana, Muslim students were opposed to the study of all religions other than Islam.[154] J. S. Pobee noted that the attitude of Muslims at the University of Ghana and certain professors considered it "a 'crime' to study Christianity." "It took years of fighting to get them to take the area of African religion seriously."[155] This attitude was not confined to African Muslims as Marxists were equally cynical. "The attitude of intellectual Muslims and Marxists to the study of African religion is [was] often exceedingly negative."[156]

The negative attitude of African Christians and Muslims is indicative of the hatred inculcated from foreign ideologies hostile against TACF. The first African Christian and Muslims who rejected the traditions of their forefathers did not know that their disdain for traditional religion was a reflection of the hatred they had formed themselves. It is important for African scholars who are practitioners of TACF to be at the forefront in studying traditional religion. Otherwise, those self-hating Africans who are at war with themselves and the culture of their ancestors will continue to spew their hatred. From the beginning Africans were challenged to reject the traditions of their ancestors and accept Arab and European cultural forms. African Christians and Muslims reject traditional culture because they cannot conceive of their traditional culture as one that is sacred, at least not on the level of Christian and Islamic cultures. They see nothing wrong with the elevation of Arab and European cultural forms to the status of religion. Those who reject their traditions for an alien cultural form are in need of psychological deliverance. Such a people are at war with themselves, and in this state of mind, they will never know peace.

Parrinder's work is highly prized and cited by many scholars of African religion.[157] He has become one of Africa's patron saints. In those African nations once controlled by the French government, the writings of Griaule and Tempels have been equally embraced.[158] However, we would be unwise to overlook that these men were dedicated Christians who were obligated to the tenets and dictates that govern their faith. Parrinder's primary obligation was to his Christian faith. He was a devoted missionary who worked for the Methodist Church in West Africa.[159] Of course his work must be seen through the cultural lens that shaped his worldview. "Any study of the religion of another person is to some extent a study by an outsider," writes Bourdillion. Parrinder may be perceived by African scholars and missionaries as a good man. Still, he could not escape the reality and limits of his whiteness. He was not an African no matter how long he lived among the people. Bourdillion writes, "There is always a danger that when we come across ways and beliefs different from our own, we narrow them down to fit into our own experience to incorporate what others think and do."

Again, p'Bitek attacked European scholarship by accusing it of being culturally restrictive and theologically inept, particularly at analyzing TACF. He criticized the Euro-Christian methods employed by Tempels and others, who believed that because they had studied African people for a few decades and lived among them, that they really knew who they were. P'Bitek attacked those who thought they knew the African simply because they studied their culture. "That what is being paraded as African metaphysics is actually an attempt by scholars who are steeped in the philosophy of Thomas Aquinas to interpret African religious ideas in terms of that philosophy."[160] P'Bitek's analysis of Western scholarship in Africa equally applies to the missionary-scholar. "Catholic scholars have also structured African religion in a spiritual pyramid or hierarchy with God at the top, although they have couched it largely in Thomistic terms."[161]

Tempels and other missionary-scholars who wrote extensively about African religio-culture cultural forms have been criticized for interpreting TACF within a Euro-Christian framework. Such arrogance and narrowness continues to plague Western scholarship. Tempels may have been highly praised for his efforts to show that the Bantus were capable of thinking, yet he remained staunchly connected to the negative ideologies that governed the West's perception of African people. In this regard, Tempels remained in league with the European Christian colonizers and those who utilized psychological warfare to destroy and destabilize African culture. The missionary objectives were clear; either to civilize African people or entice them to abandon their worldview. Temples was at least noble with his aspirations in that he set out to show that African people were capable of abstract thought. This was a bold stance taken by Temples, since most Europeans in the mid-twentieth century were convinced that Africans were not fully human. Still, Tempels (the good white liberal) was also a victim of his time and was not immune to the social pressures that preference conformity. Therefore, a close analysis of his work reveals that he did not escape the faults that plagued Western scholarship. Tempels, like Mbiti and many others, attempted to interpret TACF within a European Christian framework. This approach is incapable of yielding anything meaningful, which is why we still know very little about African traditional religion. This will not change until men and women who have not been tainted by European and Arabic religious ideologies present their findings to the world. Until then, practitioners of TACF must be actively engaged in dismantling the lies and misinformation that is presented as scholarship.

Tempels's classic text on African philosophy of religions, *Bantu Philosophy*, utilized a Thomistic methodology to categorize and interpret TACF. His use of a Thomistic methodology to investigate African phenomena contaminated his scholarship. There is no recovery from such an error because when the departure point is tainted, the findings are completely worthless. Upon further investigation of Tempels's work, one notices his inability to view African religion as a system completely separate, if not different, from Christianity. He thought it was his Christian obligation to assist God's less developed ones in making sense of the cultural chaos that engulfed their existence. *Bantu Philosophy* was written with objectives synonymous with "the ordered systems and intellectual disciplines of the Western world."[162] Although Templels does not mention the Thomistic religious schema he employed to categorize and interpret Bantu religio-philosophy, those acquainted with Thomistic schema recognize Tempels's method as Thomistic, however subtle.[163]

The study of TACF is riddled with similar errors that can be observed in the writings of others who wrote about African religion. TACF will continue to be misrepresented by those who have no interests in advancing it a sacred cultural system on par with Islam and Christianity. The late E. B. Ìdòwú was one of the leading authorities of African religion, who argued that non–Africans cannot adequately understand traditional African cultural forms. This is quite an interesting observation, since Ìdòwú was a Christian minister who was trained by Parrinder. Both Ìdòwú and Awolalu argued that non–Africans may have certain cultural predispositions which make them ill-equipped to comprehend TACF. They argued that for one to adequately understand African religion, they need to possess an African centered frame of reference. This argument is similar to what James Cone said regarding African American religion and the white man's inability to understand what only an insider can access. Cone argued that non–Africans have a different axiological grid than blacks, which prevents them from understanding Afro-

American phenomena. African scholars by far have the ability to become "better" observers and interpreters of African traditional religion than their European counterparts. Ìdòwú and Awolalu agreed that the non–African may be at too great a cultural disadvantage to understand African religion.[164]

From the beginning of the slave trade that started with the Portuguese, negative attitudes of West African culture were perpetuated as part of a strategy aimed at destabilizing TACF. "The early Portuguese visitor could not identify anything 'religious' in Africa because religion was so integrated into all of life."[165] The European invaders ignored their historical record that described Africa as home of the gods. From the mid-eighteenth century forward, European scholarship began to disassociate Egypt from Africa. If they could, these revisionists would have moved Egypt and placed it in Europe. Still, Egypt is in Africa where religion started along the Nile River which stretches deep into black Africa.

The revisionists failed to realize that religion is not a separate from society. There is no such thing in traditional communities as a demarcation between religion and culture. Such a schism would be a sign of sickness. How could a society steeped in spirituality separate belief from vocation? The connection between religion and culture remains a mystery to outsiders, especially those from cultures where religion was controlled by the state. How could they understand the African worldview that is so different from their own? There was no word in traditional African societies for religion because all is sacred. The world was a sacred entity governed by spiritual forces that upheld the cosmos. The same is true regarding the study of African religion. One cannot study TACF as an entity separate from the lives of those who live out its tenets. Christianity is expressed by faith-propositions and systems of faith that produce a different spirituality that one knowledge driven. African tradition views all life-forms as interconnected and therefore, TACF cannot be studied in isolation from equally important cultural factors. "The tendency to separate religious phenomena from their context may be partly responsible for premature generalizations regarding African religion and also for overly hasty identification of African and non–African phenomena."[166]

The European linear model is responsible for the narrow focus that pervades Western discourse. The linear model is too stringent and narrowly focused to analyze TACF. Africans view the world as a place existing on multiple levels; a world not confined to Place or Time, as opposed to the European perspective, that studies things in parts, abstracted or isolated from the whole. "Beliefs and practices abstracted from the whole of which they are parts may have quite different appearances from those which they have in context."[167] The linear model is premised on binary logic and the bifurcation of phenomena. Again, this view of reality is quite antithetical to the holism that pervades traditional African thought. There is nothing within the traditional purview which exists in isolation, including humans, animals, plants, or stones. Isolation equals death. All things are intricately connected to an overarching worldview. Even the enforcement of Christianity and Islam upon Africans was eventually accepted as an additional entity that could be added to their pantheon. Traditional Africans are tolerant and embracing of seemingly divergent views. Unity for the traditional African does not exist in conformity, but in diversity. Therefore, "Christianity and Islam make [made] their appeal in Africa in terms of new possibilities of power, humanity, wholeness, continuity, healing, and celebration. Africans frequently see them as supplementing rather than replacing their traditional beliefs and practices."[168]

Africans adopted Islam and Christianity not because they lacked a sacred cultural tradition. They knew their culture was rich and sustained their foreparents for centuries before Islam and Christianity invaded the continent. They accepted these foreign ideologies not because their culture lacked values. In fact, traditional values were worldlier and less heavenly focused then Christianity. For example, the traditional communities rejected the ideal that salvation in all its manifestations, particularly in matters of justice could be delayed. "[S]alvation is first and foremost a deliverance from the here-and-now oppression, and only secondary and remotely spiritual in the sense of life to come."[169] Africans have erred by accepting the Christian belief that justice belongs exclusively to a remote God. TACFs are based upon the Now moment. The traditional view of salvation is not a future event. We are not saved at some time in the future as taught by Christians. Either one is saved right now or salvation does not exists.

> Salvation is viewed as corporate social action against oppression. To stress the idea of personal salvation and declare hell judgment for non–Christians is considered eccentric and dehumanizing. The concerted effort is for the universal deliverance of all people everywhere from any kind of oppression by fellow human beings.[170]

Salvation is not something that only happens at death. The traditional view of death is tied to cosmic and communal harmony. Death is not simply a future event, but part of the manly life transitions one experiences throughout their stay on earth. We die each moment we let go of our ego, which Deepak Chopra described as "Edging God Out" (EGO). Traditional Africans possess a holistic view of life, which places a rather thin line between life and death. Life does not exist in one straight line that begins at birth and ends at death. There is no "real" demarcation between the two. It is here in the physical realm where one is separated from their true form. Physical death is simply the process that allows one to reconnect with all that is permanent—all that is real.[171] Many followers of TACF hold that life is rhythmic and its rhythms are infused with a divine force incapable of destruction.[172] Death is that which "stands between the world of human beings and the world of the spirits, between the visible and the invisible."[173] Death is a physical break in communal relations, but does not cancel the communal responsibility of those who pass on to the next world. Departed ones are still members of the community and maintain their position of authority in the family. Traditional Africans believe that no power exists that can separate one from the love of their family, not even the grave. "The grave is paradoxically the symbol of separation between the dead and the living, but turning it into the shrine for the living-dead converts it into the point of meeting between the two worlds. Stripping the corpse and burying it completely naked is a concrete externalization of the concept of death as birth into the hereafter."[174]

Death does not separate but catapults some to a greater status. Those who pass over into the world of spirits are in a better position to help their family. Many practitioners of TACF hold that the deceased are really never in the grave. At death the body vanishes through the process of decomposition, while the soul goes on its journey home. So long as the progeny of the dead remember one's name, they are not really dead.[175] Death is a mode of transport to the afterlife. It is not the annihilation of the energy that animates the body. It is the vehicle that carries one from the physical into the world of eternal spirits. Traditionalists believed that in ancestor heaven one could continue to honor and practice their religio-culture. "Universally, the African peoples consider death to be a separation of the material body, the flesh, from the immaterial part, the spirit or soul which continues to live on."[176] Tempels referred to the traditional view of death as "Vital Participation."[177] Death is not only a mode of transport where the immaterial is set free from the imprisoned body, it is part of the cycle of life where one returns over and again until their life mission is complete. In the Western world this phenomenon is called reincarnation, which is simply "the passage of the soul from one body to another, the lot of the soul in each being is determined by its behaviour in a former life."[178] In traditional communities names are given to children which support the idea that departed souls return to inhabit the bodies of family members.[179]

The African view of death is anchored in the knowledge that the divinities reward and punish offenders of the tradition in this life. Students of

African traditional religion argue that "the majority of African peoples claim that God punishes people and rewards them in this life. There is nothing awaiting them in death because sin is an offense against one's neighbor and is punishable here and now."[180] The Christian concept of sin has no place in traditional religious thought. Sin in traditional Africa is a breach or imbalance in the communal rhythms that govern society. The disturbance of this relationship constitutes sin. When such a violation occurs, certain rituals need to be performed to restore the delicate balance between human beings and the Vital Energy that sustains them.

It was the elders in many traditional African societies who performed the rituals to maintain ontological harmony. In parts of East Africa the father was the priest of the family who performed most of the rituals. Among the West African Tallensi, the father also served as priest. Practitioners of TACF have provided the modern world with a glimpse into an ancient model, outlining the duties of those responsible for maintaining communal balance. Not only were these ministers' representatives of the divinities in general, they also served a particular deity. "The West African religions have 'ministers' of worship who are the official intermediaries between a human community, such as a village or region, and spirits, most frequently a certain definite spirit."[181] These ministers are specialists of a certain deity and, most often, they are healers that possess an in-depth knowledge of herbal pharmacology. Ministers of African traditional religion are dispensers of sacred knowledge and possess the secrets to healing all manner of sickness and diseases. They are the "recognised masters of a sacred grove or of a place of worship by the population; he exercises his function either at a regular date for the community, or daily for those people who ask him to do so."[182] Their focus on the veneration of the deities, revolves around "prayers, purification after breach of prohibitions or faults, libations or sacrifices as well as propitiatory rites in case of sickness or danger."[183]

Most scholars of TACF hold that there is no direct worship of God the Creator in traditional communities. However correct this statement may be, it is based on the Western perspective of worship. Actually, the concept of "worship" within African traditional religion is a foreign concept and should not be used within the same context as it is understood in Western religions. Within African religion, "worship" can be described as "respect, admiration or devotion for an object of esteem."[184] The African traditional perspective of worship is culturally conditioned and based upon the people's perception of the deity. According to Awolalu, "worship depends upon and is conditioned by man's conception of God: it always has a theological basis."[185] In TACF worship is more akin to what can be called honor and veneration.

Traditional Africans may not speak of God in the affectionate language that some Christians use, as if the God-concept and one's sexual partner are the same.

Traditional Africans do petition deity and offer thanksgiving, but these thank offerings and petitions are directed to a specific deity. The divinities serve as intermediaries between the Vital Energy and the devotee. Awolalu argued that the divinities are never given supreme honor, only the Supreme Being is given ultimate praise.[186] "Worship is ... accorded to the Supreme Being to whom man owes his own being and who is the Determiner of man's destiny."[187] The African view of worship is not confined to God alone, if ever. In most cases God's functionaries and the ancestors are afforded this honor. The heart of African spirituality rests upon the divine hierarchy including the divinities, ancestors, and other spiritual entities. Life rewards those who honor the divinities and ancestors who walked uprightly. "The people believe that if worship is given to these divine beings regularly and in the right manner, all will be will with man."[188] If one fails to honor this sacred relationship calamities will inevitably follow them until that sacred relationship is restored.[189]

3

African Tradition and the Culture of Religion

The intimate relationship between the physical and non-physical realm is the most important aspect of traditional African culture. Most Africans honored traditional African cultural forms as their religion prior to Arab and later, European invasions. Throughout the various cultural forms practiced by those venerate TACF, there existed a common tradition observed even by those dispersed over a wide geographical area. For instance, the Yoruba have customs and beliefs similar to those practiced among the Dagara of Burkina Faso and the Fon of Benin. One of the most common ideals held by traditional Africans is the notion that human destiny is predestined. One's vocation should be in harmony with their life-choices, to maintain communal stability. Traditional Africans once accepted such ideas as a reality and many still believe that each human being has a unique path to journey. Many cultural groups in African and throughout the black Atlantic participate in common rituals that aim at maintaining balance between the existent and the life-forces that protect ones destiny.

For example, the Yoruba consists of several cultural groups held tightly together by a refined religio-cultural system, of which a few scholars argue have their origin in ancient Kemet.[1] Some students of TACF are convinced that Yoruba theology is similar to the system developed by Africans in ancient Egypt. The Kemites (the name ancient Egyptians called themselves and their country; meaning, land of blacks) developed a theological system that reached its apex four thousand years before the Hebrews developed the Abrahamic system, which eventually gave rise to Judaism, Christianity, and Islam. All three Western faiths point to Abraham as the founding father of their religions.[2] Or, they view Abraham as an important figure in the development of their religions. On the other hand, some Yoruba trace their origins to the world's first religious system, which first arose in black Africa along the Nile River. The traditional Yoruba are a very proud people who view themselves as descendants of noble lineage, especially those who venerate the orisha. Like the royal mythical lineage from which they descended, the Yoruba are concerned with the spiritual well-being of all human beings. The Yoruba are much the same as the Kemites, who lived in a world controlled by spirits, or what they referred to as the *neteru*. "Religion forms the foundation and the all-governing principle of life for them [traditional Yoruba]."[3] They place their existence in the hands of their Creator, whose desires are administered by divinities (orisha) that serve as mediators between Olódùmarè the Supreme Deity and the people. The rituals used to honor this unique relationship between the orisha and their devotees are performed by babalowas, who interpret the logos. Rituals are so much a part of the Yoruba way of life that for each significant life-event from birth to physical death, before birth to after death, govern every aspect of one's being.[4] Yoruba rituals are premised on myths from the Odu Corpus, which consists of liturgies, songs, and many sayings that serve the same purpose as the Chinese I-Ching.

All that is vital to understanding life's mysteries is derived from Yoruba myths. Their philosophy, theology, songs, sayings, and liturgies all originate from myth. Yoruba theology can also be found within folktales and proverbs, which are the basis of African philosophy. Mbiti maintains that African philosophy is deeply rooted within proverbs, oral tradition, and traditional mores.[5] Knowledge is transmitted orally through myths that have been preserved and safe-guarded by the priests. The oral tradition shows emphatically that Africans have always been engaged in addressing those issues of existential import, especially humanities search for the meaning of life.[6] How could a people who are the heirs of those who gave birth to "modern religion" be without such sacred knowledge?

Myths are cultural narratives that attempt to explain a people's origin.[7] They are extrapolations from oral or written narratives that provide one with meaning. Myths assisted Africans in making sense out of the world at a time when civilization was young along the Nile River. Ultimately, myths function to support the ideals people have of themselves. It's important for all cultural groups to have their own myths of origin and not to pay homage to another people's cultural narratives. No cultural group that has adopted the cultural myths of another people has ever been respected. Myths by their nature are situated within a particular cultural context and are quite meaningless when adopted by cultural foreigners. Myths provide answers about the nature of existence and the cosmos. They attempt to answer questions that experience alone cannot reveal to us. "The myths thus serve the manifold purposes of statements of doctrinal beliefs, confirmation of faith in the mind, liturgical credo, simple metaphysics."[8] Yoruba myths are likewise situated within a particular culture. They are comprised of proverbs and philosophical critiques of human nature and provide Africans with an alternative epistemology, other than the Abrahamic paradigm, which purports to be superior to all other cultural constructs.[9]

Yoruba myths are contained in the Odu Corpus, which is a body of works that belongs to the family of Qrunmila—the Oracle divinity. The Odu contains the cultural philosophy of the Yoruba people. It is a collection of responses from the Oracle that are safeguarded by priests and priestesses. Students of TACF maintain that the Odu is the most reliable corpus in the oral tradition.[10] There are at least 256 odus (headings) and affixed to each Odu are at least "one thousand six-hundred and eighty stones or myths called pathways, roads, or courses."[11] The Odu is further divided into three sections. The first consists of a verse linked to the two sections that follow, providing commentary on the first section. The sayings contained in the Odu are filled with proverbial and theological insights, which addresses a full range of questions. The Odu Corpus provides names, stories, and "appellations of the deity," which can be used to explicate Yoruba theogony.[12]

Most students of African religion hold that Yoruba liturgy has remained unchanged since its inception.[13] This is due to the strict protocol Yoruba priest must observe when performing their sacred duties. For example, "in Yoruba worship, there is nothing of the nonconformists' go-as-you-please style. A priest approaches his appointed task with awe, ever conscious of the dreadful fact that if the wrong step should be taken or the right order of service be not followed, everything might be lost and his own life and the life of the worshippers jeopardised."[14] Liturgies serve as vehicles of the sacred and are "the peoples' means of communication with their objects of worship."[15] It is a breach of African orthodoxy to call sacred objects by their wrong name, or to use sacred terms inappropriately.[16] The songs used in rituals are ballads, lyrics, and minstrelsy. "They tell stories of their past, the circumstances of their present, and their hopes and fears of the future."[17] These songs can be used to assist one in their efforts to comprehend the Yoruba people's complex history. Yoruba history can also be found in music. Their entire history is ingrained in music, which is a common characteristic among Africans throughout the world. Africans everywhere have used music as a medium, specifically designed to carry messages of sociopolitical, theological and philosophical import. Throughout the New World, Africans were forbidden to use the drum since it was a form of communication that the white man could not comprehend. Most importantly, the proverbial word is the *sine qua non* of Yoruba discourse because it shapes how one views themselves and the world around them.

Yoruba cosmology is deeply embedded within the oral tradition. Yoruba creation myths are the source of their sacred culture and are thus indispensable for explicating Yoruba theology. Yoruba myths purport that creation started in the ancient holy city Ile-Ife: "The first of creation here below; the original home of all things; the place from which the day dawns; the enchanted, holy city; the home of divinities and mysterious spirits."[18] The explication of Yoruba myths must be the departure point from which to begin any serous inquiry into the nature of Yoruba cultural forms. One cannot understand Yoruba theology without first recognizing that, for them, life began at Ile-Ife. This is the beginning from which every discussion of traditional Yoruba culture must begin. We must start with how they view their beginning, which is a perspective that honors the tradition. Otherwise, one may unconsciously use their own cultural narrative or Eden mythology to critique African myth. Ile-Ife is the place where creation began for the Yoruba and is the Yoruba's Eden. It is the sacred place through which all those who depart this life must pass. Ile-Ife is the passage to life and the place one returns after completing their life-assignment. Yoruba theology is quite modern because it upholds the universal notion, that people of every nation will exit this life by having their spirits pass through the holy city Ile-Ife. Since all life first entered the world through Ile-Ife, all life must exit through the doors it entered. German scholar Leo Frobenius was so impressed when he visited Ile-Ife in the nineteenth century that he concluded that it must be the lost Atlantis and that the Yoruba were descendants of that mystical kingdom.[19]

Yoruba Cosmology

Olódùmarè is the Supreme Creator in Yoruba traditional culture. He created all things, including the orisha. His existence, unlike that of some divinities, has no beginning or ending. Olódùmarè created all the divinities, which are equivalent to what those in the Abrahamic religions call angels or ministering spirits. The orisha are the agents of energy which assist Olódùmarè in carrying out a particular assignment. The orisha are first mentioned in Yoruba theology as assisting Olódùmarè at creation.[20] Students of African religion have argued that some of the divinities were the original inhabitants of earth. As in John Milton's *Paradise Lost*, Satan, a divinity, was cast to the earth with one-third of the angels (divinities) before human beings inhabited planet earth. Also as in *Paradise Lost*, Yoruba theology argues that earth was a watery marshland before it was occupied by human beings. This watery space served as a playground for the orisha who rejected the Creator. When

Olódùmarè decided to create the solid earth, He consulted the divinity Orisa-nla, who He supplied with a package of loose dirt in a snail shell with a five-toed hen and a pigeon.[21] Orisa-nla executed his duties as charged by Olódù-marè and after completing his assignment, he reported back to Olódùmarè. A chameleon was dispatched to inspect the work. (The chameleon is very detailed and extremely sensitive.) The chameleon first reported to Olódùmarè that the earth was not dry enough for habitation. The second report was good and so Olódùmarè continued with His on-going creation.

It is difficult to understand why many Western scholars and African Christians attempt to explicate TACF without possessing knowledge of the myths that constitute the foundation of traditional culture. Although some African Christians have knowledge of their traditional culture, they also see nothing wrong with using Western theology to explicate African myths. All creation myths have one feature in common: they reveal how a particular people understand their origin. Thus, African myths cannot be interpreted through a European lens because there is nothing universal about Western culture that would make it any less susceptible to prejudice. Every cultural group has a particular perspective that guides their thought processes. Creation myths shape a people's perception of themselves and the world. Myths of creation are used to construct a view of the world from which one develops their identity. Therefore, it is critical that all people understand the cultural narratives that detail their origin. Stories of origin provide us with a sense of belonging. Those groups who lack cultural myths or adopt another people's mythology may struggle with issues of unity.

The traditional Yoruba are a proud people who believe that the Creator chose their city Ile-Ife, not Mecca or Jerusalem, as the place from which humankind entered the world. Since they live by their own myths of origins their sense of being is more stable than those who have adopted religious myths that are foreign to their culture. Therefore, if one intends to understand traditional Yoruba ways of being, it is imperative to begin with their creation myths. The Abrahamic myths of origin should never be compared or contrasted to Yoruba myths. Yoruba myths should only be evaluated by tools forged from within traditional culture and not by outsiders who are incapable of understanding traditional Yoruba cultural forms.

Ile-Ife is the mythical location from which the work of creation started. "Ife" means that "which is wide."[22] The prefix "Ile" was added much later to differentiate it from other cities that had the same name. According to Yoruba creation narratives, earth was completed within four days and on the fifth day Olódùmarè rested.[23] After Olódùmarè was content with his creations, He dispatched his arch divinity, Orisa-nla, to go down and replenish the earth.

Olódùmarè also sent another divinity, Qrunmila, to accompany Orisa-nla. Olódùmarè sent four trees with Orisa-nla to be planted and used as food and drink: the palm tree, the silk rubber tree, whitewood, and dodo.[24] The trees were used for food and drink. The plant food was in addition to the meat from the hen and pigeon, which had multiplied upon earth.

Yoruba myths of origin maintain that at the beginning of time there was no rain on earth. Yoruba myth presents a world that did not need rain in its beginning, until the earth's inhabitants began to multiply and water became scarce. Orisa-nla requested water and Olódùmarè sent rain. Orisa-nla functioned as a co–Creator and is also the sculptor divinity who provides human beings with their physical characteristics. However, Olódùmarè alone is responsible for giving life.[25] Many creation myths depict a time in earth's history when human beings where closer to the divine than today. This brief moment of innocence was ultimately interrupted and many myths of origin seem to suggest that a gap developed between the Creator and the created. After the honeymoon between god and man ended, humanity was locked into a cycle that alternates between brief moments of harmony and extended periods of chaos.

Since Olódùmarè was Supreme and the only one capable of giving life, Orisa-nla began to envy him. Orisa-nla attempted to spy on Olódùmarè and discover how life was breathed into created beings. Orisa-nla hid in a room where those awaiting life would be breathed upon by Olódùmarè. Being wise and all-knowing, Olódùmarè knew of Orisa-nla's plans and therefore caused a deep sleep to fall upon him. He then entered the room and gave life to those waiting to enter Earth's realm. Orisa-nla awoke and found his plans thwarted and from that time, he became content with his position in the divine hierarchy. As co-creator, Orisa-nla has the authority to sculpture human beings as he desires. He decides on what physical characteristics a person will have. Those born with any kind of physical deformity are marked to accomplish a particular mission. For instance, albinos and those with other physical abnormalities are considered Orisa-nla's children. Orisa-nla is not the only divinity who knows the secrets of the origin of humanity. Qrunmila, who was with Olódùmarè from the beginning, was endowed with foreknowledge, wisdom, and other attributes that make him second only to Olódùmarè's.[26] He is the divinity that one seeks for guidance and wisdom.

The Yoruba creation narratives speak of a time when humans were in a closer relationship with God. They depict a time when people were not physically limited as they are now. At least some people possessed the power to move back and forth between the physical and nonphysical realms. This may have been the norm for each created being. The many physical limitations that constrain humanity today did not always exist. Oral tradition claims that heaven was so near one could reach up and touch God's abode.[27] This has been described as "man's golden era," a time when men and gods spoke openly without the aid of mediators. The bliss would end and be replaced with chaos. It is as though peace and tranquility cannot last long on the earth. Something eventually happens to destroy those brief moments of peace, thereby causing a disturbance between the material and immaterial realms. In the beginning this was not the case. One creation narrative attempts to explain the origin of the rift between man and god. A greedy person was ascending to heaven on a regular basis and eating too much food; hence, the Vital Force needed to prevent this from happening and therefore removed itself out of the physical reach of creation. Another story argues that a woman with dirty hands reached up and soiled the heavens, forcing God to relocate heaven.[28]

After the physical separation between Olódùmarè and his creation occurred, the orisha were assigned new roles with greater responsibilities to the extent of eclipsing Olódùmarè.[29] An important variation of this myth has the divinity Oduduwa carrying out the role ascribed to Orisa-nla. According to this version, Orisa-nla became distracted after coming to earth and was unable to perform complete his mission. One story claims Orisa-nla fell into a deep sleep and was unable to complete his assignment. Therefore, Oduduwa was sent to search for him and, finding him asleep and intoxicated from palm wine, did not awaken him but completed the mission. In some traditions Oduduwa is called father of the Yoruba people.[30] He is accepted as a god and goddess and is possibly not an indigenous deity.[31] Outside of Ile-Ife, he is only regarded as an ancestor and not a divinity at all.[32] The divine scepter remains in the hand of Orisa-nla, since "it is through him that authority to be and to rule passes to all Yoruba kings whose scepters derive from [Ile-Ife]."[33]

The concept of deity is derived from myths, philosophy, songs, sayings, and liturgies. Deity is the generic term for a Yoruba divinities or "orisha," except when the deity is called by name.[34] Many Westerners once claimed that African people were incapable of understanding deity. The eminent biographer Emil Ludwig was perplexed over the prospect of Africans possessing a concept of the divine when they were incapable of deep thought. "How can the untutored African conceive of God? … How can this be? Deity is a philosophical concept which savages are incapable of framing."[35] Ironically, this is still the mind-set of white elites, especially those who control the academy. Like Ludwig, the white elite believe that black people are intellectually inferior to whites. The overwhelming majority of university religion departments are reluctant to hire black American scholars. They too agree with Ludwig but lack the courage to publically voice what is in their hearts. Yet, it's clear from their hiring practices as discussed in Chapter 2, that universities throughout the United States have little regard for black scholarship. Ìdòwú placed the words of Ludwig in proper context with the following: "If Ludwig means by 'Deity' an abstract, intellectual concept," he might be correct in his assessment; however, since "the Deity of religion and human experience is not an abstraction but a Reality, a Being, Ludwig's premise is patently wrong, and his conclusion inevitably doomed to come to grief."[36] Ludwig along with most white scholars during his era thought it inconceivable that his white god could be conceived by Africans. In this context Ludwig was correct. How can traditional Africans or nonwhites in general conceive of a god who is a creation of European thought? It is impossible for Africans to know this god because he is a product of European cultural forms. Not even those educated Africans who are Christianized can understand the white god as well as the white man. No one can understand another people's god better than those within that cultural group because god is first and foremost a cultural creation. Even Jesus stated that he came to "save" his people from their sins. He did not come to save the world. Such thinking is simply the fantasies of Paul and others who misconstrued the words of Jesus to extend European imperialism. All gods are created from the cultures of those who give life to the god. Africans may worship the Christian's god and saints, but they have nothing to do with the cultural creation of these gods. Africans only have the power to create from within their cultural milieu. In this regard, the traditional African is certainly capable of conceiving deity. Howbeit, from within an African cultural perspective alone. He will never know the white god in its fullness, which is why many find it difficult trying to understand the white Christians in the United States and in particular their attraction to militarism. The white god is alien to the Africans axiological grid and is not capable of completing the Africans evolution. No matter how long Africans may have been prostrating themselves before the gods created by Arabs and Europeans they will never know these gods in their fullness. He can study the Koran and Bible until he is blue in the face. Still, their gods cannot be revealed to him through these sources because they are alien to black thought. God's disclosure to humanity has always been through a particular culture.

In most African societies one's name is linked to their destiny. "What is in a name?" Within African traditional societies names are not an arbitrary choosing, but connect one to his natural inclinations. Even the name or title for God in Yoruba, "Olódùmarè," has the connotation of "owner" or "lord";

"One who keeps the town's gates; one who minds broken calabashes."[37] Olódù-marè is also known as Qlofin-Qrun and Qlorun. The former occurs most frequently in the Odu Corpus as a title or alternative to Olódùmarè. Most practitioners of Yoruba culture and its offspring throughout the New World use the name Qlorun and[38] sometimes the three names are combined. Yoruba Deity uses a "threefold name to express intense emotion or urgent appeal."[39] However, as Samuel Johnson argued in his ground-breaking work on Yoruba culture, Qlorun is never used in the plural, which indicates the peoples' understanding of God's Supreme identity.[40] (Yet this observation may be tainted by the Christian lens that contaminated much of Johnson's work.)

The Yoruba conception of deity is not entirely different from others who have attempted to understand God. The Yoruba God is anthropomorphic and their view of Deity is one who is ageless, a wise counselor who is all powerful and incapable of error. Olódùmarè is the final judge. The Yoruba divinities have the authority and power to punish wrongdoers and violators of the sacred tradition. The divinities have the power to punish those who violate traditional norms, but only Olódùmarè has the authority to "[judge] man's character."[41] Olódùmarè is immortal and self-existing. His role may seem secondary to the work of the divinities but the Yoruba understand that He alone holds all things together. Olódùmarè is that "Mighty, Immovable Rock that never dies."[42] He is not a remote deity who is uninvolved in his creation as some have claimed. Olódùmarè has simply delegated his authority much like all great leaders who benefit by sharing their power. Although Olódùmarè has delegated many responsibilities to the divinities, absolute authority resides with Him.[43] Preoccupation with power relationships may be an obsession of Anglo-Europeans because they seek world dominance. It is not enough to categorize people based on their position in society. Yet in the white man's worldview, even god must be judged by the pathology of dominance that contaminates Western thought.

In the Odu Corpus Olódùmarè is depicted as the head leader to whom all matters are referred.[44] The more than 1,700 divinities render tribute and honor to Him. Yoruba theology depicts Olódùmarè as the supreme ruler of the universe and the divinities as ministering spirits who carry out his will.[45] The divinities are designated as "orisha," which was a term first used to identify the arch-divinity of Yorubaland. This original arch-divinity was killed and pieces of his body were scattered throughout the universe.[46] The pieces recovered were called "ohun-ti-a-ri-sa," from which the term "orisha" most likely developed.[47] Originally the term referred to Olódùmarè and was later used to refer to the divinities. "Orisha" is used for divinities in general.[48] Yoruba theology holds that Olódùmarè called the orisha into existence. Orisa-nla, the oldest of the orisha, is considered the father of all the ministers of Olódùmarè.[49] Orisa-nla is also called Qbatal, "the king who is great."[50] He is recognized as the offspring of God, with attributes very similar to Olódù-marè. For instance, Orisa-nla is called "A-té-rere-k'-áiye"—"He who spreads over the whole extent of the earth"—and "Alámò rere"—"The one who deals in choice clay."[51] The Odu Corpus also describes him as monogamous and one who makes his devotees prosperous.[52]

Qrunmila is an important orisha who is called the deputy of Olódùmarè. The name means "only heaven knows the means of salvation." Qrunmila is the Oracle divinity and linguist to whom his devotees pray to for an under-standing of foreign languages. He is also a doctor and has knowledge of all herbs. Every *babalawo* (Yoruba Priest) must have knowledge of herbal phar-macology. The palm tree is connected with the worship of Qrunmila because palm kernels are used for divining.[53] Each divinity has its own food, color, and hymn which is sung during funerals, child-naming ceremonies and at festivals.[54]

Most religions have an entity or force that is opposite of that which is good. Esu is the indifferent divinity within Yoruba theology. However, he is not "the Satan" as this entity is understood in Christianity. Esu is not much different from the other orisha which are energies that assist human beings in carrying out the affairs of life. All orisha are unique forces of energy which have their origin in Olódùmarè. Like the biblical Satan who had special access to the Hebrew God, Esu likewise has a special relationship with Olódùmarè. Like "the Satan," Esu reports regularly to Olódùmarè concerning the affairs of humans and punishes those who violate the rituals that govern TACF. Esu is considered the right hand of Qrunmila and for those who fail to heed Qrunmila's warnings, Esu punishes them. "In return for the service which [Esu] gives to [Qrunmila], [Qrunmila] feeds him."[55] Yet Esu, like his coun-terpart, "the Satan," refuses to be second to any divinity.[56] His power is second only to Olódùmarè. Even the great warrior Shango backed down when chal-lenged by Esu. Throughout Yorubaland many worship Esu as their main deity.[57] His symbol may be a piece of lateritic rock, "a graven image of clay or wood ... it can be an earthenware pot turned upside down, with a hole in its middle; or it can be a piece of hard rock in an earthenware dish; that has oil poured regularly on it."[58] Many Africans invoke the name of Esu to assist them in overthrowing their enemies.

Ogun is the god of iron and steel.[59] He is an excellent hunter who once used the earth as his hunting grounds before it was inhabited by humans.[60] He is called the war deity who resides at the top of the hill. Myth depicts him as one who descended from his abode at the top of the hill clothed in a garment of blood, which symbolizes his power and love of war. Ogun is the divinity who opens the way and clears the path, both physically and spiritually for those who fed him. He is the one whose eyeballs are rare to behold. He supports orphans and is the owner of innumerable houses in heaven.[61] Ogun is also responsible for placing markings or identifiable marks (scarification) on a person's body, which is said to keep them in good health. Prior to the destabilization of TACF in Yorubaland, Africans swore by Ogun in court. Hence, he is the covenant deity,[62] whose symbol is the silk cotton tree.

Sango is a national hero who was deified and is honored throughout Yorubaland.[63] His consort, Oya, is indispensable in carrying out his mission. Without the goddess Oya, Sango could do nothing. Like her Egyptian counterpart, Hatshepsut, she too wears a beard. "Her face is so terrible that none dare behold it, her wrath so devastating that it must be absolutely avoided."[64]

Sopona is another interesting orisha and is called the smallpox deity, who received his odus from Olódùmarè. He is the divinity who brings swift destruction on those who violate TACF. Sopona is the "One who kills and is thanked for it."[65] Therefore, one must not cry at the funerals of those who are the victims of Sopona. For this may anger him and he will bring swift destruction upon those who should be grateful for his deeds. He is the deity who possesses his devotees and is represented by the image of a broom made from bamboo palm without its leaves.[66]

Ela is the incarnation of the divine logos or what Christians call the Holy Spirit. Ela is the supreme force of Olódùmarè, "the one who restores order and makes the world right."[67] The Odu depicts him as the orisha that can deliver one from Esu. He is the mediator between God and humanity and many Yoruba await his return to the earth.[68] He abides in heaven but is spiritually present among those who honor the Yoruba traditions and customs.[69] Ela is the soul-force of Olódùmarè and the Yoruba's savior.[70]

African traditional religion is governed by rituals and symbols. The symbol has power to speak beyond words and implant itself deep into the human psyche. Where words fail to convey the depths of ideals, the symbol speaks and bypasses the judgmental mind. The symbol inserts itself into the soul and delivers a message unavailable in words. "Sacred symbols and rituals are the keystone of African traditional religion and life. They are major points of contact with the holy and the principal means by which Africans communicate their experience of the world and reality as a whole. In their widest connotation, the two terms cover a variety of things including words, concepts, objects, practices, institutions that make up the religious corpus of different African groups."[71]

Initiated Yoruba men and women use symbols to communicate to each other. Symbols are also used to communicate to the orisha. These sacred ideograms are not fetishes or "juju," as they were called by the French colonizers. Symbols give rise to thought and may appear as nonsense to the uninitiated but they are used to represent Deity and used for communication.[72] The symbols can serve as a representation of the orisha and one will hear Yoruba practitioners referring to their symbol as "My Orisha."[73] The reference to objects as though they are "real" is not problematic for observers of traditional African cultural forms. All things are viewed through a religious lens, including animate and inanimate objects. There is no line of demarcation between the holy and profane. The sacred and secular are linked together. Wherever Africans reside, they take their spirituality with them. Whether they attend a party or gather at a communal shrine, "African peoples do not know how to exist without religion."[74]

Unlike Islam and Christianity that are obsessed with making converts, African religion is culturally situated and could not conceive of recruiting converts as a major aspect of the tradition. One cannot simply join what is in essence another people's culture. African religion is familial-structured, which is why it does not attract the overzealous missionary types. In particular, it would not be comfortable for those outside of a TACF to embrace a way of being that is foreign to their cultural identity. In African traditional thought, one is born into a particular TACF and cannot simply assimilate another people's religious paradigm. Even Mbiti recognized the difficulty of outsiders attempting to embrace traditional African cultural forms, writing, "Europeans who claim to have been 'converted' to African religions ... do not know what they are saying."[75] Mbiti is correct and these same words were echoed hundreds of years earlier by enslaved Africans in the United States in a Spiritual: "You can't join in [the black church], you have to be born in." In essence, true religion is not something one chooses as though they were making a selection from a candy store. Religion is culturally and racially situated and it is from this departure point that one can then explore other faith traditions if they desire. Mbiti maintains that Islam and Christianity cannot address the deep existential issues that confront African converts to those religions, especially in times of crisis. African Christians and Muslims run in secret to those so-called alternative places outside the church or mosque to seek help for that which their adopted religions are culturally unequipped to address.[76]

TACF speak directly to those unique problems that challenge African people. It addresses their axiological grid which is programmed to view the world through their unique cultural perspective. Unlike European philosophy and religion whose epistemology is focused upon abstractions, TACF are experiential centered, which requires that one's needs are addressed at the affective and cognitive level. African epistemology is focused upon personal experience and has little room for conjecture or events that are disconnected from the reality they experience. It is not that Africans have no concept of the future as some have surmised. Rather, traditional Africans understood what modern science has also discovered; that the present, past, and future are one in the same. Thus, for traditional Africans the future is centered in the present. "Time has to be experienced in order to make sense or to become real."[77] The traditional African view of time is related to how some understand nature in general. Nature is not something that can be compartmentalized and manipulated like a commodity. Neither can people be manipulated for numerical purposes or as a commodity. "Since time is a composition of events, people cannot and do not reckon it in a vacuum."[78] Time is only meaningful when it is expressed in concrete terms, especially in relation to an event or natural phenomenon. "The day, the month, the year, one's life time or human history, are all divided up or reckoned according to their specific events, for it is these that make them meaningful."[79] In the Western world time is bottled up and used as a commodity, "but in traditional African life, time has to be created or produced."[80] The minutes, hours, days, and months are all connected to events that have meaning in the lives of the people. Time is as important as the events to which they are connected, especially birth, marriage, and death, and significant events that connect one to their culture and society.

Traditional Yoruba narratives serve as alternatives to Western constructs that were used to stifle the evolutionary growth and development of Africans. TACF address the plight of black people in general and provides them with a paradigm not beholden to the same constructs that has oppressed them. Yoruba theology provides Africans a deity that empowers them as human agents who are actively involved in the creation process. Neither Christianity nor Islam has provided Africans with the security available to them within their own sacred traditions. Molefi Asante maintains that "the most crippling effect of Islam as well as Christianity for us may well be the adoption of non–African customs and behaviors, some of which are in direct conflict with our traditional values."[81] TACF allow Africans to operate from a mind-set that is in harmony with their cultural DNA. The philosophy unearthed within TACF will prove invaluable when African Christian and Muslims awaken from their slumber and return to the religio-culture of their forbearers. Neither will experience authenticity relying upon another people's myths to sustain them, especially when those narratives are alien and hostile to their cultural sensibilities.

Dagara Culture and African Traditional Religion

Religion and culture are inseparable in traditional African communities. They are so closely related that even Mbiti argued that proselytism was unknown in traditional societies. Those who already live in a world of spirits do not need a foreigner's religion to save them.[82] They are already infused with divine energy. How could they conceive of embracing a thought-system contrary to their way of being? "Each people has its own religious system, and a person cannot be converted from one tribal religion to another: he has to be born in the particular society in order to participate in the entire religious life of the people."[83] By explicating the cultural practices of the Dagara of Burkina Faso, we catch a glimpse of a people who actively participate in traditional rituals. We discover how observing traditional rituals are indispensable for maintaining traditional forms of existence. Little research has focused on African culture as a form of religious redemption for Africans. Past studies have usually focused on Christianity and Islam as the only medium for African redemption. This intertextual analysis uncovers the liberative and cultural redemptive elements available within traditional African communities.

It is essential that Africans investigate the acres of diamonds within their traditional communities which have their origin in their cultural back yard. Russell H. Conwell was the founder of Temple University in Philadelphia, Pennsylvania, and traveled the world lecturing with one simple theme: the illusive riches that one searches for throughout life are available within their own back yard. The freedom that African people so desperately seek within other people's cultural myths can be obtained from the culture that gave birth to the orisha. For example, in traditional Dagara communities culture and religion are synonymous and represents a form of "salvation." TACF as practiced by the Dagara are the vehicles by which all groups have developed avenues in which to construct a mythology to birth their cultural identity. Cultural identity gives birth to self-identity. There are no nations in the world which respect themselves that will seek salvation outside of their cultural milieu—unless their culture has been completely destabilized or destroyed, as was the case for African people. Islam and Christianity made every attempt possible to completely destroy traditional African cultural forms. Until Africans on the continent and those throughout the diaspora embrace their sacred narratives,[84] black people will be unable to rise from the ashes that are quickly becoming their grave covering. (Read the classic text, *Africa: Mother of Western Civilization*, by Yosef Ben Jochannan. Here the master teacher instructs Africans how they can gather the cultural fragments that remain and reconstruct TACF that will deliver them, especially at a time when Western global influence is rapidly declining.)

The elevation of ones culture to the status of sacred is the primary means by which a people develops their intellectual and moral faculties. It is perhaps the final stage in human evolution. The veneration of ones sacred cultural narratives is essential for the survival of a people particularly if they are in a hostile environment. One cannot denigrate their primal narratives and worship the cultural narratives of another people and expect to have a clear mind. African people will never be free until they return to the sacred narratives within TACF. They must study and venerate them like they do the Bible and the Koran. They must prostrate themselves before their traditional gods much the same way they have been taught to worship the gods of Abraham, Isaac, and Jacob. A return to one's sacred narratives will provide black people with the liberation they seek in the foreign text they venerate without the side effects of a distorted identity. When one honors their cultural story and venerate their own cultural heroines, the world will have a new respect for black people. This self-imposed marginalization of black people throughout the world is the result of their lacking an understanding of their religio-cultural background. Cultural knowledge is essential for freedom.

For example, in traditional Dagara communities freedom from estrangement and the maintenance of cosmic harmony derives from within one's primal culture. As Somé recognized in his book *Of Water and the Spirit*, his forced adoption of foreign gods could not provide him with the sense of wholeness he experienced from honoring his sacred tradition. Somé offers insight into the mind-set of a people who raped, pillaged, and killed to further the Christian missionary militaristic agenda, which aims at converting the world to the white man's way of thinking by any means necessary. The missionary-colonizers acted as if they were mandated by the most-high god to civilize their lessor sisters and brothers throughout Africa. Somé offers a first-hand account of their actions to convert him over to their way of being:

> These foreigners seemed to have no respect for life, tradition, or the land itself. At first my elders refused to believe that a race of people who could cause such suffering and death could possibly have any respect for itself. It did not take long before they realized that the white man wanted nothing short of the complete destruction of their culture and even their lives.[85]

By observing traditional forms of reality and practicing Dagara rituals, Somé was freed from the brainwashing that took place in the seminary. He was saved by observing cultural forms that were not available to him from those who were converting him to imbibe Western thought. I investigate the two essential cultural elements that embody the tradition practiced by the

Dagara of Burkina Faso: cosmology and self-identity. These two factors undergird the Dagarian people's cultural perspectives and can be explicated by employing a general inquiry into those sacred elements that constitute their notion of culture. We explore the ethical and moral stances that govern their society. This yields crucial information about those essential elements that embody Dagarian philosophy. If the sacred elements within African culture as practiced by the Dagara people are not explicated, thereby removing the negative propaganda advanced by European missionaries, those who honor traditional ways of being will be forced to look elsewhere for solutions to issues that can only successfully be addressed from within the tradition.

For instance, Somé's father rejected traditional norms in exchange for what the European narrative seemed to offer him. In the end, he did not find what he was looking for because the Europeans god was not created to address the needs of African people. All gods are culturally constructed. The white god did not come to save black people. He came to save "his" people from their sin. Yet, Africans continue to bury their gods and worship at the feet of their enemies. If Africans continue to venerate another people's paradigm, they will commit cultural suicide, which is far greater than physical death. As a result of their continual assault upon their culture, millions have been killed and untold numbers are predicted to suffer a more gruesome fate. In part, those Africans who refuse to honor their ancestors and would rather bow before the gods of their enemies have betrayed their people. Unless Africans embrace their unique culture in the immediate future, there may not be any remembrance of them in the world. Moreover, if their cultural story is obliterated, losing what remains of their traditional culture, they will be unable to survive, especially after the Abrahamic faiths implode with Western imperialism. Therefore, Africans must celebrate the TACF practiced by the Dagara and others who honor their forebearers. Thus, it is important to understand the role of culture within traditional communities. Culture influences every aspect of existence and is the principal source by which a society constructs its ideology. Culture serves in shaping and refining a society's intellectual and artistic taste. Most importantly, culture serves as the departure point from which a society builds its systems of knowledge for establishing social guidelines and shapes the people's weltanschauung.

Clifford Geertz argued that all cultures are unique and there is no such thing as a *consensus gentium*. Those unique elements that make up a culture are essentially the building blocks of that society. Cultures are unique and there is no universal template that is fundamental to all cultures. Geertz argues,

Generalizations are not to be discovered through a Baconian search for cultural universals, a kind of public-opinion polling of the world's peoples in search of a *consensus gentium* that does not in fact exist, and, further, that the attempt to do so leads to precisely the sort of relativism the whole approach was expressly designed to avoid.[86]

Clyde Kluckhohn's book *Mirror for Man* outlined eleven general descriptors to identify some elements that constitute culture. (1) How a society lives independently of social or scientific observation, or what Martin Heidegger would call observing the existent in its "everydayness." (2) What is the social legacy that an individual inherits from the group? (3) Since culture encompasses a certain way of thinking, feeling, and believing, how do the people express this uniqueness, or what Robert Farris Thompson called "mystic coolness"? (4) What theories or ideas do the people have of behavior? (5) What is the anthropologist's theory about the ways in which the people exist? (6) How is the people's knowledge stored or transmitted? (7) How do the people respond to modern problems? (8) What constitutes learned behavior? (9) How is behavior regulated? (10) What mechanisms are used to adjust to natural and person-to-person issues? (11) How is history understood?[87] These descriptors are few of the questions a researcher might have in mind when studying a culture outside of his own. Others have described culture as that which "consists of whatever it is one has to know or believe in order to operate in a manner acceptable to its members."[88] This definition lends credence to Somé's testimony, especially in relation to his father's adoption of Christianity. Since his religious view was different from the colonizers, Somé's father was forced to isolate himself from the Dagara community.

Max Weber argued that humans construct culture and the webs they weave are societal building blocks. Geertz likewise interpreted culture as webs and its analysis is "not an experimental science in search of law but an interpretive one in search of meaning."[89] There is nothing scientific about interpreting culture. "Cultural analysis is ... guessing at meanings, assessing the guesses, and drawing explanatory conclusions from the better guesses."[90] Therefore it is essential that each society develop methods from their within their cultural referents, whereby they interpret and analyze phenomena that presents itself to them. These cultural reference points are not only the glue of society, but they also speak to a much larger intuition. They address those existential issues that most are unable to grasp or articulate. "[S]ocial actions are comments on more than themselves; ... Small facts speak to large issues, winks to epistemology, or sheep raids to revolution, because they are made to."[91] Goodenough wrote that "culture [is located] in the minds and hearts of men."[92]

Following a Christian dialectic, culture is equivalent to the redemptive blood that poured from the side of Jesus Christ. This mythical act of redemption signified Jesus' transition from "Son of Man" to "Son of God." Likewise, culture serves as an evolutionary transitional marker in the life of an individual and a society. As Geertz observed, "We are, in sum, incomplete or unfinished animals who complete or finish ourselves through culture—and not through culture in general but through highly particular forms of it."[93] It is those "highly particular forms" of culture that are situated within one's primal culture. The cultural referents to complete the individual's evolutionary process are not insensitive to race and gender. The evolutionary journey to full humanity is centered within the customs and traditions of one's primal culture. In African traditional communities, those particular forms of culture that assist the individual in completing the human process are available to those who honor traditional African cultural norms and customs. The notion that all cultures function the same way in completing the human process is premised upon a faulty logic. Africans cannot become fully human by observing the customs and traditions of Arabs and Europeans. The human process can only be completed for each individual when they eat the nutrients developed from within their own cultural milieu. The rhetoric of preserving one's culture when espoused by the dominant group in power, inevitably means the cultural destruction of those who are not militarily dominant.[94] Following Geertz's logic, those who are not fed the cultural nutrients that complete the human process will remain incomplete as human beings. This is a frightening prospect that happens each time a people is forced to forgo practicing their cultural norms and forced to adopt a cultural perspective foreign to their cultural DNA. Culture is not something we choose but we are born into a particular culture, and we cannot simply abandon our cultural norms and adopt another people's cultural markers without paying a high price. Self-hatred results from accepting a way of life that is out of harmony with one's heritage.

One of the hallmarks of human civilization is the ability of a people to define who they are in reference to the world in which they live. From the ancient Egyptians to the European and Arabs interpretations of the world, a people's metaphysical beliefs are crucial for establishing a positive self-identity. For example, Dagara cosmology is premised upon cultural perceptions they developed of the world. People are made of culture and culture is governed by a particular cosmology, from which one references to interpret the world. Culture is the lens for which we view ourselves and the world. "[C]ultures define themselves in terms of the ways their people perceive the cosmos."[95] Dagara cosmology is rooted in their cultural myths, which are grounded in their interpretation of the elements, earth, water, fire, minerals, and nature. All events in the physical world mirror what is happening in the unseen realm. Natural catastrophes and other occurrences that seem to defy physical reality are interpreted as a message from Mother Earth. Whether the people are experiencing floods or the lack of rain, all things are perceived as messages from the invisible realm.

For instance, an earthquake would require community elders to perform the necessary rituals to restore harmony with Mother Earth. Cosmic harmony is a common belief held by most cultural groups throughout traditional Africa. The notion that nothing happens in this world without affecting everything else is a truism among practitioners of traditional African religions everywhere. This precept is foreign for those who live under the dictates that came out of the European enlightenment. Those who subscribe to enlightenment theories believe that every event can be rationally explained. Whereas, the traditional mind perceives the world as a sovereign entity that cannot be known a part from its interactions with human beings. The earth communicates with every human being and provides them with food and shelter. In return for sustenance, human beings must honor and "protect" Mother Earth. If human beings fail to honor and respect the earth, it will dispel them as it has already done in the past.

Practitioners of TACF seem to possess a certain reverence for the earth that Westerners in general seem to lack. The Westerner seems to disregard the sovereignty of the earth and therefore, makes no connection between catastrophic events and the universe. Reason or rationality has been the god to which Western logic pays homage to. As Somé points out in his writings, when catastrophic events occur in the Western world, most people immediately make preparations to restore any external damage brought on by the events without reflecting on any deeper significance such acts might imply. "The event is seen as an attack, an insurgency that must be quickly countered, stepped over, and relegated to the past of a linear history.... It is as if people cannot tolerate the directness of Mother Earth's message to us."[96] In places where TACF are respected and observed, what the West refers to as an "act of god," would be interpreted as a message from Mother Earth. Practitioners of TACF view such acts of god as a message to the community. In the Western world one moves quickly to eradicate what they deem as the source of the problem to ensure it does not happen again. For example, 9/11. The traditional perspective is shaped from a different set of cultural values and norms. TACF preference deep reflection as opposed to swift reactions. Africans who honor the sacred traditions of their forbearers are acculturated to not react to a catastrophe without first consulting an oracle. The oracle will determine why the event occurred and what must be done to rectify the problem.

> We may not understand it at first, which does not mean that we should ask Mother Earth to repeat what she already said so eloquently, but we must come down on our knees with prayers of consternation and mourning, expressing the willingness to understand that this event in the natural world and our lives are connected.[97]

This unique way of understanding the world is derived from one's cultural values and myths. A society's values are rooted in their myths and cosmology. Dagara cosmology consists of assumptions held by the community, which informs how they live their lives. Such knowledge envelopes traditional perceptions of reality. Traditional myths and rituals house the ideals that shapes their cultural perspective. Dagara cosmology functions to provide the people with a sense of cultural identity so that they remain connected to their tradition, especially when Arab and European ways of being have challenged traditional epistemology. The myths hold a people's understanding of themselves and the world. By studying a people's myths we can develop an understanding of how their self-identity was forged.

For example, Somé's Western training reveals how he developed a certain perception of himself that was at odds with his cultural values. By studying a people's cultural narratives we can develop a much deeper understanding of the impact cultural imperialism has on those who were forced to abandon their traditions and adopt alien cultural forms. If the cultural myths that undergird traditional communities are not explicated, we risk learning from a people who could possibly provide us with solutions to our modern crisis. This is much like the rain forests where we are discovering new plant and animal life forms that seek to offer natural alternatives to conventional medicines. The plant medicines recently discovered in the rain forest have shown us how far so-called modern medicine is out of sync with our bodies.

Also, we should investigate traditional life-strategies that Africans used to maintain their traditions and overcome the effects of colonialism. First, we must recognize that those Africans who remained connected to their traditions did not rely upon the same narrative as their enemies. Whenever a people are forced to use the same texts as their enemies, they lose an essential part of themselves, because they can never be as strong as the cultural group who created the narrative. (An African proverb states that the hand that gives is over the one that receives.)

For example, the Yoruba narrative is primarily contained in the Odu Ifa Corpus. An Arab would not be as comfortable venerating the Yoruba narrative as would be an African or black American. The same is true of Christianity, which is more European then it is African. Black people cannot reach their full humanity worshipping Arab and European cultural forms. Those highly particular forms of culture that Geertz writes about cannot be addressed by narratives alien to one's primal culture. African people would have a better chance of completing their evolution by adhering to the tenets contained in the Odu Ifa. It houses the philosophy of several cultural groups throughout West Africa, and is practiced by millions throughout the Americas. It is a collection of responses from Qrunmila, the oracle divinity, and is the most reliable corpus within the oral tradition.[98]

The Dagara people also possess TACF that are more compatible with the religious DNA of black people than Arabic or European cultural forms. Traditional cosmology is diverse and capable of providing life-affirming values as any of the Western faiths. Traditional African myths of origins are just as reliable as those found within the Abrahamic traditions. "In the beginning there was no earth as we know it. In its place was a burning planet, a ball of fire combusting at high speed. Therefore, fire is the first element of the Dagara [cosmological] wheel."[99] The Dagara believe that fire exists in all things and must be tempered with another element to prevent it from destroying everything in its path. Water is the second element in Dagara cosmology and when encountered by fire, produced an atmosphere that was conducive to sustaining human life. Not only did the combustion process slow because of fire's encounter with water, but as a result of this encounter fire entered "the underworld, leaving the surface as a hot steamy place, fertile for the breeding of all kinds of life forms."[100] The divine intercourse between fire and water produced earth. The fourth element is minerals or stone, which resulted from the hardening of earth's surface. While Earth was undergoing such changes, a "steam of great density formed the atmosphere around the earth…. As the steam expanded, its pressure began to subside. The reduction of atmospheric pressure was conducive to the birth of life, and thus the fifth element, vegetative nature, came into being."[101]

Once all the appropriate elements were finally in place, Mother Earth was ready to welcome her first inhabitants. The Dagara hold that life began in mystical water. "Thus, every living form on the earth got its life signature in the waters and continues to live intimately with water."[102] Many creation myths are closely connected with water. Water serves a vital function within in traditional rituals. Animals came out of the water and evolved into human beings. "Today for instance, amphibious animals like crocodiles, sea lions, and seals are said to be beings that didn't complete their journey out of water. Their development was suspended when the atmospheric pressure stopped where it is today."[103] Those beings that eventually evolved into humans left the primordial waters and developed into higher animal forms. The early primordial waters from the underworld give birth to the first human beings.[104] This divine fluid came from the underworld and "spilled into the earth at a moment when the veil between the two worlds was thinned—the moment when the original earth flew too close to the Other World."[105] Therefore, humanity's increasing need to contact the Other World whether through spirituality or science is a human need to bridge the divide that separates the above from below. The need to communicate with the Other World is "man's" longing to reconnect to his original form.

The sacred elements that embody Dagara cosmology are thought to exist in degrees within human beings. Somé points out that various *ethnos* (nations, cultures) can be classified according to Dagara cosmological schema. For instance, indigenous cultures are characteristic of the water element. "They are mostly peace and harmony seekers."[106] By contrast, modern societies usually identify with the element fire.[107] Fire cultures "challenge everything and everyone at the great risk of cosmic disruption."[108] Individuals that embody large traces of fire are prone to instability. The fire element is the primary character trait exhibited by the elite 1 percent who control world affairs. Fire is an entity and its primary agents are those who have adopted the values that accompany this trait. The nature of a fire is to burn everything in its path. Nothing is excluded. Fire cultures burn everything, everywhere, and eventually turns in upon itself. (They implode, as can be witnessed in the United States.) Fire must eat fire or else it cannot survive. This too is the nature of a fire culture, to aggressively seek out people, places, and things to be consumed and sacrificed to the fire gods.

> Fire culture promotes consumerism and cultivates scarcity in order to increase restlessness.... [T]he culture of fire is fascinated by violence.... [V]iolence proves to be highly marketable and stimulates the fiery nature of the culture as a whole. [Hence] a fire culture is a war culture.[109]

Fire cultures exist to create and sustain their fiery nature. The United States is controlled by men of fire that are driven to appease this violent force. "Such a culture will require a lot of water to heal."[110] On the other hand, indigenous cultures are peace seekers work to maintain cosmic harmony. They are governed by the water element and need to stay around it to evolve into fully functioning beings. Water people display a deep concern for others and are communal. Water has served a vital role in many cosmologies. Those individuals and cultural groups that are tolerant of others are infused with the earth element. Earth people are adaptive and carriers of their cultural narratives. The water element played an important role in the life story of

Jesus. For example, Jesus performed many miracles around or on water. One traditional African cultural group interpreted water as

> consciousness that links us to the Other World.... Water seeks to cleanse, reconcile, and balance that which is in agitation, emotional disorder, and self-danger.... To seek water is to seek to reconcile and balance that which is ... caught in the fiery loop of speed and consumption.[111]

The earth element provides one with a sense of identity. Human beings are earth creatures and should have a natural sense of belonging here. Earth gives its inhabitants a sense of identity and "represents survival and healing, unconditional love and caring."[112] Those lacking this vital element experience a sense of estrangement. "A person without earth feels empty, alone, and confused. She or he suffers from invisibility and anonymity."[113] Individuals and cultural groups lacking this element treat Earth as though it is a commodity and will indiscriminately kill innocent human beings to control an entity that has a right to live. The earth does not belong to us. We just live here. Today, the elite are drilling into the earth for resources and poisoning the aquifers. The fire cultures have no respect for the earth or any other life-form. In fact, they are at war with Mother Earth and are making plans to go elsewhere. Fire people view the earth much like they do all other life-forms: as something to burn, pillage and exploit. When "pieces of our mother ... entered into our trade system," a great offense was committed against Mother Earth. "When the people of a culture no longer remember that they are but a thread of the web of life on Earth, then [we] they all become homeless."[114]

The mineral element is associated with memory. "Mineral is the storage place of memory, the principle of creativity, resources, stories, and symbolism."[115] Our memories are housed throughout our cells, not just the brain. Our bones are the storage place of memory—thus the saying "I have a feeling in my bones" designates the place where memory is stored. Those who possess an overabundance of minerals are skillful orators. "The person who has a mineral nature speaks a great deal because mineral expresses in discourse what is stored in coded form within the bones."[116] This element exists in plants and animals. Those individuals or societies that possess an overabundance of this element become great change agents. Nature people adapt very quickly to their environment and circumstance.

Somé argues that many Africans who adopted Western culture and rejected their traditions suffer from a crisis of identity. When people are prevented or forced to reject their cultural norms and accept another people's reality, they enter into a state of anomie. The primal need to feel culturally connected is a human desire that cannot be so easily replaced or dismissed.

The human being cannot experience wholeness outside of the cultural milieu of his ancestors.

> Whether they are raised in indigenous or modern culture, there are two things that people crave: the full realization of their innate gifts, and to have these gifts approved, acknowledged, and confirmed....
>
> This implies that our own inner authority needs the fuel of external recognition to inspire us to fulfill our life's purpose, and until this happens, we wait in paralysis for the redemptive social response that rescues us from the dungeon of anonymity. Our own confirmation or acknowledgement of ourselves is not enough.[117]

The human need to be acknowledged by others is so primal that if it does not happen in the village, town, or neighborhood, people will search for it elsewhere. For millions of black men in the United States, the prison industrial complex functions to fill our need to be recognized and affirmed. Somé seems to argue that one runs a much greater risk of experiencing identity issues when they reject their culture and adopt alien cultural forms that are really hostile to black growth and development. Also, whether one's humanity can be fully embraced within a culture designed to meet the needs of a specific people remains highly questionable. It certainly has not worked for black people in the United States. When one seeks affirmation outside of the culture of their ancestors, they are confronted with a cultural dilemma that one cannot so easily overcome. Such a people are confronted with what Somé described as "a hollowness, a void that threatens to erase meaning in everything people do."[118] Those who have lost their way can awaken and return from whence they came by performing the required rituals that restores one to wholeness.

Rituals and rites of passage serve to combat any crisis brought about through cultural abandonment or displacement. Initiations and other ceremonies are celebrated in traditional communities to prepare one for entry into a world in which they must be prepared to engage in battle. Initiatory practices in Western societies are rarely confirmed or acknowledged by the community. Community confirmation is essential to recognize initiations as a necessary part of human growth and development. Westerners do, however, practice various forms of unconscious acts of initiation, which are the result of a broken society. For instance, "Westerners meet up with tragedy, with powers beyond their control, with challenges that prevent opportunities for growth and transformation. And these challenges must be recognized as initiatory, even though this initiation is disorganized, unpredictable, and informal."[119] (Black men in American prisons is indicative of a society ill-equipped to consciously initiate their male population.) If initiations are to serve a meaningful purpose and restore one to wholeness, they must be consciously organized and confirmed by the community. A far greater "issue for Westerners is not so much the absence of initiation as it is the absence of a community to recognize initiatory passages."[120] Initiations provide "challenges presented to an individual so that he or she may grow."[121] TACF are infused with rituals that governs one's life, before birth and after death. "Ritual is central to village life, for it provides the focus and energy that holds the community together, and it provides the kind of healing that the community most needs to survive."[122] The ceremonial acts that accompany rituals serve an important communal function and no one stands alone or is left to his own devices. In traditional African society,

> only in terms of other people does the individual become conscious of his own being, his own duties, his privileges and responsibilities towards himself and towards other people. When he suffers, he does not suffer alone but with the corporate group; when he rejoices, he rejoices not alone but with his kinsmen, his neighbours and his relatives whether dead or living.[123]

Individualism or the idea of existing separate from ones community is a foreign concept in traditional thought. Traditional Africans have accepted the notion that existence is communal and human growth and development can only occur under these ideal conditions. "I am because we are, and since we are therefore I am."[124] Alternatively, as Huey P. Newton explained in his autobiography, *Revolutionary Suicide*, Africans of old would greet each other with "I am we." According to Newton, this saying implied that "all of us are the one and the multitude."[125] Oneness or unity of diversity remains the theological hallmark of traditional ways of being. Even rituals are corporal projects that aim at creating communal togetherness. "Ritual is the principal tool used to approach that unseen world in a way that will rearrange the structure of the physical world and bring about material transformation."[126] Further, "[t]he purpose of ritual is to create harmony between the human world and the world of the gods, ancestors, and nature."[127] In traditional African communities, rituals are practiced to maintain harmony with all life-forces. If communal rituals are ignored or discarded, chaos will pursue the community. For example, when Somé's father discontinued practicing the religio-cultural rituals of his tradition, he experienced a loss for which his adopted religion had no remedy. After adopting Christianity, Somé's father began to doubt the traditional values that nurtured him. Even after the death of his child, he continued to observe Christianity, which his people called the religion of the "devil." He concluded that God took his children away from him because he lacked the Christian faith to keep them alive. He later came to his cultural senses and resumed offering the traditional sacrifices that were necessary to restore harmony with the spirit world and ancestors.[128] "The truth was," writes Somé on why he didn't come to his senses sooner, "that he did not want to offend the white priest, appearing like a pagan devil worshipper in his eyes."[129]

Why would one think that they are violating god if they honor and venerate the culture responsible for their being? Who teaches them they are incorrect when they honor men and women from within their culture? Those who taught Africans that honoring traditional African cultural forms is pagan must be viewed as enemies of black people everywhere. Why do Africans or any other people have to abandon their traditional cultural values and norms to worship at the feet of an alien cultural form? Somé correctly identified his father's illness as a resulting from his rejection of his culture. Since his father initially refused to perform the rituals of restoration even after the death of his children, he became estranged from his ancestors and no longer was under their protection. Somé discovered that rituals can reduce or eliminate the fallout experienced by those who undergo long periods of exposure to alien cultural forms, including those ideologies that are hostile to African existence.

For example, after Somé escaped from the seminary he returned home and discovered that "initiation had eliminated my confusion, helplessness, and pain and opened the door to a powerful understanding of the link between my own life purpose and the will of my ancestors."[130] Somé underwent initiation when he returned home and it rescued him from the Western mind-set that he imbibed at the French seminary. The ignition restored his traditional perspective that was attacked by his teachers and training. It was through initiation that Somé was able to develop a positive image of himself and the world. "My initiation, in particular, enabled me to understand [that] … [a]t its core was the objective of restoring the damaged regions of my psyche which, as though infected by a virus, were responsible for my crisis of identity."[131] Again he writes: "I call my initiation a radical healing. My angry, vicious self was quieted, intimated by the sweeping powers of the Other World. Something like a new person was born in me."[132]

It's clear that Somé's initiation served as a conversion experience. He finally recovered from the years of "brain dirtying" that took place at the French seminary, where he was introduced to ways of seeing the world that were at odds with his cultural values. The Western view of reality condemned his traditional way of living and celebrated whiteness as the preferred aesthetic by which all else is judged. Somé's initiation reacclimated him to the world which his oppressors had taught him to despise. In the language of Christianity Somé became "born again" and re-awakened to experience his culture from anew. This transformative process is necessary for those who have been stripped of their culture and their religious worldview. If such an event does not occur in the lives of those whose ancestors were forced to adopt another peoples myths as their religion, they may live a fairly good life, but that which makes one unique—that essential ingredient that made a Greek a Greek and a Roman a Roman—"That" will be missing from their lives. That essential ingredient is found only in one's primal culture and without it, will render them incapable of experiencing authenticity. Whatever one may deem "authenticity" to be, they will remain incomplete without the nutrients found in their primal culture. Those who fail to undergo such transformative rituals will remain underdeveloped: "A person who doesn't get initiated will remain an adolescent for the rest of their life, and this is a frightening, dangerous, and unnatural situation."[133]

Such underdevelopment affects every area of one's life even their ability to learn. For instance, in traditional African communities those who experienced difficulty learning, were identified as ill. "The inability to understand, to indigenous people is symptomatic of an illness. If your psyche is disordered or deficient or overcharged, blocks are created in you that prevent comprehension and remembering."[134] After Somé escaped from the seminary where he was held for sixteen years, he had to relearn his culture. "What I noticed immediately was that native learning clashed with my previous education, creating a strange kind of commotion within me. The sensation was most interesting because my newly acquired indigenous values gradually overshadowed the concepts learned in the course of my Western education, scaring away the notion that my own culture was primitive and doomed."[135] Somé's inability to understand traditional modes of thinking was a result of the linear logic forced into his psyche while at the seminary. For example,

> I discovered that, from their [his people's] perspective, what I learned from my white teachers was considered poisonous, and even dangerous, to me and others.... With literacy had come a logic that was incompatible with the logic innate to the Dagara and other native peoples. It made me prone to doubt, incapable of trust, and subject to dangerous emotions such as anger and impatience.[136]

In essence not only was Somé physically isolated while away at the seminary, but his thoughts had become "colonized" by Western logic, a logic incompatible with traditional modes of thought. "The knowledge I had been exposed to in Western schools," writes Somé, "left a wide range of experience unexplored, and it was up to wise people in my village to help me learn to open up to all the realms of knowledge of which I at that time was ignorant."[137] Educated black people everywhere who have received their educations in Western institutions are "unofficially" required to reject their epistemic tradition and embrace Greek thought. Somé's experiences highlights how Africans or black people in general throughout the world have been educated. It is clear that the Western paradigms for imparting knowledge remain incompatible with traditional ways of knowing. Those who receive a Western-oriented education, at the expense of denying or subverting their cultural norms, experience a rupture in their psyche which is not easily repaired. The overwhelming majority of Western trained black men and women face an identity crisis of life-threatening proportion "because education [is] was a departure from home and all its values, because it meant forgetting the ancestral ways in order to survive, education fostered in me [Somé] and my colleagues a serious crisis of identity."[138] Somé continues,

> I suspect that every literate African [blacks] who went to a colonial [western] school such as mine carries, as I do, the marks of his literacy on his body. These marks are not small scars. Literacy was literally beaten into us, and to avoid pain we had to quickly master European languages. Western knowledge finds a cozy place in the African consciousness when carefully packaged inside a whip and regularly delivered.[139]

Somé makes a more stunning indictment against those missionary-educators who were embedded with the colonizers. Mission schools were established to inculturate Africans with European values. Religion was simply the medium to carry out their nefarious agenda. Since it has worked so successfully, why should the white man change now? It is such an effective strategy in which millions of black people seem so vulnerable. Western education has always served as an appendage of white supremacy and is the primary weapon used for socializing black children.

> The purpose of these schools was clear: to continue the work of European colonization on the African continent by converting natives to Christianity and the ways of the West while they were still young, susceptible, and easy to persuade.... School, to us, was a place where we learned to reject whatever native culture we had acquired as children and to fill its place with Western ideas and practices. This foreign culture was presented as high culture par excellence, the acquisition of which constituted a blessing. Going to school was thus a radical act involving the sacrifice of one's indigenous self.[140]

Cultural suicide did not subside after African nations became independent from white rule. Neither did the Emancipation Proclamation mean that slavery was over for millions of black men and women in the United States. Slavery has not ended because mental and cultural enslavement is a European strategy and weapon used to control the masses. For instance, after African nations were given permission by their colonizers to rule themselves, supposedly acquiring freedom from European tyranny and hegemony, before giving up the reins of power, the colonizers replaced themselves with African men who would continue exploiting and destroying black people. Only now the tormentors would have black faces and, in some cases, were more savage then their European masters. This too is a strategy that continues throughout the Western world and particularly in the United States, especially in those cities populated by black people. Black men are made mayors in large cities throughout the country, but the real power is in the hands of the white man from which the black mayors take their orders.

The same is true of Africa then and now. All the potential leaders have disappeared or were openly killed because they loved their people and refused to allow the white man to control their country. So the white man picks the leaders they want to represent their interests. Wherever one sees a black man in a position of power anywhere in the world, he is there at the behest of his white benefactors. (Zimbabwe may be the exception.) "Leaders emulating the totalitarian rule of colonial administrators terrorized their own people, only to find themselves driven from power by others more zealous in the business of torturing their people and kin."[141] The black puppets that represent the white power structure compete among themselves and are rewarded based on how mercilessly they treat their kinfolk. This is a vicious type of psychological warfare that has proven to be very successful. It is extremely effective at controlling the black masses and continues to be the weapon of choice, especially wherever black people are in political positions of power. The black political elite receive a Western education only to become more savage than the KKK. Many African and black leaders who were given orders to kill and maim their people (Mayor Wilson Goode was ordered to have bombs dropped on a black neighborhood in Philadelphia in 1985. Fifty to 60 homes burned to the ground and 11 people died, including children) were educated under the same Christian system as Somé. "Africans who had been educated to act on behalf of the colonizer, using the colonizers' own methods, were enlisted to maintain the prosperity of the colonial dispensation."[142]

At the end of every tragedy, a healing must take place. After the raping and pillaging of one's religio-culture by the European, there must be put into place a process by which the victims can receive healing. Again, it is the traditional rituals which many Europeans consider barbaric that black people must employ to restore harmony and the lost centuries that the colonial locust and canker worms have eaten. The African psyche is severely damaged and remains under assault from acts of barbarism and white supremacy. Thus, the African collective can be healed only by addressing their relationships with the visible worlds of nature, community, and the invisible forces of the ancestors and Spirit allies. For it is in ritual that nature, community, and the Spirit World come together to support the inner building of identity.[143]

In his book *Sacrifice in Ibo Religion*, Cardinal Francis A. Arinze unveils the negative attitude that many African Christians have for TACF and by extension, themselves. The book was the centerpiece of his 1960 doctoral dissertation written in Rome, titled "Ibo Sacrifice as an Introduction to the Catechesis of Holy Mass." The title is an obvious sign of his inability to view African religion at least culturally and linguistically as different from Roman Catholicism. The theological tools designed to correct and analyze Roman Christianity should never be used to scrutinize traditional religion or any other aspect of African culture. From the Cardinal's introduction to the conclusion, Arinze's research is riddled with derogative appellations and epithets describing the Ibo people of eastern Nigeria. I counted over fifty references in which Arinze refers to the Ibo people as pagans, a typical term that his teachers often used to describe his people and culture.

After extolling the Ibo people for their keen sense of religious observances, Arinze then writes, "Most Ibos are still pagans."[144] This is his first reference to Ibos as pagans or nonentities. Another derogative descriptor he uses is "Ibo pagan parents."[145] His questionable attitude toward TACF and the religion of his ancestors is not an aberration but represents the attitude of the majority of African Christians then and now. Cardinal Arinze concluded his dissertation as it began by referring to "Ibo pagans," to distinguish practitioners of TACF from those who venerate Arabism and Euro-Christian cultural forms. The book is riddled with negative descriptors of those who venerate traditional ways of being. Still, the book is useful and provides ample information on the function of African ontology within the Ibo tradition. There is much that is valuable within Cardinal Arinze's book and it is particularly insightful for scholars who have an eye to separate the wheat from the chaff.

The TACF that are honored by the Ibo of eastern Nigeria exhibit cultural patterns similar to Africans scattered throughout West Africa. For example, the Ibo's propensity to use proverbs is a common characteristic with the culture. Throughout Iboland the people's passion for proverbs pervades their daily discourse. "The Ibos love to use proverbs," writes Cardinal Arinze. "For them to speak always in very plain and simple language is to talk like inexperienced, little Children.... [P]roverbs are the oil for eating speech, say the Ibos."[146] Part of traditional Ibo culture is found within their proverbs. Proverbs are like a mini-universes and serve as a microcosm for African traditional religion. Within the proverb is contained in the Ibo's worldview. All that is held dear can be found in proverbs and other wise sayings. The proverbs govern religious and social behavior. "Proverbs crystallize the accumulated wisdom handed down by the ancients. They reveal profound thoughts, the soul of the people. This field is closed to outsiders."[147] Cardinal Arinze recognized the potential of traditional religion and suggested that it should not be overlooked because it is invaluable in the lives of many Ibo.

> The essence of Ibo life is found within the love of family: [T]he family order is based on the desire for social coherence.... If social changes result nowadays in a lowering of morality (juvenile delinquency, weakened professional conscientiousness, prostitution, etc.) traditional society has had, and occasionally still has a high standard of morality: stealing was rare in the village, the conduct of young people was on the whole praiseworthy and the wisdom of the elders was expressed in words which lived on. The moral life of the African religions has definite values which must not be minimised, with its sense of dignity and uprightness and simplicity.[148]

Traditional religion is centered on the family, including those not yet born and the ancestors. Children are the center of the family and are considered a sacred gift from God. Boys are circumcised on the eighth day after birth and undergo initiation at puberty.[149] In traditional Iboland and in Yorubaland, some expectant mothers refuse to give birth in modern clinics, fearing that their child may miss the sacred rite of circumcision. (Today many hospitals are now performing this operation.)[150] Some postpone circumcising their sons until they undergo initiation during puberty rites.[151] Initiation is a rite of passage that boys and girls undergo to transition into adulthood.

> The entire social and economic life of the community derives its rhythms from these customary ceremonies, rites of fecundity and of birth, of suckling and of weaning, rites of passing and initiation, rites of marriage, funerary rites. They all serve to open and close the sacrilised cycles, and being performed under the auspices of God and the ancestral Spirit, they are religious.[152]
>
> They are known to all African peoples in one form or another, and they constitute an important moment in which society accepts and adopts the "gift." Through a long and difficult process of "new birth" the child is introduced into the adult world in order to become a full-time member. For the child to enter this adult world, considerable knowledge is required: knowledge of the myths, rites and symbols which enshrine the centuries-old wisdom of the tribe; knowledge of the secret language; knowledge of everything needed for a man or woman to carry out their functions; knowledge of how to distinguish between allies and enemies and knowledge of how to recognise the presence of the ancestors.... No one can deny the effectiveness of these rites. Their influence on the young adults is such as to cause us [Roman Catholic clergy] to reexamine the methods of catechesis currently in use.[153] Rites of passage function to introduce the initiate to secret information not available to the

non-initiate. Rites of initiation are aimed at including the young person in the community and recognizing his or her genius, and moving the youth toward maturity and adult responsibility.... Initiation focuses on and is a response to some basic existential questions faced by human beings since the dawn of time.... Initiation consists of rituals and ordeals that help young people remember their own purpose and have their unique genius recognized by the community.... Rebirth or rites of passage then mark his/her passage into maturity.[154]

Some initiations are performed in secrecy and are intended to provide the community with a certain level of cohesion for maintaining social order. No matter how unrelated the initiatory events may seem to outsiders, they are designed to transform the lives of those who partake in these time honored traditions. "[R]eligious feeling impregnates the whole life and conceptions of the Africans. Thus the manifestations which seem at first to be folkloristic such as the ritual hunting and fights, are capable of constituting a catharsis, that is, a purification from the evil spirits of the universe."[155] The rite of passage marks stages of development in one's life, which are essential for assisting each member to become communally conscious. The initiation functions "to symbolise the death of the former juvenile life and the life with the new forces in the tribe. Very often this rite is performed in the course of a haunting at night in which the initiates are assembled at the very place where their ancestors became men.... Sometimes the cry of an animal sends a shiver through the young lads who are going before the mythical ancestor whose mask is an epiphany."[156]

Initiation is akin to the process in which one undergoes "psychological shock."[157] They are possibly the most important of all rites because they mark a time in human development, when one recognizes that biological changes are taken place throughout their body and mind. This transition cannot effectively happen without the community who assist the youth by preparing them to enter adulthood. In some traditions one cannot become full members of the community or enter adulthood without undergoing initiation. These rituals are not simply curiosities related to what some in the West are now calling initiations. The traditional initiation was centered within a particular TACF, and assisted the initiate in becoming a new being. "With the removal by circumcision of a feminine 'principle,' the adolescent boy sees himself committed to his virility and therefore fit for marriage."[158] Men who failed to undergo an initiation were viewed by the elders as boys. Young girls also undergo similar practices. "It can take place at the time of marriage and it is still more secret then that of the young men. The passing from the paternal home to that of the husband represents in effect a 'passage' to a completely new life especially in those tribes where marriage was achieved by effective or ritual kidnapping."[159] The initiation for women in traditional society is a sacred act and plays such an important role that some continue to observe the time-honored traditions that transition them into womanhood. Some women in traditional communities continue to maintain certain customs that are troublesome to the modern mind. For example,

> many women are still not anxious to avail themselves of the services offered them in maternity hospitals in the towns or in the dispensaries. Advised by the older women they continue with the traditional accouchement either in a sacred grove or beside their homes, so that the newly-born will make contact with the soil from the moment of his birth and that this contact with the Earth-Mother may be beneficial to him.[160]

Once the child is delivered the elders give him a secret name called a "pick-up" name. Only the elders will ever know the child's secret name. In the future whenever they speak of the child in private they refer to him by his secret name. These sacred rituals are conducted with much pomp and festivity because the traditional African views such events as orchestrated by the divinities. Therefore, they give thanks to the ancestors with festivals and celebrations. The traditional African lives within a joyful state of mind.

> An environment of festival in which he [practitioner of traditional religion] is expressing his joy in living in the society that is best for him. Dance and song play an important part in this. Through them he enters into contact with his ancestors and the spirits, and communicates with the cosmic forces. In dance and song he levels off the social differences. He has an impression of entering into communication with the invisible world in a movement which transports him, body and soul, by some correlation existing between word and actions, between the sound waves and the cries of the heart, between the pulsation of muscles and the stirrings of the soul.[161]

These sacred rituals serve to introduce members to their new identity and instill into them a sense of communal responsibility. The ontological structure governing TACF in Ibo communities like elsewhere, is comprised of three major theological precepts: (1) Supreme Being, (2) Divinities, and (3) Ancestors.[162] Chukwu (Chi-ukwu) is the Supreme Being who is accompanied by a helper spirit, Chineke, who assisted Chukwu in creating the world. Another manifestation of Chukwu is Osebuluwa, the lord who maintains the cosmos.[163] This holy triune upholds the traditional Ibo's worldview and is the ultimate referent for understanding Ibo culture and religion. Also, the traditional practitioners of Ibo cultural forms did not compartmentalize their conception of deity. In the Western faiths a psycho-social gap exists between the chroniclers of religious ideology, and the perspective of the practitioners. In fact, most African traditional societies do not draw any artificial barriers or erect lines of distinction, that categorize ideas about God as something separate from their everyday lives. The artificial barriers that exist within Christianity between culture and religion, secular and profane, are imperceptible or nonexistent within traditional African communities. Religion and morality are inseparable and govern every aspect of one's life, whether at the shrine or in the market place.

Many attributes are used to describe Chukwu. He is known as Onyeokike (Creator; *Onyekelu enu kee ani*—one who created the heaven and Earth). Multiple names and titles are attributed to Chukwu's power and benevolence.[164] Chukwu is The One who possesses all power: "No one equals Him in power. He knows everything. He is altogether a good and merciful God and does harm to no one. He sends rain and especially children, and it is from Him that each individual derives his personal '*Chi*.'"[165] It is from Chukwu that the divinities derive their power to act on behalf of those who rarely forget to honor him. The theological tenets undergirding TACF in Iboland are similar to those which govern many communities who worship at the feet of their ancestors.

In the beginning, Chukwu's dwelling was on Earth. Chaos erupted and forced Him to relocate His kingdom away from His creation. Chukwu departed due to constant tedious requests from the people.[166] Among Ibo's pantheon of divinities, Ani the earth goddess, is extremely powerful and is ranked just below Chukwu.[167] "She is the Great Mother Spirit, the queen of the underworld, the 'owner' of men, and custodian of public morality in conjunction with the ancestors."[168] Traditional Ibo women once named their children after Mother Ani,[169] who is also the gatekeeper of social norms.[170] Ibo women held a place of honor within traditional communities and practiced rituals, underwent initiations including fecundity rites, which were performed to protect them during pregnancy. Since children are considered sacred in traditional African communities, these rites addressing the needs of women is a reminder that in traditional communities they are upheld as sacred, not simply receptors of male copulation. They are God's gift to the earth and are indispensable for the well-being of the community. "In the sacred groves she is given ritual ablutions and objects of protection. She avoids looking into the distance, or staying anywhere except at home, sometimes going as far as taking with her a little earth from her home if she has to make a journey."[171]

Several helper spirits assist Chukwu in governing society.[172] Traditional Africans honor these spirits by praying and sacrificing to them. Ancestors are also given a special place of honor within African traditional religion. "The ancestors are regarded as nearest to man and as most interested in the family well-being. This explains why many families' offerings of thanksgiving and good fellowship are directed to them."[173] For example, in Madagascar devotion to ancestors serves as the apex of their theology. The ancestors function in the place of the Supreme Being and honoring them is perhaps one of the most distinctive characteristics within TACF everywhere. It is an act of sacrilege for one to dishonor or neglect to "feed" their ancestors. The ancestors are fed with sacrifices of praise, libations, and others acts of kindness. The food one feeds to their ancestors is not only physical, but more importantly, the ancestors are kept alive with these sacrificial offerings. "The unseen ancestors are part of the family and are very much interested in it. This can be said of most African peoples, but in varying degrees."[174] Those who convert to Christianity and Islam and who neglect to "feed" their ancestors risk creating an imbalance that will spill over into those critical areas of their lives. "Sacrifices to the ancestors assume, in a special way, the aspect of good fellowship, good will and the desire for communion."[175] There is a yearly feast in Iboland to honor the ancestors called Alom Mmuo.[176] Here the ancestors are honored, celebrated, and giving their proper due. Those who abandoned their cultures for Arab and Europeans ways of being risk offending their ancient mothers and fathers. "[F]ailure to worship, 'feed,' and sacrifice to the ancestors is unwarranted forgetfulness and wanton lack of filial piety and love. Those who forget their dead fathers have no right to expect their protection when the tables are turned against them."[177]

Africans believe that every person has a personal legend. Most believe that we all come to this earth to fulfill a specific mission. The notion that each person has a unique purpose or destiny is a commonly held belief within African religion. Whether on the continent or throughout the diaspora, black people in general believe that each member in the community is born with a special purpose. One's purpose and destiny is not entirely of their choosing. Some traditional narratives hold that each individual is preordained before birth to fulfill a specific mission. Not just any mission, but one they agreed upon before they entered the physical realm. The traditional Ibo people— the Dagara, the Yoruba, and the Fon—Santeria, Vodun and Condemble practitioners in the New World, all believe that each individual is born with a specific purpose. Many believe that the vocation one chooses must be in alignment with their life-purpose. If not, they will be confronted with life-issues for which there is no easy remedy.

The traditional Ibos advocated that every life is precious and protected by Chukwu. This protection is afforded to one through their Chi, which is conceived by the Ibos as a personal guardian spirit. The Yoruba describe this guardian spirit or protector of one's personal destiny as their Ori. One's Chi or Ori protects and safe-keeps their personal destiny. It watches over them to ensure that the mission assigned to them is carried out. If not in this life the next one will do. Once the individual agrees upon their life-mission, it is impossible for it not to be executed because the spirit who accepted the mission is not confined by time or place. If it takes one or thousand lifetimes the mission assigned to each of human being will be fulfilled.

Each person has a unique type of Chi that is tailored especially for one to fulfill their life purpose. One's Chi is also viewed as their twin or double. Each persons has within him or herself a double. Some believe that this double can be contacted and must be consulted to heal certain ills and to alleviate problems that must be addressed to one's twin, who dwells in the world of spirits. The human being lives in two worlds and here in the physical realm he is confined to place and time. His twin lives in the world of spirits and has no limitations. Thus, the Ibos have created numerous proverbs that explain the importance of one's Chi. "The same mother, but not the same Chi"[178] underlines the belief that each individual is unique and that no two people are the same. This proverb also implies that biology is not the sole determiner of one's character and destiny. One's Chi or destiny is preordained and guided by spiritual beings and cannot be changed. Traditional Africans also believe that one's destiny is never in the hands of another human being. One's Chi chooses the woman who will be used as a conduit to enter the earth realm. "One whose Chi was destined to be lost gets lost even when he enters his garden in his compound."[179] Every act in life is preordained and governed by one's Chi. There are no accidents in this life. From the birth to death one's life-journey is set in stone.

The belief that human beings have a personal destiny is critical for appreciating the richness and depths of TACF. For example, traditional Ibos believe that each person possesses a "genius or spiritual-double, his 'Chi,' which is given to him at conception by Chukwu and which accompanies this individual from the cradle to the grave."[180] The nature of our Chi much like karma, determines whether one will experience a life of success or failure. "The ordinary Iboman regards his Chi as his guardian spirit on whose competency depends his personal prosperity."[181] One's Chi is so vital to their well-being that it is not uncommon to hear traditional Ibos speak of themselves as possessing bad Chi. Ibos and Yoruba offer prayers and sacrifices to their Chi and Ori. "When adversities visit an individual he blames his personal guardian spirit, Chi, because his Chi has been incompetent or negligent in obtaining his requests from Chukwu."[182] It is not uncommon to hear a traditional Ibo say, "I am a man of a bad Chi."[183]

Traditional Ibos perform sacrifices to restore communal harmony and maintain balance within their lives. Sacrifices function as a medium in which an individual can realign themselves with those forces that are operating against one's well-being. For instance, if rivers overflow or if drought and disease threatens a particular region, one performs certain sacrifices to restore ontological balance. "Rivers, rivulets and lakes are believed to have guardian spirits…. 'Mammy water' [a sort of nymph] dwells at the beds of big rivers."[184] Traditional Africans perceive all life-forms as possessing in part, the same vital force that dwells in human entities. All things are infused with divinity, including rivers, trees, lakes, animals, animate and inanimate objects possess this sacred life-force. African traditionalists hold that all things are endowed with a portion of the same life force that energizes human entities. That is why sacrifices are made to rivers, trees, and other natural phenomena so as to maintain the harmony that exists in all life forms. Even nature can suffer imbalances and needs to be restored to its proper place. "Sacrifices must be offered when such laws are violated, when the water overflows its banks, or if people are constantly drowned there."[185]

Prayer accompanies such sacrifices in traditional Ibo communities. Individual prayer as known in Western religions may not have been common in early traditional African communities. Ejaculatory prayers were uttered in private but it is communal prayer, whether in public or within the family, that is most common in traditional African communities. Prayers of thanksgiving are very common wherever TACF are observed. Communal prayers are directed to the divinities or ancestors. These familial rituals are such an important aspect in the lives of traditional Africans, an Ibo woman decided against becoming a Christian for fear she would no longer be allowed to give thanks to the divinities and ancestors. "A mother recently gave as her reason for not yet becoming a Christian the objection that she would not be able as a Christian to thank the spirits and ancestors when her son returns from America."[186] The level of faithfulness and dedication shown by this woman was once the norm throughout traditional African communities. Such devotion would have remained had not Arabs and European deliberately destroyed African traditional norms, only to replace TACF with their own gods and the elevation of their traditional culture to the status of religion. The dedication of this Ibo women was once endemic throughout African life.[187] Africans wished for nothing more than life, health, and strength. It is this three-cord blessing by which many practitioners of African religion conclude their prayers.[188]

Overall, sacrifice is a major element within African ontology and is perhaps the metaphysical glue that holds traditional theology together. Sacrifice serves as the vessel through which humanity restores itself and reestablishes right relations with the vital forces. In traditional Iboland, "sacrifice is the soul of Ibo cult. If it is removed, Ibo traditional religion is almost emptied of its content."[189] Ibo ontology is based on sacrificial rites that are integrated throughout every aspect of their cultural system. Ibo culture infuses itself even into nature and all human activities.[190] "When the rain comes in April, the yam spirit, *Ifejioku*, must be worshipped before planting begins. The spirits of the family and fertility, of the farm and farming implements, of the seasons and of lightning, all receive their proper attention."[191] The theological structure that governs most African traditional societies is very similar to that which functions in Ibo communities. Sacrifice appears to be the primary medium by which ontological harmony is maintained and restored. The foundation of African ontology centers on the idea that our physical world is simply a reflection or microcosm, although somewhat distorted, of the invisible sphere which is the home of the real.

> Every Ibo ... belie.ved that an invisible universe was in action all around him, and that his term of life was short if he happened to fall foul of its denizens. He felt that it was up to him therefore to propitiate them and to treat them with courtesy and deference. That was the fundamental reason why he had such a penchant for sacrifice in all its many forms.[192]

What is said about the Ibos' "penchant for sacrifices" is applicable to most West African traditional communities. That is, ontological harmony is maintained by sacrificing to the appropriate entity responsible for maintaining cosmic and communal harmony.[193] The common usage of sacrifice within traditional African societies speaks to their knowledge of a Supreme Being, with the assistance of helper spirits who function to maintain balance. The supreme deity does not uphold the workings of the world alone. Nor does the Supreme Being require worship as is the case in Arab and European traditions. The God of traditional Africa transcended such frivolous notions and does not possess the kind of ego as does the Abrahamic gods that demand worship. Only sacrifices can appeal to the Force that is far removed from Earth. Sacrifice is a form of acknowledgment of the Supreme Being and the helper divinities for their role in maintaining balance in the world. Sacrifice in African traditional religion is a thanks offering to God and those sacred beings who assist in upholding the world.

> By sacrifice man acknowledged God's supreme dominion and excellence and offers Him adoration, worships Him with humility and joy.... Sacrifice is an offering to God by a priest of a sensible thing through its immolation, in acknowledgment of His supreme dominion and man's subjection.[194]

Sacrifices acknowledge the Supreme Being and helper spirits as responsible agents who have the power to maintain cosmic and personal harmony. Traditional Africans knew that it was the Supreme Being along with helping spirits that were responsible for all that was good in the world. The sacrifice more than any other medium was the devotee's way of saying thank you, which is the highest form of praise. "Sacrifice is an act of public worship offered in the name of a community or part of it. The community fulfils this great obligation, not by itself directly, but through a special person, the priest. Human beings have always felt the need of a special mediator between himself and the object of his worship."[195] He or she is selected by the gods and "called" into their ministry and (are) were filled with the power of Spirit. The traditional priest were not always adorned in royal attire. Certainly, the priests of Egypt and Nubia and in certain parts of West Africa wore royal apparel, but in general, as one moves farther away from Africa's religious center—the Nile Valley Civilizations—we discover that religion becomes less centralized. For example, the babalawo in Yorubaland adorned themselves in special garb, but generally throughout Africa there may be little or no distinction between a holy man and a common citizen. In Iboland priests were distinguishable from ordinary citizens by their demeanor and conspicuous dress: "[T]he priest among the Ibos is the individual you see by accident, with old rags and a dirty bag, with chalk paintings around his eyes and feathers on his head. He is seen menacing and gesticulating like a madman, perhaps with a few tense faces to form his agitated audience."[196] The locals referred to traditional Ibo priests as *eze-alusi*. He served a particular spirit to whom he offered sacrifices at the spirit's shrine.[197] Sacrifices were offered in traditional communities as part of daily existence. Every home served as a potential place from which sacrifices would be made to a particular spirit. Whenever traditional Ibos received an answer to their request, they would immediately offer another sacrifice of thanksgiving to the divinities and ancestors.[198] Traditionalists offered sacrifices to their familial spirits for good health, for the recovery of the sick, for beginning a journey and for educational success. Ibo traditional culture was highly ritualized and offering sacrifices to the gods functioned to restore broken relations and to maintain personal harmony.

African Culture and Diopian Cosmology

Cheikh Anta Diop is considered by many African and African American academics as one of the most influential thinkers in the twentieth century. Diop challenged certain presumptions about human nature and the evolution of race. His supporters recognize him as the father of Afrocentricity. This title does not ignore the role other Africans have contributed to the study of traditional African cultural forms. For many Africans on the continent and throughout the diaspora, are working diligently to correct the misinformation distributed by many white scholars, regarding the role of African people throughout world history. Diop struggled to move the African collective beyond the classroom of ideas and mere rhetoric to provide definitive answers to questions of race and origin. Among his most popular contributions was the idea that ancient Egypt was quintessentially the creation of black Africans. He argued that since the Kemites were black is a fact that must be acknowledged and become the departure point for any serious inquiry into the history of African people.

Diop utilized cultural analysis and modern scientific theories to support his theses. He maintained that Africans were the true progenitors of ancient Egyptian civilization and that the modern Egyptian is an interloper and has no right to claim any historical connection to the ancient Kemites. Diop proved rather convincingly that Africans are the true descendants of the ancient Egyptians. From the evening of their decline and at the dawn of their glory, black Africans have left more than scanty traces of their presence throughout the Nile Valley.

Diop was a scholar of immense insight who committed his life convincing other Africans that they were not simply physically different from Europeans, but that their entire psyche—that which governs mental and cultural functioning—was forged from completely different ideologies. Diop argued quite convincingly that Africa, the "Southern Cradle" of civilization, produced a different type of human being then those birthed in the Northern hemisphere. According to Diop's Two-cradle Theory, African southern agriculturalists and northern nomads view the world through different axiological lens. He bases his arguments on archeological records, scientific studies, and eyewitness accounts. Diop argued that the nature of African people is sedentary and agriculture was their primary means of survival for thousands of years. On the other hand, the Europeans nomads were placed within a hostile environment where they were forced into violence, to kill animals for food and survival. Their propensity for killing was thus encoded into their DNA. This explains their love affair with killing and scorching the earth. They were environmentally programmed according to Diop to wage war against nature because, from the very beginning, nature appeared extremely hostile towards them.

An important aspect of Diop's Two-cradle Theory surmises that ancient African societies were matrilineal prior to Arab invasions and colonialism. The Aryan families of the world have their origins in nomadic and patriarchal societies. Diop argues rather vehemently against the theory that all social units began as matrilineal and that as they became more advanced, they evolved into the more superior patriarchal communities. He holds that the two systems are irreducible and one does not naturally lead to the other. Diop advanced the theory that matriarchal societies originated in the Southern Cradle where human beings first appeared and that every matrilineal society can trace its origin to Africa. He observed from his studies that in most places where matriarchy is observed its origins can be readily traced to Africa. Diop concluded that there is little evidence indicating that Europeans transitioned from matrilineal to a patriarchal society because nomadic dwellers through-out history have had little regard for the humanity of women.

Others have supported similar ideas advanced by Diop, including some European scholars. For example, Sven Lindqvist argued that "Europe" comes from a Semitic word meaning "darkness."[199] Diop's two-cradle cosmology is premised on the idea that northern darkness cannot be reconciled to southern light. They are irreducible manifestations of being and, if seen together, would contradict natural law. The essence of Diop's cosmology is that Africans and Europeans are culturally different but are in some ways genet-ically similar. Diop proposed his biological theory in advance of science cracking the DNA code. With outdated laboratory equipment, several decades before the genome project, Diop discovered that Europeans are hybrid Africans who underwent physical and mental changes during the Ice Age. Diop's theory is no longer an unfounded accusation aimed at insulting white people. DNA studies highly support his theory on the biology of race.

For example, a study conducted at Stanford, Yale, and at the Universita della Calabria (Cosenza, Italy) found that Europeans unlike Africans "do not fit a simple model of independently evolving populations with equal evolu-tionary rates."[200] In lay terms, Europeans did not evolve as a single race but came from an existing one. What Diop advocated several decades ago regard-ing the nature of race, many dare not discuss for fear of offending the elite, who hide behind their own race theories to justify their dominance. Africans are the people from which all of humanity evolved. The earlier-mentioned study further "showed that Africans are significantly closer genetically to Europeans than to Chinese or Melanesians"—which were the other group's studied.[201] Moreover, "the distances between the African populations and Europeans are significantly smaller than the distances between the African populations and the other non–African populations."[202] It is smaller because Europeans are the offsprings of African people. From there mixtures and admixtures all the so-called races of the world emerged. The physical features are simply a result of climatic factors and other environmental changes.

African people are not superior to others simply because they are the parents of human kind. Europeans did not evolve over the long period in which the African did. This may in part explain the differences in temperament between the two groups. Diop and other leading Africanists have argued that the European "race" did not arrive until after the Ice Age 20,000 to 50,000 years ago. They further claim that all human descendants have their origin in Africa and every human being on the earth today can trace their biological origins to Africa. (Recent studies found that the Neanderthal gene may exists in at least 5 percent or less of the entire European population.) Diop advances the theory that as Africans departed Africa and headed north, they became trapped and were confronted with a climate incompatible with their nature. They were conditioned for a much warmer climate but they had traveled deep into Europe, which during the Ice Age was covered with ice stretching over a quarter mile deep. Those Africans who became trapped in Europe did not develop on an evolutionary scale at the rate the original Africans on the continent had developed over thousands of years. Those Africans who became trapped during the Ice Age in Europe are now known as Europeans or white people. The harsh climate affected their biology and overall, their evolutionary development was compromised. "Europeans diverged at a much lower evolutionary rate, or ... Europeans are descendants of a population that arose due to admixture between two ancestral populations."[203]

Diop's hypothesis of the Gramaldi man also supports his evolutionary theory regarding the cultural and biological development of Europeans. Many Africans have not studied Diop's work because it contradicts much of the information that Western education has taught them about human evolution. We all should question whether Diop's cosmology is premised upon truth or conjecture. Should his findings be discarded as though they have no relevance to who we have become? Should his work be viewed as having no bearing on African people, especially in a time when white barbarism is once again rearing its violent head? Or, should Africans be encouraged to recheck the historical record to see if Diop's theories have merit? Diop's cosmology will continue to challenge African people until they have the courage to respect the teachers from their culture. How they respond could very well determine whether they remain European servants and continue to regurgitate their cosmology or develop the courage to retake their rightful place as mother and fathers of mankind.

Again, Diop's cosmology challenges the European *consensus gentium* theory, which proposes that all societies evolved from matrilineal to patriarchal societies. European scholars decided at the close of the nineteenth century that all societies must have at one time transitioned from a promiscuous matrilineal society to a superior one controlled and dominated by men.[204] "Patriarchy is superior to matriarchy and it represents above all spirituality, light, reason and delicacy."[205] In the nineteenth and much of the twentieth centuries, this logic was the rationale advanced by most white male academics. Some of them not only viewed patriarchy as a superior system for controlling society, but also interpreted it as synonymous with "spiritual yearning towards the divine regions of the sky, with purity and moral chastity."[206] Bachofen viewed patriarchy as a religion and preached its dominance over matriarchy, which was considered to have "passive dependence on earthly life, material things and bodily needs."[207]

Diop attacked Bachofen's theory that all "civilized" societies transitioned from barbaric matriarchal beginnings and are eventually controlled by men. Africans are in an inferior social position in the world because they are still playing catch-up to Europeans, who transitioned from matrilineal societies long ago. However, Diop argued that Europeans have no historical evidence that they were ever ruled under matrilineal regimes. To the contrary, Diop maintained that matriarchy is superior in every respect to patriarchy. A matrilineal society fosters respect for human beings and all life forms. Diop criticized those who equated European Amazonian women with women who governed within matrilineal societies. The European Amazons first appeared in Western Libya and were men haters who saw no need for the male species apart from enslavement and procreation.[208] Diop argues that within a true matrilineal society there is respect between the sexes. "Amazonism, far from being a variation of matriarchy, appears as the logical consequence of the excesses of an extreme patriarchy."[209] Wherever traces of matriarchal societies are found, these communities can most often trace their origins to Africa.[210]

Black people must question the impact that living under patriarchal systems may be having on their collective growth and development. Not only the physical trauma one experiences from living in a male dominated world, but the effects on one's psyche are equally damaging. Nature teaches us that when a species is removed from its natural environment and forced to live in an atmosphere completely hostile to its nature, that entity may survive, but it will never thrive and reach its full potential. Unfortunately, this is the condition of most black people throughout the world. Human beings are resilient and can adopt life-skills to survive for a certain length of time. However, the human being will never thrive and experience fullness within a hostile environment. That is the condition most Africans and people of African descent find themselves facing today. The uprooting of Africans and replacing their cultural systems with one incompatible with their nature has had tremendous psychological and physical repercussions. No species can be uprooted from its natural enclaves and forced to thrive in an alien environment without becoming impoverished in many of the most important areas of their lives. In other words, if Africans descended from a matrilineal society that is more compatible with their nature, then deep within their collective unconsciousness is a longing to reconnect with that which has been amputated. Africans must therefore ask themselves what effect patriarchy has had upon the family, education, and their thinking process. These questions are very serious and cannot be ignored because Africans will not be made whole until they reconnect with their cultural center that may no longer be physically located in Africa, but it certainly will not be found in the cultural constructs of Europe or the United States. The conscious re-gathering of that which has been lost will be an important step for African people everywhere. It will mark the beginning of their return to wholeness. We are all seeking to be made whole in some way or another. African people have been greatly challenged on their path to wholeness for several reasons. They are a people without a cultural center. Not because they lack a sacred narrative but they were removed from their cultural referents and are being measured by a foreign yardstick. They struggle throughout their lives trying to measure up against a standard that is hostile to Africans as human beings. The Abrahamic religions are that foreign yardstick by which the Africans are being measured. Historically, Arabs and Europeans have viewed African religion and culture as barbaric and irrational. From the early conquests by the Hyksos into Africa, who declared that their god sanctioned them to kill the indigenous people, to the Arabs followed by the Christian Crusades, Westerners have used religion to justify their barbarism and those Africans who adopted their traditions seem unable to distinguish between what people say and what they do. The Christian invaders who entered Africa after the European Enlightenment received the church's blessings to raid, kill, and pillage Africans in the name of God. They understood their mission to civilize non–Christians as a way to protect themselves. European hegemony was not only driven by greed but more importantly, white tyranny is rooted in a fear that gave birth to the eugenic movement and population control theories that the elite of today still pay homage. "The only chance for the future of the [European] race is to exterminate the whole people, both male and female over the age of fourteen."[211]

Diop argued that the white man's propensity for violence was not only rooted in the fear of being racially annihilated but that his violent disposition for shedding innocent blood was forged within a hostile environment. The moist environment that produced Africans occurred under less hostile environmental circumstances. Some have argued that the less hostile environment in which African people first developed makes them appear docile, but this type of disposition is exactly what was needed for the first human species to develop and grow into human beings. Otherwise, one will be at war with not only the physical environment, but with all those who have developed into fully functioning human beings. Nature was more friendly during the early development of African people and because so, they have historically viewed themselves as being one with nature. Some even accuse them of worshiping nature but this is not the case. Traditional Africans respected nature and in some ways traditional religion has its origins within that realm. The traditional African deep respect for nature was partly based on their cosmology, which elevated the forces within nature to a sacred realm. Thus the orisha, lwa, and neteru are primarily forces of nature that assist one in living at peace with all things. The foundation of TACF are premised on one living in harmony with all things in existence. Europeans evolved within an environment that was hostile and, as a result, developed a relationship that remains at war with nature without realizing that human beings are part of nature. Thus, their war against nature is really a war waged at themselves. This adversarial relationship can readily be seen in their disregard for the environment, especially when polluting the earth means they have greater access to nature's wealth. The white-controlled governments throughout the world have placed material advancement above all else, including the respect for the earth and human life. They are at war with nature and therefore have no regard for human beings other than to enslave them to build their empires.

For example, when natural phenomena such as earthquakes arise, the white elite look for ways to control or avert the event from recurring without considering the possibility that a higher power outside of human wisdom is attempting to communicate with them. Traditional Africans understood that god speaks through nature. It is the preferred medium by which communication takes place between the two realms. In fact, god and nature were inseparable in traditional life. Africans of old developed a deep respect for the power of nature and understood that some things could not be explained by human wisdom. What we call acts of God, they viewed as a medium of communication between the created and the Creator. Traditional Africans consult an oracle in moments of crisis to determine the "why" of a catastrophe and do not exclusively focus on how they can control the event from happening in the future.

Diop and Somé claim that Europeans or white people's temperaments developed and evolved within a fiery atmosphere. Somé refers to whites as "fire people" and, in many ways, the killing and torturing taking place throughout the world is the sacrifice they are making to their fiery gods. "Because it was so useful [for their existence], it [fire] became sacred and was worshipped as such."[212] The use of fire in religious rituals are an intervention of northern nomads. "[N]owhere in Africa does there exist this multitude of domestic altars surmounted by sacred fires which must be kept burning as long as the family exist, a custom which seems to stem directly from the Northern worship of fire."[213] Fire continues to be worshipped by whites and those who emulate them. Fire served a vital purpose for white survival during the Ice Ages and it can be seen blazing at many of the Westerners' most important monuments. Fire excites the warmongers, who seem intent on using their "fiery" weapons to attack non-white nations, or even themselves. Germans, Slavs, Acheans, and Latins introduced the worship of fire to the mixed racial groups who resided along the Mediterranean basin.[214] Fire gods will not accept any sacrificial offering short of the shedding of blood. The shedding of innocent blood in particular assuages the appetite of the fire god, more than killing one's equal. All of the world watched George W. Bush wage war against the Iraqi people. Human beings around the world watched in horror; others in amazement, as the fiery skies lit overhead from the bombs that were indiscriminately dropped on mothers and their children. The bombing of Iraq was a religious ritual that fire people must perform to maintain right relations with the god they serve. Even the ancient Hebrew worshipped the gods of fire. We see this ritual continue as the fire bombs light up the skies over Palestine. We no longer have to wonder why the Israelites used fire in many of their rituals. Diop suggests the following regarding the nomad's use of fire:

> The contrast between the Canaanties [sic], leading a sedentary and agricultural life, and the Israelite nomads, is exactly the one which we have made; it confirms the theory which has been developed as to the zone of confluence of the two cradles.[215]

"It was the nomadic invaders, pastoral tribes, who introduced the worship of fire.... The peoples who introduced fire worship into the Mediterranean basin strove at the same time to eradicate savage superstition."[216] The nomadic tribes (Hyksos) brought their ideas of worship with them as they invaded the land, forcing the indigenous people from observing their traditions and making them worship their god. Diop argues the invaders into Africa brought their religions with them and forced the indigenous to abandon their gods. (Those who control the U.S. government continue this policy. They are forcing mostly Muslim countries to abandon their traditions and accept American's god, which is capitalism. Material wealth is the god of the white elite wherever they dwell.) Diop contends that even the burial rituals that were observed by traditional Africans and Europeans can be linked to their divergent views of the world. The nomadic tribes introduced cremation to the world.[217] (See Herodotus, Book IV, wherein he gives a complete description of how nomadic tribes buried their dead.)

Traditional African culture suffered its greatest lost at the hands of Arabs. Diop argues that the first blow to traditional ways of being came from the hands of the Muslims.[218] "The traditional religion withered away little by little under the influence of Islam, as did their mores and customs."[219] African traditional religion and culture were first attacked in Egypt, which was the center of TACF. Egypt is the place where modern religion can trace its beginning.[220] Case in point, "the goddess Diana of Attica was an Ethiopian," and "[a] Black Venus was worshipped at Corinth."[221] Diop's cosmology uncovers the religio-cultural gap between African and Europeans. The lenses they use to perceive the divine are not only different, but Diop suggests that the African's God is not the God white people worship. According to Diop, the Semites' (white peoples) view of God is rooted in the Edenic myth with the fall of "man" and original sin. As a result of this particular myth, white theologians struggle to explain how a righteous God made an imperfect human. Ironically, those who remain in this state of imperfection are condemned to spend eternity in hell.[222] Traditional Africans have not troubled themselves with such theological nonsense and guilt trips that confront the Christian exegetes. Africans have universally learned to accept deity under almost every circumstance because God is in control. Africans understand that circumstances are not based on what is real because they do not change what is permanent. The practitioners of TACF affirm God's goodness in good times or otherwise. They extol the wisdom of the helper-spirits, especially when faced with life-threatening circumstances that defy Western logic. The measure of traditional religion is not determined by how well one interprets abstract concepts, but how one lives from day to day. How one responds to life's daily challenges and how they deal with communal issues is the hallmark of traditional religion. This is why justice continues to be the apex of black religion wherever it is practiced. The value of any religion depends on how it interprets justice. For many practitioners of the Abrahamic religions, justice is simply an abstraction, whose meaning must remain obscured. Otherwise, we would live in a just society instead of one with laws to govern the elite and different laws for the masses. The foundations of African traditional religion was built on justice. From Maat in Egypt to the empires of Western Africa, "justice was inseparable from religion."[223]

> Acts of injustice are rare among [Africans]; of all the peoples, they are the one least inclined to commit any, and the Sultan (Black king) never pardons anyone who is found guilty of them. Over the whole of the country, there reigns perfect security; one can live and travel there without fear of theft or rapine.[224]

Black people everywhere must search the historical records to determine if Diop's theories are based on truth or fiction. All cosmologies are at best hypotheses that attempt to explain the complex nature of human existence. Diop simply attempted to entice African people to re-examine what they have been taught to distrust about themselves. Diop pleads with black people to check the historical records and there they will discover their origin and role in the world. Theories are of little import unless courageous men and women test them not just in the lab but see how they operate in the real world. Diop argued quite convincingly that Africans and Europeans operate from different axiological grids. The European mentality was forged within an environment where they were forced to use violence for their survival. They developed their thinking and culture from an environment that appeared hostile to their survival. Although Europeans may very well be the offspring of Africans, they do not have the same mental grid that governed those Africans who stayed on the continent much longer, where they had more time to evolve into human beings. The Africans who departed from the continent and became trapped in Europe during the Ice Age did not have the time to fully evolve into what we call human beings. Life may not be as sacred to them as it is to Africans because they have not fully evolved into the type of human being suited for this environment. Most of the world wants peace, but whites are a minority in the world and are constantly seeking ways to engage human beings in war. Even the European's notion of what constitutes peace is different from the African's. Nomadism appears to breed a spirit that glorifies war and celebrates the killing of human beings. As Lindqvist points out in *Exterminate All the Brutes*, the European propensity to kill is unmatched and the art of killing has its own aesthetic; thus it must be carried out in a stoic manner.[225]

The Arabization of Africa

A few notable scholars have argued that Islam is an African religion and its rise in Arabia is geographically closer to northeast Africa than to most of Asia.[226] If the geographical fault that formed the Red Sea had not occurred, the Arabian desert would be a part of the Sahara desert and Islam would indeed be an African-born religion.[227] There was always an economic relationship between the inhabitants on both sides of the Red Sea long before Islam became their religion.[228] When the first persecution of Muslims occurred, Muhammad and his followers fled to Ethiopia for safety.[229] Islamic cultural forms are intertwined with African ways of being, so much that the first *muadhdhin* (one who calls the faithful to prayer) was an African named Bilal.[230] Around 708 CE, Arab armies conquered the inhabitants of Morocco, and the Berbers of northwestern Africa were "Arabized in culture and language."[231] The Berbers eventually adopted the Arabs' religion that was enforced upon them and they began to evangelize sub–Saharan Africans. This region was known by Arabs as "Bilad as Sudan"—"The land of the Blacks."[232] The first major West African nation to adopt Islam was Senegal, around 1040 CE.[233] Al-Bakri was an Arab historian who recorded in 1067 that an African king converted to Islam and imposed this foreign culture upon his subjects.[234] The same Arab historian also noted that the Arabs began their crusade against Ghana around 1067 CE. For the first time in history, Arab warriors from Morocco made their way into Bilad as Sudan.[235] Ghana, a region devoted to maintaining the practice of traditional religion, was destroyed, and its people were forced to adopt Islam.[236] Arab-Islamic warriors were intent on propagating Arabic nationalism and traditional norms that we now call Islam. They took their crusade to the sacred kingdom of Mali and forced the people there to adopt Arab culture, which eventually became their religion.

Al-Bakri seems to suggest in his writings that a few African kings willingly converted to Islam, especially when their traditional religion failed to end a severe drought that was ravaging Mali. Supposedly, the king's traditional faith was incapable of convincing his gods to stave off a severe drought so the king of Mali converted to Islam. After he converted to Arabism the drought ended.[237] Interestingly, only the king converted to Islam, but the people did not convert to Arabism (Arab nationalism; the elevation of Arab culture to the status of sacred). Africans insisted upon maintaining their traditional religion and serving the gods from within their own culture.[238] When Ibn Battuta visited Mali from 1352 to 1353, he was appalled to find African Muslims still practicing certain African traditional cultural forms, especially those that were incompatible with Arabicism.[239] The Mali converts to Islam saw nothing incompatible about maintaining their traditional culture and adopting certain aspects of Arabism to supplement their pantheon of deities. Early Islam in Africa was at best only outwardly observed, as reported by Ibn Battuta. The people developed a nominal relationship with Arab cultural forms and at the same time remained staunch practitioners of their own cultural traditions.[240]

Many Africans eventually converted to Islam in Western Africa. The majority who converted did so either out of fear or for economic purposes. Even the kings who adopted Islam did so for political or social purposes. For example, rulers might adopt "an Islamic identity for the purposes of commercial and foreign relations while maintaining a traditional identity for rituals relating to the land, the agricultural cycle, and the ancestors."[241] The nominal attention given to Islam during its early incursion into West Africa provides a clear example of how common it was for one to outwardly convert to Islam but remain committed to traditional ways of being.

For instance, Sunni Ali ruled the Songhai Empire from 1464 to 1492. He converted to Arabism outwardly in dress and demeanor, but he persecuted Muslim scholars at Timbuktu.[242] Ali maintained authority over his subjects based upon the ancient African traditional custom that kings possess magical power.[243] The master-word was given to kings and passed down through succession. It was believed to be alive and infused with divine power and gave the king power over his subjects.[244] Sunny Ali relied upon his traditional culture and religion, not Islam, to assist him with his kingly duties. Ali tapped into TACF for strength and insight on how best to serve his people. His conversion to Islam was for political and economic purposes only. The same was true of many of the early African leaders who converted to Arabism, because of the status it afforded them. Sunny Ali never intended to replace his religion with Arabism.

> Ali like many other African rulers, saw in Islam a source of power that he wished to tap along with the traditional sources.... [H]e wanted Islam on his own terms or perhaps on traditional Songhai terms, adopting those elements which were consistent with tradition.[245]

Ali's son showed no pretensions about his disdain for the Arabs' religion and customs. He knew that Arab customs were forced upon his people and that they presented a great threat to TACF. Therefore, upon ascending to the throne he was immediately replaced by an outsider who was raised in an area where Arab culture did not have to compete with African traditional ways of being. Arabs and Europeans initially found it extremely difficult to force African people to abandon their traditional religion and culture. Both were intent upon winning the Africans over and created elaborate strategies to destabilize African traditional culture. They searched for ways to impose their religious beliefs on Africans without compromising the fundamentals of their faith. When Muhammad Ture replaced Sunni Ali's son, he made a pilgrimage to Mecca to prove his commitment and dedication to Arabism. Unlike Sunny Ali, who only pretended to honor the Arabs' traditions and culture, when Ture arrived in Mecca he was given the title of khalifa (deputy) over the land of Tukrur.[246] His title was steeped in political and traditional lure. More importantly, his appointment as deputy was partly aimed at competing with the traditional magical powers ascribed to African kings. This move by the Arab elite in Mecca was intended to unset the loyalty Africans had for their traditional customs and culture. The new titled given to Ture by the Arabs was intended to compete with the master-word ascribed to African kings.

> This change should not be exaggerated; just as the traditional king found added power through some identification with Islam, so the Muslim ruler found it advisable to follow a number of traditional practices. The difference was that, while the former incorporated Islam into traditional pattern, the latter incorporated the traditional into Islam.[247]

The incorporation of TACF into Arabism was an effective strategy used by Arabs for Islamicizing West Africa. The Roman Catholic Church used a similar strategy to Christianize certain regions of black Africa during the colonial era. Like the Arabs who tapped into certain TACF to make Islam more attractable, the Catholic Church also allowed non-offensive aspects of African religio-cultural elements into the Church. This appeared to be the most effective way by which to destabilize traditional cultural practices without appearing too engaged in a direct cultural war with traditional Africans. However, the acculturation model was not always successful in the early periods of Islam in West Africa.

For example, Muhammad Ture was forced to engage in a holy war to convert the Mossi people south of the Niger, but he ultimately failed.[248] Muhammad sent messages to the Mossi ruler that directed him to accept Islam or face death. After the Mossi ruler consulted the ancestors he declined Muhammad's offer. Muhammad invaded the country in 1498 but did not have much success.[249] He withdrew soon thereafter and the Mossi people were viewed as resistant to Islam.[250]

Muhammad's successor, Askiya Dawud, ruled from 1549 to 1583 and again found it difficult to force his subjects to abandon their traditional culture. Dawud could not persuade his subjects to abandon their "peasant" religion and accept Arabism. Thus, he was forced to maintain certain African religio-cultural practices in order not to offend his subjects, who were intent upon honoring the ancestors.[251] In the cities, Islam was more successful than in the villages were they maintained their devotion to African religio-cultural forms.[252] Like the field Negroes in the Americas who retained their African consciousness, the rural-dwelling Africans on the continent refused to abandon the religion of their ancestors.

In 642 CE the Arabs sacked Egypt at a time when the Nubian Empire was dominant but its rulers were nominal Christians.[253] Egyptians were becoming more arabicized and displayed less affection for the ancient religion practiced by their African ancestors. Arabs eventually overthrew Egypt and the Nubian government in 1275 CE. They intermarried with the indigenous population, which overtime resulted in the displacement and the destruction of the African Egyptians and their culture.[254] Those dedicated to maintaining their sacred religio-culture and customs, departed from Egypt and populated the kingdom of Sennar, which was located next to present-day Khartoum.

In 1520, the Funj people, who were black aristocrats, dominated Sennar. Soon it, too, was sacked by the Arabs and the black king "converted" to Arabism. This once-proud African society became a center for Islamic fundamentalists.[255] Similar strategies were employed throughout Africa beginning in northern Africa and eventually made their way westward. The "conversion" of African people to Islam is a misnomer, when in fact, conversion to Islam has always been synonymous with adopting Arabic ways of being and which "are the visual representatives of Islam par excellence. The Africans will always be viewed as converts to Islam and by extension, honorary members of Arab culture. In places like the Nilotic Sudan, introduction to Islam also meant that one was being acculturated for Arabization [a process that all non–Arabs undergo to become Muslim]. More than for most other Muslim peoples of Africa, for the Sudanese to be a Muslim is to be an Arab."[256] This could be said for most converts to Islam, particularly in the United States where some black Americans embraced Islam as an alternative to the "white man's religion."[257] Many of the African American converts to Islam become, in dress and demeanor, more Arab than those from Saudi Arabia.

The offspring of Arabs and non–Arabs were considered Arab and intermarriage between these children and other non–Arab people caused many to experience an identity crisis.[258] Some children displayed little or no "Arab" features and only possessed a cursory or mythical connection to Arab ethnicity. Although many would not publically admit that being Arab was once a prerequisite to be a "true" Muslim. Even today, many non–Arabs attempt to trace some part of his ancestry to Arab culture. This pathology is so deeply ingrained that many black Africans have fabricated outlandish pedigrees by insisting that they descended from full-blooded Arabs. Others are so obsessed with having an Arab identity that genealogies were manufactured to prove that they were originally Arabs. Some paid to have birth records forged to prove their authenticity as Arabs.[259] The Arabic language replaced African languages and is the preferred language in which to conduct authentic study and devotion to Islam. Of course since the Koran was "written" in Arabic, one should learn the language in which Allah first communicated with his people. Not all the black kingdoms that were sacked by Arabs gladly embraced Arab culture and religion. In a few precious areas of Nubia, the people "converted" to Islam in 1275 CE but maintained their ethnic identity and language.[260]

In the beginning, Islam remained a nominal religion throughout Africa for several centuries before it firmly implanted itself into the hearts and minds of the people. It was given external attention but was not a heart-felt faith for several centuries after its formulation. Islam's early impact into Africa was so nominal that Muslim scholars agree that its true implantation into the people's hearts took a long time before it found fertile soil within the traditional Africans mind. "Islamization was so superficial that a Muslim author [stated:] 'Islam did not make any major advances until ... the nineteenth century.'"[261] In the thirteenth century when the Arabs were spreading their tentacles from the coastal regions to the lowlands throughout Africa, Christianity was making inroads in the highlands.[262] Arabs brought their religio-culture to Ethiopia around the twelfth century.[263] Again as elsewhere, they conducted a jihad against the ruling Christian government but were temporarily defeated in 1415.[264] In 1527, Imam Ahmad waged a holy war against Ethiopia and within ten years seized control of three-quarters of the country.[265] In 1542, the Portuguese came to the assistance of Ethiopia and killed Ahmad in battle.[266] Thereafter, many Ethiopians resumed their devotion to Christianity, but some remained committed to both religions.[267]

The first Muslim incursion into sub–Saharan Africa occurred from 1000 to 1600.[268] Islam was principally of interest to African traders who conducted business with Arabs before it became a religion. The African villagers were hardly influenced by Arabism as a religion and remained dedicated to their own sacred culture. "The masses of the rural population were hardly affected, except insofar as Islam provided access to new powers which supplemented the traditional."[269] It was not until the second major Arab incursion into West Africa that many began to adopt Arab culture as their religion. "African Muslim history, beginning in the eighteenth century, is characterized by the transition from a class religion to a religion of whole peoples."[270] Sufism had more appeal to Africans than orthodox Islam. Africans could see more of their own ancient tradition wrapped in Sufism, which involved ministering to the total human being. Sufism like traditional religion, addresses the full human being and touches on every area of their lives. Sufism appealed to Africans not because it was better than their traditional religion. It simply offered something different that they could use to supplement their all-embracing sacred tradition.

> In Africa, as in other areas of Islamic expansion, Sufism played a major role, appealing to many who did not respond to traditional orthodox Islam.... Sufism arose, at least in part, as a counterbalance to legal orthodoxy, providing the opportunity for a more emotional and directly personal relationship between the believer and God, and also for a close-knit community on the human level.[271]

Sufism more akin to traditional African religion and allowed for personal and emotional expression that was missing from orthodoxy. The Arabs' initial incursion into Africa had the same effect upon the Africans as did Christianity. Both employed similar strategies designed to show how Arabism or European cultural forms were superior to African traditions. They were equally effective in "uprooting Africans and destroying traditional institutions."[272]

The second or preindustrial phase of Arab expansion into West Africa encountered resistance and competition from Christian merchants and missionaries. Both merchant and missionary were backed by the Europe Empire and this presented a major problem for Islam because now it would have to contend for converts. Christian missionaries were not only in Africa to save souls but also as representatives of European expansion that was also occurring in the New World. In fact, "religious and other motivations were not clearly distinguished in the minds of most colonists; they found it difficult to separate Christianity and European culture."[273] From the time of Constantine, Christianity has always aligned itself with the ruling power. A conflict arose between Christians and Arabs over how to divide Africa. This cultural war was not only for converts but was deeply rooted in politics, economics, and culture. "The conflict then was not only between two religions but between two cultures, each of which believed in its own inherent superiority, but one of which had the power and resources to enforce its will."[274] European culture and Christian values in some areas of Africa were preferred over Arabic and Islamic values. Arabs controlled certain regions of West Africa through trade and were valued by the Europeans during the colonial era. In the nineteenth century colonial powers set aside their religious differences and offered Muslims lucrative contracts, since they were so well entrenched within African society. They could be trusted by the white man to do their bidding, never mind that they worshipped different gods. Religion can be placed on the sidelines when economics are involved. (This in part explains the relationship between the U.S. government and the Saudis. Never mind that fourteen of the nineteen men who hijacked the plane which flew into the world trade center were from Saudi Arabia. This fact has had little or no visible impact on Saudi-U.S. relations.)[275]

One can argue that the Muslims who controlled trade in West Africa benefited from colonialism, especially from their expansion projects in urban areas dominated by Muslims. The Muslim businessmen were very well respected by the colonialists as literate and were hired as clerks and record keepers.[276] The colonist also used existing Muslim law to govern social norms, which was preferred over unwritten African oral tradition.[277] The colonists' preference for Muslim workers grew during the colonial era.[278]

For example, "in many parts of Africa there was a rapid spread—almost an 'explosion'—of Islam during the colonial period."[279] This was due in part to the need for Muslim workers who were very skilled. The Muslims' presence also functioned to resist the Christian missionaries who were viewed by Africans as representatives of the colonist.[280] "Being Muslim could be a way of gaining advantages under the colonial system and at the same time expressing a certain distance from Western culture."[281] Even the French colonizers who were representatives of Christianity were not successful in replacing traditional culture with Christianity. Islam proved more successful during the colonial area because it did not represent an occupying power. Its integration into African culture became less aggressive and felt more like a natural progression during the colonial era.[282]

Islam continues to appeal to Africans because it is a practical religion. In many ways it is more closely associated with traditional African beliefs than is Christianity. "Islam is ... a system of social obligations"[283] and is not premised upon faith propositions but real action. It is more holistic in its perspective on life, not simply based upon worship once a week. Still, African Muslims have not been able to fully embrace Islam, especially in moments of crisis. Many revert to TACF in times of crisis, which is their natural religion. They place their lives into the hands of their ancestors, knowing that their people will not abandon them in their time of need. African Muslims and Christians continue to petition the ancestors and trust their sacred traditions when faced with existential despair.[284]

4

African Culture and the Philosophy of Religion

The elements governing Traditional African Cultural Forms are found in a variety of indigenous sources. From the written records of the African Egyptians to the sacred writings of the Yoruba and the Ejagham of Calibar, Africa overflows with raw material of which the worlds creates culture was created. Africa's rich culture has given birth to a religion that provides guidance to those who honor their tradition and culture. From these rich sources one can excavate to uncover the rich sayings, proverbs, and oral histories that are abundant throughout traditional African communities. The stories and wise sayings are the raw materials from which an authentic African philosophy of religion is derived. African philosophy cannot simply look to European philosophical schema as a reference because Europe as a conglomeration of tribes that did not exist when Africa had already given birth to the oldest Philo-religious corpus in human history. Europe has given Africa very little outside of enslavement, colonization, and teaching her how to be inhumane. African philosophy emerges from the soil of Africa and is best explicated by African men and women who honor TACF.

What Is African Religion?

African traditional religion is a compilation of the cultural practices of indigenous African people. It is not a religion in the common sense of the word. African traditional religion is a way of being in the world. It is how one perceives him or herself as an entity connected to mother earth. African religion is comprised of several traditional African cultural forms. It is eclectic and embracive of divergent views. It is a nature religion and views all things including human beings as an integral part of this sacred force. The

Vital Force and its derivatives are the primary focus of TACF. As one maintains right-relations with these forces they are able to live in harmony with their neighbors and all things in existence. The aim of African traditional religion is to maintain right relations with the world, which is only possible if that relationship is first made right in the other world. The practitioners of traditional African cultural forms utilize rituals to maintain right relations with the invisible world.[1] African traditional cultural forms is not a fossil religion, but an active way of life observed by millions throughout the world. It is primarily thought of as an oral religion in the sense that it is, "written in the people's myths and folktales, in their songs and dances, in their liturgies and shrines and in their proverbs and pithy sayings."[2] Traditional religion is anti-missionary and does not seek converts. Millions of people on the continent and throughout the diaspora share certain cultural affinities that experience this sacred tradition.

For example, J. O. Awolalu holds that traditional African religion is marked by a unity that binds numerous cultural groups together. This same sentiment is shared by African scholars in the United States, including Molefi Asante, who maintains that "we have one African cultural system manifested in diversities."[3] The veneration of African culture is not unlike those New World TACF observed by millions throughout the black Atlantic world. The overwhelming majority of African cultural groups believe that spiritual forces are responsible for all existence. Although this force is called different names among various cultural groups, it is a reflection of how those divine attributes are expressed within a particular culture. Most traditional Africans believe that the Creator placed lessor spirits or divinities in charge of earthly affairs. These spirits share in the creation of human beings and are responsible for maintaining cosmic harmony. This is perhaps one of the most common characteristics within all African traditional religions, from the Egyptians to the Congolese; the belief that helper-spirts assist the Creator with the creation of everything in existence, including human beings.

The Vital Force or Prime Energy is responsible for all things that exists throughout the cosmos. Since energy can neither be created or destroyed, traditional Africans view physical death as a transition for one form to another. Death is a gateway by which one enters the afterlife. This too is a common perspective within traditional African communities. It is within this realm, which Westerners call death, where those who lived uprightly are deified and in some cases reincarnated. African religion holds its ancestors in the highest regards. An African ancestor is equivalent to those honorable men and women praised in African American Negro spirituals. Entering ancestor-hood ensures that one's family has an advocate in the spirit world who can intercede and mediate their causes. The ancestors have direct access to those forces within the spirit world because they too inhabit that space where the Vital Force resides. The divinities and ancestors reside in this spiritual realm and are fully engaged in the affairs of humanity. They watch over their family members and become their primary advocates and protectors. Not all family members will become ancestors. This position is available to those who lived an honorable life and died a good death.

Also, within this spiritual realm resides the raw materials where social mores receive their authority. It is believed in some African societies that the divinities and ancestors are the guardians of social mores. Social principles are based on the ideal that all humans are created as free moral agents. Those members in society that live a life pleasing to the spiritual entities will be blessed in this life and in the hereafter. Those who live contrary to traditional norms will not experience the abundant life. Those who live outside of the traditional norms are also expected to die a bad death.[4]

These beliefs have their basis in the idea that human beings should live in harmony with all the forces in nature, and they must especially never fail to honor their sacred traditions. One must not only be their brother's keeper, but also maintain right relation with all life-forms. Any breach in the covenant that provides for cosmic balance is construed as "sin." (Even though this particular concept is foreign to TACF, still "sin" can be viewed as an imbalance or disharmony.) Practitioners of TACF are fully aware of the consequences that result from imbalance. Failure to honor ones tradition is a dishonor which is not easily forgiven. Observers of TACF are convinced that those who offend sacred traditions will first be punished in this life and severely disciplined in the afterlife. The divinities and ancestors are responsible for executing the punishment for such offenses. When violators are made aware of their offenses they must immediately make amends, which usually requires offering a sacrifice. Without appeasing the offended divinity or ancestor thereby correcting the imbalances in one's life, one will experience a life of confusion and eventually die a bad death from the hand of the offended spirit. In traditional communities those who die bad deaths are not permitted to become ancestors or be given a proper burial.[5] Imbalances disrupts the flow of energy and maintaining balance with these forces of energy is essential to understanding traditional African religion.

TACF are given little scholarly attention especially in those places where the Abrahamic faiths dominate religious discourse. Rarely are traditional norms and values spoken of without comparing them to Christian or Islamic concepts. Yet the Abrahamic religions are foreign to traditional African cultural forms. Even many black scholars make the same mistake as their Anglo counterparts by comparing African religion with Christianity and Islam. This oversight may result from the overwhelming number of Africans who look outside of their primal culture for religious guidance. Most scholarly research is focused upon Christian or Islamic modes of being. When TACF are investigated they are usually compared with Abrahamic views, while African norms are ignored or disregarded. For example,

> sin, as a religious concept, has not received a systematic study among scholars of African Traditional Religion. Some of them who mentioned sin in their writings did so just by the way and claimed either that the Africans had no notion of sin or that they had a very poor concept of it.[6]

A few students of TACF have suggested that the Africans theological view of sin has not been developed to the extent that it is within the Christian scriptures.[7] Such observations are themselves competitive, not comparative. Awolalu charges that the African concept of sin is just as thorough and complete as that of the "Jews of the Old Testament."[8] He holds that traditional Africans have a thorough understanding of the sin concept, which is evident in their distinction between ritual sins against the divinities and those of a moral nature.

For example, Simon Maimela argued that traditional African cultural forms serve a salvific function in the lives of African people, just as Christianity or any other religion.

> The salvation offered through African traditional religions is one which speaks to the heart of the African in a way that nothing else does. For that reason any religious understanding of salvation which is pre-occupied exclusively with the salvation of the soul from the pangs of hell and eternal damnation, as the Christian faith often appears to be, will remain inadequate to meet the needs of the African world, especially if that salvation does not hold promise also for happiness and prosperity here and now.[9]

African religion is an experiential-based and not an abstract phenomenon focusing on theological abstractions that lead to nowhere but more conjecture. One would think that such questions are designed to distract one from dealing with concrete issues that affect people on a daily basis. The European has a preference for such preoccupations because, in so doing, he does not have to confront the horrors he creates throughout the world. African redemptive culture rejects utopianism as a form of salvation and is centered upon this world. Mbiti argues:

> Salvation in African religion has to do with physical and immediate dangers that threaten individual or community survival, good health and general prosperity or safety. Salvation is not just an abstraction, nor is salvation in African

religion something to be realized at the end of time. It has been experienced in the past, and it is being experienced in the present.[10]

Salvation within an African traditional perspective is centered in the Now. Freedom is not something that occurs in the bye and bye, as black Christians were taught to believe. This kind of thinking has made them docile and acceptable to various forms of dehumanization. Salvation is happening Now! It is a now event or otherwise it is a fantasy. For one to be "saved" or to become self-aware is one of the primary aims of African religion. TACF are not fixated upon ideological abstractions that will take one to the kingdom of nowhere. African religion is people-centered and focuses on the liberating activities of God in this life.[11] Rituals and sacrifices are designed to bring one face to face with the world as it truly exists. Not the one manufactured to keep one subject to the dictates of white hegemony.

The main focus of TACF is to provide people with knowledge of self and knowledge on one's enemies. This knowledge is not of things separate from oneself, nor can it be acquired by learning about things outside of oneself. True liberation cannot happen by looking outside of oneself and expecting another to save you. The traditional focus was on self-knowledge. Even the Westerner's obsession with the sin concept speaks to their need to understand themselves. Whereas the Westerners come to know themselves through the concept of sin, Africans did not view themselves as one born with such defects. From the very beginning, they were conscious of life forces that can interrupt the relationship between the human beings and the forces that control these nodes of energy. Thus, maintaining harmony is a critical component of African religion and it is their obsession with the manipulation of such forces, which makes it a modern religion. One that has its basis not only in myth, but science, which maintains that all is energy. The Africans understood this concept and it became the main focus of their religion.

The African view of imbalance is quite different from the Abrahamic concept of sin. Although both take their cue from myths, sin in traditional religion is a communal imbalance, which involves a breech in the relationship between the forces of nature and the community. Without maintaining communal harmony human beings will be unable to experience success in life. Mbiti wrote that communal imbalances are "any breach [sic] which punctuates this communal relationship amounts to sin, whatever words may be used for this concept."[12] Unlike Christian theology which primarily views sin as an individual violation that extended to the human race, contaminating even the unborn; Africans viewed sin is an imbalance that would indeed affect the entire community. Not because "we" have all sinned and fallen short of the glory of God. Human beings were out of balance the forces of nature that caused this energy to withdraw itself. Mbiti holds that God's separation from human beings was not a moral act (as it is in the Christian myth of origin) but an ontological decision.

> The separation between God and humankind was an ontological and not a moral separation. Humankind did not become a sinner by nature through these acts which brought about the loss of the primeval paradise. There is no *original sin* in African religion, neither is a person born a sinner. A person is a sinner by deed in the context of the community of which the person is a member. *Sinning* is that which injures the philosophical principal of: "I am because we are, and since we are, therefore I am."[13]

Imbalance results from a breach in the covenant human beings have with the Vital Force. Offenses occur when this intimate relationship between the divinities, ancestors, nature, and human beings is violated.[14] When such an offense happens and are brought to the attention of the community, action must be taken to immediately restore the natural order.[15] Since traditional religion is communal-based one creates an imbalance when they violate communal norms. The individual not only creates problems for himself, but jeopardizes the entire community.

For example, in the Yoruba tradition if one neglects to "feed" their orisha, such negligence places the community in danger. Awolalu, the great scholar of Yoruba tradition, holds that the African view of sin is communal. "Society, as conceived by Africans, is a creation of God and it is a moral society. In African communities, there are sanctions recognised as the approved standard of social and religious conduct on the part of individuals in the society and of the community as a whole. A breach of, or failure to adhere to, the sanctions is sin, and this incurs the displeasure of Deity and His functionaries. Sin is ... doing that which is contrary to the will and directions of Deity."[16]

Once again Awolalu's views are very sound, but his interpretation of sin appears more like Christian theologians. Although he interprets sin as an individual transgression of a moral order, he maintains the traditional view that its removal is highly ritualistic. Sin is alleviated or removed through the use of rituals of appeasement or rituals of reconciliation. The ritual of restoration may include spitting in one's mouth, washing or shaving the body, or even sacrificing a human being.[17] Although human sacrificial offerings were banned during the colonial era, the practice continued in secrecy during extreme communal crisis. Awolalu holds that human sacrifice was the ultimate gift-offering to God. This offering functioned as a medium to transfer the sin of the community to the victim. The victim served as a ransom or scapegoat for the sins of the community.[18]

For example, there is an annual festival in Nigeria known as the Edi Festival, where the community commemorates a time when their heroine Moremi delivered them.[19] Moremi vowed that upon her people's deliverance she would offer a sacrifice to the river goddess Esimirin. After they were delivered she honored her vow, but Esimirin would not accept an animal sacrifice. Moremi was required to offer the best thing she had—her only son. This annual celebration honors this mythical event and most importantly reminds us all that only what is most sacred can appease the gods. The Edi Festival commemorates this cosmic principal by celebrating Moremi who gave her best to save her people.[20]

Awolalu wrote that the Edi Festival serves as an important reminder of what is required to recreate the traditional systems that were uprooted and destabilized by Arab and Europeans. Moremi's son was a human scapegoat who took away the sins from the community. This holy sacrifice made things right between the community and the spirits that were offended. This practice is rooted in the idea that not all of humanity should suffer for human error, and that a way of escape is available that spares the community. Awolalu noted that when an animal sacrifice is used at the Edi Festival, people place their hands upon it before it is led to the sacred grove. As they place their hands on the animal they cry out, "Take diseases away! Take misfortunes away! Take impurities away! Take death away!"[21] The people believe that their offences are transferred to the animal and right-relations with the spirit world have been restored. The individual is only safe when the community is in harmony with the vital forces of life.

The maintenance of communal harmony is premised on the idea that anything that blocks communication with the divinities creates an imbalance, which prevents ones from communing with spirit. This blockage must be removed before the free flow of spirit can move in one's life. The restoration of this energy safeguards the community, provides deliverance from natural catastrophes, and combats anything that oppresses the human spirit. Any abstract ideas about the role of salvation in African religion is indicative of a foreign ideology that has creep into the African psyche.[22] African tradition is premised on a system of rewards and punishment in this life. The human being is obligated to strive to live a life of good character and to avoid those things that prevent them from fulfilling their destiny.[23] One must strive to live a life free from those obstacles that produce disharmony between the *sunsum* (personality) and the *okara* (soul). This is the duty of every practitioner of TACF.[24] Those who deviate from the path established by tradition will wander into the forests of sin. Those who exhibit patience, maintain truth, love others and honor their elders are exhibiting the fruits that attest to their salvation in this life. Such an individual will not be disappointed in the next life where they well be welcomed by their ancestors.[25]

All violations of traditional mores or TACF are weighed on the scale of righteousness. Some sins are viewed as hereditary and others are the results of violating cultural norms. In traditional Yoruba communities lying was considered a moral violation and a transgression against Deity.[26] Adultery and lying were viewed as offenses connected to one's Ori—destiny. Transgressors of traditional norms who neglected to offer the necessary sacrifices to appease the offended deity would be punished. If any believed they escaped the all-seeing eye of spirit their impending demise would reveal their sinister ways. The divinities abhor lying and require all people to love truth and justice. The oracle Ejiogbe says, "Be truthful, be just! Oh, be truthful, be just!"[27]—implying that the divinities are righteous and only support those who love truth and advocate justice. Also, in traditional Yoruba communities stealing was considered an offense for which immediate punishment would be rendered by the gods. The Odu Ogbe-Ale warns that there is no escape from the all-seeing eyes of god. "If the earthly king does not see you, the heavenly king is looking at you. Thus declares the oracle to the one who steal under the cover of darkness, who says that the earthly king does not see him. God sees the thief and will surely punish him."[28]

There are also odus that admonish children to honor their parents. If they do otherwise they should expect to incur the wrath of the divinities. "If a child respects his father, everything he embarks upon will always be well. He will be a perfect gentleman."[29] Its unfortunate that many such proverbs and cultural norms were targeted and systematically dismantled by Arabs and Europeans. Nevertheless, Africans had (have) an extremely rich culture that is more than adequate for providing the religio-cultural nutrients they seek for in the Arab and European faiths.

Instead of honoring their forefathers as admonished by many proverbs, millions of African children are taught to dishonor their tradition and are in violation of the cultural precepts established by their ancestors. "The unfortunate acceptance of foreign cultures have [*sic*] to a large extent affected African children in respect for elders and we appear to be moving into a confused and dual culture."[30] Traditional norms have been severely challenged and compromised because of the foreign religio-cultural incursions into Africa that not only depleting the continent of its natural resources, but also introduced their traditions as superior to African ways of being. These foreign traditions have shown little respect for traditional modes of existing. At least from the viewpoint of advancing TACF as a viable medium to assist Africans.[31] Unfortunately, millions of African Muslim and Christians will remain in the wilderness until they turn away, or at least critically analyze, the foreign cultural forms which they have thoroughly imbibed. The Africans on the continent and millions throughout the diaspora who have imbibed other peoples norms that are foreign to their cultural DNA will remain estranged from their real potential until they embrace what they have been taught to hate. They unknowingly worship Arab and European cultural norms and values, without realizing that the elevation of their culture to the status of sacred is the only alter of which they should prostrate themselves.

Chirevo Kwenda argued that TACF are more than worthy of elevation to the status of sacred. He accuses Western scholars of misrepresenting African traditional cultural norms when they fail to promote it as a sacred cultural form on the same level as other religions. He maintains that one errors when they assume that salvation must take the route of escape from the present. TACF are not centered upon an eschatological event hoped for in the distant future. Christian utopianism must be rejected in all its guises because salvation is not a destination. Salvation is an experience that is either happening now or it is a lie. The desire to maintain personal immortality through the ancestors signifies that traditional Africans did not limit themselves to the present moment. Freedom and salvation were connected to their view of ancestor hood because death was not final but a transition to another state of being.[32] Kwenda charges that Mbiti mistakenly associated TACF as a rescue from the monster of death. However, death is not final nor does it represent the threat that it does in the Abrahamic faiths. Practitioners of traditional African cultural forms hold that their spirit will reincarnate until "it" fulfills the mission it was assigned. Reincarnation is type of salvation that no less represents deliverance from death than other forms of liberation.

Mbiti is also wrong in thinking that "rescue from the monster of death" can only be achieved through a mythology of future bodily resurrection. For the existential embodiment posited by the notion of reincarnation, whether partial or complete, is no less serious a proposition than future bodily resurrection.[33]

Ancestor-hood is a crowning metaphysical moment in one's existence. In some traditional cultural groups, passing from the physical into the realm of ancestors, implied that one had finally received their just reward. This honor is available to those who conduct themselves according to traditional values and mores. Through the elaborate use of rituals, salvation avails itself to every member in the community, and even transgressors of traditional norms can redeem themselves. By performing rituals of restoration, Africans who are estranged from traditional norms can restore their relationship and reconnect to the life forces that complete the human process. Ritual aims at restoring and purifying the transgressor by putting "Entities in their proper places—an ancestor at the head of a clan of healers, the nature spirit back with nature, the ancestress back in her tree shrine, the afflicted person back in good relationships with all these as well as the community."[34] The ritual aims at correcting imbalances and restoring ontological harmony. Rituals do not provide absolute purity but seeks instead, "in the Douglasian sense," to put "things back in their proper places."[35]

African religion is cosmos-centric and aims at redeeming living and nonliving entities. Human and nonhuman elements encompass the spectrum of the life forces of which man must live in harmony. Traditional religion revolves around a spiritual axis that aims to address the range and dimension of human interactions. TACF are guided by an ethic that hold a deep respect for right living. The traditionalists were not focused entirely upon one's actions, which are only a manifestation of a deeper malady. The circumstances surrounding human actions are but a minute reflection of deeper reality, which has not unveiled itself. African traditional religion is cosmos-centric in that its vision aims at seeing beyond the illusion of circumstances. Its ethics are based upon traditional moral codes that governed African communities prior to the Arab and European invasions. Western scholars continue to debate whether religion gives birth to morality or vice versa. Yet, students of African traditional cultural forms hold that moral codes have their basis in religion. J. Estlin Carpenter wrote that "the historical beginning of all morality is to be found in religion; or that in the earliest period of human history, religion and morality were necessary correlates of each other."[36] Geoffrey Parrinder shared a similar view and argued that within TACF morality or social codes are derived from religion.

> [T]he morality of West Africa is entwined with religion, for the people undoubtedly have a sense of sin. Their life is not overshadowed with a constant feeling of sinfulness, however; the African's happy disposition is well known. If a man breaks a taboo, he expects the supernatural penalty to follow, and his friends will desert him, or even punish him further.... If lightening [*sic*] strikes a man or a house, he is judged at once to be an evil doer, without question, for he must have offended the gods.[37]

The Veneration of African Religion

Christian Gaba has written extensively on African traditional culture and argued that it is best understood by observing African modes of worship.

(A better word for "worship" in a traditional African context is veneration.) God and his saints may be worshipped throughout Christianity, but the ancestors and orisha are venerated within African traditional cultures.

For example, among the Anlo Ewe of southwestern Nigeria and southern Benin, Dagbe (salvation) is activated through rituals. Dagbe can also imply abundant life, prosperity, and good living. Students of TACF maintain that prosperity is one of the primary markers of abundant life. Dagbe signifies that all is well with one's neighbors and especially that one is in right relations with the orisha. Prosperity must be experienced in this life, otherwise, it is not authentic, but simply an abstraction that awaits one in the next life. The late E. Bóláji Ìdòwú argued that the African concept of salvation (dagbe) is akin to the Hebrew's "shalom." This word conveys that one is complete or whole, experiencing abundance and "well-being in body, mind and soul."[38]

The Vital Force is the source of Dagbe. The Anlo rituals highlight their deep trust in the power of spirits to sustain their existence. Gaba recorded numerous Anlo proverbs and prayers which illustrate their belief in the salvific power of deity, prayers such as "Take them [offerings] to the abode of Mawu, the Creator, and in return bring to us everything that makes for abundant life."[39] He further observed several rituals which suggested that salvation is always in the hands of the divinities. Those who honor their cultural traditions are never left to fate, because their lives are watched over by guardian spirits. The Anlo believe that spiritual entities are responsible for worldly affairs. The orisha and lwa are involved in the affairs of life and even the creation process. Prayers uttered at shrines by the faithful indicate that the Anlo were well aware that divinities and ancestral spirits are the real source of their salvation.

For instance, "O Grandfather Nyigbla; today we have gathered in your sacred grove. Give life to all your male servants. Give life to all your female servants too. Grant abundant life and prosperity so that we continue to serve you."[40] Dagbe (salvation) does not proceed directly from the Supreme Being. African theology is familial-oriented and those who pass over into the spiritual realm remain an active member of the community. Therefore, the ancestors and divinities are not necessarily subordinate to the Creator. Spiritual entities carry out the work of the Creator and their assistance in such delicate matters does not lessen God's authority. It is also important to point out that within traditional Anlo communities the Creator offers Dagbe to all regardless of their moral status.[41] This openness to all members of the community regardless of their "moral" status is akin to universalistic ideals advocated by New Age gurus who hold similar views. Anlo communal members can participate in the ritualized communal meal without first passing a moral fitness exam. Communal fellowship is unconditional because "every human being in Anlo thought qualifies to participate in the salvation that God offers to men."[42]

Dagbe is available to every member in the community and each person has the opportunity to accept or reject the communal support and fellowship available to them. Yet, the gatekeepers of their sacred customs are afforded special recognition. For example, during the communal meal where Dagbe is offered a select number in the community share a special beer or blood meal. Only those who are living a life that brings honor to their family and ancestors partake in this special offering. The communal members deemed worthy to participate in this ritual meal receive a special blessing.[43] Those members who have not fully embraced the traditions only receive a portion of Dagbe commensurate with their level of commitment. Their prosperity or lack thereof demonstrates the presence or absence of Dagbe in their lives. One who "enjoys good health and immeasurable success in all endeavors right through life and eventually ends in ripe old age ... provides proof [of] participation in Dagbe."[44]

There are indeed other factors that determine one's life fortunes. For example, one's personal destiny is preordained and certain ills or bad luck may be part of their *Chi* or *Ori*. Ultimately, the divinities are responsible for assisting human beings in fulfilling their life-mission. If one is not in good relations with the orisha they can expect to experience many mishaps throughout their lives. Those who fail to complete their life-assignment in this life are expected to reincarnate until they complete their life mission. Ills connected to one's destiny must not be allowed to prevent one from fulfilling their life-mission. Even though the assignment may continue into several lifetimes human destiny remains in the hands of the divinities. These helper-spirits are appointed by the Creator to assist human beings, and they are also responsible for controlling certain aspects of nature.

One's destiny cannot easily be altered since it is not entirely under human control. The traditional Anlo word "dzitsinya" implies that one's destiny or conscience is sealed at birth. Dzitsinya is the life force received from God at birth, and this force serves as one's inner guide. Dzitsinya is related to Chi among the Fon and Ori in Yoruba culture. These ideals are also connected with the traditional African belief in predestination. Westerners have had many historical debates over the theological role of predestination from the time of John Calvin. These debates continues within many Christian funda-mentalist circles over whether one can lose their salvation. Gaba recorded several prayers uttered by the Anlo that seems to suggest that salvation is not certain. There is no guarantee that one will be "saved" or delivered from their enemies. "May the wicked people perish in twos and threes.... Those who may scheme that [your] children and grandchildren should not live, may they become the victims of their own machinations and perish in large numbers.... Should anyone undermine him that he should fail in his employment, may that person utterly fail in any venture."[45]

These prayers suggest that evil threatens one's Dagbe, but that there are rituals that are performed to combat those antilife forces. Salvation in traditional African theology suggest that human beings must be given every opportunity to live a full life by overcoming the obstacles that threaten human freedom. In traditional Anlo communities the *nuxe* (prevent-pay sacrifice) is used to restore one's communal standing and provides them access to Dagbe. "The belief in the efficacy of sacrifice to assuage the wrath of spiritual beings and to afford peace to the human race is so strong that provision is made in the traditional religion to avert every misfortune, including sickness, barrenness, famine, flood, war and unemployment."[46] One must be conscious of offenses before presenting their offering because "sacrifices are made to gods and ancestors in time of peace to prevent disaster in the community, and in time of outbreaks of disaster to purify the community of any epidemics or calamities."[47] Sacrifices serve a twofold purpose: First, they avert calamity and secondly, to maintain and restore communal harmony. Once an offender confesses their faults before a priest or elder the sacrificial rituals can begin.

For example, "every year brings me the same round of misfortunes.... [I] consulted the diviners and I was advised to perform some rites. For the rites I must obtain cowries ... the basic fruits of the earth ... white clay ... gin ... chicken ... soft drink.... As I present myself before you, Vizaze, all the misfortunes that are after me, grant that they leave me alone.[48] A ritual is recited after the confession: I wipe away death ... sickness ... poverty ... trouble ... indeed all manner of misfortunes from the person of me, Naki. May the days of my life here be long and full of prosperity and peace. May my earthly life reach its natural evening safely."[49]

Apart from confessing one's faults to restore communal relations with the offended deity there are countless Anlo rituals that utilize sacrificial animals. "As long as one offers the head of an animal, one's head can no longer be claimed. Today I have offered the head of a chicken in exchange for her head. Henceforth her head is fully her own."[50] Such is the logic behind the common practice of sacrifice within TACF. Sacrifices are offered to the tutelary deity of the sacrificer and to other spirits good and indifferent.[51] A successful sacrifice will appease good spirits and force the bad ones to select another victim.[52] At the conclusion of the ritual a portion of the sacrificial meal is eaten with the community, signifying that the offender has been received back into the fold as a member of society. Sacrifice is at the heart of most African traditional religio-cultures and is the most important practice within Anlo society. The role of sacrifice is also an important feature in the Christian scripture, implying that human effort is not sufficient to assuage guilt. Prayer alone is insufficient to provide the community with the power to attain freedom. Spiritual requests must be accompanied by sacrifice to secure freedom and deliverance from oppressive spirits.[53] Salvation is deliverance from material lack and physical ills. Sacrifice has its origins in cultural myths, which are premised on the idea that human beings should live a life free of physical and spiritual oppression.

Myth enshroud the philosophy from which a people develop the norms and mores that govern their society. It is from these cultural myths that a people develop the lens by which they view themselves and the world. Myths serve as a medium and are a "language of expressing truths or realities for which history does not supply a full explanation."[54] They are the building blocks that comprise the foundation from which traditional customs and norms are derived. In this regard, students of TACF corroborate the Durkheimian idea, which advocates that the sacred and social are closely integrated.[55] This is especially true for African traditional religion because in traditional communities there is no separation between the sacred and profane. The foundation of traditional communities have their origin in myths, which existed "*before* a system of beliefs, which coming *afterwards*, justifies this prior level of reality."[56]

African traditional myths are more than simple conjectures or feelings of nostalgia glorifying one's historical past. Luc de Heusch maintains that myths are made from things that are real. "I take [myth] to be a significant component of social reality, the way a society talks about itself not in order to justify the existing order but in order to constitute its own empirical reality through an original language."[57] Communal norms are grounded within cultural myths that one taps to constructs their worldview. Myths form the foundation of every society and are voiced "through a genealogy, sacred texts, or ancestors."[58] Genealogical mythoform are very important for understanding the formation of one's cultural values and making sense of history. Myths are laced with principles that connect each generation to the present and future. Myths of genealogies are vital for maintaining cultural identity.

For instance, the Dogon's myths of origin are connected to four ancestors who came down from heaven and established their society. The four ancestors were begotten by an androgynous being that descended from heaven carrying a fish inside itself, which was the egg that gave life to all humanity.[59] God sacrificed this being by cutting its body into four sections, which represents the four major Dogon families.

> The myth is the ultimate referent of a social and religious order. Its fundamental principles are found throughout much of West Africa. It is a genuine charter of international relations in the upper Niger River valley where it defines relationships among different cultural and linguistic groups.[60]

Myths as the "ultimate referents" governed traditional communities throughout Africa prior to Arab and European expansionist pogroms. Traditional myths housed their cultural norms that were fundamental for providing Africans with a stable society. However, myths have not completely disappeared but continue to function in the modern world. Western society has its origins in myths from which there most cherished ideals are derived. Myths governing the Western world have their origin in the Abrahamic religions. For example, the myths of the ancient Hebrews gave birth to Judaism, which gave birth to Christianity. (Some would argue that Islam is a composite of the latter faiths.) All three are considered Western religions or Abrahamic faiths because each accepts Abraham as important to the founding of their religion. The Jewish, Christian, and Islamic religions provided Western society with its mythical foundation. "This [Abrahamic] myth was the referent of a social order wherein three parties [warrior aristocrats, priests and commoners] recognized the authority of kings by divine right."[61]

The Protestant Reformation challenged certain aspect of these myths, which guided Western thought for nearly three thousand years. The reformation ushered in a new interpretation of these myths and Protestantism challenged the old myths much like Socrates confronted the Greeks blind allegiance to the old myths that governed Greek thought. The Protestant Reformation was partly an attack upon these ancient myths challenging Roman Catholicism and attempting to make it reinterpret its myths of origin. "Protestantism made this order [old myths] quake down to its very foundations."[62]

Max Weber also argued that Euro-Christian Protestantism and its myths are the foundation of modernity and in particular gave birth to capitalism. "Profits were not generated by capital in compliance with a fundamentally economic logic," writes Heusch. "They were produced through a reinterpretation of the myth that constituted the ultimate reality of this civilization. Profits arose out of this myth just as the dog and the pig sprang out of the Obukula ravine on a faraway Melanesian island in order to give people other reasons for living together—a reason such as exchanging seashells."[63]

African myths are held together by symbols rooted in divine kingship. Divine kingship mythology undergirded traditional norms that maintained social order throughout Africa. For example, "in the traditional society the king was not only the head of the government but also the living representative of the kingdom, the chain binding the past to the future and the living to the dead.... On his health and on his good fortune often depended the vitality and fortune of the country; also in many tribes regicide was not uncommon, either when the king became powerless or when he was impotent. This deed had the character of a religious sacrifice and had to be carried out according to the rites."[64]

The political structure in traditional Africa was likewise founded on myth. "In African thought the exercise of power was part of the religious universe, and something of that mentality has survived to the present."[65] The traditional political system was established in accordance with certain myth, particularly the wandering hunter mythoform.[66] An indigenous community provided the hunter shelter in exchange for game. This narrative gave rise to the deification of kings and the authority given to them throughout traditional communities is derived from this myth. The wandering hunter mythology gave rise to such thoughts that permeate traditional African logic. The most meaningful ideals are expressed in symbols, which serve as existential reference points, that causes one to reflect upon that which speaks beyond language.

Christopher Ejizu asserts that symbols are the "keystone of African traditional religion and life."[67] The symbol represents that which cannot be seen or expressed with language. Symbols speak to the depths of humanity's yearning to communicate with forces outside the physical realm. Human beings yearn to communicate with that which cannot be named or described. Traditional culture is enmeshed within symbols that attempt to address the need for humans to see beyond the veil. "The traditional African mind perceives the universe as a forest of symbols," writes Ejizu. "In which the sacred is believed to pervade and manifest itself in and throughout all of nature, animate and inanimate."[68] The symbol illuminates the mysterious, which hides itself within the mundane. The universe is symbol-driven and likewise traditional Africans believed they could better communicate with deity through symbols. Traditional Africans were to some degree culturally programmed to interpret the world through symbols. Symbols are divine mediums used to communicate the mind of God. Many of these traditional objects may upon first glance appear crude or unsanitary. However, these objects are not cherished for their aesthetic value but are designed to point one in the direction of the sacred. The sacred vessel may appear outlandish but it is anointed and infused with power to liberate the imprisoned mind. Their very appearance is intended to cause a shift in perception. There are two major types of symbols used throughout traditional Africa. The first is purely natural and the second is classified as work objects.[69]

Purely natural symbols includes things such as land, rivers, animals, hills, colors, and numbers. These symbols serve as mediums that reveal the mind of God. For example, the Ibo of Nigeria are noted for their use of natural symbols. They view the earth as a feminine deity and believe that specific spirits inhabit the natural environment. The Niger River, the kola nut, the white clay chalk that the priests place around their eyes, and the palm leaf are natural objects commonly used by practitioners to shift perception. In southern Sudan among the Dinka certain colors and the configurations of cattle serve as signs and messages from the spirit world. Nature is a medium much like the Christian pastor who serves as a vessel of the Holy Spirit. Also, the Congolese who inhabit the tropical forest regions of the Congo venerate trees as sacred symbols and divine mediums.[70] The forest is not simply representative of Deity, but is itself Divine and infused with mystical powers.

The work class symbols used by priests and healers includes objects which are made of natural substances shaped by artists. Clay figures of sacred deities and images of altars belong in this category. Among the Akan of Ghana the ancestral stools and Adinkra cloth are work class symbols *par excellence* of ancestral royalty. "The *Adinkra* cloth symbols [such as] *Gye Nyame*, *Onyamedua* and *Nyame bewu na mawu* express vital attributes of God [omnipotence, supremacy and immortality respectively]."[71]

Rituals are also infused with symbolic meaning and express humanities need to live in harmony with the life forces that comprise the cosmos. Rituals function to "encompass a complex variety of behaviour patterns including verbal forms like prayer, songs, incantation, and other forms of corporal movements like pouring libation, prostration, dancing."[72] The use of rituals varies among the different African cultural groups. Unlike the Abrahamic religions that demand conformity traditional African cultural forms advocate diversity. African unity is expressed not in conformity but by its openness and diversity. "All African people participate in the African Cultural System although it is modified according to specific histories and nations."[73]

Rituals revolve around natural and seasonal events that have their origin in cultural myths. There are life-cycle rituals that are performed throughout one's lifetime. These rituals include initiations, circumcision, and, for some, induction into the priesthood and secret societies. There are also rituals connected to agricultural cycles. "Agriculture itself from many of the cosmological myths is divinely sanctioned and many important crops like yam, grains, and animals are sacred and closely linked to certain invisible beings and powers."[74]

Elaborate rituals are performed to honor the ancestors because, in the traditional worldview, death is not final and does not deny one the honor due throughout life and beyond. The remembering of one's departed ensures that familial bonds are never broken. One's immortality is intimately connected to familial rituals that must be maintained beyond the death of a loved one. Those who fail to honor such traditions not only dishonors the love one, but places the community in jeopardy. "A culture that is in touch with its spiritual connection is a culture that is poised to evolve," writes Somé.[75] Honoring family members in life and beyond the grave allows one to remain connected to their lineage. Traditionalists place a high value on family and the veneration of the ancestors is the highest form of respect given to elders. Ancestors and divinities are historically and culturally connected to certain families. Those families in particular are obligated to feed their ancestors by regularly calling out their names, pouring libations, and praying to them in moments of crisis.

Other important life-cycle rituals are performed at birth. The naming ceremony is extremely important because one's name is intimately connected to their destiny. There is an African proverb which implies that God cannot be mocked or fooled—because God knows your name. Puberty rites are also critical for adolescents and function to help youth transition into adulthood. Observers of TACF are expected to contribute to the well-being of their community by partaking in the sacred rites and rituals that perfect their humanity.

Prayer is also highly ritualized and is directed to the ancestors and divinities. "Prayer is a fundamental aspect of traditional ritual life."[76] Petitions for health and prosperity are a common request. If a deity or ancestor continuously fails to answer one's petition they may be rejected by the practitioner. If a deity "fails to deliver on a request sought in prayer, that deity will be censured, treated with contempt, and ultimately abandoned by the people."[77] The deity in African religion are not abstract or distant, but are a type of family member who is expected to assist their loved ones. In this regard, one of the sole purposes of deity is to assist the devotee in attaining and maintaining their material and physical well-being.

For instance, Kwame Gyekye argued that traditional Africans expect their deity to assist them in their efforts to live an abundant life. Traditional African cultural forms are praxis oriented and, if they fail to be practical and of immediate use they will be discarded. This thinking partly explains why many Africans converted to Islam and Christianity and why some temporarily abandon these faiths in moments of existential crisis and look for immediate answers to their problem in the tradition of their forbearers. African traditional cultural forms operate in the now moment or else they are of little value to those in need of assistance.

The Christian doctrine of redemption serves an important theological purpose, but it is of little or no use to the family that is starving or whose crops have failed due to lack of rain. Deities that cannot respond to the needs of their devotees must be deserted because African religion is praxis-oriented and the devotee expects a positive response to his requests. According to Booth this partly explains why some Africans abandoned their traditional religion to embrace Islam and Christianity. The Abrahamic religions promised to meet all their physical and spiritual needs at a greater level. Segun Ogungbemi wrote that African religion is a practical faith that must yield fruit, otherwise, it will be rejected and exchanged for something more promising. "Religion is employed as a means to legitimize individual and social needs and accomplishments."[78] Ogunbemi contends that religion is perhaps the sole factor that undergirds traditional societies and those who initially rejected TACF in exchange for another people's gods did so because they were offered greater opportunities. He accused Mbiti and other scholars of overemphasizing the role of religion in traditional African society. Instead, he believes that other variables may account for Africans' deep respect for the numinous.

For example, Ogunbemi charges that TACF in Yoruba are much less spiritual and more materialistically oriented than has been recorded. In fact, Ogunbemi argues that in Yoruba culture the orisha who failed to answer the request of their devotees were quickly abandoned.[79] Ogunbemi claims that when Christian colonizers first invaded Yorubaland many Africans abandoned their tradition in exchange for the materialistic culture promised by the Christian colonizers. "The new converts destroyed religious objects of the traditional gods because they [believed] that the Christian God was more powerful and more reliable in meeting their existential needs."[80] Many abandoned their faith for a culture whose religion was premised not on spiritual development but on controlling the material wealth of the world. Christianity certainly had more to offer Africans such as food and new road constructions. This move away from the spiritual into the material has without question become African's greatest sin. Not just in Africa but throughout the New World, materialism has become the new god by which black people prostrate themselves. Wherever black people have abandoned their traditions for Western materialism, one finds an overabundance of greed and chaos within that community. The drive for material wealth causes many to lust for the superficial which has led to the destruction of millions of black men throughout the world. This was not the case in communities where TACF were honored and observed. For instance, Ìdòwú writes that lying and stealing increased with the rise of Islam and Christianity in West Africa.

Again, the traditionalists believed that rituals can heal imbalance in whatever guise it appears. The prayer ritual is the highest form of communication in traditional African societies. It occurs between the petitioners and divinities or ancestors. The ritualization of prayer is the "Quintessential religious activity among traditional Africans. It is the highest form of prayer which involves the articulation of the worshipper's deep sentiments of acknowledgment and submission to God, divinities and ancestral beings, not only through uttering of words in prayer, but more importantly through the consecration and offering of some physical animate and/or inanimate thing or object."[81]

Prayers are directed at divinities and ancestors, especially when they are celebrated at annual festivals and on holy days. Among the Ashanti people of Ghana the priests of Nyame (God) offer animal sacrifices at Nyame's Temple. The may sprinkle the altar with animal blood, which is a custom also practiced by the ancient Hebrews.[82] The use of sacrificial blood was a common practice of the Ewe and Fon, the Igbo of Nigeria, the Dinka of Sudan, and the Gikuyu of Kenya.[83] The use of ritual blood for communing with deity is a well-established practice throughout traditional Africa. Animals, such as goats, dogs, chickens and birds, may be used as sacrifices. In Yorubaland dogs and tortoises were the preferred animals sacrificed to Ogun, the divinity of iron and war.[84]

The rationale for ritual sacrifice is connected to the myths undergirding traditional African cultural forms. The core of African ontology is centered on the ideal that harmony is a sacred force that prevents chaos and disorder. Sickness and misfortunes result when one is in a state of imbalance. This happens when there is a breach in the relationship between the divinities, ancestors, nature, and the existent. The divinities move swiftly to judge those responsible for upsetting the balance that keeps things in their rightful place. When such imbalances occur within the community immediate action is required to prevent or delay judgment. Ritual sacrifices are performed to restore communal equilibrium, which ensures that communal norms are continuously maintained.

Sacrifices have their origin in restoring communal and cosmic equilibrium. They serve to attack the evil that is responsible for introducing disorder into the community. Ejizu labeled this type of intervention as "joyless sacrifices." Such sacrificial rituals of restoration may involve casting out evil spirits and other forces intent on causing harm and creating disasters. The joyless sacrifice "drives away the attacking spiritual being and thereby liberates the afflicted person, object, thing, place, as well as restore the disbalanced cosmic equilibrium."[85] Traditional society relied upon such sacrifices as a means to prevent physical and natural catastrophes. Africans believed deeply in the efficacy of sacrifice and were convinced that good forces can be approached and called upon to assist them in times of crisis. These forces were expected to restore, repair, and maintain the harmony needed for good health, prosperity, and divine protection.

Modernity has challenged traditional African thought and the destabilization of TACF have proven to have a devastating effect on black people throughout the world. The assault from Islam and Christianity challenged the cultural myths, which formed the foundations of traditional ways of being. Students of African religion have argued that these outside attacks have negatively affected Africans on the continent and beyond. While a few of the non–African cultural groups appear to have benefited materialistically from colonialism, in many ways Africa has remained stagnated, and has actually regressed, especially since the rise of Western hegemony. This unholy aggression has crippled what remained of the traditions that governed African ways of being for thousands of years. The continent has been systematically bombarded with a barrage of attacks, which challenged the traditions that were already imprisoned by Arab-Islamic and Euro-Christian expansionist pogroms.

Ejizu maintains that Christianity and Islam have been powerful forces responsible for destabilizing traditional African cultural forms, which has forced many to adapt to changes they were not prepared to experience. "Missionary religions [Islam and Christianity] have systematically been pursuing policies and strategies that successfully win over hundreds of millions of traditional Africans to their respective faiths."[86] These alien hostile faiths that millions of Africans now pay homage destabilized traditional cultural ways of being and left many in a state of confusion. As a result of the military strategies used by Arabs and Europeans to destroy TACF Africans are betwixt between two worlds. Many have lost their way and are uncomfortably finding their identities in the Abrahamic paradigms much like a lad trying to wear military amour designed for a man. The old gods and spiritual beings have been forgotten and replaced by another people's gods that are foreign and even hostile to African thought. Traditional African cultural forms were challenged by these foreign faiths in much the same way Socrates confronted Greek thought with his introduction of rationalism. The intrusion into Africa by Christians and Arabs likewise forced many to reject the old paths in exchange for a lifestyle at war with African ways of being.

Christianity and Islam have especially challenged those who once whole-heartedly accepted their traditions. Ejizu declares, "The traditional divinities and spiritual beings that formerly undergirded different aspects of life and ensured social order and cohesion have been routed. Their images and symbols have tumbled and their ritual fallen into disuse."[87] These foreign incursions into Africa also impacted the invaders, especially their myths of origin and racial dominance. Modernity continues to challenge the Abrahamic religions and the arrogance by which they place their perspective above all others. Since they have no equal to contest their dominant discourse they have turned inward and are fighting themselves. (Judaism against the Arab Palestinians Muslims and Christians against Muslims worldwide.)

Change is inevitable and we should not be surprised when it happens. However, it is usually gradual and at times imperceptible, but in Africa it was thrust upon them. Africa was hijacked by outside religious and cultural fanatics who were intent upon forcing their worldview down the throats of the "heathens." At least in the ancient Greek world the people had an opportunity to reject the sudden changes of which Socrates and others attempted to force upon them. Socrates was put to death for attempting to force radical changes upon the Greeks by challenging the traditionalist perspective from which they derived their worldview. Africans had no such defenders and those who did stand up to protect TACF were deemed a criminal and put to death. There were no laws or international courts to defend those who wanted to maintain traditional ways of being. Those courageous enough to confront the intruders were put to death with such brutality to serve as an example for those who defy the Western perspective of which they were expected to imbibe. As a result of their helplessness Africans were in many ways forced to accept Islamic and Christian ideologies, which resulted in the near-destruction of their sacred traditions.

The Western governments were the glue that held the unholy trio of Islam, Christianity, and Colonialism together. Although economics may have been the driving force behind the Europeans invasion into Africa, their presence served to destabilize African traditional norms and values. The colonial militia accompanied with their missionaries labeled Africans and TACF as "pagan." TACF and the people who venerated their sacred tradition were perceived as an evil that should be eliminated. The colonizers (today the colonizers would be viewed as terrorists) viewed African culture as "barbarous" and a threat to European expansion.[88] Many missionaries advocated that their God mandated them to dismantle African religion and culture. They could not stand to see these "pagans" live in a world of "darkness," especially without experiencing the joy that comes from serving Jesus. The more vigorously missionaries fought to dismantle African traditional culture the more their work was viewed positively by the faithful and correlated with their love of God.

Many similar strategies were used by the missionaries to bring the "savages" into the knowledge of the one true God. The missionary was not content with the pagans simply knowing God in the general sense of the word. The God Africans were taught to know and worship was created in the white man's image. He alone could civilize the African and thus, Africans were programmed to seek this god to heal their ills and give them joy. In those places where Christians could not reach the pagans, the Arabs and their god were there to complete this holy work. The missionary was obligated by their god to Christianize Africans. Ejizu claims that the first group of missionaries in West Africa were primarily responsible for dismantling traditional customs. Thus making it easier for those who followed them to convert the pagans. "Intermittent waves of iconoclasm by missionary agents and converts led to the destruction of sizeable numbers of many traditional religious symbols, sacred places like shrines, sacred groves, images of divinities and other ritual artifacts."[89] With a strategy so effective and systematic, Christian missionaries were assured of their success and labor. When Africans abandoned their "idols" and confessed faith in the Christian God the missionary could rest assuredly knowing their work was not in vain.[90]

Yet, throughout the many onslaughts and attacks from those intent upon destroying African ways of being, there remained a faithful remnant who continued to honor the religion of their ancestors. How could they abandon the religion of their ancestors who were responsible for their existence? There is such a deep respect for family and history that practitioners of traditional religion instituted elaborate rituals that served to defy death. Honoring the lives of men and women who lived exceptional lives is an African religio-cultural obligation, akin to what Westerners associate with worshipping God. Paul John Isaak of the University of Namibia maintains that "evoking the authority of the past gives bedrock support to current political and religious actions. It also allows for a period when social relationships are affirmed, reconciliation is encouraged and the solidarity of the community is expressed."[91]

Memorial rituals confirm the traditionalists' love of their people and culture. These sacred acts of memory are indicative of a people that reverence family and believe the maintenance of such relationships are essential for maintaining communal stability. When one forgets or neglects their cultural heritage a communal rupture occurs that is not easily repaired. Whenever the community becomes fractured, traditional rituals must be enacted to correct the chaos, which results from forgetting one's past. Remembering ones cultural history and venerating those who sacrificed themselves to keep alive Africa's sacred heritage is a sacred honor that must not be forgotten. Even those Africans who have embraced Christianity and Islam must not forget to venerate their ancestors much the same as the Arab and European honor their gatekeepers. Honoring those who struggled to keep African traditions alive "marks one of the recognized milestones in a person's journey in life and as one passes from one stage to another, each stage is celebrated with special rituals. Hence, rituals have come to be known as rites of passage."[92]

Rituals of remembrance are perhaps one of the most important acts observed by practitioners of TACF. For instance, the funeralization of one who passes into to the spiritual realm is the crowning event of their life journey. This sacred act must be performed with the utmost respect and precision. Those passing on are now entering the realm where they become familial spirits, which one can now access and consult in time of need. Those who die a good death are expected to become ancestors and accompany the divinities in the spirit world. In many respects death is the culmination of human evolution which begins at birth. Physical death marks the moment a person reaches the end of one of many journeys. Death is the culmination of one's life-lessons and the celebration of one's physical existence. It is the ultimate celebration given to those who are transitioning from one form to another. Death does not mark the end of one's familial obligations. To the contrary, it actually marks the beginning of a new stage of growth and development, which takes place in the spiritual realm. Death is not final because the traditionalists hold that we are eternal beings made of energy who have no beginning or ending. Those who lived uprightly by honoring their ancestors and cultural heritage can now work directly on behalf of their family. They are more effective now because they dwell in the spirit realm where they are not limited as in the physical. Death is the most sacred of all rites because it is the gateway to the afterlife and the place where one achieves the status of ancestor. Those who lived a good life are finally "saved" when they enter the spiritual realm where they are once again beckoned to commune with the ancestors.

Wherever TACF are venerated death is not something one fears. "The death of a person does not gradually slide him or her into oblivion, a vague region or a hell; instead, such a living-dead being creates an occasion for history."[93] There are at least two types of tradition identified by traditionalists. A good death allows one to continue their evolution in the spirit realm, which is their place of origin. In this realm they have the power to assist their loved ones as they complete their earthly mission. They will not interfere with the life-lessons that their loved ones must experience. They work as guides to assist them as they carry out their assignment. Those who died a bad death will not have the opportunity to evolve in the spirit realm until they repair the imbalances that occurred in their lives during their time on earth.[94]

In the case of those dying a bad death attention and care were not given to the burial or body of those who failed to honor traditional ways of being. In the days of old those who died a bad death could not be buried at local grave sites. The death rituals assisted traditional Africans in celebrating the end of one's life. Death was something to embrace and not the enemy spoken of in the Christian scripture. Death "rituals are not superstitions and irrational actions but were premised on how traditional people regarded "funerary rites as absolutely realistic to their situation."[95] Although death was not perceived as a hostile intruder, still it created disorder. "Death seems to be an intruder into the intended pattern of things," writes Awolalu. "It is the cutting off of the vitality of one's existence. It is the supreme and final crisis of life which is of great concern to almost all thinking human beings."[96]

Unlike the traditional concept of death Awolalu's analysis of TACF are unfortunately at times evaluated through the lens used by Christian theologians. Christianity in general does not view death as the culmination of life activities, but as an enemy that brings an end to one's familial relationships. Awolalu further suggested that in Yoruba tradition that they too viewed death similar to that of white Christians. For example, Socrates maintained that human beings consist of an immaterial substance that survived physical death. Awolalu argued that Yoruba hold a similar view without acknowledging that this perspective was introduced by African Egyptians nearly four thousand years before Homer produced the Iliad. It has commonly been accepted throughout African traditional communities that there is an immaterial substance that exists in every human being. This substance or divine energy choses a body as a vessel in which to enter the world. In Yoruba tradition Olódùmarè would seal one's destiny before birth. Human beings are therefore preordained and come to earth to carry out a particular mission.

For example, the traditional Yoruba advanced the notion that "whenever a soul is to incarnate, it kneels before Olódùmarè, the Creator and states what … it wants to achieve on its mission on earth. Olódùmarè then commissions it; the destiny is sealed, and it becomes unalterable."[97] African Americans also speak of death much like their Yoruba brothers and sisters. Many elderly African Americans speak of death as a vehicle that will carry them home to be with their loved ones. (I often heard my grandmothers and other family members, when death was approaching, say they were ready to go home to see their family members who proceeded them.) The Yoruba use the same language when they speak about death as a vehicle that will carry them home. Death is not an enemy in traditional African thought, but a heavenly bailiff who calls his children to return home. Physical death is but a transition or journey in which one must cross a river to get to the other side. It is on the other side of the river according to many Negro spirituals, where one will find rest for their weary soul. Upon crossing the river that separates the material from the immaterial one enters the place inhabited by the ancestors. After successfully reaching the other side they are dressed in the eternal garments they adorned themselves prior to inhabiting a body.[98]

Education, Culture and Cosmology

Arabism and numerous destabilization strategies contributed to the erosion of African traditional culture and the destruction of education. The need for formal education in Africa during the colonial era and thereafter has been linked to the destruction of TACF. The colonial era marked a time when traditional Africans were forced to send their children away from the village to be educated within an environment which assaulted their humanity. The village which once served as the center for inculcating traditional epistemology was replaced by a system that perceived Africans as less than human. Ejizu argued that although there was a need to provide children with education, the type of education they received presented serious problems that eroded the stability of family life.

For instance, certain rituals and familial cult obligations were abandoned and could not be maintained while the children were away from the village. "The duration of many initiation ceremonies and traditional rites like marriage, title-taking and funeral are being modified in many societies to accommodate the long periods which the youth spend in school and many other different circumstances of present-day life…. Traditional divinities, their agents, symbols and rituals, have greatly been displaced by civil courts and law enforcement agents as instruments of social control in most African societies."[99]

Although Africa has been under assault since Alexander in 332 BCE, and again in the 7th century CE beginning with the Arab invasions, Ejizu remains optimistic about TACF ability to survive and reinstitute those traditions that were destroyed. Even though many rituals and symbols that once governed traditional communities have changed or fallen into disuse, many TACF have been reinterpreted, especially by those enslaved and brought to the Americas. Throughout the New World TACF continue to flourish even within a hostile environment. The symbols that comprise the core of traditional religion have not been completed destroyed or erased from cultural memory. The values that held African traditional culture together are undergoing a metamorphosis much the same way as they were forced to undergo in Cuba, Trinidad, Jamaica, Brazil, and throughout the black Atlantic world. Africans have learned how to adapt to an ever-changing world, especially under hostile conditions. Still, Africans will have to work much harder to regain those sacred elements which were partially destroyed with the Arab invasion and throughout the colonial era. What remained of Africa's sacred cultural traditions were either lost or misinterpreted by white scholars and missionaries. This effort to misconstrue TACF is a part of the ongoing psychological warfare against black people throughout the world.

For example, Diop argued that white scholars deliberately obliterated the historical record of African people's contribution to world civilization. Diop maintained that restoration of the historical record would only happen when African scholars reconnect Egypt to Africa. He further surmised that it was impossible to understand traditional African cultural forms without possessing an understanding of their origin, which began along the Nile River and reached their apex in Egypt. Therefore, Egypt cannot be left in the hands of Europeans or Arabs because neither had anything to do with its creation. Africans contributions to world history will remain obscured and incomplete without Egypt. "One cannot make any approach to an intimate knowledge of African religious systems except by a cordial appreciation of their philosophy, because these systems which have so long remained hidden even from the most perceptive research workers, possess a logic and are more elaborate and coherent than is generally supposed."[100]

Some Western scholars have argued that even African philosophy is a product of Europe. A few have argued that African philosophy is simply a critique of European philosophy. If this is correct one cannot expect to find anything of value from that which is currently presented as African philosophy. What passes for African philosophy is in reality European regurgitations of African ideas. The African Catholic bishops addressed a similar issue by positing the following: "Can it be said that there exists in the traditional societies a philosophy, in the Greek sense of the term, that is, a striving after wisdom? Rather let us say that this Wisdom exists. It is there. The old man in the solitude of his cabin, the Council of Elders under the palaver tree, the Master of Initiates in the sacred grove of the circumcised, these are not seeking wisdom. They possess it already, and their anxiety is to impart it to the young generations, just as they have received it from those that went before them."[101]

Many post enlightenment European philosophers once held that African philosophy is a misnomer. They assumed that Philosophy by its very nature is Greek and Africans that are a communal people could not possess philosophy. How could they have philosophers when philosophy arises from individuals and not from groups? The notion that philosophy is the result of an individual and not communal serves as an attack upon those places where the community is the life center. Traditional African societies were communal-centric because the individual had no meaningful existence outside of the community. "Knowledge," says the proverb of Popo of Benin, "is the trunk of a baobab tree that no human can span."[102] The ideals that enshrine a people's way of being are never in the hands of one person alone. Even though knowledge is the product of the community, there are unique roles served by the individual.

For instance, each person comes into the world with a special gift that they share with the community from which they receive their power. One of the primary presuppositions of African philosophy is "the dynamism of being—'*Ntuisme*.'"[103] This implies that human beings are equipped with the affective skill to ponder those life issues that are of existential import. "What we think important is our attitude to life."[104] The ability to reason and find meaning in the world is a skill available to every human being. "[E]very being possesses a vital dynamism as well as properties which can be possessed by those who have knowledge and power. Magic, which is an attempt to capture those dynamisms and properties, fits in with the logic of this presupposition."[105]

Another presupposition undergirding African ontology is the traditional practitioners view of harmony as the energy that envelopes cultural values. The traditional African holds that there is a direct relationship between cosmic harmony and individual misfortunes. "One of the bases on which the African mode of life rests is 'participation' or the profound communion with the universe."[106] It is perhaps important to point out that this relationship is based on "communion" with the universe not worship of the universe. Although some do indeed view Mother Earth as an entity worthy of veneration. Still, maintaining cosmic harmony with all things in existence is the *modus operandi* of African traditional religion. Harmony among human beings, animals, nature, and the divinities is vital for maintaining peace in life. Imbalance is a disorder or "sin" that must immediately be dealt with. If not chaos will pursue those who are out of alignment with the forces of life.

The Abrahamic focus on what constitutes "imbalance" or transgression places more emphasizes on moral offenses. The Abrahamic paradigm is focused on the individual trespassing against each other more than one's relationship with all life forces. The only time when they extend their perspective to view the cosmos as an entity is when they are seeking ways to harness or even destroy it. "The westerner's major project is that of liberating and transforming the world, even though he has not yet obtained the technical means of doing so. On the other hand, African traditionalists focused on how to live a life in harmony with humanity and with nature. While firmly preserving a certain type of individualism, the traditionalists does not easily detach himself from his close ties to nature. For him the first evil is disintegration. The good thing is integration and participation."[107]

Practitioners of traditional African cultural forms do not view themselves at odds with the natural world. Nor do they struggle to tame or dominate the environment because human beings are an integral part of nature. Traditional Africans have never viewed themselves as being at war with nature, but instead seek to become one with it. Those who are disconnected from nature are in essence at war with themselves. Those who pollute the environment for material gain are waging a senseless war against themselves. Nature will expel them from the earth before they are successful at destroying Mother Earth. Traditional Africans view themselves as earth-entities continuously seeking balance with all things, especially fellow human beings. "Man [Traditional Africans] sees himself in harmony *with* man, with those who are living, just as with those who have departed."[108] This sense of unity with all things extends to animated and inanimate beings. Both animals and minerals are endowed with the Life-Force that animates all things in the physical and nonphysical realms. Practitioners of TACF view their relationship with the physical world as part of the eternal cycle of life. Not even physical death has the power to separate one from those who pass on into the nonphysical realm. Death does not have the power to sever familial ties in traditional African families. One does not fully cease to exist until their family no longer remembers their name. Only then, when they are no longer honored by their descendants is the "process of dying ... completed."[109] After the living-dead are forgotten they enter the realm of collective immortality. "This is the state of the spirits who are no longer formal members of the human family," writes Mbiti. "The departed in this state become members of the family or community of the spirits, and if they appear to human beings they are not recognized by name and may cause dread and fear."[110]

Familial power and cultural values are the hallmark of traditional ways of being, which is why the ancestors serve a vital role in maintaining communal and personal harmony. African traditional theology is rhythmic, forever seeking balance so that human beings can share in all of life's abundance and joy. For example, "African ontology is basically anthropocentric: man is at the very centre of existence, and African peoples see everything else in its relation to this central position of man."[111] Human beings are the focal of the TACF, which is the medium responsible for maintaining the delicate balance between humans, divinities, ancestors, and nature. Any breach in this relationship can cause problems that may threaten all of humanity. For instance, uncommon natural catastrophes or phenomena that threaten cosmic balance, including "[u]nusual events … which do not fit into this rhythm, such as an eclipse, drought, the birth of twins and the like, are generally thought to be bad omens…. The abnormal or unusual is an invasion of the ontological harmony."[112]

The aim of traditional theology seeks to maintain balance with all life forces, especially between human and nonhuman entities. Traditional African narratives are replete with stories of how certain families are associated with specific animals, plants, rivers, and mountains. It was taboo (a sin) to kill certain animals or cut down sacred trees, which the people believed were endowed with the same life force as human beings. Various trees and plants were venerated and served a vital role in maintaining the ontological balance needed to prevent communal disasters.

For instance, Somé argued that among the Dagara of Burkina Faso, certain trees and animals serve as mediums of communication between the unseen world and the visible realm. Trees were not simply viewed as a source of creature comfort to be cut down, but were revelatory vehicles that the Vital Force used to communicate to human beings. Trees and animals share in the sacred breath that sustains all living things and to destroy them for profit has created an imbalance between the visible and invisible sphere.

The earth is also a sacred entity and is the temporary home of human beings. Some venerated it as a god with a living soul. The selling and commodification of Mother Earth is antithetical to traditional African ways of being. Minerals and lakes, rivers, mountains and oceans, are sacred revelatory mediums that spirits use to communicate to human beings.[113] One cannot be at war with nature without experiencing chaos from within. A theological perspective that fails to view nature as a sacred entity will partly be responsible for creating a society at war with Mother Earth. TACF are premised on the notion that human beings are not simply a part of nature, but are infused with the same energy that emanates the cosmos. The traditional African perspective is one that "makes man look at God and nature from the point of his relationship with them."[114]

African Symbols and Word Power

The symbol is a presuppositional element that functions within African ontology. In the processus of the *mens Africana* the image tends towards its own realization. Because it is a signifier it calls it forth it tends to produce it. The term "imaginal" has been coined to describe this faculty of intuitive cognition, expression, and action at a distance.[115] One scholar remarked that the African mind appears naturally governed by symbols. In the emergence of an image or of a representation there is already an intervention into life. The pregnant woman who sees the marks of a rope on the ground will make an instinctive detour to avoid this image, which evokes a possible danger to the child she is carrying within her, strangulation from a distance by a "magic tail."[116] In traditional African thought there exists a direct relationship between language and image.

African languages are full of imagery and the word is close to the reality which it expresses. The verb often reproduces the substantive merely by the addition of prefixes or suffixes. In this way one obtains expressions rich in concrete terms which are much used by the storytellers and poets.[117]

Like the image, it carries within itself the dynamism of its own realisation. What people call the "Magic of the Word" is manifested in the case of those "Bearers of the Word" who are the "griots" in some hierarchized societies. In fact in East Africa among the Chamite Bantus, it is a mark of honor to call a person a *mugambi*, a word which means "orator" or more accurately "he who possesses the word" and can use it to express his thoughts with exactness and elegance.[118]

The griot was the man who carried the people's history and expressed it with such exactness that even modern historians would find it difficult emulating such elegance. Upon the death of a griot the body was buried in a sacred baobab tree, which was a sign of respect and fear. "The people are afraid that even after [the griot's] death this word may remain effective and constitute a danger."[119] Only recently in some traditional African communities have griots been buried in common graves. "The [griots'] baobab tree is both their grave and the receptacle of their word."[120] The baobab tree was the symbol used to identify griots who were the philosophers and teachers in traditional Africa.

Sacred symbols were also employed to identify family and villages throughout traditional Africa. For example, Somé discusses how symbols were understood and used for divination and clairvoyance throughout traditional communities. "The universe is seen as a forests of symbols. Visible things and for invisible things, just as masks evoke and make present the ancestral spirits, and mirrors call up the gift of clairvoyance. The Peul shepherd can know of things to come while contemplating his flock. The flock is for him the symbol of the world. In looking at the distribution of his cattle and particularly of the colours, he can interpret a situation and provide people with good advice. A particular kind of colour grouping symbolises a future event. When the elders have difficulty in making a decision they watch the play of the children, who are considered as 'angels' and as interpreters of the spiritual powers."[121]

Human beings can also be used as mediums whose behavior may symbolize a future event. Traditional Africans even viewed the world as a divine medium capable of communicating through virtually any vessel it chooses. Unlike Christianity whose medium of divine law is confined to past events inscribed in the book, every human being is possessed with the ability to become a vessel and emissary of the Vital Force. The traditional African looks everywhere and under every table to hear from the divine because the entire world is a medium of which human beings are the main vessel. "When one begins to understand this particular type of mind [traditional African perspective], what seemed to be mere ignorance or superstition becomes coherent and logical, in the logic of symbolism. This logic can be reduced to three laws: the law of continuity, the law of similitude, the law of contrast."[122]

Unfortunately, this particular schematic does not directly emerge from traditional African thought, but was first articulated by David Hume. P'Bitek argues against using non–African paradigms to explain African phenomena. The African religious worldview is (was) shaped primarily from its cultural cosmology. It is African myths that gave birth to African thought, which is not dependent upon European constructs. African creation myths are rich and remain untapped sources that can be used to express African thought. African cosmologies remain untapped because African scholars have generally ignored the redeeming values of their myths and have instead spent most of their academic life explicating Abrahamic myths. Although there is a need for an inquiry into the Abrahamic religions by Jews, Europeans, and Arabs, unfortunately, this paradigm has been the exclusive focus of academic investigation. Meanwhile, African cosmology is largely ignored and whenever it is investigated it is usually conducted by those whose primary aim is to show that TACF are incomplete by themselves and have their fulfillment in the Abrahamic faiths. "The principle [sic] intuitions of African thought on the origin and the meaning of life are expressed in a manner which is reflected in the cosmological myths, which furnish to the religious conscience the bases of an interior construction and of its dynamism.... It is equally probable that these [cosmologies] are exceptional in Africa and that only a very small number of races have developed and transmitted them."[123]

The human being is at the center of inquiry into the nature of existence and must serve as the departure point when conducting any serious research into the origin of African religion. "The only [theology] that interests the man of Africa is an anthropocentric one."[124] In general, African theology's primary focus is on humanity and their estrangement from the spirit world. The theme of African cosmology focuses on a mythical world where rituals of restoration are employed to make things right. Something happened that disrupted communal stability and imbalance between the forces of life entered the world. Imbalance is perhaps the best traditional African definition of what Western theology describes as sin. After disharmony entered the world, creating an imbalance between the forces throughout the cosmos, Africans became engaged in a struggle to maintain balance between these forces, which was necessary for good health and prosperity. The maintenance of communal and cosmic harmony is the hallmark of African traditional religion. Such ideals are influenced by myth and are infused within symbols. Again, symbols and rituals function to transmit values aimed at maintaining communal balance. "Sacred symbols and rituals are the keystone of African traditional religion and life. They are major points of contact with the holy and the principal means by which Africans communicate their experience of the world and reality as a whole."[125] The traditional African interprets reality through "a 'forest of symbols.'"[126] The symbol functions to provide ideological stimulation to "illuminate the sacred."[127]

African traditional cultural forms are very much alive but remain unilluminated to those imprisoned to Western logic. Some students of African traditional culture continue to compare and/or contrast African cultural forms with those of the Abrahamic faiths. For instance, E. D. Adelowo attempted to prove in a comparative study of Yoruba and Abrahamic religions that African creation stories share an affinity with Western stories of origin. This may indeed be true, but it is not the reason why such comparisons are made. In most cases Africans and well-intending white students of African culture make such comparisons to show that Africans may be capable of abstract thought.

For example, Adelowo begins his study of TACF by analyzing the Hebrew creation myth, which holds Yahweh to be the creator of all things on earth. Adelowo maintains that Yoruba make a similar claim as their Western counterparts in that they also describe Olorun as creator, the king who adorns himself with the "skyey-heaven."[128] Olorun refers to one who is creator and owner of the sky.[129] Adelowo points out that contrary to once popular opinion, African people do have a monotheistic view of God like the superior Western beliefs that push the one god theory, much like a dope pusher sells drugs.

However, as a theologian committed to advancing Western hegemony, Adelowo wrote many articles simply to prove that the traditional African concept of a Supreme Being is not unlike the Abrahamic's view. Adelowo argued that neither the Yoruba nor the Abrahamic faiths confront the "why" of creation. The most theologians have ventured to address this matter suggest that God conceived of the idea of creation and executed it alone. God's intentions for human life is primarily communicated to human beings through revelation. Adelowo should have questioned whose interpretation of revelation God discloses God-self. Revelation in traditional religion does not confine itself to a specific medium because all things can serve as a vessel bearing a messages from the divine. All of nature can function as mediums and modes of revelation. Anything can be a vessel of God's power. The Abrahamic paradigm that is the foundation of Western hegemony, which attempts to dominate sacred discourse, is not the only narrative that one can choose to govern their perspective.

For example, Yoruba creation myth maintain that sixteen men were led by Orèlúeré to populate the earth. They entered through the holy city in Yorubaland Ile-Ifè. While the sixteen were on earth, Òrisànlá was given the charge by Olódùmarè to form human beings out of clay. Olódùmarè supplied the Vital Force or breath that gives life.[130] The Akan of Ghana also have creation narratives that purport to explain the origin of their existence and culture.[131] One myth purports that the leaders of a specific ethnic group entered the earth-realm through holes in the ground. The forebears of the Akan cultural group are believed to have entered through holes in the earth near Nkoranza in an area surrounded by sacred groves.[132] The myth maintains that an earthworm bore a hole in the earth to make a path for the ancestors to travel, which represent the seven families who populated the earth. The worm was followed by "seven men and several women, a leopard and a dog."[133]

There are many similar myths throughout Africa that explain the origin of existence. Some of them claim that human beings emerged from water; others, from trees. There are myths of origin that support the theory that human life has it origin in God.[134] The important thing to understand about these myths is that they are similar and that they attempt to speak to a common cultural curiosity. They depict Africans as a communal people who have their origins in an African culture. Thus, honoring one's cultural heritage is the central message that undergirds every African creation myth.

Unlike traditional African societies that place human beings at the center of creation, modern science advances the theory that all creatures are made from the same substance. A few TACF oppose such thinking and holds that human beings are made of a substance quite separate from that of animals.[135] In the Yoruba tradition to refer to someone as an animal (*eranko*) is the ultimate insult. For one to speak of a human being as akin to an animal is an offense that few traditional Africans would commit. Traditional society holds that human beings are part material and partly immaterial.[136] The material encompasses one's biological nature, while the immaterial constitutes their spiritual nature. The head is the most important part of the physical body because it is the first member exposed to light. Therefore, in several African traditions one's head symbolizes their essential nature and is the locus of one's personality—soul.[137]

The heart symbolizes affection and character. A Yoruba proverb states that a strong-hearted person will escape mental traps that overthrow the simple because the mind (heart) is the battlefield where warfare is won or lost. If one cannot win the spiritual battles that first attack the mind-heart they will find it impossible to succeed in life.

Blood is also an important element in African lore and ritual. Awolalu maintains that blood serves a vital role in traditional society which is why it is used in rituals and sacrifices. Many believe that blood has mystical powers to liberate those who violate traditional norms and values. The shedding of blood, much like the eating of the deceased king's heart, transmits power and re-establishes the link used to communicate with forces that inhabit the unseen world.

Life-Force or energy is an important element in African theology. It encompasses the spiritual forces that comprise the immaterial part of human beings. This energy is called by many names throughout traditional African communities. Some call it èmi (Yoruba), *yiegh* (Nuer), or *ava* (Lugbara).[138] This is the energy that Olódùmarè breathed into created beings. It is what Westerners mean when they say the spirit has gone out of a person. This life-force is housed in the soul, which has been described as the "principal of life in man or animal, the spiritual part of man in contrast to the purely physical; the spiritual part of man considered in its moral aspect or in relation to God and His precepts; the whole person or an individual [chiefly an enumeration]."[139]

The life-force is the energy that lives in one's soul and survives physical death. Some African cultural communities distinguish between soul and breath. The Lugbara hold that *orindi* (soul) resides in the heart; *ava* (breath) in the lungs.[140] The word "*orindi*" is a correlation of what in the West is called a ghost. The Akan of Ghana speak of the soul (*sunsum*) by distinguishing personality from spirit-soul, 'kra.[141] The 'kra leaves the body upon death and seeks out another body to complete the soul's life mission. The idea that the 'kra seeks a body is commensurate with the popular African belief that one's destiny is chosen before birth. The 'kra initially chooses a body in which to carry out a specific mission and upon completion of its mission, it returns from whence it came. Otherwise, it will seek out another body until its mission is completed. The 'kra leaves the body only at death, but the sunsum is capable of leaving one's body at night while one is dreaming.

The Nuer (Nupe) people refer to the soul as *kuci*, that part of the being that is considered immaterial.[142] Kuci, like the 'kra, is an understructure that survives physical death. It is sometimes seen as an ancestral spirit returning to co-habit a body. Kuci is not available to animals. In Yoruba tradition it is one's inner person, *óri-inú*, that is where the essence of life resides. One's ori is predestined and is akin to Plato's forms, the Akan's 'kra, and the Nuer's kuci. One success or failure in life is attributed to their ori. The Yoruba have numerous sayings that acknowledge the power of one's ori. If one's destiny is preordained for failure one's ori cannot will otherwise. Yet, one can pray and perform the necessary oblations and sacrifices, which will bring them a certain level of happiness despite possessing a bad ori. The ori in Yoruba tradition is also viewed as one's double, which exists in the spirit world. The idea that all people have a double in the spirit world is a common belief throughout traditional Africa.[143]

The Ibos of Nigeria express this same idea with the word "chi." One's chi functions exactly as *ori* in Yoruba tradition. A person's chi is also their double, which is endowed with good or bad characteristics. If someone is constantly experiencing sickness or misfortune the traditionalist believe it is due to possessing a bad chi. One's chi can be appealed to through the use of sacrifices or contacted by priests in the hope of correcting the problems besetting their destiny.

For example, the Akan believe that one's 'kra is predestined much like the Nuer kuci, the Yoruba *ori*, and the Ibo's chi. The notion that human beings are simply replicas of a more perfect form is also a scientific idea expressed in quantum physics. The Yoruba believe that each person is given an ori-destiny from Olódùmarè before coming to earth. It is Olódùmarè who fixes one's destiny. Hence, the Yoruba say, "that which is affixed to one cannot be rectified with medicine."[144] Many cultures in West Africa express the view that children are born with a *bea* (manner) that is fixed. The term "nkrabea" (manner of taking leave) implies that when a child is born, a ghost or spirit leaves the spirit realm and takes residence in the child. This entity expresses its desire to perform a particular mission within the child. "Nkrabea" expresses this concept, which is closely aligned with destiny and fate. A proverb captures this idea: "*Onyame nkrabea nni kwatibea* [What Nyame has destined cannot be evaded, there is no evading fate]."[145] The Mende of Sierra Leone express these same sentiments with the word "nga-Fa" (soul), which they believe comes from Ngewo, destiny or fate. One's *nemi* is incapable of alteration, which is why it is important to seek a vocation that is in agreement with one's destiny.

After exploring the traditional African view of human destiny it appears to some that Africans are fatalistic, since one's fate cannot be altered and is sealed at birth. Even though one's life mission cannot be changed there are ritual provisions designed to appeal to one's ori. Through these means one can at least live a content life. It is also evident from our analysis of destiny within TACF that Africans are communally driven and seek a corporate solution to ills that affect their society. They see themselves as one another's keeper. A Yoruba proverb states, "If a member of one's household is eating poisonous insects and we fail to warn him [to desist] the after-effects of his action would rob neighbours of sleep."[146] The destiny of Africans lies in corporate salvation, which is a concept that has been lost in the modern world. Either the collective will find safety or there will be no permanent refuge for black people anywhere. Africans on the continent and in the diaspora must embrace the African dictum, Man is created for a purpose: namely for the purpose of fellowship. He is not left to the whims of his passions and lusts. His rights and obligations are prescribed, his duties are enjoined and his relations to others are regulated.[147]

African traditional religion and TACF in general function in the lives of millions of black people throughout the world. These cultural forms are codified in numerous rituals and cosmological systems. Embedded within the various African religio-cultural forms is a deep respect for traditional ways of being in the world. It is their view of the numinous that shapes the core of African social structures. "In this dimension, religion establishes a specific relationship between man and God, and the sociocosmic environment…. In its finality the African religion aims at enhancing in the believing man his profound desire of openness to others and to the Divine Absolute. The African man looks towards and tends towards the Supreme Being on whom he sees himself as dependent."[148]

The constant need to maintain a relationship with the Supreme Being or spiritual forces can be witnessed in the lives of black people throughout the world. This relationship was maintained by the day-to-day activities that occurred in traditional villages, where the religious and social sphere collapsed to feed the people's insatiable desire to please benevolent and at times, even hostile spiritual forces. "[An] African's religious practices are traditionally not distinct from his other activities. He makes no difference between his religious practices and, say, his administration of justice or hunting exploits. Whether he is traveling or farming, or tending cattle, or dancing, he is deeply involved in a religious experience."[149]

African religion is a spiritual and physical experience, which is unlike other systems of thought. TACF are not built upon propositions that one discards as though changing garments. Religion, or more correctly spirituality, in Africa is the lifeblood of the people and forms the basis for the philosophy undergirding African thought. African religion is connected to the traditional moral codes by which each member is expected to abide: "The African's religion is the basis of his morality.... There are no religious classes of the type that has come to be almost constitutional to Christianity.... [T]he African learns about his religion through imitation, observation, active participation in religious ceremonies, etc."[150]

Religion permeates every aspect of African existence. Whether one is attending a social gathering or preparing to take a journey, religion serves as the reference and the guide to which one appeals. "Traditional African society remains a culture guided by religious norms: The first thing to realise is the close bond that exists between religion and social life. The African religions impregnate the whole life of the community. They are the beginning and end of everything. Reduced to essentials, their worldview, their vision of the world, is a unifying factor, because it does not imply any clear-cut difference between profane and sacred, between matter and spirit. In its view the living and the dead, the visible cosmos and the invisible world merely constitute one and the same universe, and the antinomies of good and evil, life and death, which spring from antagonisms inherent in existing beings do not vitiate the unity of this world-vision."[151]

The African vision of the universe is premised on a "logical development of a system of thought, differing from Cartesian logic, and having coherence between its constituent elements: dynamism of being, participation and 'Sympathy,' the power of the image and of the Word in symbolism."[152] In traditional thought, there is no line of demarcation separating phenomena into binary categories, such as this or that, in or out, with "us or with the terrorists," and so forth. The separation of phenomena into neat categories that can be manipulated have been used by some governments to justify their propensity for violence. George W. Bush expressed the height of such rhetoric in his remark "You are either for us or against us" with regard to the war on an ideology used by the weak to fight against the strong.

In the African worldview multiple possibilities exhaust the either/or logic which is embedded throughout Western discourse. Traditional thought is non-linear. All ways of thinking are considered and linked to one another. "Social, political and economic organisation is in relationship with the system of beliefs and religious representations. The very techniques, such as those of the smith and the weaver, are linked with religious beliefs and practices."[153]

The social and secular realm is intricately connected to the religio-sacred worldview. One cannot adequately conduct fieldwork in Africa without understanding the relationship between persons, the society, and religion. "Every approach to the native religions requires a very deep knowledge of the social life of the various groups.… [M]any of their myths and rites provide the explanation of certain structures or certain aspects of their social life.… That is why religious beliefs and social structures throw light on each other."[154]

The Roman Catholic Church has used African bishops to conduct studies into the strange relationship between Africans and the religio-cultural forms practiced by their ancestors. The Vatican has directed African bishops to conduct fieldwork into the nature of religion and culture so the Church can acquire a better understanding how best to acculturate and evangelize Africans.[155] The Church has been actively involved in an evangelization campaign throughout the continent, supposedly with the goal of leading Africans to the Christian scriptures. Yet in the past when the colonizers first invaded West Africa they were accompanied with their missionaries who were but adjuncts of the colonizers, who were more concerned with exploiting Africa for its resources than in saving souls. Wherever we see the work of the Church in Africa it would be naïve to think it separate from the capitalist vision held by those intent upon re-colonizing Africa. They are also aware that Africa is rich with many cultural elements, which should not be sacrificed on the altar of acculturation. Those "worthy elements" within TACF that are deemed compatible with Christianity should be saved and used by the Church. This is simply one of the missions of the Roman Catholic Church on the continent of Africa. The others have already been written in the history books and those who fail to respect the lessons of history will certainly become victims to a much crueler form of exploitation.

African Traditional Culture and Psychology

Philip Bartle has defined culture as "everything which human beings learn that makes them human: a super organic level of complexity based on the organic [biological] level, but transcends the inorganic [physical] level."[156]

Culture is a complex web of ideas that encompasses the physical and metaphysical sphere in which human beings operate consciously or otherwise. The multiple elements that make up culture are primarily transmitted through symbols. These symbols are highly religious and serve to transmit ideas that are beyond language. According to Gyekye, "Religion—the awareness of the existence of some ultimate, supreme being who is the origin and sustainer of this universe and the establishment of constant ties with this being— influences, in a comprehensive way, the thoughts and actions of the African people."[157]

The power of religion is so embedded throughout traditional African cultural forms that it is difficult for an outsider to distinguish between secular and sacred ways of existing. This is because the sacred-profane binary does not exist within traditional African communities. Traditional Africans do not distinguish between their daily activities and their relationship with the numinous. All is sacred and therefore "religion enters all aspects of African life so fully— determining practically every aspect of life, including moral behavior—that it can hardly be isolated."[158] African traditional religion may at times be difficult to observe outside of public places such as shrines or festivals. However, every event, act, and gesture is religiously significant in traditional society. Whether one is farming in the field or drinking gin at a shrine, they are engaged in an important religious function. "For the Africans, life is religion and religion is life. It is unimaginable for the Africans, following their traditional environment and culture, to think of human life divorced from religion."[159]

Traditional African communities and practitioners of TACF throughout the diaspora have traditionally viewed religion as inseparable from morality. "Religion supplies the basic principles of morality which if faithfully adhered to, helps man to live well or reform himself should he have erred."[160] In traditional communities it was an acceptable norm that all members of the village believed in divine forces, which governed their lives and ruled the cosmos. The belief in deity was widespread throughout all of Africa and not an imported ideology, as is the case with Islam and Christianity. The continent is filled with thousands of artifacts and symbols along with other historical markers of world significance that attest to the people's historical relationship with God.[161] The spirituality that governed traditional communities has its basis in African culture and values. Most African scholars maintain that traditional religion is closely aligned with culture.[162] (Throughout the book, I have referred to this closeness with the term "religio-culture.") Religion in Africa is a communal reality and the idea of one converting from one religio-culture to another is not an African concept, but a reflection of the foreign invasions that swept across the continent.

For example, in the pre–Arab era and before colonialism, Africans were born into a particular religio-culture and could not conceive of abandoning their familial norms for a foreign perspective. It was inconceivable in pre–Islamic Africa for one to abandon TACF and adopt a stranger's culture as their religion. African religion is familial-based and the abandonment of one's religio-culture is tantamount to rejecting their family. "One cannot detach oneself from the religion of the community, for to do so would be to isolate oneself from the group and to disrupt one's sense of communal membership and security and lose much of the meaning of life."[163]

The thought of seeking isolation to be made pure or to achieve sanctification is not an African ideal. Individualism is a Western construct rooted within the Abrahamic traditions. Aloneness in traditional Africa meant certain death. African culture is communal oriented and detests individualism. Mbiti asserted that African religion and culture encompass beliefs, moral codes, ideals of origin, and other socioreligious laden variables that functioned to provide social norms. "Religion, belief in the ancient supernatural conglomerate of gods, goddesses, spirits and their associated ritual systems provided the main engine of each community's recognized law and custom."[164]

It was their belief in traditional ways of being that provided Africans social stability, which acted as a form of social control. Tamuno laments that after the Islamic and Christian incursions into West Africa crime begin to increase. "Such newer faiths as Islam and Christianity seriously threatened the bulwarks of the ancient moral code of conduct applicable to each rural community."[165] Ìdòwú also was saddened by the negative impact of Christianity and Islam upon the traditional moral systems, which were responsible for maintaining law in the villages.[166] Those foreign faiths even justified their disdain for traditional modes morality and used their scripture to support their position.

For example, the Western notion of future punishment as opposed to the traditional swift and certain judgment by the divinities was undermined by certain Christian doctrines. Within Christian dogma, one may indeed violate laws but can simply confess their faults and repent of their violations before death. If they failed to confess their faults after death they would be judged by spending eternity in hell. This ideology greatly challenged the traditional model, which functioned as a deterrent to crime. The traditional model had no such concept of one being sentenced to an eternal hell for crimes committed on earth. Regardless to the nature of those crimes one would pay for them in this life. Immediate punishment served as a great deterrent throughout traditional communities.

The Arabs and Europeans introduced Africans to several modes of behavior that functioned to uproot or destabilize traditional ways of being. The concept of individualism threatened the sociocultural African identity system, which was based upon communal and collective identity.[167] Islam began its incursion into West Africa between the seventh and fourteenth centuries and because many of its religious tenets were based in Arabism, they introduced foreign elements into Africa that destabilized and trampled upon the tradition that served Africans for centuries.[168]

The spread of both Islam and Christianity were forms of Western hegemony that continue with a renewed interests in Africa. These incursions were affective in destroying the practices of many practitioners of TACF. Still, not all was destroyed and many Africans on the continent and throughout the diaspora are showing a renewed interests in the religion of their ancestors. Adolphe Amadi argued that although Africa received a "fatal" blow from the colonial powers, "African cultural reality persisted and still persists and though driven underground, has survived. This is to say that against the outwardly more powerful and glamorous Western tradition, there remains an African identity which colonialism scorched but did not exterminate."

Traditional religion is a spiritual movement that is not confined to space or time. There are countless rituals and practices that govern the various religio-cultural groups who honor these traditions and there remains a commonality shared by them all. Each community mines from the rich African traditions and have developed elaborate systems for communing with the spiritual world. African traditional religion does not force its adherents to subscribe to certain beliefs in order to be accepted. It does not require its followers to preach their beliefs to others through evangelization. African religion has its origin in spiritual principles that are humanistic, which advance the view that human beings are free moral agents who must be allowed to live out their lives free from human obstructions. Those systems of control that attempt to imprison individual autonomy and human freedom must be rejected by all human beings who are intent upon fulfilling their life mission.

Ikenga-Metuh argued that other factors in addition to religion may account for the basis of traditional social codes. Is it possible for a society to have moral codes whose foundations are secular, he asked. Ikenga-Metuh argued that most traditional African moral system arises from their religion. Placide Tempels maintained that the Bantu people's moral codes emanated from their religion and[169] Ìdòwú echoed the same sentiments: "Our own view is that morality is basically the fruit of religion and that, to begin with, it was dependent upon it. Man's concept of the Deity has everything to do with what is taken to be the norm of morality. God made man; and it is He who implants in him the sense of right and wrong."[170]

Other scholars counter this view claiming that morality does not have to derive its moral codes from religion. "Since there is no single sovereign god like Job's, one cannot feel entitled to rewards for following a code of conduct pleasing to him or deserving of punishment for knowingly transgressing it. One lives according to one's mundane lights, guided by the moral and jural sanctions of society."[171]

The question of whether religion is the foundation of morality or if a society derives its moral codes from another source has been contested in Western discourse since Socrates posed the question, "Do the gods love something because it is holy, or is a thing holy because the gods love it?" Some scholars have argued that religion is the basis of morality in African societies. A few have contended that the autonomous free will of rational creatures is the primary factor that governs morality.

For example, Kant surmised that all rational beings are capable of living moral lives. "No external authority, not even God can provide a criterion of morality," writes Ikenga-Metuh, "because the truth [or] falsity of such an externally imposed moral [norm] would still be decided by ... human reasons."[172] Kant likewise theorized that the human inclination to apprehend the good, truth, and just is indicative of humanity's *a priori* knowledge.[173]

Like their Western counterparts African scholars also struggle with the question of the source of societal moral codes. Although most followers of TACF agree that religion is the fuel that ignites traditional African moral systems. Traditional Africans live out their existence through concrete experiences expressed primarily through the medium of religion. Monica Wilson wrote that scholars who advocate that religion is not the basis of morality in Africa have misunderstood the vast array of symbolism that attests to the power of religion over one's life.[174] Ikenga-Metuh attributes Wilson's remarks to overgeneralizing between the different religio-cultural groups in Africa.[175]

Tempels wrote that the basis of Bantu morality was in their religion, while Fortes and other scholars theorized that morality does not derive from religion but has its basis in social norms.[176] Those who support Tempels's theory are by far the majority because they base their position on the evidence which shows that religion and culture are socially derived institutions.

Mbiti also maintained that religion is pervasive throughout every aspect of traditional life. A society's value system has its basis in culture. Therefore, culture can be understood as a system of belief's which encompasses the social fabric of a people. This includes the way one eats, dresses, makes love, buries their dead, sings, laughs and cries. These expressions form cultural patterns which create societal norms to which one is expected to conform. Societal norms and mores establish "complex ways of behavior associated with the universal needs of reproduction and the care of the young."[177] Cultural patterns governing communities function as a cultural umbrella, under which are housed one's value system.

Various forces in society shape culture. In almost every case the forces that shape culture are not products of the dominant class. The underclass have a great effect on shaping particular kinds of cultural patterns, such as clothing, automobiles, and disposable products in general. There are also certain charismatic individuals in every society who serve as transmitters of culture. These men and women who shape and transmit culture are endowed with special skills and possess the insight to interpret and articulate the unspoken language of their people.[178] Although, certain individuals serve a vital role in transmitting and shaping their people's religio-cultural norms, in traditional African communities moral values are a composite of several variables. "In the African traditional society, moral values are not the creation or the invention of the society, much less of the individual. Moral values are the expressions of the transcendental moral order which is beyond man and to which both man and the society must conform."[179]

Only those members who conform to societal expectations and possess good character assist in the shaping of African cultural values.[180] Those who challenged the sacred traditional norms were expected to suffer divine consequences because inappropriate behavior has widespread repercussions. Ethics in traditional society were not simply a personal matter but are a major concern for the entire community because African ontology is communal and based upon harmony. The violation of this holy cohesion may result in a chain of misfortunes that threaten the entire village. "When the balance of the moral order is upset by a serious violation the whole society suffers. Every evil act in African traditional ethics is [an] anti-social act which has adverse effects on the whole society."[181]

"Most African scholars hold that religion in Africa is the center of everyday existence. Religion provides sanctions for the moral obligations and responsibilities of the members of the community. Misfortunes and disasters that befall individuals, clans, or communities are very often interpreted as the consequences of, or perhaps, as punishment sent by the supernatural powers for bad conduct or failure to fulfill certain moral obligations to kinsfolk or community."[182] It is clear that religion in Africa must be socially relevant because it is communally based, and part of the people's daily activities. Religion cannot be a personal matter. African religion by its very nature is a communal and cosmic centered. Its focus is upon maintaining harmony in the village and with ones neighbors throughout cosmos. There is little place for individualism outside of the special men and women who administer and preserve those sacred traditional cultural forms. In traditional African society to exist is to live among others, for "the individual does not and cannot live his life alone. The individual exists because others exist and he owes his existence to other people in the society."[183] Communal living is a reality in traditional ways of being and corporate existence brings about communal suffering. Therefore, traditional Africans have come to understand the importance of communal joy and also how to suffer as a people. "To be born into a human community is to be born into a religious community and to find oneself, as one grows and matures, participating more and more in the ceremonial rites and festivals of that [religious] community."[184]

The practice of traditional African cultural forms is a living religion observed by millions of people around the world. It is a spirituality or way of being in the world based upon a diversity of forms. It is not governed by propositions or faith statements. African spirituality is cosmic-centered and experienced by those who venerate TACF and is accepted as an absolute reality by millions. It has suffered greatly from the onslaughts and attacks from Arabs and Europeans and these forces, along with other factors, has caused it to lose its "character as truth with the increasing influence of missionary activity—Islamic and Christian, and [it] was proclaimed as nontruth, as despicable, as the last and most primitive thing—paganism, heathenism, fetishism, etc."[185]

In the 1950s Europeans allowed African countries to govern themselves after occupying most of West Africa for nearly three hundred years. Thereafter, many Africans began to experiment with various African cultural forms, which were suppressed under the reign and terror of colonialism. Africans returned to their language and began dressing in traditional garb. Renato Berger wrote that many professors at the University of Ibadan began wearing traditional garb in formal and public outings.[186] This return to an African consciousness continued with renewed interest in traditional art and music. There were even debates as to whether the people should reject the language of the colonizer and use an African language for official discourse. It was a subtle move towards fully embracing TACF, which prompted an intellectual and outward return to the former paths.

According to Berger and other scholars cultural shifts are better understood through the lens of religion than by any other medium. "The study of religion is, in a sense, the most intimate study of the people who practice the religion. It is here that one really sees—if one is let in—the souls of the people in their nakedness."[187] Here Ìdòwú implies that Africans are intimately connected to their religio-cultures and that religion is inseparable from their identity. The Western assault from the colonial powers and the Abrahamic faiths were weaponized, which tore at the center of African anthropology and psychology. Such strategies were in essence an attack against TACF, which housed the religio-cultural soul of African people. Berger points out that in the future scholars should study the damage that foreign occupation has on one's culture and psyche.[188] An objective approach should be employed that is not beholden to European ideology or the Abrahamic religions. Berger maintains that such an inquiry should comprise of a holistic approach, or a method he terms as "integral consciousness." This methodology rejects the linear European model and incorporates a science of integral consciousness that rejects the binary structure and employs a phenomenological approach. Berger believes this approach to be less biased because it "does not claim for itself absolute intellectual demonstrability and 'measurability' of one single scientific fact, but considers all phenomena of life; [second, it] does not consider only a single science at the expense of the others, as it is often done by the acknowledged sciences, but puts them in relation to all the others and with life."[189]

The integral-consciousness methodology is an open attack against the linear model that undergirds the Western paradigm. The prevailing theories preferences certain elements and ignores others. Such "objective" methods cannot be used to investigate the complex webs that govern African phenomena. TACF are multidimensional and require a multivariate approach. The integral-consciousness method includes ways by which the inquirer can measure non–Western categories of interests such as magical, mythical, and mental, in tandem with other phenomena that are significant for obtaining accurate data.[190] This method may prove more effective in the study of African religion since the Abrahamic approach is biased against non–Western ways of being.

Berger identified two main reasons that account for Western bias against nonwestern phenomena. First, Western scholars have difficulty in assessing and categorizing traditional African cultural forms because of their heavily layered and multidimensional nature. Also, traditional African cultural forms are highly complex because they are difficult to identify since they are integrated throughout every aspect of society. The African religio-cultural sphere is a complex arena that requires the inquirer to understand abstract rituals such as magic, divination, and numerous African cosmological systems. Many of these systems employ methods that are completely different from the linear models that govern Western systems of thought.[191]

Secondly, since African religion is not usually associated with a founding prophet many researchers have difficulty identifying the tenets that govern TACF.[192] Berger holds that Westerners do not always possess the cultural tools to understand African phenomena, which leads to greater levels of mis-conceptions. Therefore, many Western scholars are forced to either ignore important African customs or dismiss them as irrational. Some have rejected crucial African systems and "banished the magical back to its darkness as black magic, superstition, the sinister power of a world which Christianity and the Enlightenment have both condemned to death."[193]

African religio-cultural systems have generally been condemned by the West because they do not conform to Western patterns of thought. Carl Jung and other psychologists were among the first Westerners to explicate the symbolism associated with African ritual systems. Jung showed that the symbolism employed in what he deemed as "primitive" rituals also existed among the so-called enlightened populations. The primitive patterns in traditional societies speak to the same human needs that those in the "cultured" societies long to address. Jung maintained that enlightened societies have simply masked such longings. Berger argued that "the same religious contents as existed and still exist in the so-called primitive societies in a legitimate form have been expelled by rationality, so that they had to take refuge in the interior of the human soul."[194]

While the psychological drive that directs the traditionalists to conduct rituals and sometimes appear fanatical may not be outwardly present in those who live in modern world, their absence is not indicative of human advancement, but in many ways is a clear sign of repression. Jung holds that what appears to some as irrational behavior is in fact an appropriate psychological expression. These same forms of expression need an outlet in modern society if a people are to maintain their sanity. The modern person has not transcended the need to communicate with a force greater than themselves. "The only transformation they have undergone is that they exist in the psyche of the modern rationalists and atheists in a distorted form or, if they have kept their former shape, the individual, being allowed to realize their message only in his dreams, has become sick or neurotic."[195]

The rationalist approach for addressing those certain human needs cannot be ignored. Authentic beings recognize this universal need and resort to religion or some other means by which they connect to those metaphysical elements that address psychical needs. Those who abandon what appears to be nature's proclivity to express itself through ritual, develop a pathology that manifests itself to the detriment of the society. The human need to express itself via ritual or other non-rational means may be a part of human nature's proclivity to reach out to those nonmaterial elements that comprise human existence. Traditional forms of expression that involve highly styled rituals and ceremonies as modes of communication may be attempts to express what Freud refers to as humanity's original religious patterns that are wired into our consciousness or DNA structure. Jung later extended this view and claimed that the human proclivity to suppress one's sexual nature was not the sole reason for humanities stagnation on the social evolutionary ladder. Humanity's evolutionary retardation may stem from the suppression of our religious nature and the refusal to feed that primal hunger through the use of ritual and other non-cognitive forms of expression.[196]

The countercultural movements are reflections of the human need to feed the immaterial part of their being. The ritualized nature of subcultures acts as a form of expression that provides the psyche with the nutrients needed to prevent it from becoming schizophrenic. The hippie movement in the 1960s was an example of human beings having a need that the dominant cultural forms failed to address. "[T]he solemn dresses of the hippies and their followers, their preference for ceremonies, for Indian philosophy and music, for burning incense, for dancing in a ritual way, for jazz-singing and jazz-dancing in the Churches, and similar other manifestations, show very clearly that religious needs refuse to remain repressed in the sick souls of European neurotics, and look for new ways in which to realize themselves."[197]

The countercultural movements reveal that human beings are indeed *homo religiosus* and that certain forms of secularism are valid modes that serve a ritualistic function.[198] These psychical rituals practiced by the hippie movements is one of the basic elements within traditional African cultural forms. The numerous African systems that employ the use of elaborate rituals and other mediums for addressing ones physical and nonphysical needs use ritual as the vehicles to assuage the human need to communicate with the spiritual world. It is within this realm that humans' deepest needs are met. Only within this sphere can cosmic harmony be maintained or restored. Within the realm of magic the ontological breaches are repaired and "sin" is forgiven. Inside the spiritual realm is where traditional Africans communicate with living and nonliving entities. Berger writes that neither Europe nor Christianity with all its technology has been able to address ones needs within the spiritual realm. Only in traditional Africa and places where similar rituals and TACF are practiced does one find nourishment for their entire being. African religion is a spiritual system that aims at restoring cosmic balance between human and nonhuman entities. It is not only focused upon saving the individual, but the entire cosmos. Saint Paul wrote that the cosmos awaits redemption. All of nature groans in anticipation of its release from the estrangement it finds itself facing in the dessert of life.

Geoffrey Parrinder made great contributions to the study of traditional African cultural forms. However, like most whites he too rejected the idea that some West African religions may have their origin in Egypt. He argued that J.O. Lucas and other scholars who advocated this theory were not objective scholars and were in fact overly passionate. Nonetheless, it should be noted that Parrinder has also been criticized or dismissed outright by some scholars. His complete rejection of black people's relationship to Egypt and Egypt's historical connection to West Africa sheds light on his inability to view Africans with the same respect provided to Europeans or Arabs. His inability to view black Africans as creators of the world's greatest culture is equivalent to denying that a causal relationship exists between Christianity as practiced in Russia and in Ireland. Parrinder argued that the research of J. O. Lucas, who outlined the similarities between African Egyptians and West Africans, might be of value to the Yoruba tradition he represents. However, Parrinder claimed that Lucas may be too emotional to present an objective study of TACF. "But one feels that it is time for new research into Yoruba religion to be made, and one could wish that one who is a Yoruba, like Archdeacon Lucas, would present an entirely new study. Such a study, one might suggest, would be even more valuable if it were purely objective, and kept quite free from speculations as to the Egyptian or other origins of Yoruba religion."[199]

It should be noted that Parrinder's assessment of Lucas might be correct in some regards. However, Parrinder errs by suggesting that a purely objective study of African religion can be conducted. If so, by who? His own work is certainly not purely objective. Most, if not all of his research is interpreted from a Christian frame of reference. This Euro-centric framework as the ruling paradigm by which all others are judged has created serious problems that continue to plague Western scholarship. Further, Parrinder's rejection of Lucas's theory sheds light on his own inability to acknowledge that Africans were indeed capable of producing the world's richest culture. Parrinder even claimed that the divination systems used throughout West Africa was imported from elsewhere: "The Ifa system of divining, with its combination of sixteen figures written on a board, so popular in Nigeria and Dahomey, may well have come to these erstwhile illiterate peoples from the Sudan or further north."[200] It should now be clear that Parrinder's Eurocentric lens prevents him from being the objective scholar he admonished his students to become. Although he has made many contributions to the study of TACF that have been brought to the attention of academia, he has never attempted to respect African religion as a sacred culture on par with Christianity and Islam.

Aside from the Eurocentrism that evaded his low thoughts of Africans as capable of creating the world's first system of religion, Parrinder has advanced the study of TACF throughout the Western world. Still, modern scholars have identified four major errors in his research. He has been criticized for presenting African religion as an ahistorical phenomenon as compared to the value given to Christianity and Islam.[201] Second, some scholars argue that he lacks an adequate sociocultural critique of TACF.[202] Third, his work has been labeled by some as too general and insubstantial. Other scholars such as Mbiti, Benjamin Ray, and K. A. Opoku have attempted to avoid these three criticisms in their work.[203] Fourth, Parrinder has been criticized by some African scholars because of his Christian, Euro-centered bias that tainted his analysis of African religio-cultural phenomena. It has been suggested that his Euro-Christian background also prevented him from objectively assessing TACF and African phenomena in general.[204] Further, Parrinder has made no attempt to advance African religion as a faith comparable to Christianity and Islam. His status as a Christian missionary further outrages his critics, who call him "a former missionary who has not repudiated the Christian missionary enterprise and so must exhibit the worst possible form of bias."[205]

Yet Parrinder continues to have his defenders. H. W. Turner of the Department of Religious Studies at the University of Aberdeen, Kings College in Scotland, argued that most work on African religion would have to be rejected if based upon the fourth criticism of Parrinder. He notes that the scholars who conducted eighty-five percent of the early studies on African religion were closely aligned with the Christian church.[206] In this regard we must agree with Okot p'Bitek's bitter critique when he argued that the study of African religion has barely been addressed until men and women not beholden to Christian and Islamic dogma begin to conduct serious studies of TACF. African religion will continue to be articulated by men and women who are consciously or otherwise at war with black people and possibly through no conscious fault of their own.

Many leading practitioners of TACF employ methods for analyzing African phenomena that involve viewing the individual inseparable from their environment. Traditional healers hold that all sickness has an origin that must first be addressed before any attempts are made to treat outward manifestations that fail to address the root cause of a disease. Many traditionalist and those wherever TACF are venerated hold that illness is an entity that can be appeased or addressed through ritual. Sickness can range from acute diseases to one's inability to develop and use their cognitive skills. For instance, mental retardation is perceived as an assault upon human beings from a hostile energy. "[T]he inability to perceive, the inability to understand, to indigenous people is symptomatic of an illness. If your psyche is disordered or deficient or overcharged, blocks are created in you that prevent comprehension and remembering. To open up the channels in you so that whatever energy you need can flow freely is not the task of the teacher; it is the task of the shaman."[207]

Many traditional oriented Africans on the continent and throughout the diaspora feel that the source of illnesses can be known by consulting a diviner. After one's energy is restored the priest or healer "will repair the spiritual state so that the spiritual healing can be translated into healing of the physical disease. You have to heal in the Spirit World before you can heal in the physical world."[208] African psychology and pharmacology addresses the source of illness not simply as a biological disorder, but as a manifestation of disharmony that occurs when one's Chi or Ori is blocked or under attack. Indigenous pharmacology is premised upon the theory that human beings are primarily spiritual creatures who temporarily reside in a material body. Healing can be achieved only when one's true form is first healed in the spirit world. Thus, it is the duty of healers to contact the spiritual realm, which is the only way that human beings can be assured of complete healing. "Healers who bring energy from the Spirit World through the gateways are known as gatekeepers. A gatekeeper can trace the shadow from this world back to its origin in the spiritual world and act as an intermediary, as a bridge, since he or she understands the relationship between the different aspects of the reality of this world."[209]

African religion is premised upon maintaining communal and cosmic harmony between all the forces in nature. Thus, healing aims at restoring any imbalance within the individual that is needed to maintain good health. "To effect healing it is necessary, first of all, to re-establish harmony between the major elements which constitute the human person. Such healing will not be efficacious if it does not at the same time restore relations with the environment and the Supreme Being, spirits, ancestors and other people."[210]

Some African Muslims and Christians still hold dear many of the traditions that govern traditional African ways of being. A few scholars advocate that those who become Christian or Muslim, even centuries after adhering to the tenets of these foreign faiths, have a difficult time discarding the religion of their ancestors. Their inability to divest themselves of traditional African ways of being has created a sense of separation that may have an ethical basis. Some scholars argue that Christianity does not possess the principles that operate the African psyche. Ethical principles inherent in traditional African cultural forms are conspicuously missing from Christianity, which "does not sufficiently take notice of the local Spiritual base. Also, in moments of crisis, the Christians live in Christianity [Christian practices: Masses,

Sacraments] while they carry out traditional religious practices which give them satisfaction."[211]

This duality may be the result of living within two worlds created from different cultural forms, which are alien to each other. The adoption of another people's cultural system to be venerated as a religion, has forced many Africans to wear masks. The outward mask embraces Christianity or Islam on a superficial level, while at night they take off these mask and seek answers from men and women who commune with their forebears. Under these artificial circumstances authenticity and healing is unable to occur. "Healing begins when the mask is released from the self, for people can't transform when they are hiding behind them."[212] The mask separates one from their true self and such schism creates chaos. The true nature of a human being cannot blossom and come to flower behind a mask. "If we live a life that denies or ignores our true and natural self, we open ourselves to some of the most painful emotional and psychological problems that a human being can know.... Meeting for the first time the person who lives behind the mask is usually a powerful and emotional experience, but from the point of view of the indigenous world, that is the person you came to this life to be."[213]

The inability to express oneself is perhaps one of the primary sources of sickness. Unexpressed emotions create negative energy that accumulate within the body and become toxic. If the denial of expressing oneself continues and they refuse to face the "man in the mirror" over time sickness or premature death will certainly occur. Within traditional African ways of being one is expected to freely express their emotions. The inability to do so is indicative of major blockages to one's chi or life-energy, which will lead to brokenness. "If we cannot express ourselves emotionally with the members of our own community, something deeply important is missing. And when emotion is missing, usually we are missing as well, unable to be fully present either to ourselves or to one another."[214]

5

African Religion in the New World

The Caribbean Islands have been inhabited since the fourth century according to the Western historical record. There are over 40 million people in the Caribbean and at least another 40 million outside the islands who are of Caribbean descent.[1] The early inhabitants were known as the Ciboneys or Guanahatabeys. The Tainos were the largest population of whom some believe migrated from South America. When the Spaniards started their exploration of the New World, an event some now refer to as "Campaigns of Terror," the Ciboneys began migrating to Western Cuba and the Southern Peninsula of Haiti, where they intermarried with the local population. Traces of their biological traits have been dispersed throughout the Haitian population.

Since receiving independence most of the Caribbean Islands have been dominated by white powers from Europe and the United States. The United States controlled many of the islands throughout the 20th century.[2] What began with the Spanish incursion into the Americas over five centuries ago continues today with the same malicious disregard for the sovereignty of the local population. Very soon after the Spaniards' arrival in the Caribbean they quickly became obsessed with the natural resources that littered the land. The indigenous were adorned in gold and pearls and, in certain regions of the New World like South America, were awash in natural resources.

The white man's entrance into the Caribbean and South America is a microcosm of their involvement with indigenous populations throughout the world. When we study how they displaced the original inhabitants of these islands we are given a clear portrait of the strategy they used to destabilize and destroy other indigenous populations throughout the world. The study of these strategies allows one to develop a greater appreciation of the Caribbean and its people, especially how a remnant were able to survive European barbarism and recreate ancient cultural forms. When we investigate the methods and strategies used by Europeans to "civilize" the indigenous population, we catch a glimpse into the philosophy undergirding their current civilizing project in the Muslim world.

For example, throughout the Western world students are taught that the early Europeans who arrived in the Americas did so as friendly "explorers." However, nowhere in the Americas can we find the European humane in their efforts at "civilizing" the indigenous. Still, the Western world has lionized those men who killed and tortured human beings as servants of God. Our children are taught to venerate these men and whenever their past deeds are brought to light, those who question their deeds are condemned as unpatriotic. Yet, most of the men, including Christopher Columbus, were not humanitarians. At most, they were capital adventurists in search of riches. Some have labeled Columbus and his crew, including those who followed after him, as the first international terrorists in the New World.

For instance, Columbus gave his men specific orders when they landed in the Caribbean to "spread terror," which would ensure that the natives remain submissive. From the beginning of the Europeans' arrival the indigenous people were programmed to fear the white man. If they questioned their behavior, they could lose their lives. "In retaliation for the slightest offense, disrespect, or show of resistance, the settlers [another term for invaders] would go on an indiscriminate killing rampage without regard for the guilt or innocence of those being killed. Using their military advantage, this wreaked havoc on the local population in the name of subduing them. Their swords, lances, and crossbows far outmatched the Tainos spears and clubs. Most fearsome were the ferocious dogs let loose to hunt and tear locals to pieces and the horses were used to charge crowds, mowing down and trampling some and sending others into flight."[3]

The Europeans wielded complete control over the indigenous and used their power to indiscriminately torture and rape Taino women. Columbus's crew terrorized the indigenous with impunity and fifty years after his arrival, most of the Taino population was exterminated. Also, because of forced rape of women by Columbus' crew, an extremely large mestizo population was created, leaving behind them a lasting trait that some argue remains "characteristic of the Hispanic societies in the Americas."[4]

Caribbean religion is as mestizo as are the people who comprise these various cultural groups throughout the islands. This cultural tension, in part, gave birth to New World cultural forms that in many ways are uniquely Caribbean. What also emerged from this creative tension is a complex religio-cultural system that has created the most fluent and dynamic New World cultural forms in the Western hemisphere.[5] These unique Caribbean cultural forms were created in an atmosphere of chaos. Not random chaos, but as a strategy that has historically been used by minority Anglo powers around the world to destroy and destabilize nonwhite populations. The destabilization of the indigenous population throughout the Caribbean forced upon the islanders a cultural complex that has no easy remedies. In general, the islanders suffer from an identity crisis initially caused by the colonizers, who deliberately separated the populations based on race and language.

For example, "the present division of the region into Anglophone, Francophone, Hispanic, and Dutch Caribbean's is a legacy of colonial conflicts and partitions of the islands by Europeans. This has created feelings of kinship based not on proximity but on language and former association with European Powers."[6] Still today, long after independence the Caribbean Islands remain under the cultural and political influence of their former colonizers. "European ideas and aesthetics continue to greatly influence political and social institutions throughout the Caribbean. Their continuing influence holds sway over the economy, education, and legal system. The Caribbean continues to be riddled by ... the melody of Europe and the rhythm of Africa." This idea has been supported by other scholars of Caribbean studies who reached a similar conclusion. "One of the ways of characterizing contemporary Caribbean culture[s] is to say that, while Europe rules in the official social institutions of politics, economics, education, and law, other ethnic groups, particular Africans, tend to rule in folk and popular culture, including religion, music, dance and, increasingly, the visual and performing arts."[7] In a similar context the same can be said about African Americans, who are the creators of today's popular music and "cool" culture. Wherever "popular" music is heard anywhere in the world one can trace its origins to enslaved Africans in the United States.[8]

These "African rhythms" have not only influenced popular culture, but, they have equally shaped the religious perspectives of millions of people throughout the Caribbean. In this regard, religion in the Caribbean and throughout the Americas can rightly be understood as an "African New World Belief System." These New World African Cultural Systems can perhaps, more accurately be described as Traditional African Cultural Forms (TACF). Africans were enslaved and placed throughout the New World in hostile environments and for survival purposes had to discover new ways of how to maintain their humanity. In the white man's New World where Africans were perceived as less than human, they reinterpreted and "recreat[ed] their cultural systems of belief within a restrictive social structure in a new and unfamiliar environment."[9]

Religion played a major role in shaping New World African cultural and spiritual identities. It was religion and not race, which was first used to justify the Atlantic slave trade. Papal Bulls issued by Pope Nicholas V (1454) and Pope Calixtus II (1456) authorized the enslavement of Africans, supposedly to convert them to Christianity. Africans were viewed by the Church as "captives of a just war."[10] At the time these Papal Bulls were issued poor indentured whites were used throughout Europe as cheap labor. Slaves in early Spain were of a lighter hue than African Moors. The word "slave" has its origin among the Slavs of Eastern Europe. (It is of interest to note that if the Slavs happened to be seen outside of Europe, they would have been classified as mestizo or mulatto.) Dark-skinned people throughout the Mediterranean area were first placed into servitude by aristocratic Arabs. Throughout the medieval era, African men were generally described as "warriors, conquerors, rulers, boards, and musicians."[11]

When Columbus set sail in 1492 to explore what has become the New World it marked a crucial time in world history. Prior to 1492, Africans (also known by some as Moors) ruled Spain for eight hundred years. With the first voyage of Columbus and those who followed, the "dark-skinned" Moorish rule of Spain would come to an end. The Moors had ruled the Iberian Peninsula for eight hundred years and in 1492, it was back in the hands of the Europeans. It was with a renewed sense of pride that the Europeans, under the leadership of Columbus, entered the Americas. The European was once again back in power, which he believed was his rightful place. The Muslim blackamoors were defeated and Jesus would once again reign as king of the world. Mary and the saints were back on the throne and Muhammad was defeated. Allah was dead. This new sense of spiritual pride infused the Roman Catholic hermeneutic, which was used to justify the Europeans barbarism and violence in the New World. A new Christianity was born and the Dark Ages were finally over. The new victorious Christianity that entered the "Americas was one branded by Spain's re-conquest of the Iberian Peninsula from the Moors.... One cannot question the conquest and slave trade without contextualizing them in the light of Catholicism's struggle to regain Spain and Portugal."[12]

It was the blackamoor darker-skinned Muslims of possible "mixed" racial origins who were the prime enemies of the Roman Catholic Church. The dark-skinned Muslim was associated with conquerors, dominators, and world rulers. After all, they ruled what was for all practical purposes the capital region of Europe for 800 years. The blackamoors also introduced into Europe a more refined way of living. They exposed Europeans to a lifestyle that the average European was not at all accustomed. For when the European was still in the Dark Ages the Muslim world was at the peak of one of its greatest renaissances.

Religion was one of the major factors used to justify European bar-barism, much like today where Western nations use democracy to justify white barbarism. The Roman Catholic Church was the leading institution that authorized aggression and promoted European barbarism. The Catholic Church used its influence and economic and religious power to advance its inhumane agenda throughout the world. For example, Pope Alexander VI's justification for controlling the resources of the New World was to civilize and Christianize the indigenous populations. Religion has always been used to justify white barbarism. In the past it was couched in theological termi-nology, such as "When Christ came into the world, he divested all heathen powers of their authority and became the sole sovereign over human kind. Before returning to heaven, Christ passed the authority onto Peter, the first Pope, and to succeeding Popes, who are Christ's representatives here on earth. Therefore, Popes had the authority to assign jurisdiction of any territory to "Christian princes." Based upon this psychotic hermeneutic, Pope Alexander issued a Papal Bull, "assigning all newly discovered land beyond an imaginary line in the Atlantic to Spain, given responsibility to Christianize the local people."[13]

Christendom has historically aligned itself with oppressive regimes whenever it was not leading from the front. For instance, from the time of Emperor Constantine in the 4th century, the Roman Catholic Church, which is the global face of Christianity, has been engaged in one campaign of terror after another. Today in the United States Evangelical fundamentalists lead the rhetoric of cultural destabilization in the name of evangelizing the lost. The American Christian fundamentalists usually support those who share a similar ideology of global domination even if they are not Christian. The Christian fundamentalists claim to be against abortion, yet support U.S. global domination through which millions of innocent people have been slaughtered. Such men and women have aligned themselves with the same kind of aggressive Christianity first instituted under Constantine's regime. The Protestant Church either remains silent over the innocent blood shed by U.S. soldiers or they too find the words to justify their support of white barbarism. In this regard, the U.S. government has replaced the Roman Empire by adopting its radical fundamentalist ideology. In many ways, the American government is beholden to an ideology that is as hostile as radical Islam. Like the Islamic fundamentalists throughout the Middle East and Northern Nigeria, radical Christians in the United States are engaged in a ferocious battle to force their legislators to enact laws that support their nar-row vision, which is the Christian version of sharia law.

The cozy relationship between governments and extreme forms of radicalism has its religious roots in Western religion. For one can rightly argue that "the history of the Roman Catholic Church in the colonial era is marked by complicity with the support of Spanish colonial domination and exploitation of indigenous peoples and African people's throughout the Caribbean."[14] The deeds of the Catholic Church must be regarded, at least during the colonial era, as an inhuman because it openly supported the killing of indigenous populations and later the enslavement of Africans throughout the New World. They justified the use of violence as a means to control the people's resources and land. There is no other way of truthfully speaking about the Catholic Church's role in the destruction and destabilization of indigenous cultures. In the language of today, the Roman Catholic Church, especially between the 9th to 15th centuries, was a terrorist organization.

Another example of the Church's complicity with violence and oppression occurred after Haiti gained its independence from France. The Catholic Church converted millions of Africans to Christianity, but when it came down to choosing between religion and ethnicity, they sided with their white French brothers. Race trumps religion every time when one is forced to choose between whiteness and otherness. At least when there is disagreement between whites and non-whites, historically, white people have always chosen their own over nonwhites. Only money or the control of resources can force whites to choose otherwise.

Case in point, Saudi Arabia's relationship with the United States is an exception to what is otherwise a truism. The U.S. government maintains an economic relationship with the Saudi dictatorship, even though 14 of the 19 terrorists who crashed into the World Trade Center were Saudis. This is a perfect case of money and resources taking precedent over the rhetoric of democracy preached by American politicians. Also, when Cuba was seeking independence from Spain, once again, the Catholic Church sided with their Spanish brothers. Such behavior is indicative of an institution without moral principles. One would be foolish to trust theological rhetoric over action and experience. History is a much greater teacher than abstract theological principals, which never seem to pass the real tests of life.

Religion and Theology

Some students of Caribbean religion believe that it lacked theological structure and coherence until the mid-twentieth century, when it was articulated by Caribbean and European theologians.[15] Unfortunately, this idea is premised on the assumption that for any religion to be valid, it must meet several European standards. Yet, how could one believe that religion in the Caribbean lacked structure until it was discovered by European theologians? This erroneous idea goes against everything we know about the Africans in Haiti and Cuba, who possessed complex and elaborate theological structures in the early 19th century. Also, the indigenous populations throughout the Caribbean maintained a rigorous knowledge of the sacred, which infused every area of their lives. All of the indigenous groups throughout the Caribbean subscribed to a unique cosmology based on their cultural values and norms. They visualized the world as one filled with spirits that were responsible for maintaining individual and cosmic harmony. In particular, when Africans arrived in the Caribbean they brought with them one of the most complex theological systems in the world. The Africans theological system was well formed and unknown to the uninitiated. Much like today, most Christian practitioners have little knowledge regarding the theological tenets that undergirds Christian discourse. How then could the Caribbean populations be without a theology until the mid-twentieth century? Unless one's Eurocentrism has blinded them from viewing the indigenous and Africans as human beings capable of abstract thought. There are those throughout academia who maintain that religion and culture has no value unless evaluated through a Eurocentric lens. Of course it is equally clear that such men and women are indeed quite delusional and perhaps they are suffering from a superiority complex that plagues Western thought. If we observe the religious systems of other people and fit it neatly into our own pre-conceived categories (white perceptions), this can comprise an assertion of the superiority of our own point of view and an assertion of a difference in status and power between the observer and the observed.

Africans who entered the New World came from over 200 highly complex and diverse cultural groups throughout West Africa. Their theological perspectives had been fine-tuned and articulated since the decline of the Egyptian Empire. This is true of the Fon of Dahomey and the Yoruba of Nigeria and Cameroon. The Africans brought their own theology to the Caribbean. It was highly refined and in many ways unknowable to the European mind. What is new about Caribbean theology may be its conscious collaboration with other African cultural forms, especially the fusion that occurred between the different cultural groups and the indigenous populations. There are indeed new ways of expressing religion in the Caribbean, but how to speak anew is the nature of religion. This new way of speaking about the divine does not mean that they lacked a coherent theology.

For example, the Afro-Cubans brought to the New World an ancient writing system much like the hieroglyphs in Egypt. How could such a people lack theological coherence? Most Caribbean cultural groups did not have a written system, but still possessed a clear theology that governed their ideals of the sacred. Those who prefer to state otherwise in the face of evidence are once again trapped in the white superiority hermeneutical circle, which has already destroyed Western academia, especially those disciplines who claim to conduct objective bias-free scholarship. When scholars make statements of judgments without revealing their position, the findings are always contaminated. Such superiority logic is akin to that advanced by the European explorers to the New World. The Europeans justified their confiscation of the land because the indigenous "lacked" the concept of land ownership. A similar ideology was used by the early white explorers in South Africa, who also justified the taking of African land because they failed to till the land and also lacked the concept of land ownership.

Supposedly Caribbean theology is found in the writings of scholars who are from the Caribbean, the United States, and Europe. The aim of Caribbean theology is "contextual, decolonized, missonological and ecumenical."[16] This definition of Caribbean theology seems very imperialist—much like the same theological language used by the Catholic Church to justify the extermination of indigenous populations throughout the Americas. Why would a colonized people develop a mission oriented theology? This goes against the nature of indigenous and African theological cultural values. For example, within most indigenous cultural groups one does not engage in missionary activity because you cannot join another people's culture—you must be born into or marry into these cultural groups. We cannot accurately speak of Caribbean theology as mission oriented, which is another way of talking about Western hegemony. Caribbean theology cannot be dictated by a Eurocentric agenda and still call itself Caribbean. It will not survive in these foreign garbs because it arose in response to an imperial and militaristic form of Christianity, which at the time was stifling their humanity. Caribbean theology came to fruition because of the violent form of Christianity that was sweeping across the Americas and it exists not because of Euro-Christianity, but in response to its virulent nature towards the indigenous and African populations. Caribbean religion and theology has its origins in protesting Euro-Christianity, and if it is to stay authentic, it must remain in dialogue with oppressed people everywhere.[17]

The Caribbean is viewed by most in the West as part of the Third World. These same people rightly view black Americans as a minority group connected to this Third World. However, there is much friction that has been manufactured between Caribbean blacks and those in the United States.

Edmonds and Gonzalez wrote that this tension more than any other factor is what has given rise to a Caribbean theology. The theology of the Caribbean was created to distinguish itself from black theology in the United States. Yet, this is a skewed extrapolation of the gap between Caribbean blacks and those on the mainland. In reality, the tension that may exist between the two groups was created and propitiated by their common enemy. We should not forget that Caribbean theology was born from the white Christian fundamentalist threats to their humanity. Those who claim otherwise have a very narrow view of black history throughout the New World.

Edmonds and Gonzalez also argue that the tension between blacks on the island and those on the mainland is based on several factors. However, its real origins are in the lack of historical knowledge that black people have of their common history. The tension between Caribbean and mainland black people has no real political, social, or economic basis. Blacks throughout the New World share a common cultural and historical heritage. The tension that exists between them was fabricated by a common enemy. Until this is understood and the external forces responsible for creating the tension are revealed, black Caribbean and African Americans will fight the "white" man's war, which is aimed at annihilating each of them. The white elite, also called the 1 percent, will continue to put forward the lie that black people in the Caribbean and those in the states are different. In fact, they are both victims of white exploitation and unbeknown to both groups, they share a common fate.

Africans in the Caribbean and those in the United States have a common heritage that they must draw from. The African heritage goes beyond one's religious differences because the Europeans and Arabs have used religion as a weapon to divide black people for nearly two thousand years. If black people simply focus on superficial differences they will continue to perpetuate the myth put forward by white scholars; that is, black people are in a war against each other. What else could explain the high murder rate in black communities throughout the world, especially in the United States? There may indeed be some black academics in the United States who ignore the people of the Caribbean in their theological analysis. These men and women are the minority and, in the majority of cases, do not represent the black populations. At the same time there are some in the Caribbean, especially those who consider themselves "non-black," who only look to Europe or Latin America to shape their theological sustenance and worldview.[18]

Black theologians in the United States are not focused on that population who look to Europe for spiritual direction. They do however aim to reach black people everywhere with their message of collective hope and cultural redemption. The advocates of black theology in the United States have not abandoned the Caribbean people. Still, Delroy Reid-Salmon contends that there is a rupture between Caribbean people and black theologians in the U.S.[19] Delroy's analysis is based on misinformation and a misreading of the real situation. This kind of bickering and making false accusations against each other plays into the hands of their enemy. All the "major" black theologians in the United States are committed to reaching the black populations throughout the world. James Cone in particular, who is considered the father of black theology, is committed to developing a theology that reaches oppressed people everywhere. There is no preference for black people in North America, which does not extend to black people everywhere. Africa, not North America, must be the departure point from which all black theologians begin their inquiry into the origins of black spirituality. Otherwise, they will remain off-centered and prone to the distractions that may have lead Edmonds, Gonzalez, and Reid-Salmon down the wrong paths to a faulty conclusion.

Religion and Culture

In the United States and wherever people who classify themselves as white dwell, the word culture usually presupposes race. It is a word that is never neutral but loaded with meaning. It many instances it is a code word that usually represents non-whites. Every U.S. politician must master the skill of using such code words. Otherwise, their political career will be cut short because they must learn how to speak to several audiences every time they open their mouths. In the Caribbean, race and culture is a much more complex phenomenon than in the United States. We cannot appreciate the richness and depths of cultural diversity throughout the Caribbean without viewing it through the dynamic lens of race. For throughout the Americas, especially the Caribbean, people are extremely race conscious. Questions of race and the formation of identity must therefore become the departure point for any serious dialogue about the Caribbean. Exploring the role of cultural identity in the Caribbean demands that the enslavement of Africans and the destruction of indigenous peoples become the departure point to begin dialogue. There can be no meaningful discussion about the Caribbean without first deconstructing the role of race and racism in particular. In fact, everything in the New World must be viewed through the lens of race. Race may not be the only departure point from which to begin dialogue, but it certainly is one of the major factors that must be acknowledged if one intends on getting to the kernel of the matter.

Some students of Caribbean studies have argued that the genocide of indigenous populations and the enslavement of Africans was carried out with such brutality and precision that its ongoing effects are responsible for the current socio-political system, which continues to stifle individual growth and development. The political systems throughout the Caribbean have their roots in colonial thought. The origins of colonialism are rooted in white supremacy theories that may no longer be outwardly present, yet continue to taint the thinking of every nonwhite person throughout the Caribbean. For instance, those who classify themselves as "white" still believe that they are superior to non-whites. The advocates of white supremacy have used the Christian scripture and pseudo-science to justify their supposedly superior status. These ideas are no longer openly expressed but remain the governing ideology behind the socio-political structures throughout most of the New World.

In addition, the "culture and heritage of the dominated—black slaves— were suppressed and strangled, and the ruling minority—white Europeans— imposed a new identity upon them."[20] The proponents of the Plural Society Theory (PST) argue that the Caribbean is comprised of various cultural groups that lack coherence. As a result of too much diversity the people are fragmented and incapable of having any unity among themselves. PSTs maintain that due to this "fragmentation" and "disparate parts," those cultural groups that were once unified prior to colonialism no longer have any "shared culture, no shared participation in common social institutions that could provide a precondition for social stability."[21]

We cannot deny that the institution of slavery and colonialism were extremely effective in destroying the social foundations of the indigenous and African populations. Slavery and colonization robbed them of their cultural heritage and as a result, one cannot expect a people stripped of their cultural identity to have anything in common. Thus, people of the Caribbean islands have little or no memory of where they came from. How could they understand the African communal ideals and values which governed them prior to their bondage? They emerged from different cultural groups in Africa and were scattered throughout the Americas, which left them without a cultural center. A people lacking a cultural reference point will find it difficult, if not impossible, to establish a positive self-identity. Without possessing a cultural identity one has no link to their heritage and cultural values. Left in this nomadic condition, Africans, who are a communal people, entered the realm of animals—unaware of their existence. Once a people enters the non-human realm they become feared by the "civilized" and must be controlled. Thus, to suppress the behavior created by slavery and colonialism, some cultural theorists argue that the colonizers had only one means by which to control the people: "Force is the only social mechanism that holds these societies together."[22] This is the logical conclusion taken by the advocates of PST. Once the people were enslaved and later colonized the only way to control them was by using brute force, which is a military strategy that is used by the CIA and rogue governments throughout the world. For example, we see this same strategy used by the U.S. and their adjuncts in Iraq, Libya, and Afghanistan. The United States government created the situation in Iraq and Libya, much like the Europeans gave birth to the Caribbean dilemma. Overall, the strategy remains the same, but these powers have now resorted to a more brutal form of violence to control the monsters they created.

The Creolization Theory (CT) is another academic attempt to explain the on-going conditions that affect the Caribbean and its people. Advocates of CT maintain that the cultural fragmentation in the Caribbean is best understood as a form of creolization and syncretism, which occurred between the various cultural groups scattered throughout the islands. It is not an aberration but a natural process, which occurs whenever too many different cultural groups are forced to contend for limited space. Creolization theorists maintain that "discrete cultural elements that have been transported to the Caribbean environment have undergone a process of transplantation to produce distinct cultural forms that reflect both the history and the social and geographic environment of the region."[23]

Critics of CT point out that the blending of African, indigenous, and European cultural forms, unfortunately, is premised on the belief that every essential cultural element within African tradition either did not survive the middle passage, has disappeared, or were sacrificed and subsumed by more dominant cultural forms.[24] Yet, how could this be, since traditional African cultural forms are very prominent throughout the Caribbean? These TACF are kept alive by millions of practitioners throughout the Caribbean. Black people throughout the Caribbean including Haiti, Trinidad, and Jamaica continue to faithfully observe the sacred rituals practiced by their ancestors. African religion and culture has never fully surrender itself over to the Western construct, nor has it lost those essential elements, not even when Africans were in captivity. Its authentic character remains intact despite undergoing what is best described as a "creole-fusion" and "creole transformations." African symbols, ideals, and artifacts that remain in memory, however fragmented, are those sacred "indissolvable ingredients" that cannot be destroyed. It seems as though certain African cultural forms were wired into African peoples' DNA. These "indissolvable" elements within TACF are the "bones, gristle, and hard seeds that never fully dissolve, even after they have contributed their substance to the broth. These indissolvable ingredients are the survivals and recreations of African traditions within religious-cultural complexes."[25]

The Black Atlantic World

The New World, or the Americas, are partly a European creation. It was initially comprised of European administrators, enslaved Africans, and de facto enslaved indigenous populations. This New European creation brought into existence a new way of thinking about humanity. A new vocabulary was created of which new ways to speak of, and about, the divine were created, especially after the arrival of Africans who introduced new ways of thinking about the divine. They did not come to the Americas without viable culture or as blank slates for Europeans to inscribe their history upon them. Their minds were filled with mythic narratives about gods giving birth to divine men. Most of the enslaved Africans came from West Africa and brought their sacred cultural worldview with them. When Europe was in the throes of barbarism conducting one savage conquest after the other, West Africa was experiencing a cultural renaissance.

Therefore, considering the real background of the Africans brought to the New World, it would be greatly misleading to perpetuate the myth that they entered the Caribbean lacking a religio-cultural etiquette. As a result of their theological grounding we cannot adequately or correctly speak of a "Creole African Religion." For it is more accurate to speak about this Caribbean phenomenon as an "African Creole Religion." This is a very important distinction because African sacred thought remains the dominant cultural form manifested in a variety of styles throughout the Caribbean.[26] Regardless of how TACF manifest themselves throughout the Caribbean they remain authentically African.

It is a waste of time for white scholars and those under their influence to continue perpetuating inaccurate information regarding African people. African people did not come to the Caribbean without religion and culture but arrived with a fully articulate sacred tradition. They engrafted certain elements from the indigenous people's tradition because it is the nature of African religion to respect the religious views of others. The Roman Catholic Church possesses a large pantheon of saints much like African orisha or helper-spirts. This aspect of Roman Catholicism greatly appealed to Africans. After all, they were in a condition akin or worse than imprisonment and housed within a strange and hostile environment. In the Catholic Church the saints were viewed by Africans as possessing attributes similar to their lwa and orisha. Therefore, the enslaved Africans embraced certain Christian ideals that were similar to those they were already familiar with. Decades after a much fuller syncretization occurred between African and Western cultural forms, Africans did embrace certain questionable aspects of the Roman Catholic tradition. Theologically, only those elements within indigenous and Roman Catholic culture that were compatible with African cultural forms were assimilated so they could remain connected to their ancient tradition.

For example, the indigenous populations throughout the Americas had more in common with Africans then Europeans. Both viewed nature as a sacred entity that was alive and capable of sustaining various types of life forms in addition to human species. They believed that human beings were a part of nature and not at war with it. Nature was the Great Mother that was worthy of veneration. She was a Divine Being who was given respect and honor. On the other hand, the type of Christianity the Europeans brought to the New World was one at war with nature. They were in particularly at war with human nature. They subscribed to the Abrahamic ideal, which viewed human beings as inherently evil because they were formed in sin. The body was especially evil and sex was dirty and should only be used for procreating. The human being was born corrupt. These ideals gave rise to the theology underpinning the mindset of those early Europeans who entered the Americas. This theology and way of thinking was foreign to Africans and the indigenous populations in the Caribbean.

The Europeans introduced an aggressive form of Christianity to the New World. It was stepped in imperialist ideology and hegemony. Its vision was guided by "Old Testament" conquer—theology and especially the taking of other people's land. African and indigenous ways of being were non-dogmatic and they had no desire to make converts, which is the hallmark of Christianity and Islam. Enslaved Africans freely borrowed certain ideals from indigenous and Roman Catholic traditions. In part, such theological borrowing was a result of the environment they found themselves facing in the Americas. They were naturally open to new ideas from the various cultural groups throughout West Africa. At the same time, they were equally concerned about the nature of the religion advocated by their captors. Edmonds and Gonzalez argue that the "colonial era in the Caribbean was marked by an explosion of religious traditions that both drew from and challenged the normative of Christianity."[27] The African and indigenous populations challenged Christianity for the sake of their cultural survival. The Christian rhetoric espoused by the colonizers and enslavers hardly matched their behavior. It was the Africans' attempt to understand themselves and their condition that forced them to construct a theology in alignment with their cultural memory and self-image. They were more than the wretched condition in which they found themselves. Within this context, bordering upon a state of anomie, they created and re-interpreted their sacred tradition.

This New World interpretation of African culture has given birth to several re-interpretations of African cultural forms. These African cultural forms are what some scholars mistakenly describe as Caribbean religions. Some refer to this phenomenon as Creole-Fusions or Creole transformations. The name given to these Traditional African Cultural Forms is not as important as knowing the source of these "new world adaptations of traditional religion and culture." What American and European scholars call Creole or Caribbean religion is better described as "transatlantic reinstatements."

For example, Santeria, Vodun, Palo Monte, Abakua, Shango Baptist, and countless other TACF are all reinterpretations of African cultural forms. They represent the evolution of African New World values and systems of thought. With the re-interpretation of African values throughout the Caribbean came new mythological expressions. The New World African aesthetic challenged the Euro-Christian hermeneutic and forced its proponents to re-interpret their theology. The Africans' New World vision gave birth to new interpretations of the divine, which forced some Christians to question their static relationship with the divine. For instance, Espiritismo is a European creation that found its way to the Caribbean and attached itself to certain African cultural forms. It has since been adopted by several African Creole traditions as another medium in a world controlled by the Abrahamic hermeneutic.

The African Creole traditions in the Caribbean are rooted in several African cultural forms of expressions that are housed in many traditions in West Africa. Wherever African traditional cultural forms exist they have an intimate connection with the spirit world. Africa is the home of deities and those divinities can better be understood as nodes of energy, which assist human beings in living a fulfilled life. With the aid of these helper-spirits one can expect to live a rich and meaningful life. The divinities enrich our lives and reside in a place where illusion cannot exists. They dwell beyond the physical realm where one can see past the illusion. Human beings therefore need assistance from the orisha (helper-spirits) and the ancestors to help them experience the world as it truly exists.

Theology (Yoruba-Santeria)

Traditional Africans view the world as a place composed of energies that reside with the orisha. These forces assist human beings as they navigate the paths that one must journey in life. The spirit world is the center of TACF, regardless of how far removed one may be from traditional African life, because the orisha are not confined by space and time. It does not matter if one is a Christian or Muslim. People of African descent believe in an unseen world that is inhabited by spirits, especially one's ancestors. Even the black church seems at times to unconsciously operate as a re-interpretation of TACF, even though such knowledge was no longer in their immediate conscious grasp. This is especially true of the black Holiness and Pentecostal churches in the United States and the Independent Christian Churches in Africa and Jamaica. In those places that "unconsciously" adhere to certain TACF, Jesus is just another orisha who is called upon to assist the devotee throughout life. In the black church, Jesus is the primary orisha, who is called upon much like other African divinities to assist one in time of need. He is praised, venerated, worshipped, and held in highest esteem. Offerings of thanksgiving and praise are given to him for the joy and fulfillment he brings to one's life. Is this not the same role of all African deities? The role of Jesus in the black church whether as savior or lord serves the exact function as the orisha, Iwa, and neteru, which were venerated by their ancestors.

Santeria is perhaps the most popular reinterpretation of any TACF in the Caribbean, and especially in Cuba. Like most African New World cultural forms, Santeria is a Yoruba-based re-interpretation of Yoruba culture and mythology. It, too, has adopted several elements from the Roman Catholic Church, which lately have become problematic, especially for the non–Latino followers of this tradition. There is currently a movement under way to re–Africanize several Yoruba-based religions in the New World.[28] A few Cuban scholars suggest replacing the term Santeria—way of the saints, with Regla Lucumi—rule or way of Lucumi, which is less Euro-Catholic.[29] This designation places less emphasis on the Roman Catholic influence within this African tradition and attempts to replace such problematic terms with "pure" Yoruba theology. *Regla de Ocha*—rule of orisha—is also more African than Santeria. Regla, as it is called, presupposes its African origin and emphasizes the role of spirits, which is the heart of African religion.[30] Santeria/Regla is an African-based spirituality that has its origins in the Yoruba tradition of West Africa. Its theological structure is extremely complex, especially for Westerners who have been trained to think within an Abrahamic framework. Santeria emanates from an ancient cultural system, of which some trace its origins to African Egyptians.

The aim of Yoruba theology is to shed light on the cultural myths and rituals that are the bedrock of Yoruba spirituality. Most traditional societies believe that there is a supreme being who created all things in existence. Such knowledge does not always equate with its Western equivalent, or role of a supreme being. The Abrahamic religions are in some ways obsessed with the idea that societies that lack the concept of an all-powerful single entity have not fully evolved as human beings. This belief has given birth to religious wars that continue throughout the world. Those supposedly lesser evolved societies that lack certain theological concepts or possess a perspective not beholden to the Abrahamic paradigm, especially the single god theory, are depicted as less developed. In the name of civilizing the heathens, wars are waged and the killing of innocent people is justified in the name of furthering civilization or, of late, democracy.

The traditional African view of the Creator is one who does not work alone. Intermediaries or helper-spirits work in conjunction with the Creator. Not only did they assist the Creator in creating the world, but some helper-spirits are also responsible for the creation of human beings. In particular, the divinities assist human and non-human entities in maintaining right relations with everything in existence. Helper-spirits function in many other roles, but their primary duties involve assisting human beings as they complete their life-mission. They have different names depending on the cultural groups and region. For example, the African Egyptians called their pantheon of spirits the *neteru*. In the Yoruba tradition these same spirits are called *orisha*. In the Fon tradition, which found its way to Haiti, they are referred to as the *Iwa*. Regardless of the name given to these nodes of energy, these divinities emanate from a single source. All things are comprised of this energy or life-force. Everything in existence is sustained by this energy, which cannot be created or destroyed. Traditional Africans believe that they are the products of this energy and possess the *Ashe*, or potential to make things happen.

In the Yoruba tradition this energy or potential is described as Ashe. This node of energy originates from the Vital Force. This "divine cosmic energy … is the animating energy in the universe, whether operating in the spiritual sphere, the human sphere, or the physical/material sphere. It is the principle or force necessary for the accomplishment of anything positive."[31] Ashe is potential energy, but once activated by rituals, it becomes kinetic energy. The rituals in Yoruba-based Santeria are designed to strengthen and activate one's Ashe. The health of one's Ashe determines their overall success in life. In Yoruba and Yoruba-derived religions throughout the New World, there is no cult of worship for the Supreme Being; only those nodes of energy called divinities are venerated.

For example, Olódùmarè or Olurun is the owner of all things in Yoruba tradition. Yet, the orisha are the principle players in Yoruba theology. The divinities are key players throughout life's drama because they are the mediums between the physical and spiritual realms. These spirits must be fed and venerated by their devotees. In return, they assist them throughout life and make certain that those obstacles that prevents one from experiencing abundance are eliminated or removed. The spirits have no limitations as do human beings, who are entrapped between the physical and spiritual realms. Thus, the spirits have access to knowledge not readily known to humans. Since they are acquainted with both worlds, they can best guide their devotees throughout life's journeys. Therefore, the orisha are the foundation of Yoruba religion and theology and without them, there would be no contact or knowledge between the real and the illusionary.

For example, every orisha is equipped with specific skills that are needed by their devotees to carry out their life assignment. The orisha provide their devotees with the knowledge and energy necessary to complete the mission that was assigned to them before birth. The deities are also responsible for maintaining harmony throughout the cosmos. Some are protectors of water, earth, thunder, healing, love, dreams, and war. Every human characteristic and trait is under the authority of an orisha—especially those devotees who have surrendered their lives over to a particular orisha.

Throughout Yorubaland there were more than one thousand orisha recognized by the babalawo. Knowledge of the pantheon did not survive the middle passage and today in the Caribbean where the tradition continues, less than 30 orisha have remained alive in memory. Of course in recent years many have traveled to Africa to re-acquaint themselves with those orisha who did not survive the middle passage. Today there are only eight primary orisha recognized by Santeros in Cuba.[32] One comes into a mature relationship with the orisha through possession, divination, and celebrations. Divination is the most important mode of divine communication in Yoruba-Santeria. It allows one to interact with the sprit that carries them beyond the superficial into the place where only truth resides. Sprit possession and divination afford the devotee the opportunity to know themselves beyond the ego, which is one of the primary goals of African religions. It introduces one to their life mission and allows them to foster an intimate relationship with the spiritual forces that guide them throughout their lifetime. In the state of possession, one discovers why they are here and what they must do to fulfill their personal legend. Divination and possession teaches one how to operate from their core and not from the ego.

In the Yoruba–Santeria tradition, divination is referred to as Ifa. The process begins when the babalawo cast the "Opele, a sacred chain of over eight oval-shaped medallions, babalowa's are able to diagnosis a person's condition and prescribe a remedy."[33] Only men can become a babalawo and they must be knowledgeable of the Yoruba mythic cultural traditions. The babalawo acquires his skill-set through many years of intense study and apprenticeships. He must be familiar with the unique character traits of each human being's "archetypical legend [Patakis Odu]." Such readings may require the client to present a gift to a particular orisha, or to perform a unique ritual, such as sacrificing an animal to restore balance and wholeness into their lives.[34] The babalawo may also divine or provide their client a reading by using the Ikin (sixteen sacred palm nuts) to assist them in interpreting one's destiny. Divining with the Ikin in traditional Africa was reserved for royalty, but throughout the New World, the Ikin is used to determine the life-mission of a babalawo.[35]

The art and science of divining is a sacred gift and skill that takes years to develop. The babalawo spends most of his life becoming efficient at divining. Still, there are not enough diviners to serve the many in need of help. Thus in Cuba, Santeros and Santeras (priest and priestess) assist the babalawo in fulfilling the needs of the many seeking guidance and assistance. The Santeros and Santeras divine with a diloggun, which is used much like the Opele. It consists of sixteen cowrie shells that are interpreted by reading the Obi—coconut rinds.[36]

Afro-Cuban Origins

Africans were captured on the continent and taken to Cuba to work on plantations between 1774 and 1865. The actual number of enslaved Africans brought to Cuba is not known, even though some claim otherwise. How could we know how many Africans were brought to Cuba or elsewhere, since the illegal trading of enslaved Africans continued even after it was officially outlawed? Therefore, we do not have accurate figures regarding how many Africans were enslaved and brought to Cuba. We do however know that some came from parts of Western Africa heavily influenced by Yoruba and Congolese traditions. Once in Cuba, they re-connected to their African traditions through the cabildos that were established by the Roman Catholic Church to control and Christianize them.[37] The cabildos were structured according to one's national origin (*Naciones*, or ethnic group). The early cabildos were in some ways akin to the early African American churches that emerged after slavery, which also served a similar function to control and Christianize African Americans. The cabildos functioned to serve religious and social needs of African Cubans. The black church in the United States and the cabildos in Cuba were both created by the white church to control African people's aspirations and hamper their desire for freedom. The Church and the cabildos were created to benefit the establishment but once again, Africans used what was meant to destroy them to keep their cultures alive.

The rationale undergirding the creation of these institutions in hindsight is quite clear. Both the Protestant Church in the United States and the Roman Catholic Church in Cuba understood that when one is kept in a condition where life-affirming cultural elements are not fully celebrated, the people will be unable to experience their full humanity. This strategy was quite successful in the United States, but not in Cuba. In Cuba, Africans used the cabildos to maintain their cultural memory and to re-create new ways of relating to the divine. The Protestant Church that controlled the slave industry in the United States forbade Africans from preserving any connections with their cultural history. This is not to say that the Catholic Church in Cuba celebrated the African's love of their tradition, but there were other factors at play in Cuba that did not exists in the states.

In North America the Protestant church aggressively fought to destroy every remnant of African cultural forms. This strategy was quite effective and we witness its lingering negative affects throughout the black community in the United States. More than any other New World Africans, black Americans appear to have lost their connection with their African heritage. Although the cabildos were not created for Africans to maintain their cultural heritage, this is exactly what happened because in Cuba African elders were committed to retaining their connection to TACF. In the cabildos Africans remained connected to their culture and religious traditions. They were forbidden from openly celebrating their religion, but they hid their orisha in the "guise of Roman Catholic iconography." This was an ingenious act and perhaps more than any other factor accounts for the reason why enslaved Africans in Cuba where able to stay connected with African culture, unlike their counterparts within the United States. Of course there are several other factors that account for black Americans' disconnect from their cultural heritage.

For example, the southern part of the United States was ground zero for North American slavery. Southern Protestantism lacked the pantheon of saints found in Roman Catholicism. In American Protestantism there were no saints to hide the orisha. Enslaved black Americans did not have access to the Catholic saints, where they could disguise their gods and keep them alive. All they had was Jesus, which is why he remains the patron orisha of the black church in the United States. Jesus is more prominent than God the Father. In many ways, he remains the primary orisha in the black Christian world. Religion scholars usually associate the African orisha with Roman Catholic saints without explaining that "the orisha, not the saints, were always the focus of ritual attention."[38] This point is usually ignored by scholars of African "Creole" religions, but we cannot fully appreciate the creolization of African religion without understanding that the Roman Catholic saints were simply symbolic stand-ins, representing the gods who were left behind in Africa. The white saints who were related to the enslavers of African people were the same image chosen by the early Africans to hide their orisha. They kept their sacred tradition alive by hiding it within the same images and theology that justified their enslavement. After all, it was the Roman Catholic Church which first gave its blessings to the European monarchies, theologically justifying and authorizing them to enslave Africans. How brilliant must it have been for those African men and women who recognized that the saints and orisha shared similar attributes. By absorbing certain aspects of Roman Catholic theology, Africans in Cuba were able to keep alive their cultural identity and hence the "cultural focus of their civilization was maintained." It did not matter the garb in which the sacred clothed itself. What was important is that African culture remained alive and would be passed down to the next generation of Africans in Cuba. The white portraits of the saints was not their main concern, as it has become for those who are now attempting to re–Africanize the Yoruba traditions throughout the New World. The image of these saints were of little importance because Africans were able to "rephrase the chromolithographs to fit their own religious language."[39]

Also, the enslaved Congolese in Cuba were already familiar with Roman Catholicism because many were exposed to Christianity prior to their arrival in the New World. For example, the Congo cosmogram or Yowa is a sacred African symbol, somewhat shaped like the Christian cross, although it is not at all related to Christianity. The Congo cross (Yowa), as an African cosmological symbol, "signifies the equally compelling vision of the circular motion of human souls about the circumference of its intersecting lines. The Congo cross ... refers to the everlasting continuity of all righteous men and women."[40]

Throughout most of the New World wherever TACF have been reinterpreted, the white Roman Catholic saints are held in high esteem and many practitioners only possess a cursory knowledge of the African deities represented by the saints. This was not so in the beginning, although African religion has always been organic and culturally diverse. There have always been several competing strains or versions of Yoruba theology practiced throughout the Caribbean and the Americas. For example, as early as 1863, numerous African cultural ideals were competing for dominance and were finally unified under the leadership of Oba Tero and Latuan (Timotea Albear) and

Lorenzo (Ociriaco) Suma.[41] They called their religion *Regla de Ocha* and under this designation, African men formed cabildos and used them for disseminating information. Yet the Catholic Church initially created the cabildos to keep an eye on the African. When the slave trade officially ended in Cuba, the cabildos were forced to re-invent themselves. Africans once again had to adopt new ways to preserve their cultural traditions after the cabildos were viewed by the Cuban government as a potential threat to their control over black people. Also, the end of slavery signaled an end to the supply of new enslaved Africans. It was the newly arriving Africans, who brought with them their culture and ideas that may have been forgotten by the transmitters of TACF.

After slavery officially ended, national affiliation was no longer a prerequisite to become members of the cabildos. Once the enslavement of Africans in Cuba was discontinued, ritual initiation became the determining factor for cabildo membership. When cabildos became more organized and financially independent of the Catholic Church, the Cuban government grew more suspicious of them. The government began to fear the financial independence of the cabildos and the ever growing influence they wielded in the community. The Cuban government especially feared their potential to protest against the government's control over black people. As a result of such unwarranted fears, the government reacted by requiring cabildos to register and apply for a license. They prohibited drumming during ceremonies and placed strict regulations on the requirements for establishing a cabildo. The government banned old-style cabildos in 1888 and removed their legal status as religious institutions.[42]

In particular, the white Cuban government developed an even greater fear of a black insurrection when in the late 1800s, George Emmanuel began to unify the cabildos into a national political party. The Cuban government reacted swiftly by appealing to white Cuban nationalism and especially their tentative relationship to Europe. The government passed laws targeting cabildos and "confiscated religious articles, [established] proscriptions against the use of drums, and [instituted] studies to understand and eliminate sorcery and witchcraft."[43] Again in 1912, the Cuban government began another campaign of terror aimed at destroying African people and their culture. The racist Cuban government resorted to the preferred white strategy for controlling the masses and "massacred 1000 Africans after they established the Cuban independent party of color."[44] The government feared the independent party of color because they would have an inordinate amount of influence over Africans and other Cubans of color. The Cuban government fought back by destroying the cabildos, which functioned as the nerve center of black consciousness. The cabildos were legally outlawed and forced to go underground, which resulted in the black social and religious cultural movements going underground and re-emerging in private homes. Once again, TACF were forced underground where they underwent more changes, which added ever greater strength and character to the cultural forms they carried with them across the Atlantic.

African creole culture departed from the public cabildos and entered the Ile, which were comprised of a "Familia de Saints," lead by house priest and keepers of the tradition. It was during this era, when TACF were forced into hiding, that new African cultural forms were birthed. The house priest became historical figures in black Cuban history because they kept the sacred tradition alive at a time when one could be killed for upholding African traditions. Those house priests who kept African religion alive in practice and memory have since been recognized as the keepers of the tradition. They are now honored in Santeria history for having the courage and risking their lives to keep African culture alive. The persecution of Africans in Cuba during this era, and the house priests' love of African culture, is a testament to the power of this sacred tradition.

African religion and culture did not die when the Cuban government banned the cabildos from organizing. The government intended to kill black culture, but the dedicated house priest and faithful followers of African culture continued to give of themselves to keep the tradition alive. Thus, throughout the 1920s and 1930s, Afro-Cubans gave birth to an African creole-fusion called Afro-Cubanism. This movement marked the resurrection of African religion and culture. It spoke loudly to those haters of black humanity that they could not kill what is real. Death only comes to the temporal, while the permanent last forever. Afro-Cubans again resurrected their African traditions and refused to accept the world that the white Cuban government was forcing upon them. The Africans created a world of their own based upon the cultural values passed down by their ancestors. They embraced the African values based on their cosmology and rejected the foreign ideology forced upon them, which would only lead to ever greater degrees of chaos. For chaos and confusion are the primary elements associated with those who imbibe an alien peoples worldview. Afro-Cubanism was a New World expression of a TACF, and once again signified that black people were "rejecting modernism, with its valorization of empiricism. Science, and technological progress, Afro-Cubanism adjudged the purer, nobler primativity of a healthy approach to life."[45]

In some ways, Afro-Cubanism attempted to articulate Santeria in ways acceptable to white Cubans, who were in fact the most staunch critics of

African culture. Afro-Cubanism was a watered down version of African culture, which whites and mixed-race Cubans could embrace without feeling overwhelmed by blackness.[46] The attempt to water down African Creole religion in Cuba did not set well with dedicated practitioners of TACF. Even this scaled-down version of African culture did not satisfy the Cuban government, which distrusted religion in whatever form it appeared. The adherents of Afro-Cubanism and their adoption of Marxist historical materialism was at odds with the government's communist worldview. Still, the short-lived revolution did provide a brief reprieve for advocates of Santeria, since one of the revolution's aims was to restore relations with the Roman Catholic Church. Of course there was no such move made to even remotely embrace African culture. "While the revolution had to work out an accommodative relationship with the Catholic Church, no such accommodation was granted to Afro-Cuban religion. Santeria and other African-based religious traditions were effectively driven underground. Any public practice of these traditions was relegated to folkloric performances."[47] TACF were regulated to the status of "folkloric" and there remained for most of the 20th century.

Palo Monte is a Congolese African cultural expression that is practiced throughout Cuba and elsewhere in the New World, including the United States. It was brought to the Americas by enslaved Congolese men and women. There are several derivatives of Congo-influenced cultural forms scattered throughout the New World. In Cuba it is known by some as *La Regla De Palo Monte*, or *Regla Congo* or just *Palo*. It was practiced in several regions throughout the sub–Sahara regions of Africa, but in Cuba it is heavily influenced by the Yoruba tradition known as Santeria or *Regla de Ocha*. The Yoruba tradition, more than any other African tradition in New World, is by far the most influential African cultural form in use throughout the Americas.[48]

Some view Palo Monte (the essence) as perhaps the most syncretized of African-Cuban religions. It is referred by some as "religion cruzada," because it is mixed with several African and non–African cultural forms.[49] The Congo civilization was once comprised of present-day Congo-Brazzaville, Gabon, and northern Angola. The name "Congo" was used by enslavers to designate Bakongo people, regardless of what region they came from. When the Congolese arrived in Cuba, some were from Congo and others from Angola. There was a fusion among the Congolese cultures in Cuba, which birthed another unique New World African cultural form. The blending together of the different African cultural groups was a natural event because they shared common cultural ideas.[50]

For instance, there are several versions of Congolese religions in Cuba.

Briyumba, Mayombe, and Kimbisa are considered the most structured of the Congolese cultural forms in Cuba. The core of Congo theology is centered on ancestor veneration and African metaphysics. Congo cosmology is very complex and only the initiated can fully appreciate its rich mysteries. The Congo cosmogram is a cross that represents re-incarnation and humanity's relationship with this world and the one beyond. A practitioner and observer of this sacred sign attempted to explicate its significance. "God is imagined at the top [of cross], the dead at the bottom, and water in between [intersecting line on cross]. The four disks [circles at each end of cross] at the points of the cross stand for the four moments of the sun, and the circumference of the cross the certainty of reincarnation: especially the righteous Kongo person will never be destroyed but will certainly come back in the name or body of progeny, or in the form of an everlasting pool, waterfall, stone, or mountain."[51] When an initiate of this rich African cultural form progresses through the appropriate stages and is ready to be enthroned, they stand upon the sign of the Congo cross, which signifies that he is "capable of governing people, that he knows the nature of the world, that he has mastered the meaning of life and death."[52]

In addition to the Kongo cosmogram there are the minkisi, which consists of herbal medicines, groves, and sacred trees that are at the heart of Kongo cosmology. For example, Kongo healing and divining tradition survived the middle passage and in various forms remains widely practiced throughout the New World. From Brazil, the southern United States, Cuba, and Haiti, it has a faithful following who continue to live by its principles.[53] The Congolese viewed the minkisi as sacred herbal medicine given to them as a divine gift from Mpungu (God). Mpungu placed this power to heal in the hand of kings (Mfumu). The king was the supreme authority, impartial, and lived righteously.[54]

The Kongo viewed their city much like the Yoruba honored Ile-Ife as the birthplace of humanity. Mbanza Kongo was their mythical birthplace, a city not made by hands. The Nkongo (inhabitant of the capital of Kongo) thought of the earth as a mountain over a body of water which is the land of the dead, called Mpemba. In Mpemba the sun rises and sets just as it does in the land of the living. The water is both a passage and a great barrier. The world, in Kongo thought, is like two mountains opposed at their bases and separated by the ocean. At the rising and setting of the sun the living and the dead exchange day and night. The setting of the sun signifies man's death and its rising his rebirth, or the continuity of his life. Bakongo believe and hold it true that man's life has no end, that it constitutes a cycle, and death is merely a transition in the process of exchange.

Mayombe is the more popular of Congolese religions or cultural forms observed in Cuba. Palo Monte in general has more of a negative view than most Kongo religions, but shares many common attributes with other African cultural forms, such as there is no cult or worship of the Supreme Being. Samia, the Supreme Being, has no followers, which is a common practice throughout most traditional African cultures. Practitioners of Palo Monte can theologically be viewed as Universalists in the Western sense because they hold that there is a cosmic spirit Nzambi, who governs all earthly and spiritual affairs. Nzambi is part of the Congolese Trinity, Mayombe, Brillumba, and Kimbisa. Nzambi is a cosmic force that pervades all life forms. This all-pervasive force is omnipresent and exists in all things, organic and inorganic. Nzambi is the divine manifested in the physical realm and in the words of the Christian scribe Paul, in Nzambi we move, we live, and we have our being.

The liturgy of Palo Monte is priest-centered. This heavy focus on the leader is akin to the hierarchy observed throughout black Christendom in the United States. It, too, like other African and creole African cultural forms, has no direct cult of worship for the Supreme Being. It is entirely Jesus-centered, whose followers serve as an orisha much like their African ancestors who venerated certain divinities. Unbeknown to the majority of black Christians, Jesus has replaced the orisha that were lost and forgotten during the middle passage. In some cases, especially in the black American mega-churches, Jesus-centrism has been replaced by the charisma of the pastor. The mega-church is exclusively clergy-centered and the majority of mega-churches in the United States have replaced Jesus and the African orisha with their pastors.

Palo theology is rooted in the Bantu religions of Africa. In Cuba the priest or nganga is not a central figure of the liturgy but the focus is instead upon a cauldron, which is symbolic of the world in miniature. The cauldron represents the world in "microcosm over which the priest can exert control."[55] The nganga remains active by being "fed" through sacrifices that are offered by its followers. The nganga is neutral and has the power to do good or evil, depending on how it is manipulated. The cauldron carries or holds the "mpungus," which are the spirits of the ancestors and other spiritual forces.[56] Once the mpungus that inhabit the cauldron become activated, they can work miracles or perform curses. One must write down his or her *firma* to activate the spirits in the cauldron. Every human has a distinct *firma* or signature which must be safely guarded at all times because if someone has access to another's firma, and want to do them harm, they can do so by manipulating the spirits within the cauldron. If one intends to bring harm to an enemy they must write his *firma* in black and expect the results to occur.

Most importantly, the nkisi was also used by Congolese-Cubans to protect them against the evil of slavery. Both prendas and nkisis were Kongo-

Cuban cosmological symbols that could heal, or when necessary, be pro-grammed to kill one's enemies. The Europeans referred to these sacred objects derogatively as charms, but they were certainly not toys for children or the uninitiated to play with. In the hands of skillful men and women they could be programmed to "mystically attack slaveholders, and other enemies, and for spiritual reconnaissance."[57] The nkisi was used throughout the black Atlantic world, including New Orleans and Charleston, South Carolina, where High John the Conqueror is a black American nkisi. Johnny the conqueror commonly used in the southern part of the United States, is also a Congolese nkisi "reinstatement" used primarily by African Americans.[58]

The seven-star nkisi is one of the most celebrated Congolese symbols in Cuba. It symbolizes the world in miniature and is celebrated in the forests. "The stars come down to this charm. There is an hour in the night when the nkisi is left by itself in the forest, so that the stars may come down, to enter into its power. When you see something brilliant coming down—it is a star, entering an nkisi."[59] In Haiti there is a symbol that performs a similar function, which is called Pacquets-Congo. There are many creolizations of this sacred Congolese symbol in use throughout the Americas. The names given to it are different, but it clearly remains a New World expression of an African Con-golese sacred cultural form. Like Prendas in Cuba, the pacquets of Haiti are cosmic securing points—*ponto de segurar* between the living and the departed.[60]

The nkisi has been defined by one practitioner as "the name of a thing we use to help a person when that person is sick and from which we obtain health; the name refers to leaves and medicines combined together … it is also called nkisi there is one to protect the human soul and guard it against illness for whoever is sick and wishes to be healed. Thus a nkisi is also some-thing which hunts down illnesses and chases it away from the body. An nkisi is also a chosen companion, in whom all people find confidence. It is a hiding place for people's souls, to keep and compose in order to preserve life."[61]

According to those who venerate traditional African cultural forms, the nkisi is not simply a lifeless charm but is alive. It heals the sick because it represents the source of life. "Thus, the nkisi has life; if it had not, how could it heal and help people? But the life of an nkisi is different from the life in people. It is such that one can damage its flesh [*Koma Mbizi*], burn it, break it, or throw it away; but it will not bleed or cry out … nkisi has an inextin-guishable life coming from a source."[62] The nkisi medicine is "spirit-embody-ing and spirit-directing." This medicine (*bilongo*) is very much alive and has a soul (*mooyo*). This *mooyo* is the source from which the nkisi derives its power. The medicines inside the nkisi are spirit-directed and are equipped to "hunt down evil or … make a person more decisive in daily affairs."[63]

6

Traditional African Cultural Forms in the Caribbean

The Abakuá Society of Cuba has its roots in the Ejagham and Efik cultural groups of southern Nigeria. The Ejagham and Efik people gave rise to this ancient secret society that entered the Americas when enslaved Africans arrived in Cuba. The word Abakuá may be a Creolized version of "Abakpa," which is the West African community that honored this sacred tradition. Africans from southeastern Nigeria and the southwestern Cameroon gave rise to an African cultural form that in many ways serves at the center of African theology in the New World. Robert Farris Thompson points out in *Flash of Spirit* that the Ejagham exploded the "myth of Africa as a continent without a writing tradition."[1] The Ejagham developed a writing script called nsibidi (cruel letters). It is purely African in origin and does not borrow from Arab or European writing systems. Nsibidi is an ancient African hieroglyph or ideographic writing system that was brought to the New World by Africans. Nsibidi signs "embody many powers, including the essence of all that is valiant, just, and ordered."[2]

The Ejagham and Efik regions were once viewed as the land of secret societies. The Ejagham elite used nsibidi to communicate, decorate clothing and pottery, and for initiation rituals into their secret society. Nsibidi was everywhere and only the initiated could decode its powerful messages. Those who mastered this sacred art form received much respect for their knowledge of this mysterious communication system. Nsibidi was also used by those wielding power to enforce societal laws and norms. The Nsibidi Society was comprised of "law and order" men who served their community as both judge and jury. They were the "traditional executioners" of their society: "Men who killed convicted murderers or launched preemptory strikes against outside enemies—these men formed what was called the Nsibidi Society."[3]

The Nsibidi corpus was primarily used by men of the Leopard Society for communication that only the initiated understood. In a sense, these ideographic symbols were not unlike the ancient Egyptians hieroglyphics, which also were used by the priest and elite to record information and for communication. Only the initiated or elite had access to this rich source of knowledge. Nsibidi likewise served to "exalt the power of privileged persons and pointed to a universe of aesthetic and intellectual potentiality."[4]

Africans have never been without letters and have used symbols and hieroglyphics to communicate and record their ideas for thousands of years. How the first people who gave birth to the human race could have been the only people in world history who did not develop a writing system has perplexed the savviest of men. Since the African Egyptians have been excluded as black Africans by enlightenment scholars, Africans have been viewed as illiterate and without script. Yet, the Ejagham have proven otherwise as Thompson argues throughout *Flash of Spirit*. The "educated persons [westerners] continue to assume that black traditional Africa was culturally impoverished because it lacked letters to record its central myths, ideals, and aspiration. The Ejagham and other traditional African communities and especially those who entered the New World, developed a creole offshoot of nsibidi in Cuba that attest to Africans history with the written script."[5]

Nsibidi came to the public's attention in 1839, when Cuban police raided the home of a black man. There they found papers with strange symbols or letters. In Cuba these sacred letters have become known as *Anaforuana*, *Ereniyo*, and *Gando*; their meaning depends on the contexts surrounding the writing. There are at least five hundred letters or nsibidi symbols that have been identified in Cuba. "These signs are written and rewritten with mantraic power and pulsation. Mediatory forces, the sacred signs of the Anaforuana corpus, indicate a realm beyond ordinary discourse. They are calligraphic gestures of erudition and black grandeur, spiritual presences traced in yellow or white chalk [yellow for life, white for death] on the ground of inner patios or on the floor of sacred rooms, bringing back the spirit of the departed ancestors, describing the properties of initiation and funeral leave taking."[6]

Ejagham cosmology houses the origin of the Ngbe called the Leopard Society. Ejagham myth has enabled the followers of this sacred cultural form to view human existence much like a theatrical play. Thompson described Ejagham cosmology as that akin to Greek theatrics. "Play for sake of formal excellence, transcending, like the Greeks, their material existence through acts of aesthetic intensity and perfection. Their culture naturally made them the envy of neighboring civilizations ... who eagerly borrowed the artistic fire of the Ejagham."[7]

For example, men in the Ejagham communities were equivalent to the

European philosopher, who had leisure to contemplate the meaning of life. Most labor was performed by women or hired hands so the male could spend his time hunting, being an artist, or perfecting his warrior skills. His culture supported this unique role allowing him time to focus his attention on other matters such as, "the pursuit of excellence in the making of string-net costumes, body-painting, poetry, mime, and processioneering. He developed new dances or entire dramas and sold them with their appropriate emblems to less talented neighboring civilizations."[8]

Ejagham women were the true transmitters of their sacred culture. Their Nkim—fatting-houses—were at one time the source of legends. Here women were instructed on how to be artist, mothers, and transmitters of their rich cultural heritage. Most importantly, in the Nkim women were taught nsibidi and how it is sewn into cloth and painted onto pottery.[9] European writers of Ejagham culture praised these women as "mastery of outline ... far beyond the average to be expected from Europeans." Another writer remarked, "The women of old Calibar are not only surgical operators, but are also artists in other matters. Carving hieroglyphs on large dish calabashes and on the seats of stools; painting figures of poetized animals on the walls of homes."[10]

The women of Ejagham also made Mbufari nsibidi, which are elaborate designs and symbols sewn into cloth. Variants of this tradition are still practiced throughout the New World, especially in the United States where Southern black women sew quilts covered with symbols. They may no longer have memory of these symbols, yet they continue to honor this sacred African cultural form.[11] The patterns and designs sewn into fabric were messages of praise and "acts of creative consciousness."

Nnimm cosmology was as rich and multilayered as the messages sewn into the cloth. According to a Nnimm creation narrative, the first women came from heaven with feathers in the hair. The Nnimm woman were compared to the forests with all its beauty and mystery. They were unlike their European counterpart and were as complex as was the mythology surrounding their existence. They were described by one observer as "multi-textured manifestations of potentialities, resisting the pigeonholing of women as purely instruments of labor. Fear of what these women had intuited and stored within their objects provided checks against injuries that might have been committed against them by men or other women."[12] Ejagham women were respected and feared because some "believed that Nnimm women were privy to ancient secrets first given by—or seized from—beings in the river or the sea."[13]

The feathers or blood-red plumes that adorned the heads of women in Nnimm lodges throughout Western Africa re-emerged in Cuba. The Nnimm tradition did not fully survive the Middle Passage intact but certain aspects of the tradition were successfully re-interpreted in Cuba. The Ngbe Society's main function was to protect the Supreme Force of the cosmos, mother of the sounding leopard, Ebongo. Once in Cuba, Ebongo underwent a creole-fusion and was replaced by Sikan. The African Cuban's re-interpretation and replacement of Ebongo with Sikan, retained much of its original mythology with only minor creole adaptations. The Nnimm reinvented itself in Cuba from the fragments that survived the West African holocaust. African Cubans recreated an old myth within an environment that depicted them as less than human. After surviving one of Africa's worst holocausts, a remnant was able to recreate their myths and in doing so, were able to maintain their humanity.

For example, once in Cuba, Sikan took the place of Ebango and became associated with the sacred drum—"drums of silence."[14] In Western Africa the Ejagham drums were sacred instruments that communicated to the devotee and to those in the spirit realm. In Cuba these sacred symbols are sometimes called the "sese" drums, and were used at the funerals of Abakuá members.[15] The Cubans associated the sese drum with the voice of Sikan—a "powerful female spirit at the heart of their society."

Ngbe cosmology is rooted in Western Africa mythology that has been reinterpreted by New World Africans. According to an Abakuá informant in Cuba, Tanze was an ancient king of Ejagham, from which the myth emerged. "A long, long time ago, when the king died, his spirit became a fish, which a women captured, discovering thus in the river the fortune of the kings of Ejagham. And a man came and took this power away from her, killed this woman, and set up the religion [The Leopard Society]. Lord Tanze was a departed king who enacted the body of a fish and then became the body of a female drum."[16]

Another version of the same myth states the following: "The sacred fish lived for a while in its calabash and then it died. A grand Efut priest, Nasako, began the rites to recapture its spirit within a sacred object in which its mighty voice could sound again. Nasako removed the skin from the body of the fish. Later, in his sanctuary, he traced the first symbol of the leopard society, upon the skin of the fish … the symbol of renaissance and immortality. Over the skin of Tanze, Nasako initiated the seven sons of Ngbe, the founding persons. These represented the seven clans of Efut. These seven chiefs, born in the beginning, included titles which have come down to us in the Ngbe hierarchy, such as it was elaborated among Efut: Mo, Kongo, Ekuemon, Isue, Mpego, Iyamaba, and Nrikamo. Their souls are present today in the seven plumes [of the Abakua lodge] … Nasako then began to build a sacred object for the spirit of Tanze, a base in which his voice could again resound. He covered, with Tanze's sacred skin, the mouth of the calabash in which the fish had lived … but this skin covered calabash gave back the voice of Tanze weakly. It was but a shadow of his voice. Nasako's divining-instrument, Manongopablo, then spoke, saying it was imperative to bring the instrument to stronger life with Sikan's blood. And Nasako then ordered Sikan's sacrifice." This is the origin of living, roaring voice of the living leopard and mystic fish. "The voice was the moral terror that forced an erring person to mend his ways that commended hardened criminals or murders to be killed, that announced a reported incidence of adultery or some other crime against the well-being of the town. Tanze, within the council hall became the source of certainty."[17]

Abakuá may be a creolized version of the Nigerian word, "Abakpa," signifying that one is an original member of the community. The Abakuá Society was comprised of lodges where the initiated swore an oath to secrecy and to protect the sacred voice of Ekue, which served as a "manifestation of God."[18] The Abakuá were associated with dock workers and more independent than their counterparts. The members were all male and were feared by the white Cuban government, and this fear was enough that eventually led to their persecution.

In the beginning only Africans of "pure" blood could join the Society. Eventually, they opened their doors to creoles and others of "mixed blood." This lead to even greater problems for the Society and marked the beginning of their downfall. From this point forward, they were forced to re-invent themselves, which has become the hallmark of all African religions throughout the New World. Adies Petit was one of the first of "mixed blood" to join the Abakuá Society. In 1863 Petit opened his own lodge and began initiating whites. He was viewed as a traitor by many Africans but this hospitable act did not prevent the Cuban government from attacking them. The Abakuá were disciplined and organized and the possession of these two traits alone by a black man are enough of a threat to incur the wrath of a racist and tyrannical government.

Also, because the Abakuá were well disciplined, they were role models for other Africans who aspired to develop similar life skills. Enslaved Africans needed to re-invent themselves and the Abakuá were viewed by many Africans as cultural lights in a land of darkness. They exemplified the sacred principles associated with Africa's classical traditions. The Abakuá had the power to influence many others and their potential to affect positive change among their people became a great threat to the Cuban government. For the Abakuá possessed the power to assist others in acquiring the skills necessary to re-invent themselves. Such traits have historically been feared by those who aim to physically and mentally enslave another human being. A clear-minded black male in the Americas has always been perceived as a great threat to the white establishment. Western hegemony is partly based on keeping the black masses in perpetual ignorance because when black men open their eyes, they begin to love themselves and may attack their real enemy instead of killing each other. A conscious black man signals an end to white supremacy. Thus, the racist Cuban government feared the Abakuá and their potential to re-center African men. Therefore, they began deporting and repatriating Africans to Africa and other parts of the Caribbean. They were deported under the pretense that they were witches. Actually, the Cuban government feared these men because their eyes were open and they began to organize by aligning themselves with pro-independent movements. Eventually, African Cubans created their own party and this became the proverbial straw to break the Cuban government's back. Enough was enough and the Society would have to be destroyed.

African Writing Systems in the New World

Africa was once the center of imparting knowledge throughout the world. The first writing system was created in Africa along the banks of the Nile River south of Egypt. In Cuba there are three types of nsibidi that have their origins in southeastern Nigeria. Nsibidi, or cruel letters, were primarily used by members of secret societies in southwestern Cameroon and southeastern Nigeria.[19] Its style defies Western logic. The Europeans have known for centuries that Africans created the world's first writing system and have used various forms of writing to communicate, record, and preserve their culture. (See the writings of Dr. Bruce Williams, associate researcher of the Oriental Institute, University of Chicago, who wrote on March 1, 1979, in the *New York Times* that the origin of the Egyptian hieroglyphic system lies among black people in the Sudan. He announced the discovery of a black kingdom known as Ta-Seti, which preceded the first Egyptian Dynasty by twelve generations.) The Manding and Akan have also used scripts that pre-date the European Enlightenment that introduced many Europeans to literacy for the first time in history. Nsibidi is an example of an ancient African writing system that reemerged in Cuba and elsewhere in the New World, including Suriname and St. Vincent. In Cuba there are at least three types of writing that have been identified; Anaforuana, Gando, and Ereniyo.

Anaforuana has been described as "Creole concentrations upon certain ancient themes ... reaffirmations of what happened in Africa at the founding of the lodges ... evocations, sacred authorization emblems, importing force to what is done here in Cuba."[20] This style of writing serves liturgical and secular purposes and evokes the same "crossroad imagery" found within the Yoruba tradition. Nsibidi speaks to everyday events and communicates to those in the invisible realm. Anaforuana signs assisted African Cubans in reliving their culture in the New World. They used these signs to remember their family and life in Africa.

For example, the sign of a calabash and seven plumes stimulated their memory to remember Africa and their rich cultural heritage. The primordial calabash signified that "Sikan captured the sounding fish of God within the waters of Ndin."[21] Nsibidi ensured that "creative intelligence" would remain alive within the memory of enslaved Africans, even though they were uprooted from the familiar and placed within a hostile environment. The African writing system that emerged in the New World should not seem strange, especially since we know that at least one of the Egyptian dynasties were ruled by "black Africans." This being the case, why should anyone question the presence of a writing system in Western Africa? It is "surprising only to those who still believe that Africa alone among the continents was without letters, before the arrival of whites, without a means for recording and transmitting moral and folklore. The transformation of Ejagham Nsibidi writing into the creolized offshoot in Cuba known as Anaforuana is one of the signal achievements of the black New World."[22]

Cuba is just one of the places where New World Africans brought their cruel letters. Throughout the New World we catch a glimpse of these reinterpretations of African writing systems. What we have is a black Atlantic writing system brought to the New World by enslaved Africans. In Haiti we have ground signatures called Véve and in Brazil, we have *pontos riscados*, which are derivatives of a common African writing system that survived the middle passage. Nsibidi defies Western logic because it was given to Africans by mermaids.

Another myth states it was given through a vision where "bells and gongs echoed beneath the water."[23] Nsibidi is rhythmic and possesses the vocal elements of "repetition, call and response, and correspondence." Nsibidi was first used by the elite and initiates of African secret societies throughout West Africa. In addition to the Ejagham and Efut, other African cultures used letters to communicate. The women who controlled the fattening houses were masters of nsibidi, especially its usage in clothing and pottery.

For example, the African women who mastered this writing system were held in great esteem and many believed they possessed secret information, such as "Knowledge of supernatural underwater transformations, lore about fish that were really leopards, leopards that were really kings, and many other forces."[24] The initiated and elite used nsibidi to communicate much the same as the ancient Egyptian elite and priests, who used hieroglyphs to not only record the sacred but particular forms of hieroglyphs to record daily activities. Likewise, the secret societies in Africa allowed the elite and initiated to keep their communication hidden from the general public. The Ejagham and Efut secret society members and social elites were the keepers of justice and transmitters of the culture. The letters used for communicating were better understood by the elite but these cruel letters or signs also represented the "heart, the depth, of Ancient Ejagham societies." Anaforuana served the same purpose in Cuba as it did in Africa: to venerate traditional African cultural forms and provide the devotee with power to transcend the mundane.

Vodun

Vodun is an African synthesis of Yoruba, Fon, Bakongo, and Roman Catholic influences. It is also shaped by Native American spiritual principles that are similar to traditional African cultural forms. Vodun is highly syncretic but has never relinquished its African center over to Roman Catholicism. It remains very much a traditional African cultural form and is only "partly informed by the saints of the Roman Catholic Church and by their attributes."[25]

Vodun theology was integrated with other African cultural expressions prior to its arrival in the New World. Thompson described Vodun as perhaps "one of the richest and most misunderstood religions of the planet." He further speaks of the "greatness of Vodun art," and in particular, their writing system which is itself an artistic expression. These grand paintings or signatures, as they are called in Cuba, serve as lines of communication between the Lwa (divinities/helper-spirits) and their devotees. The Vévé and Haitian "flags of meditation" are "perhaps the religions two most beautiful expressions."[26]

Vodun is the most organic of all the New World African expressions. It was greatly intertwined with the religion and culture of its neighbors in Nigeria before its re-transplantation in the Caribbean. When the Dahomey and Yoruba kingdoms were not fighting each other, they were intermarrying and freely exchanging their theological and cultural heritage. Many Dahomey (Republic of Benin) and Yoruba were enslaved and forced to work on plantations throughout Hispaniola. Enslaved Africans enriched the French economy which made Haiti their most prosperous colony. Once Vodun arrived in North America and particular New Orleans, it lost most of its theological richness. Most of the enslaved Africans in New Orleans were more influenced by Congolese culture and theology than by the Dahomey-Yoruba tradition.

For example, the Congolese embraced a nominal form of Roman Catholicism in 1491, when the king declared his kingdom Christian. St. Anthony, one of the most popular saints in New Orleans, was also the patron saint of the Congo. Even today Vodun is heavily influenced by Congolese theology. The Kongo cross or Yowa is perhaps one of the most complex African cultural symbols in the black Atlantic world. Congolese cultural forms combined with Dahomey and Yoruba culture, Roman Catholicism, and Indigenous spirituality. Thus, Vodun is highly syncretic and remains a misunderstood African New World spirituality. Even though it gathered from several cultural groups to shape its spirituality, it takes from none. Vodun advances a rather recent scientific view of the world, that all things in existence are held together by an invisible energy. This energy is controlled by the Lwa—helping-spirits. These spiritual entities control all life activities, including natural and supernatural phenomenon. The Lwa's carry within themselves this "invisible energy that animates the world."[27] All things in the physical and non-physical realm are under the control of these nodes of energy. Human beings are the primary expression of this energy par excellence, especially those who surrender their lives over to the lwa. Only after surrendering to these forces does one become a vessel and will be assisted by these forces throughout their lives. The lwa will guide and protect their devotee and most importantly, live inside of them. Thus, not even physical death can displace this power.

Once a relationship is formed between the devotee and Lwa the individual can then expect to receive favors from his lwa such as guidance, protection and special knowledge. The Lwa exists in both worlds and therefore have access to knowledge and information not available to humans confined to the physical realm. With this special knowledge (Konesans), the devotee has access to past and future events. This contract is premised upon the relationship established between the Lwa and devotee. The devotee must "feed" the Lwa to remain in good standing. Long as the lwa is honored, celebrated and properly fed, it will continue to "ride" its "horse." The devotee aligns themselves with the Lwa through a set of elaborate rituals, which "takes place most forcefully through initiation ceremonies."[28] Once the alignment between the devotee and lwa is completed, the individual becomes the property of the Lwa. They are then required to "feed" the Lwa through rituals and ceremonies that must be strictly maintained. If this relationship is neglected by the devotee, they run the risk of placing their relationship with the lwa in jeopardy. This will create a great amount of instability in their lives. Any strain in the relationship between the Lwa and devotee can also produce cosmic instability. When one is estranged from their Lwa the world becomes imbalanced. When this happens chaos will fill the void created from the estranged relationship between the devotee and the lwa. This imbalance creates mental and physical instability and if not repaired, can eventually lead to the death of the devotee.

Therefore, to maintain individual and cosmic harmony requires that one must nurture their relationship with lwa. The Vodun ceremonies are the primary place where Lwa are "fed." The ceremony is where the "Vodouisants assume the responsibility to honor and serve the Lwa and to assist them with life's challenges."[29] After the lwa are properly fed they will confirm their presence by mounting their "horse"—the devotee. Once they possess the devotee they can then begin to communicate to them. During "the possession Lwa temporarily displace the personality and consciousness of the persons who serve as their horses and use their bodies to communicate with the community."[30]

Vodun is communal oriented much the same as most traditional African cultural systems. Traditional African cultural forms share this basic fundamental and cannot exist outside of a community. For example, an Afro-Mexican informant of Costa Chica remarked that she could not conceive of a community without the Mandé-influenced round home, redondos. When shown a picture of a group of houses she stated the following: "This drawing does not represent a house, know why? Because the other round houses are missing, and without them, there's no balance, between man and man."[31] In other words, there is no individual existence at least not meaningful, outside of a unique community—one that shares in common cultural and spiritual values.

Overall, Vodun is a holistic African cultural expression that serves to address the total human being. Vodun is communal and seeks to bring the individual into right-relations with the cultural principles that uphold communal values. Its myths are rooted in TACF observed by practitioners in Haiti and those throughout the New World who honor this tradition. Vodun is influenced by the Yoruba, Fon, Kongo, Native American, and Roman Catholic traditions. Even though it has been nominally influenced by non–African traditions, currently there is a movement under way to "re–Africanize" Vodun. Many students of Vodun are not happy with the Roman Catholic influences, especially its iconography, since many of these white saints have become the objects of worship. Both Vodun and Santeria are being re-evaluated in an attempt to remove the "whiteness" that has stained this sacred traditional African cultural form. "The attempt at re–Africanization is driven by the belief that returning Vodun to its "pure" African roots will bestow more authority and legitimacy on the tradition."[32]

Revival Zion and Spiritual Baptist

Traditional African cultural forms have undergone many changes throughout their re-transplantation in the New World. Many non–African scholars celebrate what they call "Creole Religions" because this term slightly negates the influence of its African foundation. Non-whites have indeed been a part of the re-formation of African religion throughout New World. Yet it wasn't until the mid-twentieth century that African cultural forms in the Caribbean would spread beyond the black community.[33] The attempt to re–Africanize Creole religions in the Caribbean aims to correct the revisionist history in academia and elsewhere. It will be difficult but not impossible to de–Europeanize African religion in the New World. The process of removing the foreign garments used to cloth African deity and replace them with their original garb will be a difficult challenge, but one that must be done.

For example, Revival Zion in Jamaica has been moving away from their African roots for centuries and embedding itself within the Pentecostal church. Since arriving in the Caribbean over two hundred years ago, it has nearly been absorbed by Pentecostalism. Revival Zion was created to serve the poor and underclass but its current association with Pentecostal megachurches and their prosperity gospel is waging a war against the poor. The prosperity gospel's primary theological dogma argues that the poor have misunderstood God, and this, more than any other factor, accounts for their poverty. The proponents of the prosperity gospel fail to mention how an unjust socio-political system with its preference for the corporate elite functions in the destruction of social systems. Unfortunately, many megachurches are clearly aligned with corporations and wealthy donors. Revival Zion has replaced its historical mission to serve the poor with mega-church philosophy, which condemns the poor for their poverty.

The Spiritual Baptists or Shango Baptists in Trinidad are also being challenged to re-evaluate their theology. This has proven difficult for an Afro-Christian movement that embraces Orthodox Christianity, and especially those who want to re–Africanize what started as an African-center tradition.

The Shango Baptist serves God with two hands—Christianity with one hand, and the Yoruba orisha tradition with the other. Many "Shouting Baptists," as they are called by some, are content with its theology and would not dare change it. They have no desire to challenge what has served their fore-parents for hundreds of years. Shango Baptists and Revival Zion are indeed "African Creole" cultural expressions that may be more or less Christian, depending on their location. In some ways, both of these traditions are deeply African because of their willingness to embrace new paradigms and their ability to adapt to new environments. An openness to other mythoforms to enrich one's tradition is a common feature of African spirituality. African spirituality's willingness to adopt new ways of being in the world distinguishes it from the Abrahamic traditions, which justifies killing in the name of their singular god. African-based cultural expressions possess an openness to embrace new deities and this ability to adapt to new environs may be the primary reason why TACF survived the middle passage. The ability to re-invent itself places African religion in an exalted category, especially when we consider the cultural destruction of non-white people throughout the world. Sometimes the annihilation of "other" people's cultural forms takes place in the name of Moses, Jesus, and Muhammad. In this regard, African cultural expressions can serve as a vehicle in which we can emulate and learn how true religion presents itself. Authentic religious discourse must be non-dogmatic and humane to all, especially to people of different races and religio-cultures. Only a religion capable of adapting to a new environment and remain adverse to militarism should be tolerated in the New World.

Black Atlantic TACF are dynamic, adaptive, and ever-expanding their view of the divine. This is a unique trait rarely witnessed because the Abrahamic religions openly support militarism and use their theology to justify all forms of oppression, especially when aimed at non-white populations. Traditional African cultural forms throughout the Caribbean were borne from a different hermeneutic. "Once formed, these traditions never become static cultural artifacts but were dynamic, evolving traditions that responded to new influences and adapted to the changing realities in the region."[34] It was those ancient African humanitarian characteristics—a preference for embracing change instead of fear—which allowed African religion in the New World to adopt certain features of Roman Catholicism and other local traditions. It was natural for Africans to accept ideas from other people's culture, long as they did not conflict with theirs.

Traditional cultural forms are pervasive and pervade every area of one's life. They consciously seek to engraft ideas outside of their historical and cultural confines. Yet this does not weaken or even contaminate the tradition. African spirituality is richer because of its ability to take within certain elements from other cultural systems. The followers of traditional African cultural forms are enriched as it extends its definition of an all embracing spirituality. In so doing, the tradition remains vital and is not so easily uprooted. "They retain African orientations and aesthetics in the way in which they understand and deploy their faith to deal with exigencies of life."[35]

The Revival Zion and Shango Baptists subscribe to certain Christian tenets but have also maintained their preference for certain TACF. They do not possess a fully articulated theology like Santeria and Vodun. Still, there are clear aspects within these Afro-Christian traditions, which have retained many African cultural elements. For example, God as the Supreme Being is acknowledged, but is afforded no direct worship. This is a common trait in most traditional African cultural systems and is observed even by those who have adopted other people's culture as their religion. Still, unconsciously, they too abide by this ancient African theological tenet by not providing direct worship to the Supreme Being.

Case in point, African American Christians have unconsciously elevated Jesus to the status of an African orisha. Jesus is venerated in liturgy with songs of praise and worship but very few songs are sung with the same fervor to God. In this regard, Jesus remains the sole focus in every major black church in the United States. Likewise, in Revival Zion and Shango Baptist traditions, Jesus has been elevated to the status of an orisha. The Supreme Being is "transcendent and removed from the milieu of everyday life. Jesus and the Holy Spirit is the vital presences that are believed to empower and sustain the lives of adherents as they struggle to sustain themselves spiritually, socially, and materially in this world."[36]

African spirituality is experiential and the seeker in pursuit of truth is encouraged to "feel" the divine for themselves. Experience as opposed to belief is a critical African theological tenet that can be witnessed in Revival Zion and Shango Baptist churches. Both traditions place more emphasizes on having an experience with the divine than on orthodoxy. In many ways these traditions are consciously "oriented to having experiences of the divine in the body and marshalling spiritual resources to deal with aspects of everyday existence, such as health issues, material resources, and social relationship."[37]

Revival Zion has its origins in Obeah and Myal West African TACF. The Native Baptist Movement emerged from within a climate created by these two traditions. African American clergy attempted to Christianize these ancient African cultural forms and merge these African expressions with the expressive and experiential form of black Christianity, first articulated in the

Americas by enslaved Africans. Later, it was further shaped by Alexander Bedward's theology and these factors gave birth to the African Pentecostal movement in Jamaica.[38]

George Liele and Moses Baker introduced practitioners of Obeah and Myal to African American experiential Christianity. Liele was also the co-founder of the First African Baptist Church in Savannah, Georgia. His interpretation of Christianity was African-centered and lent itself to the kind of hermeneutic that practitioners of Obeah and Myal were somewhat familiar. The primary focus of Obeah spirituality was centered on magic, or the control and manipulation of spiritual forces. Myalism focused its spiritual energy on healing and the use of herbs to restore and maintain one's physical and spiritual health. The "Myal men," as they were called, focused upon making connection with "cosmic energy." Cosmic energy is a divine force they believed was available to its leaders so they could heal the community and provide them with solid leadership.[39]

Many students of traditional cultural forms in Jamaica assume that Myalism and Obeaism were sworn enemies constantly at war with each other. Those who advocate such tension existed between the two African cultural forms believe that these theological wars began in West Africa from whence the cultural groups originated. Others assert that they were most likely from the same cultural group and were simply focusing upon a different aspect of a common African tradition.[40] Aside from speculation it is clear that both Myal and Obeah were traditional African cultural forms, struggling to re-interpret themselves in Jamaica. "Drawing upon African heritage, they constituted a religious ethos with beliefs and practices that countered the Christian ethos of the dominant class."[41]

Another scholar of African creole religion made similar comments regarding Myal and Obeah, as African cultural forms that served several functions, one of which was to combat racism, which was a European value. "This [Myal and Obeah] tradition has been a powerful catalyst for Afro-Jamaican resistance to European valves and control."[42] Obeah and Myalism are African expressions that provided enslaved Jamaicans with a cultural connection to their home, during a time when they were perceived by the white world as non-human. These sacred African cultural forms expressed by the Myal and Obeah tradition, reminded the enslaved of their rich cultural heritage and re-assured them in spite of white barbarism that they were highly valued as human beings. The Obeah and Myal TACF assured enslaved Africans that they were indeed fully human, even in the midst of a people who treated them worse than dogs. These African spiritual systems were the only thing of value available to Afro-Jamaicans, which assisted them in maintaining their cultural connection to their home and their humanity. More than any single factor, African spirituality allowed enslaved Jamaicans to maintain their humanity in the face of European barbarism. African Jamaicans resorted to magic and herbs to heal their troubled mind and body. Magic and healing rituals accomplished what the type of Christianity the slave masters offered them could not provide.

In West Africa the Myal tradition was known as *Mwela*—breathing power or cosmic energy, which was possessed by spiritual leaders. This sacred energy was used by spiritual leaders to address communal needs, not simply for one's personal use. The Myal tradition, much like the Ejagham and Efik of Calibar, originated from secret societies that were scattered throughout West Africa. The knowledge possessed by the initiates from these societies was complex and strictly secret. Such knowledge within these secret groups gave rise to the theology adopted by the Myal in Jamaica.

For example, many traditional African religions are known throughout the Western world as "dance religions." The Myal dance is performed by its members to assist them in reaching a state of possession, which serves to "connect the participant to sources of spiritual or cosmic energy." The dance may seem strange to outsiders, but focusses on preparing the initiate to communicate with the spirit world. Spirit possession allows one to transcend the ego and enter into a realm where they can hear from the divine. Practitioners of traditional African cultural forms were known for combining the intellect with intuition, much like the pairing of male and female deities that provides one access to "cosmic energy." When one aligns themselves to this force they find healing for their mind and body. Once in alignment with this divine energy they begin to restore the broken relationships with deity and ancestors. The restoration and balance to one's life was actually the focal of Myalism. It, like most African cultural systems was designed to assist human beings in this life. African tradition cultural forms have always aimed to "equip its members to deal with everyday personal and community problems and with the greatest evil of all, their enslavement and exploitation of colonial plantations."[43]

Spiritual Shango/"Shouting" Baptist

The Shango Baptist tradition of Trinidad is an African Christian religion which accepts most of the major Christian tenets. However, certain aspects of its liturgy and theology are African, or New World adaptations of an African religion. The liturgy is similar to the African American Christian tradition, which shuns orthodoxy and is experiential-oriented. The Spiritual Baptists trace their roots to African American immigrants brought to Trinidad around 1812. These men fought with the British during the Revolutionary War and brought their unique style of Christianity to Trinidad, such as the typical African expressions like call and response, spontaneity, spirit possession, and speaking in an unknown tongue. The African American aesthetic combined with Afro-Trinidadian spirituality laid the foundation for the Spiritual Baptist tradition.[44]

This particular theory of its founding has been questioned by some, but the "trumpet songs" which serve a major role in the Shango tradition have their origin in Negro spirituals. The Spiritual Baptists have maintained a cultural and theological connection to their African spirituality. They continue to venerate certain Yoruba orisha who were brought to Trinidad by their enslaved ancestors. The orisha are venerated in various forms by millions of black people throughout the Caribbean. These spiritual entities assist their devotees in confronting issues of health, finding success in relationships, and comforting them during moments of crisis.

In Trinidad and Cuba only about 30 orisha are recognized by most practitioners of traditional African cultural forms. Most of the pantheon were lost or forgotten during the dreadful middle passage. The Catholic saints replaced some orisha with Peter, Raphael, Anthony, Barbara, and a host of other saints. Originally, these white saints were not the focus of worship but only represented a comparable energy possessed by African spirits. Today, there is a movement in Trinidad and throughout the Caribbean to re–Africanize the orisha tradition. The re–Africanization of African deity has been described as the "Yorubanization of Orisha." This is a genuine attempt to restore the orisha to their original African identity, as understood by the Yoruba of Nigeria. The Roman Catholic white saints are an insult to many Yoruba practitioners in Africa and especially those devotees of African religion in the African American community. The attempt to re–Africanize the orisha tradition throughout the New World is more than one simply waging a battle against whiteness. It is a noble effort to "purge non–African elements from the religion and to make it conform to Yoruba religion as practiced among the Yoruba in Nigeria."[45]

The Shango Baptist liturgy is centered on fasting, shouting, possession, divination, and mourning rituals. There leaders are called Mothers and Fathers, terms that are also used in African American Pentecostal and Holiness Christian traditions. (Today in the African American Pentecostal and Holiness Church, "church mothers" still serve a prominent role.) The teachers instruct novices on baptism principals, how to interpret dreams, visions, and other ritual preparations.[46] Provers are those who test the sincerity of new believers, especially those who claim to be "saved." Preachers expound upon biblical principles, while Pointers provide spiritual direction to new converts. Nurses are care-givers for children or actual health practitioners that assist the congregants. Shepherds watch over children, especially during the services.

The most important element within Shango theology are the orisha. The orisha are spiritual entities or nodes of energies that serve humanity for good or ill. They make their "appearance in possession rituals, where they displace the personalities of the individuals they possess and use those believer's bodies to dance and to deliver a message to those assembled. They often communicate through dreams and visions and divination rituals performed by priests reading obi seeds [kola nuts] or gazing in water."[47] Hyperventilation may occur when the orisha enters one's body. This is a sign that the evil inside one's body is leaving them. The individual will be restored to wholeness once this uninvited entity is removed. Animal sacrifice outside the temple is also used to restore individual and cosmic balance. Only when one is completely free of energies that are hostile to human growth and develop can they receive the "right hand of fellowship." This implies they have been fully initiated, empowered from on high, and are full-fledged members of the Church.[48]

Yoruba in the New World

"The man in touch with his origins is a man who will never die."[49] Those who are estranged from their culture of origin and its traditions will remain at war with themselves. Traditional Africans venerated their ancestors and could never imagine abandoning them for foreign myths. Traditional African cultural forms survived the middle passage and were re-transplanted by enslaved Africans throughout the New World. The Yoruba tradition more than any other African cultural form has provided the black Atlantic world with its deepest connection to traditional ways of being. When we speak of Condemble in Brazil, or Lucumi and Santeria in Cuba, and to some extent Vodun in Haiti, we are speaking about an African cultural form whose foundation is based in Yoruba thought.

Robert Farris Thompson wrote in *Flash of Spirit* that the Yoruba are the "creators of one of the premier cultures of the world." The Yoruba were at the height of civilization when most of Europe was still in the Dark Ages. "At a time, between the tenth and twelfth centuries, when nothing [artistic] of comparable quality was being produced in Europe, the master sculptors of Ile-Ife were shaping splendid art."[50] Yorubaland was comprised of city-states and very early in their history they created aesthetics that continue to be observed by millions of black people throughout the New World. New World Yoruba cultural traditions have taken many forms since their emergence in the New World. Yoruba spiritual traditions are known by several names throughout the black Atlantic world. In Cuba it is called *Regla de Ocha, Santeria,* or *Lucumi,* after the Yoruba word *Olukumi*—my friend. Once Yoruba entered the Americas there was a fusion of deities from several African traditions, followed by the absorption of indigenous and European cultural forms. Many scholars usually omit that there was a major syncretization of TACF prior to Africans entering the New World. Instead they focus their discussion on why African religion in the New World is dependent on Roman Catholic saints. This is true to an extent, but long before the people of Yorubaland entered the New World, they had already begun the process of infusing traditional Yoruba deities with the deities of their neighbors. Especially of note is the relationship between Yoruba and Dahomey deities. Once these TACF entered the New World, there was an even greater synchronization between various African traditions, including the blending of Congolese, Dahomey, Ibo, and Yoruba traditions.

Eventually Africans were introduced to Roman Catholicism and were attracted to the saints. At first they did not venerate these foreign deities, but only used them to shield their gods because they recognized similarities between the orisha and the saints. With the knowledge of their gods' "attributes, [they] worked out a series of parallelisms, linking Christian figures and powers to the forces of their ancient deities."[51]

Many Yoruba were captured and taken in large numbers to Cuba, Brazil, Haiti, and Trinidad. Even today there are parts of Haiti where some still speak with the Yoruba dialect. Those who populated the New World "emerged from ... Ketu Yoruba men and women captured by the Dahomeans turned up in Haiti and Brazil, where to this day they are called by the Dahomeans word nago."[52] Africans were forced to re-invent themselves upon arriving in the Americas. They loved their traditional culture and did everything in their power to remain connected because it was the source from which they derived meaning as human beings.

Any people removed from their culture and transplanted in a hostile environment will experience great levels of confusion and despair. For all practical purposes, African cultural forms should not have survived the middle passage. Not even the fragments that were stored in their collective memory and later used to reinterpret their sacred culture. Yet, it was the retransplanting of traditional culture within an alien environment that gave it new meaning. Thompson described the reinterpretation of African traditional cultural forms in the New World as one of the "great migration styles in the history of the planet."[53]

Africans entered the New World with a profound knowledge of their sacred traditions. More importantly, they taught their enslavers the true meaning of human hood by maintaining their humanity, in a condition Chinua Achebe described as "mankind's greatest crime against humanity." Both the enslaved Africans and the indigenous populations throughout the Americas provided Europeans a glimpse of humanity that they were not accustomed to seeing. In many ways Africans and Native Americans taught their enslavers and colonizers how to be human. Even though we may all have the "potential" to become fully human, reaching our full humanity is not a certainty, but an evolutionary possibility.

Upon arriving in the New World Africans began to re-construct a new theology based upon their unique experiences. Out of this re-construction they replaced pure African deities with a "Creole image" of divinity. The blending of the old and new allowed Africans to expand their theological perspective and most importantly keep their traditions alive. African traditional religion was amenable to this kind of expansion because it is non-dogmatic and lacked the missionary zeal found in Islam and Christianity. African traditional cultural forms could not have survived the brutal transplantation from an embracing environment to one at war with their humanity if it had been a zealot religio-culture. Syncretism, or the blending of different cultural forms, is not a sign of weakness but one of strength. It is like retelling a myth with a thousand voices. Contrary to acceptable opinion the syncretism that occurred between African deity and Roman Catholic saints is not as simple as it appears. "Outwardly abiding by the religious practices of the Catholics who surrounded them, Africans covertly practiced a system of thought that was a creative reorganization of their traditional religion. Luminously intact in the memories of black elders from Africa, the goddesses and gods of Yoruba entered the modern world of the Americas. They came with their praises [oriki], extraordinary poems of prowess that defined the moral and aesthetic reverberation of their presence."[54]

In essence, syncretism from a New World perspective is a "creative reorganization" of ancient and new ideas. This was an effective strategy that allowed Africans to maintain their way of being within a hostile environment. The New World Africans kept their culture alive by mastering the skill of creative reorganization and that was an act of African genius. In addition to learning from their sacred spiritual traditions, they also taught us how to maintain those essential aspects of traditional values even within a hostile environment.

Any meaningful discussion of New World African religions should begin with the Yoruba tradition. It is the largest non–Abrahamic African traditional religio-culture in the New World. The Yoruba tradition is considered the "most salient surviving African belief system in the New World."[55] Regardless to its many names, Regla, Lucumi, Santeria, Shango Baptist in Trinidad, or Roots in the United States; it is an African traditional cultural form expressed anew. It has provided the world with a glimpse into the richness of African culture. "The Yoruba remain the Yoruba precisely because their culture provides them with ample philosophic means for comprehending and untimely transcending, the powers that periodically threaten to dissolve them. That their religion and their art withstood the horrors of the middle passage and firmly established themselves in the Americas ... reflects the triumph of an inexorable communal will."[56]

When those enslaved Africans influenced by the Yoruba and Fon tradition began arriving in Haiti to work the sugar and cotton plantations, another blending of Yoruba and Dahomey cultural forms occurred. The cultural blending was not confined to the Yoruba and Dahomey population, but enslaved Africans from Congo were involved in this mixture. In this regard, Vodun is an African cultural form that was again "re-blended," when several African cultures came together in Haiti. They gave rise to what some call "Creole religion." This is not the same Creole religion that one speaks about when discussing the influence of Roman Catholicism on Vodun. This is an "African re-blending" of "classical religions of Congo, Dahomey, and Yorubaland [which] gave rise to a Creole religion."[57]

New World Vodun is divided into two parts, which is a reflection of the African traditions most reflected in those unique aspects of the religion. For example, Rada, named for the Africans from Arada, is considered the "cool side" of Vodun. Petro is the "hot side" from the Congo tradition. The two traditions of Vodun are simply different aspects or emphases placed on certain cultural ideals deriving from common African cultural forms. These African ideals "fused similar religious aspects of different African cultures."[58] It's important to remember that the Yoruba and Dahomey deities were already fused long before they entered the Americas. For instance, the Yoruba Supreme Deity, Olorun, and the Fon Mawu, combined to become *Bondieu* in Haiti. Ogun fused with GU and became Papa Ogun in Haiti. The Ewe, Fon, and Yoruba cultural forms had already undergone a major fusing prior to their arrival in the Caribbean. Once in the Americas, they combined the Congo and Roman Catholic spiritual traditions with their organic and ever expanding pantheon.[59] Syncretism is in fact an ancient African tradition as old as the culture. Its roots are in the common African cultural forms that combined to give birth to Vodun and other TACF. Roman Catholicism was later engrafted into the Africans theological world view not to give value to the religion, but a conscious act of necessity for the survival of African culture.

Yoruba Theology

Yoruba myths reveal the complexity of traditional African cultural forms and how they have shaped African thought. African cultural myths are multilayered and seek to address questions involving the nature of existence, one's life purpose, and how human beings participate in the ongoing creation process. Everything in the universe is energy and therefore Yoruba theology is highly focused on entities that are representatives of this Vital Force. The orisha that comprise the Yoruba pantheon can be viewed as nodes of energy which assist the Creator in the ongoing evolutionary process. All things are evolving and vibrating throughout the cosmos and within Yoruba thought—this creative process is known as Ashe.

Ashe is pure energy that emanates from the Vital Force. It governs all things in existence. Ashe is the ruler of all things and there is no force good or otherwise, that exists outside the purview of it influence. Ashe has been called the "principle of all that lives or acts or moves ... everything which exhibits power, whether in action or ... in passive resistance like that of the boulders ... the orisha are only part of such forces, the part that is disciplined, calmed, controlled."

Eshu is the Yoruba orisha associated with divine energy that emanates from the Vital Force. He is at times incorrectly associated with the Christian devil. Yet, Eshu is a much more complex entity which does not lend itself to such simple equivalents. He is incorrectly associated with the "Christian and Moslem [sic] Devil wherever Yoruba religion has come into contact with theologies which promulgate a more exclusive concept of evil." Eshu is the orisha who safeguards ashe, much like the Egyptian Thoth. Eshu is also the possessor of the Word, Energy Incarnate, and the Divine Paradox. These are only a few of the theological attributes associated with Eshu-energy. Eshu is also known throughout the black world as the trickster deity and venerated by millions of practitioners of TACF. Some consider him the most powerful of all Yoruba deities second only to the Creator.

The attributes of Eshu have also been described more "more serviceable than other saints ... whatever evil you would want him to do you go to him because we have the privilege of talking to him as much as we talk to the saints. "I talk to him just as I talk to the saints but I would not serve him." Eshu is second only to Olorun the Supreme Deity, and all other deities must pay him his "respects" or suffer the consequences. He serves an important role in Yoruba theology and is known across the black Atlantic world by several names. Eshu is the cosmic representative of chaos and rebirth, "because he is chaos itself in certain of his aspects, he can either permit or subdue chaos." There are many New World alters erected in his honor.

Eshu is a very popular New World orisha and, among many things, represents the complexity of African experiences. Eshu is the archetypical deity who symbolizes the different, and at times, conflicting aspects within an individual or cultural group. For instance, Juana Elbein dos Santos implies that Eshu is an arch-type of human nature. "Each individual is constituted and accompanied by his own personal Eshu, the element which permits his birth, ultimate development and progeny ... in order that [Eshu] can fulfill harmoniously a person's cycle of existence, the person must without fail restore, through sacrifices, the ashe devoured, in a real or metaphoric way, by his principle of individualized existence."[60]

In the Afro-Cuban re-interpretations of African cultural forms, elaborate myths depict Eshu as one who "devours himself but once again returns when proper sacrifice, centered upon a piece of stone, is made. The Afro-Cuban Eshu mythoform is an "intricate retelling of the Yoruba belief that the highest form of morality is sharing and generosity."[61] In many of the Yoruba-Santeria homes in Cuba and throughout the Americas, practitioners honor certain symbols that represent Eshu, although they claim not to worship or venerate these images. All must pay their respect to Eshu because he is the divine Logos and the mouthpiece of god. Eshu is the "messenger of the gods, not only carrying sacrifices, deposited at crucial points of intersection, to the goddesses and to the gods, but sometimes bearing the crossroads to us in verbal form, in messages that test our wisdom and compassion. Sometimes he even "wears" the crossroads cap, colored black on one side, and red on the other, provoking in his wake foolish arguments about whether his cap is black or red, wittingly insisting by implication that we view a person or thing from all sides before we form a general judgments."[62]

All that is in the visible world and in the realm of the ancestors is a representation of ashe. The orisha are the primary representatives of this divine incarnate force. It has been described by some as pure potentiality, power to "make things happen." We are all intimations of this power and yet the orisha are the premier vessels in which ashe is most active. According to Yoruba cosmology, ashe first entered the earth through a viper earthworm, and snail.

It was through these animals that ashe was made available to humanity. Ashe is a "morally neutral power" or pure potential, "power to make things happen." The orisha are messengers of ashe and there have been many "Aviators of Ashe" upon the earth. This potentiality has appeared in "multiple forms, multiple aviators."

For example, in traditional Yorubaland the king was considered "Master of Ashe." He was divine and second only to the orisha. This explains why kings throughout traditional Africa performed certain priestly functions. In traditional African communities and in the New World where TACF are observed, one has to undergo an initiation to "receive" ashe. Once ashe implants itself into the devotees psyche, it is "sealed in a small incision cut at the upper-most portion of his shaved head and placed within the container of one's personal Osun bird-staff with disk and bells." In New World Yoruba traditions, the Osun Bird is usually associated with one's personal destiny. In Dahomey the bird staff was associated with mental and emotional faculties representing "universal thought: the triumph of the mind over the annihilating circle of destruction and disease."[63]

Conclusion

The world has drastically changed since *African Traditional Religion in the Modern World* was first published ten years ago. We have witnessed the rise of barbarism and violence under the guise of fighting terrorism. This has proven to be so pernicious that even the most hawkish warmongers must search for new language to justify their propensity for shedding blood. Many would agree that 9/11 was the event that those thirsting for blood used to justify what was apparently already in their hearts. The ideologues behind the American New Century were looking for opportunities to birth an American vision that would keep the country in a state of perpetual war. Their vision of the New World focused not on diplomacy aimed at keeping the citizenry at peace, but the American New Century project was committed to using brute force to solve what was once political differences between nations. Under George W. Bush the United States placed the American people in a vulnerable condition that not even Western religion can provide us with a solution. In fact, there are some who argue that the wars in which the U.S. government is engaged are religious in nature. Even though it does appear that the U.S. government is waging a war against Islam, this analysis is only partial and fails to view the crisis in its totality. The U.S. government is not at war with Muslims because if it were the Saudis would not possess the special status they have with the government and their corporate adjuncts.

The U.S. government appears to be controlled by a corporate elite that some have labeled as the 1 percent. No one can deny that representative democracy has died in America and the people are at the mercy of the corporations who control foreign and domestic policy. The people are in need of a participatory democracy, but it appears as though this cannot happen as long as corporations control the electoral process.

Some may wonder what the U.S. government has to do with African traditional religion. First, the United States has set up military bases throughout many nations in Africa. Africom is the recolonization of Africa and as before, the French, British, and United States are deciding what parts of the continent it will control and take back from the Chinese. With these white powers back in control of Africa—not that they ever relinquished power—what does that mean for those who live on the margins and have not imbibed the religious traditions of the Arabs or Europeans? Many traditional Africans are being forced from their lands to make room for Western expansionist projects. The African political leadership is weak and are easily manipulated and bribed by the white powers, much like their ancestors who sold Africans into slavery in the past.

Who can stand up to such a force? Boko Haram and other terrorist organizations throughout Africa have attempted to fight against Western hegemony. However, their contaminated hermeneutics are without moral values and even though their hatred of Western imperialism may be valid, the religious ideology guiding their sick minds has made them a danger and menace to society. Yet some would argue that the terrorism practiced by the Taliban, ISIS, and Boko Haram is not unlike the torture taking place in Guantanamo Bay, Cuba. One cannot torture others in the name of preventing torture and be any less animalistic.

African people were forced to reject their tradition and imbibe the religion of their tormentors. Since it happened over one thousand years ago (Arabs, 7th–14th centuries CE, and Europeans, 14th to 20th centuries) many think it harmless that they are drinking from the wells of foreigners. How could abandoning the traditions of one's "pagan" ancestors have anything to do with the conditions black people are facing today? These questions have been raised indirectly by many before me. However, none believed they were connected to the conditions Africans are facing on the continent and black people throughout the world are confronting. Wherever black people dwell in the world they are treated by whites as less than human. Why would they not be? They have no religion of their own. They rejected the tradition of their ancestors and expect to be respected by those who birthed cultural systems from which derived their religions. The African should not be respected by anyone in the world, because when he rejected the "religion" of his ancestors, he in essence rejected himself. Why should a people be respected who hates themselves?

The black man is treated like an outcast wherever he goes. Why should anyone view him as their equal? Maybe he can redeem himself by returning to what he was taught to hate. Most black people have no idea of their history and that the Nubians gave birth to the ancient Egyptian dynasties. They provided Egypt with the hieroglyphs and its pantheon of deities, and yet most black scholars continue to speak about traditional African culture as not possessing a written script. How could this be? Who benefits from keeping black people in a state of ignorance?

I wrote this book knowing that most black people in Africa and throughout the diaspora hate themselves. In my city in the United States, African American men kill each other every night. Those who escape the bullets die of premature deaths at a rate 62.5 percent higher than any other ethnic group. There are many African American men in my city who convert to Islam when they are incarcerated. It would be of more value to them if they could convert before running afoul of the criminals' justice system. Christianity does not seem to do any better because most black people trust in Jesus and still their condition has not changed.

Could it be that the black condition is connected to their abandonment of the practices handed down to them from their ancestors? Many were forced to abandon those time-honored practices, such as initiations, that functioned to reprogram one's thinking. Maybe the high incarceration rate of black men would lessen if the men underwent an initiation. Would things get better if black men were taught self-knowledge as the key to their freedom, and secondly, the knowledge of their enemy as they most important of all educational principles?

Yet black people are at war with themselves because they have been programmed to hate themselves. From birth they are taught to question their looks and adopt a white aesthetic as the standard by which all that is lovely is judged.

I do not think that traditional culture is superior to all other cultural forms. However, I know that we are cultural animals and that we are culturally programmed to respond to certain cultural nutrients that are needed for our full growth and development. The nutrients that come out of the European cultures cannot provide Africans with the sustenance needed for their spiritual growth, which is why Islam and Christianity have taken Africans as far as they can go. They must now return home to complete the process of becoming fully human.

Chapter Notes

Introduction

1. "In some countries, there are efforts by some people to revive ATR as a kind of defense of the culture of the Africans against Christianity and Islam, which are considered by them as foreign. ATR continues to exert its influence on many converted Christians and Muslims. Such Christians and Muslims revert to some practices of the ATR at moments of crisis in life such as marriage, birth, initiation rites, sickness, setbacks, the beginning of big enterprises, and funerals" (Chidi Denis Isizoh, *The Attitude of the Catholic Church towards African Traditional Religion and Culture: 100 Excerpts from the Magisterial and Other Important Church Documents*, p. 159).

2. Derrick Bell, foreword to *Critical Race Feminism: A Reader*, p. xv.

3. Cited in Laurenti Magesa, *African Religion: The Moral Traditions of Abundant Life*, p. 6, quoting Burleson, *John Mbiti: The Dialogue of an African Theologian with African Traditional Religion* (Ann Arbor: University Microfilms International, 1986), 12.

4. *African Religion*, pp. 8, 9–10.

5. Mercy Amba Oduyoye, *Daughters of Anowa: African Women and Patriarchy*, p. 12.

6. Clifford Geertz, *The Interpretation of Cultures: Selected Essays*, p.49.

7. John S. Mbiti, *African Religions and Philosophy*, p. 3.

8. Benjamin C. Ray, *African Religions: Symbol, Ritual and Community*, p. 1.

9. A.B.T. Byaruhanga-Akiiki, "Africa and Christianity: Domestication of Christian Values in the African Church," in *Religious Plurality in Africa: Essays in Honor of John S. Mbiti*, edited by Jacob K. Olupona and Sulayman S. Nyang, *Religion and Society* 32 (Berlin and New York: Mouton de Gruyter, 1993), p. 186.

10. Molefi Asante argues this point rather succinctly in his book, *Afrocentricity*.

11. Malidoma Patrice Somé, *Of Water and the Spirit: Ritual, Magic, and Initiation in the Life of an African Shaman*, p. 9.

12. See Somé's comments in chapter 4 of this book at notes 130–132.

13. See Somé's remarks in chapter 4 of this book at note 85.

14. Oduyoye, *Daughters of Anowa*, p. 12.

15. Malidoma Patrice Somé, *The Healing Wisdom of Africa: Finding Life Purpose through Nature, Ritual, and Community*, p. 29.

16. Geertz, *Interpretation of Cultures*, p. 49.

17. Ibid., pp. 38–39.

18. Somé, *Of Water*, p. 61.

19. Ibid., p. 95.

20. James H. Cone, *Black Theology and Black Power*, p. 118.

21. Somé, *Of Water*, p. 96.

22. Mbiti, *African Religions*, p. 27.

23. Ibid., p. 16.

24. Kwame Gyekye, *An Essay on African Philosophical Thought: The Akan Conceptual Scheme*, p. 43.

25. Ibid., p. 42 (emphasis in original).

26. Ibid., p. xxxv.

27. Ibid., p. xxxvi.

28. Marcel Griaule, *Conversations with Ogotemmêli: An Introduction to Dogon Religious Ideas*, pp. 1–3.

29. Gyekye, *An Essay*, p.13.

30. E. Bólájí Ìdòwú, *Olódùmarè: God in Yorùbá Belief*, p. 7.

31. Gyekye, *An Essay*, p. 15.

32. Ibid., p. 51.

33. For more information on this topic, see Emmanuel Chukwudi Eze, ed., *Race and the Enlightenment: A Reader*.

34. Gyekye, *An Essay*, p. 150.

35. Ibid., pp. 42–43.

Chapter 1

1. Isizoh, *The Attitude of the Catholic Church towards African Traditional Religions and Culture*, p. 110.

2. Ibid.
3. Ibid.,109.
4. Ibid.
5. Ibid.
6. Tokunboh Adeyemo, *Salvation in African Tradition*, p. 39, citing John S. Mbiti, *Concepts of God in Africa*, p. 179.
7. Harry Sawyerr, "Sacrifice," in Kwesi A. Dickson and Paul Ellingworth, eds., *Biblical Revelation and African Beliefs*, p. 59.
8. Adeyemo, *Salvation*, p. 39, quoting Mbiti, *Concepts*, p. 179.
9. E. Bólájí Ìdòwú, *Olódùmarè: God in Yorùbá Belief*, p. 120.
10. Adeyemo, *Salvation*, p. 35.
11. Ibid., 37.
12. Ibid., 28.
13. Ibid.,
14. Isizoh, *Attitude*, p. 268.
15. Adeyemo, *Salvation*, p. 33.
16. Mbiti, *Concepts*, p. 179.
17. Adeyemo, *Salvation*, p. 34.
18. Ibid.
19. David Westerlund, *African Religion in Western Scholarship: A Preliminary Study of the Religious and Political Background*, p. 34.
20. Adeyemo, *Salvation*, p. 34.
21. Ibid.
22. Ibid.
23. Ibid., 35.
24. J. Omosade Awolalu, *Yoruba Beliefs and Sacrificial Rites*, p. 99.
25. Ibid.
26. Ibid., 102.
27. Ibid.
28. Ibid.
29. Ibid.
30. Ibid.
31. Ibid.
32. Ibid.
33. Isizoh, *Attitude*, 173.
34. Ibid., 236.
35. Ibid., 215.
36. Ibid., 216 (emphasis in original).
37. Ibid., 86–87.
38. Ibid., 87.
39. Ibid.
40. David K. Glenday, "God Spoke to Our Wise Men: Dialogue with African Traditional Religions," pp. 12–13.
41. Ibid., 13.
42. Ibid.
43. Ibid., 10.
44. Ibid., 12.
45. Samuel G. Kibicho, "Revelation in African Religion," p. 171.
46. Isizoh, *Attitude*, p. 70.
47. Ibid., 77.
48. Ibid.
49. Ibid. (Emphasis in original.)
50. Ibid., 78.

51. Ibid.
52. Ibid.
53. Ibid.
54. Ibid., 79.
55. Ibid., 133.
56. Ibid., 133–34.
57. Ibid., 79.
58. Ibid., 79–80.
59. Ibid., 258.
60. Ibid., 188.
61. Ibid., 190.
62. Kibicho, "Revelation," p. 166.
63. Ibid.
64. Ibid.
65. Samuel G. Kibicho, "The Teaching of African Religion in Our Schools and Colleges and the Christian Attitude towards This Religion," p. 30.
66. Ibid.
67. Kibicho, "Revelation," p. 167.
68. John S. Mbiti, *African Religions and Philosophy*, p. 29.
69. Ibid.
70. Ibid.
71. Ibid., 30.
72. H. van Geluwe, "Media of Revelation in African Traditional Religion," p. 40.
73. Ibid.
74. Ibid.
75. Ibid., 41.
76. Kibicho, "Revelation," p. 167.
77. Ibid.
78. Ibid., 168.
79. Ibid.
80. Ibid.
81. Ibid.
82. Mbiti, *African Religions and Philosophy*, p. 271.
83. Kibicho, "Revelation," p. 169, citing a 1972 course syllabus from Nairobi.
84. Kibicho, "Teaching," p. 30.
85. Ibid., 31.
86. Ibid.
87. Ibid., 32.
88. Ibid.
89. Kibicho, "Revelation," p. 169.
90. Ibid.
91. Ibid., 171.
92. Ibid.
93. Ibid.
94. Kibicho, "Teaching," p. 33.
95. Ibid., n. 12.
96. Ibid., 33–34.
97. Mbiti, *African Religions and Philosophy*, p. 74.
98. Kibicho, "Teaching," p. 34.
99. Ibid., 35.
100. Ibid., 36.
101. Ibid.
102. Ibid., 37.
103. Geluwe, "Media," p. 41.

104. Ibid.
105. Ibid.
106. Ibid., 42.
107. Malidoma Patrice Somé, *The Healing Wisdom of Africa: Finding Life Purpose through Nature, Ritual, and Community*, p. 89.
108. Isizoh, *Attitude*, p. 105.
109. Ibid.
110. Ibid.
111. Ibid., 106.
112. Geluwe, "Media," p. 42.
113. Somé, *Healing Wisdom*, p. 62.
114. Ibid.
115. Geluwe, "Media," p. 43.
116. Ibid.
117. Ibid., 44.
118. Kibicho, "Revelation," p. 173. According to Somé, the moment one enters the earth realm, traditional Africans believe that, using nature rituals, an individual can maintain the relationship necessary to have proper communion with nature, God, and the ancestors. However, how is one made aware of this delicate ontological balance between humanity, nature, and the Supreme Force? Somé surmises that nature has the ability to awaken one to one's divine purpose for life. "In order to crack open something in yourself to allow you to be aware of the presence of ancestors' spirits, you have to walk into nature with your emotional self, not with your intellectual self.... If nature is the only hospitable place that can hold the spirits that leave the cities and towns, then it is beyond thought what will happen if nature, already so endangered, is destroyed" (Somé, *Healing Wisdom*, p. 54).
119. Kibicho, "Revelation," p. 173.
120. Ibid.
121. Mbiti, *African Religions and Philosophy*, p. 56.
122. Geluwe, "Media," p. 47.
123. Ibid.
124. Ibid.
125. Ibid.
126. Kibicho, "Revelation," p. 175.
127. Ibid., 173–74.
128. Ibid., 174.
129. Ibid., 175.
130. Ibid.
131. Ibid.
132. Geluwe, "Media," p. 42.
133. Isizoh, *Attitude*, p. 133.
134. Kibicho, "Revelation," p. 172.
135. Ibid.

Chapter 2

1. E. O. Babalola, "The Reality of African Traditional Religion: A Yoruba Case Study," p. 50. Many scholars or priests who advance negative views of ATR were once a part of that religio-culture. It is as though certain Africans who adopt Western religio-culture develop a hatred for the culture that gave them birth. However, analyzing ATR through an Islamic or Judeo-Christian lens is a serious academic error that needs correction. Any methodology used to analyze, observe, or pass judgment upon ATR must use tools and assessment measures that are developed from within the tradition. Otherwise, it is impossible to analyze and classify African religio-cultural phenomena honestly or accurately.
2. Ibid., 51.
3. See Justin S. Ukpong, "The Problem of God and Sacrifice in African Traditional Religion," pp. 187–203.
4. "Black Faculty in Religion Departments at the Nation's Highest-Ranked Universities," p. 28. Update June 2014: Only a few changes have occurred since 1995. For example, the University of Pennsylvania Religion Department has hired an African American female. Rice has two African Americans faculty in their religion department; Northwestern, one. Brown remains lily white (with an Arab here or there) along with Stanford, Michigan State University, Yale, University of Virginia, and UC Berkeley; at least according to their websites. I point this out not that they may hire someone of African American descent. This observation is important because it is a reflection of the entire country's open return to a form of protectionism that has always accompanied greater levels of fear, which inevitably leads to more subtle forms of racism, primarily directed at African Americans. As former Secretary of State Dr. Condoleezza Rice made perfectly clear with her brilliant analysis of America's inherent dislike or hatred of her former slaves' offspring: "We are never going to erase race as a factor in American life. It is a birth defect with which this country was born out of slavery; we're never really going to be race blind. I think it goes back to whether or not race and class—that is, race and poverty is not becoming even more of a constraint." Furthermore, as the United States continues to flex its international muscle to retain its military dominance throughout the world, because it has lost all moral authority, race will once again rear its ugly head as is the case with the U.S. government backing of a neo–Nazi regime in Ukraine or their supposedly sworn enemy, Al Qaeda, who they financially support in Syria. We can no longer deny that we are now witnessing an open return to barbarism as reflected in our national foreign policy. It is the same kind of barbarism that ushered Europe into the Dark Ages. They emerged from the darkness only to briefly experience what they called a Renaissance that was short-lived. The U.S. government's display of irrational exuberance is akin to the behavior of Joseph

Goebbels, who used propaganda to control the German people. His weapon of choice was also the media: "Let me control the media and I will turn any nation into a herd of pigs." The media in the United States is state controlled.

5. Okot p'Bitek, *African Religions in Western Scholarship*, pp. 14–15.

6. Ibid., 15.

7. Ibid., 17.

8. Ibid., 18.

9. Ibid.

10. Ibid.

11. Ibid., 19.

12. Ibid.

13. Ibid., 20.

14. Ibid.

15. Ibid.

16. George W. Bush, who was "elected" president by the U.S. Supreme Court and with the suppression of the African American vote, stated after the September 11, 2001, terrorist attacks that every country would have to choose between two options: Either they were with the United States, which supposedly opposed terrorism, or they were for terrorism. This propensity to divide the world or knowledge into two camps is the hallmark of Western epistemology. It is very narrow and stifles the intellectual growth of many.

17. P'Bitek, *African Religions*, p. 22.

18. Ibid, 22–23.

19. Ibid., 40.

20. Ibid., 41.

21. Ibid., 46–47.

22. Ibid., 47, quoting Mbiti, *Concepts*, xiii.

23. P'Bitek, *African Religions*, p. 50.

24. Ibid., 53.

25. Ibid., 80, 88.

26. Ibid., 88.

27. Ibid., 111.

28. Ibid., 113.

29. Ibid.

30. Newell S. Booth, Jr., "Islam in Africa," in Newell S. Booth, Jr., ed., *African Religions: A Symposium*, p. 338.

31. P'Bitek, *African Religions*, p. 113.

32. Ibid., 102, 104.

33. Ibid., 104.

34. Ibid.

35. Ibid., 104–5.

36. Ibid., 105.

37. Ibid.

38. Ibid., 107.

39. Ibid., 108.

40. Ibid., p. 119. For more information on Africa's need to establish or recognize its own thought system, see Kwame Nkrumah, *Africa Must Unite*.

41. P'Bitek, *African Religions*, p. 123.

42. Gates, p. 47.

43. P'Bitek, *African Religions*, p. 17.

44. Ibid., p. 125, in the epilogue by Ali A. Mazrui.

45. Ibid.

46. Ibid.

47. Ibid.

48. Ibid., 126.

49. Ibid., 127.

50. Ibid., 129.

51. P'Bitek, *African Religions*, p. 102.

52. See Booth, "Islam in Africa," esp. pp. 312–22.

53. Chidi Denis Isizoh, *The Attitude of the Catholic Church towards African Traditional Religion and Culture*, pp. 174–75.

54. Ibid., 175, quoting "*Redemptoris missio*," 52; cf. Final Report II, chap. 6 of the Second Extraordinary General Assembly of the Synod of Bishops, 1985.

55. Ibid.

56. Ibid.

57. Ibid.

58. Ibid.

59. Ibid., 176, quoting John Paul II, *Discourse to the University of Coimbra*, May 15, 1982; *L'attività della Santa Sede* (1982), p. 389.

60. Isizoh, *Attitude*, p. 210.

61. Ibid., 212.

62. Ibid., 177.

63. Ibid.

64. Ibid., 178.

65. Ibid., 220–21.

66. Ibid., 222.

67. Ibid., 179.

68. Ibid., 179–80.

69. Ibid., 196.

70. Ibid., 199 (emphasis in original), citing "*Ad gentes divinitus*," 22.

71. Ibid,. 199–200. (Emphasis in original.)

72. Ibid., 200.

73. Ibid., quoting "*Redemptoris Missio*," p. 52.

74. Isizoh, *Attitude*, 249, quoting "*Gaudium et spes*," p. 58.

75. Isizoh, *Attitude*, pp. 263, 266. (Emphasis in original.)

76. Ibid., 224.

77. Ibid., 226.

78. Ibid., 133.

79. Ibid., 134. (Emphasis in original.)

80. Ibid.

81. Ibid., 134, 135.

82. Ibid., 141.

83. Ibid., 142.

84. Ibid., 144–45.

85. Ibid., 148.

86. Ibid., 164.

87. Ibid., 165.

88. Ibid., 164–65.

89. Ibid., 170.

90. Ibid., 182; see p. 183, where a history of cultural displacement by the Christian church is cited.

91. Ibid., 170–71.
92. R. M. Githige, "African Traditional Religion Today: Its Prospects for the Future: A Review of Scholarly Opinions," p. 1.
93. Ibid.
94. Ibid.
95. Ibid., citing John S. Mbiti, *African Religions and Philosophy*, p. 219.
96. Githige, "African Traditional Religion Today," p. 1.
97. Ibid.
98. Ibid.
99. Ibid.
100. Ibid., 2.
101. Ibid.
102. Ibid.
103. Ibid.
104. Ibid.
105. Ibid.
106. Ibid.
107. Ibid.
108. Ibid.
109. Ibid.
110. Ibid., 3.
111. Ibid.
112. Ibid.
113. Ibid., 4.
114. Ibid.
115. Ibid.
116. Ibid., 5.
117. Ibid., 6.
118. Ibid.
119. Ibid.
120. John S. Mbiti, *African Religions and Philosophy*, p. 22.
121. Githige, "African Traditional Religion Today," p. 6.
122. Mbiti, *African Religions and Philosophy*, p. 19.
123. Ibid.
124. Ibid., 16.
125. Ibid.
126. Ibid.
127. Ibid., 17.
128. Githige, "African Traditional Religion Today," p. 6.
129. Ibid.
130. Ibid., 7.
131. Patrick J. Ryan, "'Arise, O God!' The Problem of 'Gods' in West Africa," p. 161.
132. Ibid.
133. Ibid.
134. Ibid.
135. Ibid.
136. Ibid., 169.
137. Kwesi A. Dickson, "Research in the History of Religions in West Africa," p. 91.
138. David Westerlund, *African Religion in African Scholarship: A Preliminary Study of the Religious and Political Background*, p. 17.
139. Ibid.
140. Ibid.
141. Ibid.
142. Ibid.
143. Ibid., 18.
144. Ibid., 26.
145. Ibid.
146. Ibid.
147. John S. Mbiti, *Introduction to African Religion*, p. 10.
148. Westerlund, *African Religion*, p. 27.
149. Ibid., 22.
150. Ibid.
151. Ibid.
152. Ibid., 23.
153. Ibid.
154. Ibid.
155. Ibid., 25, n. 7.
156. Ibid., 14, n. 2.
157. Ibid., 18.
158. Ibid.
159. Ibid.
160. Ibid., 75.
161. Ibid., 76.
162. Ibid., 75, citing Placide Tempels, *Bantu Philosophy*, p. 15.
163. Westerlund, *African Religion*, p. 75.
164. E. Bolaji Idowu, *African Traditional Religion: A Definition*, p. 98; J. O. Awolalu, "The Yoruba Philosophy of Life," p. 61.
165. Newell S. Booth, Jr., "An Approach to African Religions," p. 10.
166. Ibid., 2.
167. Ibid., 2–3.
168. Ibid., 9.
169. Tokunboh Adeyemo, *Salvation in African Tradition*, p. 94.
170. Ibid.
171. Ibid., 63.
172. Ibid.
173. Ibid., 64.
174. Ibid.
175. Ibid., 71.
176. Ibid., 65.
177. Ibid., 66.
178. Ibid., 71, citing "Reincarnation," in James Hastings, ed., *Encyclopedia of Religion and Ethics*, pp. 425–41.
179. Adeyemo, *Salvation*, p. 71.
180. Ibid., 70.
181. Isizoh, *Attitude*, p. 108.
182. Ibid., 108–9.
183. Ibid., 109.
184. J. Omosade Awolalu, *Yoruba Beliefs and Sacrificial Rites*, p. 97.
185. Ibid., 98.
186. Ibid.
187. Ibid.
188. Ibid., 99.
189. Ibid.

Chapter 3

1. See Jonathan Olumide Lucas, *Religions in West Africa and Ancient Egypt.* Parrinder disputes the connection between ancient Egyptian religion and Yoruba.

2. See Maulana Karenga, "Restoration of the Husia: Reviving a Sacred Legacy," in Maulana Karenga and Jacob Carruthers, eds., *Kemet and the African Worldview: Research, Rescue, and Restoration,* pp. 83–99.

3. E. Bólájí Ìdòwú, *Olódùmarè: God in Yorùbá Belief,* 5.

4. "Before a child is born, the oracle is consulted and due rites observed; when the child is born, the oracle gives directions about it; at every stage of life—puberty, betrothal, marriage, taking up a career, building a house, going on a journey and, in fact, the thousand and one things which make up human existence here on earth—man is in the hands of the Deity whose dictate is law, and who is waiting on the other side of this life to render him as he deserves" (Ibid.).

5. John S. Mbiti, *African Religions and Philosophy,* p. 3.

6. Mbiti provides an adequate definition of what religion is: "[I]t is an ontological phenomenon; it pertains to the question of existence or being" (Ibid. 15). Existence or being is entirely a religious phenomenon. The human being is a religious being. The entire universe is viewed by traditional Africans as one in unison with nature. Thus, the African mind is one in harmony with nature. The environment for the African, historically, has been viewed as friendly. This has not been the case for Europeans, due to the harsh environment in which they had to survive.

7. See David Leeming, *The World of Myth: An Anthology.*

8. Ìdòwú, *Olódùmarè,* p. 7.

9. Tsenay Serequeberhan, "The Critique of Eurocentrism," in Emmanuel Chukwudi Eze, ed., *Postcolonial African Philosophy: A Critical Reader,* pp. 141–61. The author points out that the European construct, from its beginning, was intent upon dehumanizing non–European people, especially Africans. Serequeberhan shows throughout this essay that, starting with Immanuel Kant, the king of European philosophy, Africans have been looked at by these so-called great minds as less than human. The general European philosophical construct is the "shrine at which the great minds of Europe (past and present) prayed and still pray. It is that which serves as the buttress and justification and thus enshrines the 'normality' of the European subjugation of the world" (Serequeberhan, "Critique," p. 146).

10. Ìdòwú, *Olódùmarè,* p. 7.

11. Ibid., 8.
12. Ibid., 9.
13. Ibid.
14. Ibid.
15. Ibid.
16. Ibid., p. 2. When the Portuguese arrived in Africa and observed the religious practices of the people, they labeled them "fetishes" because they did not understand them. European exploiters of African people would later call Africa a place governed by "insensible fetish." "Juju" was another derogative term used by Europeans in relation to African religion. They referred to the sacred religious objects as "Juju," derived from the French word "jou" (toy).
17. Ibid.10.
18. Ibid., 11.
19. Ibid., 14.
20. Ibid., 18.
21. Ibid., 19.
22. Ibid., 20.
23. Ibid.
24. Ibid.
25. Ibid., 21.
26. Ibid.
27. Ibid., 22.
28. I am researching whether the disharmony that occurs in most African creation myths is a Western idea, especially since we know that Africans everywhere converse with God and the spirit world as though it is "right here." The harmony-disharmony cycle in creation myths may be a Western construct. It is only in the West that the "God is dead" movement was given academic credence, which still has its corollary in so-called postmodern thought.
29. Ìdòwú, *Olódùmarè,* p. 22.
30. Ibid., 23.
31. Ibid., 26.
32. Ibid., 28.
33. Ibid.
34. Ibid., p. viii.
35. Emil Ludwig, *African Ideas of God,* p. 1.
36. Ìdòwú, *Olódùmarè,* p. 30.
37. Ibid., 33.
38. Ibid.
39. Ibid.
40. Samuel Johnson, *The History of the Yorubas: From the Earliest Times to the Beginnings of the British Protectorate,* p. 26.
41. Ìdòwú, *Olódùmarè,* p. 42.
42. Ibid., 43.
43. Ibid., 49.
44. Ibid.
45. Ibid., 56.
46. See Barbara Watterson, *Gods of Ancient Egypt,* which outlines in detail similar stories that took place in other parts of Africa, especially Egypt.
47. Ìdòwú, *Olódùmarè,* pp. 59–60.
48. Ibid., 61.

49. Ibid., 62.
50. Ibid., 71.
51. Ibid., 71, 72.
52. Ibid., 73–74.
53. Ibid., 75–79.
54. Most African American Christians usually sing the "Negro" spiritual "Precious Lord" at home-going services.
55. Ìdòwú, *Olódùmarè*, p. 80.
56. Ibid., 81.
57. Ibid., 84.
58. Ibid., 85.
59. See Maulana Karenga, *Odu Ifa: The Ethical Teachings*, pp. 59–63.
60. Ìdòwú, *Olódùmarè*, p. 85.
61. Ibid., 87.
62. Ibid.
63. Karenga, *Odu Ifa*, pp. 54–55.
64. Ìdòwú, *Olódùmarè*, p. 91.
65. Ibid., 97.
66. Johnson, *History*, p. 28.
67. Ìdòwú, *Olódùmarè*, p. 102.
68. Ibid., 104.
69. Ibid., 106.
70. Ibid.
71. Christopher I. Ejizu, "African Traditional Religious Rituals and Symbols," p. 243.
72. Ìdòwú, *Olódùmarè*, pp. 64–66.
73. Ibid., 64.
74. Mbiti, *African Religions and Philosophy*, p. 2.
75. Ibid., 4.
76. Ibid., 3.
77. Ibid., 17.
78. Ibid.
79. Ibid., 19.
80. Ibid.
81. Molefi Kete Asante, *Afrocentricity*, p. 5.
82. Mbiti, *African Religions and Philosophy*, p. 101.
83. Ibid.
84. Many scholars argue that Egypt may be the home of the world's oldest religion.
85. Malidoma Patrice Somé, *Of Water and the Spirit: Ritual, Magic, and Initiation in the Life of an African Shaman*, p. 3.
86. Clifford Geertz, *The Interpretation of Cultures: Selected Essays*, p. 40.
87. Ibid., 4–5.
88. Ibid., 11.
89. Ibid., 5.
90. Ibid., 20.
91. Ibid., 23.
92. Ibid., 11.
93. Ibid., 49.
94. Ibid., 4.
95. Malidoma Patrice Somé, *The Healing Wisdom of Africa: Finding Life Purpose through Nature, Ritual, and Community*, p. 163.
96. Ibid., 164.
97. Ibid., 165.
98. Ìdòwú, *Olódùmarè*, p. 7.
99. Somé, *Healing Wisdom*, p. 166.
100. Ibid.
101. Ibid.
102. Ibid., 166–67.
103. Ibid., 167.
104. Ibid.
105. Ibid.
106. Ibid., 169.
107. Ibid.
108. Ibid.
109. Ibid., 171.
110. Ibid.
111. Ibid., 172.
112. Ibid., 173.
113. Ibid., 174.
114. Ibid.
115. Ibid., 177.
116. Ibid., 178.
117. Ibid., 27.
118. Ibid.
119. Ibid.
120. Ibid., 28.
121. Ibid.
122. Ibid., 24.
123. Mbiti, *African Religions and Philosophy*, p. 106.
124. Ibid., 110.
125. Huey P. Newton, *Revolutionary Suicide*, p. 332.
126. Somé, *Healing Wisdom*, p. 23.
127. Somé, *Of Water*, p. 32.
128. Ibid., 34.
129. Ibid., 33.
130. Ibid., 3.
131. Somé, *Healing Wisdom*, p. 9.
132. Ibid.
133. Somé, *Of Water*, p. 23.
134. Somé, *Healing Wisdom*, p. 29.
135. Ibid., 7.
136. Ibid., 8.
137. Ibid.
138. Ibid., 6–7.
139. Ibid., 6.
140. Ibid., 4.
141. Ibid., 5.
142. Ibid., 4.
143. Ibid., 17.
144. Francis A. Arinze, *Sacrifice in Ibo Religion*, p. 6.
145. Ibid., p. 9. To mention a few: "Ibo pagans" (pp. 10, 11), "pious pagans" (p. 11), and six references to Ibos as pagans on p. 14.
146. Ibid., 3.
147. Ibid.
148. Isizoh, *Attitude*, pp. 123–24.
149. Arinze, *Sacrifice*, p. 3.
150. Ibid., 4.
151. Ibid.
152. Isizoh, *Attitude*, p. 113.
153. Ibid., 213.

154. Somé, *Healing Wisdom*, pp. 276–77.
155. Isizoh, *Attitude*, p. 113.
156. Ibid., 112.
157. Ibid.
158. Ibid.
159. Ibid., 112–13.
160. Ibid., 111.
161. Ibid., 114.
162. Arinze, *Sacrifice*, p. 8.
163. Ibid., 9.
164. Ibid.
165. Ibid., 10.
166. Ibid., 12.
167. Ibid., 15.
168. Ibid.
169. Ibid.
170. Ibid.
171. Isizoh, *Attitude*, pp. 110–11.
172. Arinze, *Sacrifice*, p. 16.
173. Ibid., 42.
174. Ibid., 19.
175. Ibid., 43.
176. Ibid., 48.
177. Ibid., 19.
178. Ibid., 116.
179. Ibid.
180. Ibid., 15.
181. Ibid.
182. Ibid., 13.
183. Ibid.
184. Ibid., 14.
185. Ibid., 15.
186. Ibid., 24.
187. Ibid.
188. Ibid., 25.
189. Ibid., 22.
190. Ibid.
191. Ibid.
192. Ibid., p. 34, quoting from J. Jordan, *Bishop Shanahan of Nigeria*, p. 126.
193. Arinze, *Sacrifice*, p. 34.
194. Ibid., 33.
195. Ibid., 62.
196. Ibid.
197. Ibid., 63.
198. Ibid., 42.
199. Sven Lindqvist, *"Exterminate All the Brutes,"* p. 7.
200. Anne M. Babcock, et al., "Drift, Admixture, and Selection in Human Evolution: A Study with DNA Polymorphisms," p. 839.
201. Ibid., 840.
202. Ibid.
203. Ibid.
204. Cheikh Anta Diop, *The Cultural Unity of Black Africa: The Domains of Patriarchy and of Matriarchy in Classical Antiquity* (London: Karnak House, 1989 [original: *The Cultural Unity of Negro Africa* (Paris: Présence Africaine, 1963)]), 5.
205. Ibid., 6.
206. Ibid., 21.
207. Ibid.
208. Ibid., 108.
209. Ibid., 108–9.
210. Cheikh Anta Diop, *Precolonial Black Africa: A Comparative Study of the Political and Social Systems of Europe and Black Africa, from Antiquity to the Formation of Modern States*, pp. 50, 59.
211. Lindqvist, "Exterminate," p. 62.
212. Diop, *Cultural Unity*, p. 26.
213. Ibid., 35.
214. Ibid., 41.
215. Ibid., 43.
216. Ibid., 44, quoting a passage from Piganiol, *Les Origines de Rome*, pp. 93–101.
217. Diop, *Cultural Unity*, p. 77.
218. Ibid., 61.
219. Ibid.
220. Ibid., 68.
221. Ibid., 71.
222. See Karen Armstrong, *A History of God: The 4000-Year Quest of Judaism, Christianity, and Islam*. She argues that Western theology has had difficulty in explaining God's justice or theodicy.
223. Diop, *Precolonial*, p. 124.
224. Ibid., 127, quoting a passage from Ibn Battuta, *Voyage au Soudan*, pp. 19–20.
225. Lindqvist, *Exterminate*, p. 38.
226. Newell S. Booth, Jr., "Islam in Africa," in Newell S. Booth, Jr., ed., *African Religions: A Symposium*, p. 297.
227. Ibid.
228. Ibid.
229. Ibid.
230. Ibid.
231. Ibid.
232. Ibid.
233. Ibid., 298.
234. Ibid.
235. Ibid.
236. Ibid.
237. Ibid., 299.
238. Ibid.
239. Ibid.
240. Ibid.
241. Ibid., 299–300.
242. Ibid., 300.
243. Ibid.
244. Ibid.
245. Ibid.
246. Ibid.
247. Ibid.
248. Ibid., 301.
249. Ibid.
250. Ibid.
251. Ibid.
252. Ibid.
253. Ibid., 303.
254. Ibid., 304.

255. Ibid.
256. Ibid., quoting I. M. Lewis, in I. M. Lewis, ed., *Islam in Tropical Africa*, p. 5.
257. This identity crisis plagues many African Americans, especially in the Germantown section of Philadelphia where for many, it is a badge of honor to "out–Arab" the Arab Muslims in dress and devotion.
258. Booth, "Islam in Africa," p. 304.
259. Ibid., 305.
260. Ibid.
261. Ibid., quoting Mahmud Brelvi, *Islam in Africa*, p. 156.
262. Ibid.
263. Ibid., 306.
264. Ibid.
265. Ibid.
266. Ibid.
267. Ibid.
268. Ibid., 309.
269. Ibid.
270. Ibid.
271. Ibid., 310.
272. Ibid., 314.
273. Ibid., 318.
274. Ibid.
275. Ibid.
276. Ibid., 320.
277. Ibid.
278. Ibid.
279. Ibid.
280. Ibid.
281. Ibid.
282. Ibid., 321.
283. Ibid., 332.
284. Ibid., 336.

Chapter 4

1. J. Omosade Awolalu, "Sin and Its Removal in African Traditional Religion," p. 3.
2. Ibid.
3. Molefi Kete Asante, *Afrocentricity*, p. 2.
4. Awolalu, "Sin and Its Removal," pp. 3–4.
5. Ibid., 20.
6. Ibid., 4.
7. J. K. Parratt, "Religious Change in Yoruba Society," p. 118.
8. Awolalu, "Sin and Its Removal," p. 5.
9. Simon S. Maimela, "Salvation in African Traditional Religions," p. 72–73.
10. John Mbiti, "God, Sin, and Salvation in African Religion," p. 67.
11. Ibid.
12. Ibid., 63.
13. Ibid., 64. (Emphasis in original.)
14. Ibid.
15. Ibid., 65.
16. Awolalu, "Sin and Its Removal," p. 9.
17. J. Omosade Awolalu, "Scape-Goatism in Yoruba Religion," p. 4.
18. Ibid., 5.
19. Ibid.
20. Ibid.
21. Ibid., 6.
22. Malidoma Patrice Somé, *The Healing Wisdom of Africa*, p. 75.
23. J. C. Thomas, "The Ethical Philosophy of J. B. Danquah," p. 38.
24. Ibid.
25. J. A. Omolafe, "The Socio-Cultural Implications of Iwa in Yoruba Traditional Thought," p. 81.
26. S. A. Adewale, "Crime and African Traditional Religion," p. 56.
27. Ibid., 59.
28. Ibid.
29. Ibid., 62.
30. Ibid., 63.
31. Ibid., 65.
32. U. E. Umoren, "Religious Symbols and Crime Control in Annang-Land," p. 71.
33. Chirevo V. Kwenda, "Affliction and Healing: Salvation in African Religion," p. 2.
34. Ibid., 8.
35. Ibid., with reference to Mary Douglas, *Purity and Danger*.
36. J. Estlin Carpenter, *Comparative Religion*, p. 10.
37. Awolalu, "Sin and Its Removal," p. 6, quoting E. G. Parrinder, *West African Religion*, p. 199.
38. Christian R. Gaba, "Man's Salvation: Its Nature and Meaning in African Traditional Religion," in *Christianity in Independent Africa*, p. 389.
39. Ibid., 390.
40. Ibid.
41. Ibid., 391.
42. Ibid., 392.
43. Ibid.
44. Ibid., 394.
45. Ibid., 395.
46. S. A. Adewale, "The Significance of Traditional Religion in Yoruba Traditional Society," p. 9.
47. Ibid., 8.
48. Gaba, "Man's Salvation," p. 396.
49. Ibid.
50. Ibid., 397.
51. Ibid.
52. Ibid.
53. Ibid., 398.
54. John S. Mbiti, "Flowers in the Garden: The Role of Women in African Religion," p. 70.
55. Luc de Heusch, "Myth as Reality," p. 200. (Emphasis in original.)
56. Ibid.
57. Ibid.

58. Ibid.
59. Ibid., 201.
60. Ibid.
61. Ibid., 202.
62. Ibid.
63. Ibid.
64. Chidi Denis Isizoh, *The Attitude of the Catholic Church towards African Traditional Religion and Culture*, p. 120.
65. Ibid., 121.
66. Heusch, "Myth," p. 202.
67. Christopher I. Ejizu, "African Traditional Religious Rituals and Symbols," p. 243.
68. Ibid.
69. Ibid.
70. Ibid., 245.
71. Ibid.
72. Ibid., 246.
73. Asante, *Afrocentricity*, 2.
74. Ejizu, "African Traditional Religious Rituals," 246.
75. Somé, *Healing Wisdom*, 78.
76. Ejizu, "African Traditional Religious Rituals," 251.
77. Kwame Gyekye, *African Cultural Values: An Introduction*, p. 16.
78. Segun Ogungbemi, "A Philosophical Reflection on the Religiosity of the Traditional Yoruba," p. 61.
79. Ibid., 63.
80. Ibid.
81. Ejizu, "African Traditional Religious Rituals," 153.
82. Ibid.
83. Ibid.
84. Ibid.
85. Ibid., 254.
86. Ibid., 255.
87. Ibid.
88. Ibid., 256.
89. Ibid.
90. Ibid.
91. Paul John Isaak, "Death and Funerals in African Society: A Namibian Perspective," p. 60.
92. Ibid.
93. Ibid., 62.
94. Ibid., 64.
95. Ibid., 67.
96. J. Omosade Awolalu, "The Concept of Death and Hereafter in Yoruba Traditional Religion," p. 57.
97. Ibid., 58.
98. Ibid., 65.
99. Ejizu, "African Traditional Religious Rituals," 256.
100. Isizoh, *Attitude*, 74.
101. Ibid., 80.
102. Ibid.
103. Ibid., 81.
104. Ibid., citing a Ugandan remark reported to the Second International Congress of Africanists, held in 1967 in Dakar.
105. Isizoh, *Attitude*, 82.
106. Ibid.
107. Ibid.
108. Ibid. (Emphasis in original.)
109. John S. Mbiti, *African Religions and Philosophy*, p. 25.
110. Ibid., 26.
111. Ibid., 90.
112. Ibid., 25.
113. Isizoh, *Attitude*, 82–83.
114. Mbiti, *African Religions and Philosophy*, 48.
115. Isizoh, *Attitude*, 83.
116. Ibid.
117. Ibid.
118. Ibid., 84.
119. Ibid.
120. Ibid.
121. Ibid.
122. Ibid., 85.
123. Ibid., 99.
124. Ibid.
125. Ejizu, "African Traditional Religious Rituals," 243.
126. Ibid.
127. Ibid., 244.
128. E. Dada Adelowo, "A Comparative Study of Creation Stories in Yoruba Religion, Islam, and Judaeo-Christianity," p. 30.
129. Ibid., 31.
130. J. O. Awolalu, "The African Traditional View of Man," p. 102.
131. Gyekye, *African Cultural Values*, 8.
132. Awolalu, "African Traditional View," 102.
133. Ibid.
134. Ibid., 103.
135. Ibid.
136. Ibid.
137. Ibid., 104.
138. Ibid., 105.
139. Ibid., 106, citing the definition from *Webster's International Dictionary*.
140. Awolalu, "African Traditional View," 107.
141. Ibid.
142. Ibid.
143. Ibid., 109.
144. Ibid., 110.
145. Ibid., 111.
146. Ibid., 112.
147. Ibid., 114.
148. Isizoh, *Attitude*, 149–50.
149. Ibid., 234.
150. Ibid., 233–34.
151. Ibid., 75.
152. Ibid., 75–76.
153. Ibid., 176.
154. Ibid., 117.

155. Ibid., 163.
156. Philip F. W. Bartle, "The Universe Has Three Souls: Notes on Translating Akan Culture," p. 86.
157. Gyekye, *African Cultural Values*, 3.
158. Ibid.
159. S. N. Ezeanya, "The Contribution of African Traditional Religion to Nation Building," p. 14.
160. Ibid., 18.
161. Gyekye, *African Cultural Values*, 4.
162. Adewale, "Significance of Traditional Religion," 7.
163. Gyekye, *African Cultural Traits*, 4.
164. T. N. Tamuno, "Traditional Methods of Crime Detection and Control in Nigeria," p. 32.
165. Ibid.
166. E. Bóláji̇́ İdòwú, *Olódùmarè: God in Yorùbá Belief*, p. 211.
167. Tamuno, "Traditional Methods," 30.
168. Ibid.
169. Emefie Ikenga-Metuh, "Religion and Morality in Traditional Africa Beliefs: Assessment of View-Point," p. 93, citing Placide Tempels, *Bantu Philosophy*, p. 122.
170. E. Bóláji̇́ İdòwú, *Olódùmarè: God in Yorùbá Belief*.
171. Ikenga-Metuh, "Religion and Morality," p. 93, quoting Meyer Fortes, *Oedipus and Job in West African Religion*, p. 53.
172. Ikenga-Metuh, "Religion and Morality," 92.
173. Ibid.
174. Ibid., 92–93, citing Monica Wilson, *Religion and the Transformation of Society*, p. 76.
175. Ikenga-Metuh, "Religion and Morality," 93.
176. Ibid.
177. P. Ade Dopamu, "Traditional Values: A Means to Self-Reliance," p. 14.
178. Ibid., 16.
179. Ibid., 17.
180. Ibid., 18.
181. Ibid.
182. Gyekye, *African Cultural Values*, 17–18.
183. Adewale, "Significance of Traditional Religion," 11.
184. Gyekye, *African Cultural Values*, 17.
185. Renato Berger, "Is Traditional Religion Still Relevant?" p.15.
186. Ibid., 15–16.
187. Ibid., 15, citing E. Bolaji Idowu, "The Study of Religion, with Special Reference to African Traditional Religion."
188. Berger, "Is Traditional Religion Still Relevant?" 16.
189. Ibid.
190. Ibid., 19.
191. Ibid., 19–20.
192. Ibid., 20.

193. Ibid.
194. Ibid.
195. Ibid.
196. Ibid.
197. Ibid., 21.
198. Ibid.
199. Geoffrey Parrinder, "The Possibility of Egyptian Influence on West African Religion," p. 63.
200. Ibid., 64.
201. H. W. Turner, "Geoffrey Parrinder's Contributions to Studies of Religion in Africa," p. 158.
202. Ibid., 158–59.
203. Ibid., 159.
204. Ibid., 160.
205. Ibid., 161.
206. Ibid., 161–62.
207. Somé, *Healing Wisdom*, 29.
208. Ibid., 73.
209. Ibid., 75.
210. Isizoh, *Attitude*, 215.
211. Ibid., 151.
212. Somé, *Healing Wisdom*, 270.
213. Ibid., 272.
214. Ibid., 311.

Chapter 5

1. Ennis Edmonds, et al., *Caribbean Religious History: An Introduction*, 15–16.
2. Ibid., 6.
3. Ibid., 37–38
4. Ibid., 41.
5. Ibid., 221.
6. Ibid., 6.
7. Ibid., 7.
8. For more information on this topic see James Cone, *The Spirituals and The Blues*.
9. Margarite Fernandez Olmos, *Creole Religions of the Caribbean*, 21.
10. Edmonds, *Caribbean Religious History*, 182.
11. Ibid., 181.
12. Ibid., 48.
13. Ibid., 34.
14. Ibid., 45.
15. Ibid., 207.
16. Ibid.
17. Ibid.
18. Ibid., 208.
19. Ibid., 242.
20. Ibid., 9.
21. Ibid.
22. Ibid., 9.
23. Ibid. 11.
24. Ibid.
25. Ibid., 4.
26. Ibid., 93.
27. Ibid.

28. Ibid., 205.
29. Ibid., 93.
30. Ibid., 94
31. Ibid.
32. Ibid.
33. Ibid., 95.
34. Ibid.
35. Ibid.
36. Ibid.
37. Edmonds, *Caribbean Religious History*, 98.
38. Ibid., 99.
39. Thompson, *Flash of Spirit*, 177.
40. Ibid., 108.
41. Edmonds, *Caribbean Religious History*, 99.
42. Ibid., 100
43. Ibid.
44. Ibid.
45. Ibid.
46. Ibid., 101.
47. Ibid.
48. Ibid., 102.
49. Ibid., 103.
50. Thompson, *Flash of Spirit*, 104.
51. Ibid., 109.
52. Ibid.
53. Ibid., 107.
54. Ibid.
55. Edmonds, *Caribbean Religious History*, 105.
56. Ibid.
57. Thompson, *Flash of Spirit*, 125.
58. Ibid., 132.
59. Ibid., 124.
60. Ibid., 127.
61. Ibid., 117.
62. Ibid.
63. Ibid., 118.

Chapter 6

1. Thompson, *Flash of Spirit*, 227.
2. Ibid.
3. Ibid., 228.
4. Ibid.
5. Ibid.
6. Ibid., 229.
7. Ibid.
8. Ibid., 230.
9. Ibid.
10. Ibid.
11. Ibid., 217–233.
12. Ibid., 235.
13. Ibid., 239.
14. Ibid., 236.
15. Ibid., 237
16. Ibid., 241.
17. Ibid., 243.
18. Edmonds, *Caribbean Religious History*, 107.
19. Thompson, *Flash of Spirit*, 227.
20. Ibid., 252, 260.
21. Ibid., 253.
22. Ibid., xvii.
23. Ibid., 244.
24. Ibid., 247.
25. Ibid., xvi.
26. Ibid.
27. Edmonds, *Caribbean Religious History*, 109.
28. Ibid., 110.
29. Ibid.
30. Ibid., 111.
31. Thompson, *Flash of Spirit*, 204.
32. Edmonds, *Caribbean Religious History*, 206.
33. Ibid., 119.
34. Ibid., 121.
35. Ibid.
36. Ibid.
37. Ibid., 122.
38. Ibid.
39. Ibid.
40. Ibid., 123.
41. Ibid., 122.
42. Ibid., 125.
43. Ibid.
44. Ibid., 146.
45. Ibid., 140.
46. Ibid., 150.
47. Ibid., 141
48. Ibid., 236.
49. Thompson, *Flash of Spirit*, 158.
50. Ibid., 4.
51. Ibid., 17.
52. Ibid.
53. Ibid., xvii.
54. Ibid., 18.
55. Ibid., 17.
56. Ibid., 16.
57. Ibid., 164.
58. Thompson, *Flash of Spirit*, 165.
59. Ibid., 167.
60. Edmonds, *Caribbean Religious History*, 22.
61. Ibid.
62. Ibid., 19.
63. Ibid., 47–50.

Bibliography

Adebajo, Sola. "Kóri: The Yoruba Deity of Children." *Orita (Ibadan Journal of Religious Studies)* 21 (1989): 65–77.

Adelowo, E. Dada. "A Comparative Study of Creation Stories in Yoruba Religion, Islam, and Judaeo-Christianity." *Africa Theological Journal* 15 (1986): 29–53.

Adewale, S. A. "Crime and African Traditional Religion." *Orita* 26 (1994): 54–66.

_____. "The Cultic Use of Water among the Yoruba." *Orita* 18 (1986): 28–39.

_____. "Sacrifice in African Traditional Religion." *Orita* 20 (1988): 91–106.

_____. "The Significance of Traditional Religion in Yoruba Traditional Society." *Orita* 15 (1983): 3–15.

Adeyemo, Tokunboh. *Salvation in African Tradition*. Nairobi: Evangel, 1979.

Alyenjina, Funso, et al. "Orisa (Orisha) tradition in Trinidad. *Caribbean Quarterly* 45 (1999): 35–50.

Amadi, Adolphe. *African Libraries: Western Tradition and Colonial Brainwashing*. Metuchen, NJ: Scarecrow, 1981.

Ani, Marimba. *Yurugu: An African-Centered Critique of European Cultural Thought and Behavior*. Trenton, NJ: Africa World, 1994.

Arinze, Francis A. *Sacrifice in Ibo Religion*, ed. J. S. Boston. Ibadan: Ibadan University Press, 1970.

Armstrong, Karen. *A History of God: The 4000-Year Quest of Judaism, Christianity, and Islam*. New York: A.A. Knopf, 1993.

Armstrong, Robert. "African Religion and Cultural Renewal." *Orita* 6 (1975): 109–32.

Asante, Molefi Kete. *Afrocentricity*, rev. ed. Trenton, NJ: Africa World, 1988.

_____. *The Egyptian Philosophers*. Chicago: African American Images, 2000.

_____. *The Painful Demise of Eurocentrism*. Trenton, NJ: Africa World, 1999.

_____, and Abu Abarry. *African Intellectual Heritage: A Book of Sources*. Philadelphia: Temple University Press, 1996.

Asante, Molefi Kete, and Kariamu Welsh Asante. *African Culture: The Rhythms of Unity*. Trenton, NJ: Africa World, 1985.

Awolalu, J. Omosade. "The African Traditional View of Man." *Orita* 6 (1972): 101–18.

_____. "The Concept of Death and Hereafter in Yoruba Traditional Religion." *West African Religion* 18 (1979): 57–69.

_____. "Scape-Goatism in Yoruba Religion." *Orita* 19 (1987): 3–9.

_____. "Sin and Its Removal in African Traditional Religion." *Orita* 10 (1979): 3–22.

_____. *Yoruba Beliefs and Sacrificial Rites*. New York: Athelia Henrietta, 1996. Originally London: Longman, 1979.

_____. "The Yoruba Philosophy of Life." *Presence Africaine* 73 (1970).

Babalola, E. O. "The Reality of African Traditional Religion: A Yoruba Case Study." *The Nigerian Journal of Theology* 6 (May, 1991): 50–63.

Bartle, Philip F. W. "The Universe Has Three Souls: Notes on Translating Akan

Culture." *Journal of Religion in Africa* 14 (1983): 85–114.

Bell, Derrick. Foreword to *Critical Race Feminism: A Reader*, ed. by Adrien Katherine Wing. New York and London: New York University Press, 1997.

Bell, Hesketh J. *Obeah: Witchcraft in the West Indies*. Westport, CT: Negro University Press, 1970.

Berdyaev, Nicholas. *The Meaning of the Creative Act*. New York: Collier, 1962.

Berger, Renato. "Is Traditional Religion Still Relevant?" *Orita* 3 (1969): 15–25.

"Black Faculty in Religion Departments at the Nation's Highest-Ranked Universities." *The Journal of Blacks in Higher Education* 7 (Spring 1995): 28, 30–31.

Blakely, Thomas D., Walter E. A. van Beek, and Dennis L. Thomson, eds. *Religion in Africa: Experience and Expression*. David M. Kennedy Center for International Studies at Brigham Young University Monographs 4. London: James Currey; Portsmouth, NH: Heinemann, 1994.

Booth, Newell S., Jr. "An Approach to African Religions." In *African Religions: A Symposium*, edited by Newell S. Booth, Jr., 1–11. New York, London, and Lagos: Nok, 1977.

_____. "Islam in Africa." In *African Religions: A Symposium*, edited by Newell S. Booth, Jr., 297–343. New York, London, and Lagos: Nok, 1977.

Bowcock, Anne M., Judith R. Kidd, Joanna L. Mountain, Joan M. Hebert, Luciano Carotenuto, Kenneth K. Kidd, and L. Luca Cavalli-Sforza. "Drift, Admixture, and Selection in Human Evolution: A Study with DNA Polymorphisms." *Proceedings of the National Academy of Science USA* 88 (February 1991): 839–43.

Bryant, M. D. "African Wisdom and the Recovery of the Earth." *Orita* 27 (1995): 49–58.

Budge, E. A. Wallis. *The Book of the Dead*. New York: Bell, 1950.

Byaruhanga-Akiiki, A. B. T. "Africa and Christianity: Domestication of Christian Values in the African Church." In *Religious Plurality in Africa: Essays in Honour of John S. Mbiti*, ed. Jacob K. Olupona and Sulayman S. Nyang, *Religion and Society* 32, 179–95. Berlin and New York: Mouton de Gruyter, 1993.

Canizares, Raul Jose. "From Afro-Caribbean Cult to World Religion." *Caribbean Quarterly* vol. 40, no. 1 (1994): 59–63.

Carpenter, J. Estlin. *Comparative Religion*. London: William Norgate, n.d.

Chevannes, Barry. "Revivalism: A Disappearing Religion." *Caribbean Quarterly* 24 (1978): 1–17.

Clark, Austin H. "An Ingenious Method of Causing Death Employed by the Obeah Men of the West Indies." *American Anthropologist* vol. 14, no. 3 (1912): 389–561.

Cone, James. *Black Theology and Black Power*. New York: Harper and Row, 1989.

Consentino, Donald. "Vodun Vatican: A Prolegomena for Understanding Authority in a Synthetic Religion." *Caribbean Quarterly* 39 (1993): 100–107.

Cox, James. "Missionaries, the Phenomenology of Religion and 'Re-Presenting' Nineteenth-Century African Religion: A Case Study of Peter McKenzie's 'Hail Orisha!'" *Journal of Religion in Africa* vol. 31 (2001): 336–353.

Dammann, E. "A Tentative Philological Typology of Some African High Deities." *Journal of Religion in Africa* 2 (1969): 81–95.

Dickson, Kwesi A. "Research in the History of Religions in West Africa." *Religion*, special ed. (1975).

Diop, Cheikh Anta. *The African Origin of Civilization: Myth or Reality?* Trans. Mercer Cook. Chicago: Lawrence Hill, 1974. Selections from *Nations nègres et culture* (Paris: Présence Africaine, 1955) and *Antériorité des civilisations negres: Mythe ou vérite historique?* (Paris: Présence Africaine, 1967).

_____. *Civilization or Barbarism: An Authentic Anthropology*. Trans. Yaa-Lengi Meema Ngemi. Ed. Harold J. Salemson and Marjolijn de Jager. New York:

Lawrence Hill, 1991. Originally published in French in 1981.

_____. *The Cultural Unity of Black Africa: The Domains of Patriarchy and of Matriarchy in Classical Antiquity*. London: Karnak House, 1989. Originally published as *The Cultural Unity of Negro Africa* (Paris: Présence Africaine, 1963).

_____. *Precolonial Black Africa: A Comparative Study of the Political and Social Systems of Europe and Black Africa, from Antiquity to the Formation of Modern States*. Trans. Harold J. Salemson. Brooklyn, NY: Lawrence Hill, 1987.

Dopamu, P. Ade. "Health and Healing within the Traditional African Religious Context." *Orita* 17 (1985): 66–80.

_____. "Traditional Values: A Means to Self-Reliance." *Orita* 25 (1993): 12–21.

Echekwube, A. O. "The Historical-Philosophical Background of African Traditional Religion." *Orita* 23 (1991): 1–14.

Ejizu, Christopher I. "African Traditional Religious Rituals and Symbols." *Pro Dialogo* 87 (1994): 243–58.

_____. "Oral Sources in the Study of African Indigenous Religion." *Cahiers des Religions Africaines* 23 (1989): 37–47.

Eze, Emmanuel Chukwudi, ed. *Race and the Enlightenment: A Reader*. Oxford and Malden, MA: Blackwell, 1997.

Ezeanya, S. N. "The Contribution of African Traditional Religion to Nation Building," *Nigerian Dialogue* 3 (1979): 13–19.

_____. "Women in African Traditional Religion." *Orita* 10 (1976): 105–21.

Fandrich, Ina J. "Yoruba Influences on Haitian Vodou and New Orleans Voodoo." *Journal of Black Studies* vol. 37, no. 5 (2007): 775–791.

Farrow, Stephen. *Faith, Fancies, and Fetich, or Yoruba Paganism*. New York: Athelia Henrietta, 1996.

Felder, Cain Hope. *Troubling Biblical Waters: Race, Class, and Family*. Maryknoll, NY: Orbis, 1990.

Gaba, Christian R. "Man's Salvation: Its Nature and Meaning in African Traditional Religion." In *Christianity in Independent Africa*, ed. Edward Fasholé-Luke, Richard Gray, Adrian Hastings, and Godwin Tasie, 389–401. Bloomington and London: Indiana University Press, 1978.

_____. "Prayer in Anlo Religion." *Orita* 2 (1968): 71–78.

Gates, Henry Louis. *Thirteen Ways of Looking at a Black Man*. New York: Random House, 1997.

Geertz, Clifford. *The Interpretation of Cultures: Selected Essays*. New York: Basic, 1973.

Gehman, Richard. "African Religion Lives." *Evangelical Missions Quarterly* 27 (1991): 350–53.

Geluwe, H. van. "Media of Revelation in African Traditional Religion." *The Ghana Bulletin of Theology* 4 (1975): 40–47.

Genovese, Eugene. *Roll, Jordon, Roll: The World the Slaves Made*. New York: Vintage, 1974.

Githige, R. M. "African Traditional Religion Today—Its Prospects for the Future: A Review of Scholarly Opinions." *Utamaduni: A Journal of African Studies in Religion* 1 (October 1980): 1–8.

Glenday, David K. "God Spoke to Our Wise Men: Dialogue with African Traditional Religions." *Worldmission* 27 (1976).

Gonzalez, Michelle. *Afro-Cuban Theology: Religion, Race, Culture, and Identity*. Gainesville: University Press of Florida, 2006.

Green, Ronald. "Religion and Morality in the African Traditional Setting." *Journal of Religion in Africa* 14 (1983): 1–23.

Greschat, Hans-Jürgen. "Understanding African Religions." *Orita* 2 (1968): 59–70.

Griaule, Marcel. *Conversations with Ogotemmêli: An Introduction to Dogon Religious Ideas*. Trans. Ralph Butler, Audrey I. Richards, and Beatrice Hooke. Oxford: Oxford University Press, 1965.

Gyekye, Kwame. *African Cultural Values: An Introduction*. Philadelphia and Accra: Sankofa, 1996.

_____. *African Philosophical Thought.* Philadelphia: Temple University Press, 1995.

___. *An Essay on African Philosophical Thought: The Akan Conceptual Scheme,* rev. ed. Philadelphia: Temple University Press, 1987.

Hackett, Rosalind I. J. *Art and Religion in Africa.* Religion and the Arts Series. London and New York: Cassell, 1996.

Henry, Francis. "Religion and Ideology in Trinidad: The Resurgence of the Shango Religion." *Caribbean Quarterly* 29 (1983): 63.

Heusch, Luc de. "Myth as Reality." *Journal of Religion in Africa* 18 (1988): 201–15.

Hood, Robert. *Begrimed and Black: Christian Traditions on Blacks and Blackness.* Minneapolis: Fortress, 1994.

Ìdòwú, E. Bólájí. *African Traditional Religion: A Definition.* London: S.C.M., 1973.

_____. *Olódùmarè: God in Yorùbá Belief,* memorial ed. New York: Wazobia, 1994. Originally published in 1962.

_____. "The Study of Religion, with Special Reference to African Traditional Religion." *Orita* 1 (1967).

Ifesieh, Emmanuel. "Vatican II and Traditional Religion." *AFER African Ecclesial Review* 25 (1983): 229–37.

Ikenga-Metuh, Emefie. "Religion and Morality in Traditional Africa Beliefs: Assessment of View-Point." *West African Religion* 18 (1979): 92–102.

_____. "The Religious Dimension of African Cosmogonies." *West African Religion* 17 (1978): 9–21.

_____. "Search for Methodology of African Religion." *Cahiers des Religions Africaines* 22 (1988): 117–29.

Isaak, Paul John. "Death and Funerals in African Society: A Namibian Perspective." *Journal of Constructive Theology* 4 (1998): 59–72.

Isizoh, Chidi Denis. *The Attitude of the Catholic Church towards African Traditional Religion and Culture: 100 Excerpts from the Magisterial and Other Important Church Documents.* Lagos and Rome: Ceedee, 1998.

Janzen, John. "Self-Preservation and Common Cultural Structures in Ngoma Rituals of Southern Africa." *Journal of Religion in Africa* 25 (1995): 141–62.

Johnson, Samuel. *The History of the Yorubas: From the Earliest Times to the Beginnings of the British Protectorate.* London: G. Routledge and Sons, 1921.

Kalilombe, Patrick. "The Salvific Value of African Religions." *African Ecclesiastical Review* 21 (1979): 143–57.

Karenga, Maulana. *Odu Ifa: The Ethical Teachings.* Los Angeles: University of Sankore Press, 1999.

_____. "Restoration of the Husia: Reviving a Sacred Legacy." In *Kemet and the African Worldview: Research, Rescue, and Restoration,* ed. Maulana Karenga and Jacob Carruthers, 83–99. Selected papers from the proceedings of the first (1984, Los Angeles) and second (1985, Chicago) conferences of the Association for the Study of Classical African Civilizations. Los Angeles: University of Sankore Press, 1986.

Kibicho, Samuel G. "Revelation in African Religion." *Africa Theological Journal* 12 (1983): 166–77.

_____. "The Teaching of African Religion in Our Schools and Colleges and the Christian Attitude towards This Religion." *Africa Theological Journal* 10 (1981): 29–37.

Kingsley, Mary H. *Travels in West Africa, Congo, Francais, Corisco and Cameroons.* London / New York: Macmillan and Co., 1897.

_____. *West African Studies.* London / New York: Macmillan and Co., 1899.

Kowanba, John. "The Mumuye Concept of God and Spiritual Beings." *TCCN Research Bulletin* 17 (1986): 31–36.

Kwenda, Chirevo V. "Affliction and Healing: Salvation in African Religion." *Journal of Theology for Southern Africa* 103 (March 1999): 1–12.

Leeming, David. *The World of Myth: An Anthology.* New York: Oxford University Press, 1990.

Lewis, Maureen Warner. "Yoruba Religion in Trinidad—A Transfer and Reinterpretation." *Caribbean Quarterly,* vol. 24, No. 3–4 (1978): 18–32.

Lindqvist, Sven. *"Exterminate All the Brutes."* Trans. Joan Tate. New York: New, 1996. Originally published as *Utrota varenda jävel* (Stockholm: Albert Bonniers, 1992).

Lopes, Nel. "African Religions in Brazil, Negotiation, and Resistance: A Look from Within." *Journal of Black Studies* vol. 34. no. 6 (2004): 838–860.

Lucas, Jonathan Olumide. *The Religion of the Yorubas: Being an Account of the Religious Beliefs and Practices of the Yoruba Peoples of Southern Nigeria, Especially in Relation to the Religion of Ancient Egypt*. New York: Athelia Henrietta, 1996. Originally published in Lagos in 1948.

_____. *Religions in West Africa and Ancient Egypt*. Lagos: Nigerian National, 1970.

Ludwig, Emil. *African Ideas of God*, ed. W. E. Smith. London: Edinburgh House, 1950.

Madu, Raphael Okechukwu. *African Symbols, Proverbs, and Myths: The Hermeneutics of Destiny*. New York: Peter Lang, 1992.

Magesa, Laurenti. *African Religion: The Moral Traditions of Abundant Life*. Maryknoll, NY: Orbis, 1997.

Maimela, Simon S. "Salvation in African Traditional Religions." *Missionalia* 13 (1985): 63–77.

May, Daniel J. "Journey in the Yoruba and Nupe Countries in 1858." *Journal of the Royal Geographical Society of London* vol. 3 (1860): 212–233.

Mbiti, John S. *African Religions and Philosophy*, 2d rev. and enl. ed. Oxford and Portsmouth, NH: Heinemann Educational, 1989. Originally published in 1969.

_____. *Concepts of God in Africa*. New York: Praeger, 1970.

_____. "Flowers in the Garden: The Role of Women in African Religion." *Cahiers des Religions Africaines* 22 (1988): 69–82.

_____. "God, Sin, and Salvation in African Religion." *The Journal of the Interdenominational Theological Center* 16 (Fall 1988/Spring 1989): 59–86.

_____. *Introduction to African Religion*, 2d rev. ed. Oxford: Heinemann Educational, 1991. Originally published in 1975.

McCartney, John. *Black Power Ideologies: An Essay in African-American Political Thought*. Philadelphia: Temple University Press, 1992.

Mendonsa, Eugene. "The Soul and Sacrifice amongst the Sisala." *Journal of Religion in Africa* 8 (1976): 52–68.

Miller, Ivor. *Voice of the Leopard: African Secret Societies and Cuba*. Jackson: University of Mississippi Press, 2009.

Murphy, Joseph. *Santeria: African Spirits in America*. Boston: Beacon, 1993.

Nevius, Jim. "In the Spirit: A Review of Four Books on Religion in Jamaica during the Pre—Post Emancipation Era." *Caribbean Quarterly* (2002): 71–81.

Nkrumah, Kwame. *Africa Must Unite*. New York: International, 1975.

_____. *Consciencism*. New York: Modern Reader, 1970.

Oduyoye, Mercy Amba. *Daughters of Anowa: African Women and Patriarchy*. Maryknoll, NY: Orbis, 1995.

Ogungbemi, Segun. "A Philosophical Reflection on the Religiosity of the Traditional Yoruba." *Orita* 18 (1986): 61–67.

Olupona, Jacob K. "Rituals in African Traditional Religion: A Phenomenological Perspective." *Orita* 22 (1990): 2–11.

Omolafe, J. A. "The Socio-Cultural Implications of Iwa in Yoruba Traditional Thought." *Orita* 22 (1990): 69–86.

Ozaniec, Naomi. *The Elements of Egyptian Wisdom*. Rockport, MA: Element, 1994.

Paden, William. *Interpreting the Sacred: Ways of Viewing Religion*. Boston: Beacon, 1992.

Parratt, J. K. "Religious Change in Yoruba Society." *Journal of Religion in Africa* 2 (1969): 113–28.

Parrinder, E.G. "Islam and West African Indigenous Religion." *Numen* vol. 6 (1959): 130–141.

Parrinder, Geoffrey. "The Possibility of

Egyptian Influence on West African Religion." In *Proceedings of the Third International West African Conference Held at Ibadan, Nigeria, December 12–21, 1949*, 61–67. Lagos: Nigerian Museum, 1956.

P'Bitek, Okot. *African Religions in Western Scholarship*. Kampala, Nairobi, Dar es Salaam: East African Literature Bureau, [1971].

Raboteau, Albert. *Slave Religion: The "Invisible Institution" in the Antebellum South*. Oxford: Oxford University Press, 1978.

Ray, Benjamin C. *African Religions: Symbol, Ritual, and Community*, 2d ed. Upper Saddle River, NJ: Prentice-Hall, 2000. Originally published in 1976.

Ryan, Patrick. "'Arise, O God!' The Problem of 'Gods' in West Africa." *Journal of Religion in Africa* 11 (1980): 161–71.

Saul, Mahir. "Islam and West African Anthropology." *Africa Today* vol. 53 (2006): 3–33.

Sawyerr, Harry. *God: Ancestor or Creator? Aspects of Traditional Belief in Ghana, Nigeria, and Sierra Leone*. London: Longman, 1970.

_____. "Sacrifice." In *Biblical Revelation and African Beliefs*, ed. by Kwesi A. Dickson and Paul Ellingworth, 57–82. London: Lutterworth, and Maryknoll, NY: Orbis, 1969.

Serequeberhan, Tsenay. "The Critique of Eurocentrism." In *Postcolonial African Philosophy: A Critical Reader*, ed. Emmanuel Chukwudi Eze, 141–61. Cambridge, MA, and Oxford: Blackwell, 1997.

Shaw, Rosalind. "Agency, Meaning, and Structure in African Religion." *Journal of Religion in Africa* 18 (1988): 255–65.

Shorter, Aylward. "The Study of African Traditional Religion." *Bulletin of the Pontifical Council for Interreligious Dialogue* 70 (1989): 77–82.

Somé, Malidoma Patrice. *The Healing Wisdom of Africa: Finding Life Purpose through Nature, Ritual, and Community*. New York: Tarcher/Penguin, 1998.

_____. *Of Water and the Spirit: Ritual, Magic, and Initiation in the Life of an African Shaman*. New York: Tarcher/Putnam, 1994.

_____. *Ritual: Power, Healing, and Community*. Portland, OR: Swan Raven, 1993.

Somé, Sobonfu. *The Spirit of Intimacy*. New York: William Morrow, 1997.

Tamuno, T. N. "Traditional Methods of Crime Detection and Control in Nigeria." *Orita* 26 (1994): 25–41.

Tarver, Michael, et. al. *The History of Venezuela*. New York: Palgrave Macmillan, 2006.

Thomas, J. C. "The Ethical Philosophy of J. B. Danquah." *Africa Theological Journal* 10 (1981): 36–45.

Thompson, Robert Farris. *Flash of the Spirit: African and Afro-American Art and Philosophy*. New York: Vintage, 1983.

Tokunboh, Adeyemo. *Salvation in African Religion*. Nairobi, Kenya: Evangel, 1997.

Turner, H. W. "Geoffrey Parrinder's Contributions to Studies of Religion in Africa." *Religion* 10 (1980): 156–64.

Ukpong, Justin S. "The Problem of God and Sacrifice in African Traditional Religion." *Journal of Religion in Africa* 14 (1983): 187–203.

Umoren, U. E. "Religious Symbols and Crime Control in Annang-Land." *Orita* 26 (1994): 67–78.

Walker, David. *David Walker's Appeal, in Four Articles; Together with a Preamble, to the Coloured Citizens of the World, but in Particular, and Very Expressly, to Those of the United States of America, Third and Last Edition, Revised and Published by David Walker, 1830*. Intro. James Turner. Baltimore: Black Classic, 1993.

Warner-Lewis, Maureen. "Trinidad Yoruba: Its Theoretical Implications for Creolisation Procesesses." Caribbean *Quarterly* 44 ((1998): 50–61.

West, Cornel. *The Cornel West Reader*. New York: Basic Civitas, 1999.

Westerlund, David. *African Religion in Western Scholarship: A Preliminary Study of the Religious and Political Background*. Stockholm: Almqvist and Wiksell, 1985.

Wilberforce, William. *An Appeal to the*

Religion, Justice, and Humanity of the Inhabitants of the British Empire, in behalf of the Negro Slaves in the West Indies. London: J. Hatchard and Son, 1823.

Williams, Joseph J. *Hewbrewisms of West Africa: From Nile to Niger with the Jews.* Baltimore, MD: Imprint, 1999.

_____. *Voodoos and Obeahs: Phases of West India Witchcraft.* New York: L. Macveagh Dial, 1932.

_____. *Whisperings of the Caribbean: Reflections of a Missionary.* New York and Cincinnati: Benziger Bros., 1925.

Wilpert, Gregory. *Changing Venezuela by Taking Power: The History and Policies of the Chavez Government.* New York: Verso, 2007.

Wright, Richard. *Black Power: A Record of Reactions in a Land of Pathos.* New York: HarperCollins, 1995.

Zuesse, Evan. "Divination and Deity in African Religions." *History of Religions* 15 (1975): 158–82.

Index